E. R. Hagemann

· FIGHTING REBELS AND REDSKINS ·

FIGHTING REBELS AND REDSKINS ✕ EXPERIENCES IN ARMY LIFE OF COLONEL GEORGE B. SANFORD 1861–1892

Edited and with an Introduction by
E. R. HAGEMANN

Norman
University of Oklahoma Press

STANDARD BOOK NUMBER 8061–0853–3

LIBRARY OF CONGRESS CATALOG CARD NUMBER: 69–16719

Copyright 1969 by the University of Oklahoma Press, Publishing Division of the University. Composed and printed at Norman, Oklahoma, U.S.A., by the University of Oklahoma Press. First edition.

To the Memory of My Father
Frederick Louis Hagemann (1885–1961)

·ACKNOWLEDGMENTS·

I HAVE RECEIVED MUCH HELP in the preparation of this book, and I wish that I could acknowledge all my obligations. Particularly and especially do I thank my friend William W. Wallbridge, of Short Hills, New Jersey, chemist and industrialist and son-in-law of Colonel George B. Sanford. Mr. Wallbridge's generosity and kindness have known no bounds through the years. I am also indebted to him for providing a color transparency of the portrait of Colonel Sanford, as well as a grant for the purpose of printing it in color. I also wish to thank the members of the reference staff of the University Research Library, University of California, Los Angeles, who have rendered cheerful and accurate aid for many years, dating back to my brief tenure in the Department of English; and I especially thank Mrs. Ruth Berry, Miss Ardis Lodge, David Smith, Richard Zumwinkle, and William Osuga. The same expression of gratitude is extended to the staff of the Library, University of Louisville, Louisville, Kentucky, and specific praise to Mrs. Martha Gregory, of the Interlibrary Loan Department. I owe more than I can say to the research committee at Louisville, who contributed generous grants from very limited funds to the research and writing. Two generous grants from the Toward Greater Quality Committee and from John A. Dillon, Jr., dean, Graduate School, University of Louisville, made possible the publication of this book. The staff of the Reference Department, University of Kentucky, Lexington, and the staff of the Louisville Free Public Library have also given me helping hands when needed.

I must mention the many efficient and gracious gentlemen in the

National Archives, Washington, D.C., and the Photoduplication Service of the Library of Congress. Miss Elizabeth J. Dance, research librarian, the Valentine Museum, Richmond, Virginia, ferreted out many photographs for me. Mrs. Arthur W. Felt, assistant librarian, Missouri Historical Society, found valuable data and helped identify some obscure persons. James de T. Abajian, librarian, California Historical Society, San Francisco, helped in much the same manner and freely did research for me. Miss Ann K. Harlow, chief, Readers' Services Division, Library, United States Military Academy, West Point, has been one of the most helpful librarians. The Arizona Historical Society encouraged me by publishing some very minor articles of mine on the history of Arizona.

One final word: I must acknowledge my debt to, and my admiration for, Ezra J. Warner's *Generals in Gray* (Baton Rouge, 1959) and *Generals in Blue* (Baton Rouge, 1964). These two superb volumes were the basis for much information and the source of constant pleasure. They cannot be improved upon.

E. R. HAGEMANN

University of Louisville
January 15, 1969

·CONTENTS·

·ILLUSTRATIONS·

·MAPS·

· FIGHTING REBELS AND REDSKINS ·

·INTRODUCTION·

IN THE SPRING OF 1861, when George Bliss Sanford was appointed a second lieutenant in the First Regiment of Dragoons, the United States Army, although beginning to expand in response to President Lincoln's call for 75,000 volunteers and due for reorganization in the coming summer, was small, tightly organized, and stationed throughout the United States and the Territories at approximately 106 forts, barracks, arsenals, stations, and other posts, in six military departments. The Table of Organization shown in the *Official Army Register* for 1861 as of 1 January provided for 1,117 commissioned officers and 11,907 enlisted men, or an aggregate of 13,024.[1] Headquarters was in New York City. This for a nation which in 1860 had recorded a population of about 31,500,000.

By present-day standards, the administrative organization of the Army was absurdly uncomplicated. At the top was Brevet Lieutenant General Winfield Scott, seventy-five years old and unable to ride a horse. There were 4 brigadier generals. The Inspector General's Department numbered 2 officers; Quartermaster's Department, 40; Medical Department, 115; Corps of Engineers, 48.

---

[1] This is a minimum or fixed figure. The *Register* states (p. 42): "By the act of 17 June 1850, 'to increase the rank and file of the Army,' &c., section 2d, the President is authorized, whenever the exigencies of the service require it, to increase to *seventy-four* the number of privates in any company 'serving at the several Military posts on the Western frontier, and at remote and distant stations.' . . . There being *one hundred and eighty-one* companies serving at, or in route to, these distant stations, the authorized increase in the number of privates is 5,098; making the 'total enlisted' (as the troops are now posted, or in route) 17,005, and the 'aggregate' 18,122."

There were nineteen regiments, tailored to the exigencies of the service: two regiments of dragoons, two of cavalry, one of mounted riflemen, four of artillery, and ten of infantry. Under the Table of Organization, Sanford's regiment, the First Dragoons, had a minimum strength of 35 officers and 615 enlisted men, a maximum strength of 35 and 855—fewer than a present-day battalion. The First Dragoons was further organized into ten companies (or troops), each officered by one captain, one first lieutenant, and one second lieutenant (this is, of course, the ideal complement). The enlisted personnel included four sergeants, four corporals, two buglers, a farrier, and 50 privates (minimum or fixed), for a total of 64.

The military geographical departments numbered six: Department of the East, headquarters at Troy, New York; the West, headquarters at St. Louis, Missouri; Texas, headquarters at San Antonio; New Mexico, headquarters at Santa Fe (Sanford was eventually to have reported for duty to this department); Utah, headquarters at Camp Floyd, Utah Territory; and the Pacific, headquarters at San Francisco.[2]

Determined to make the Army his career (he was not yet nineteen), Sanford must have realized what lay ahead of him in the way of promotion, rewards, and satisfaction. It was not uncommon for an officer to serve as long as forty years—there were ancient captains and majors scattered through the *Register*—and promotions were long in coming and based almost entirely on seniority. The Civil War changed the situation, but not much. When the fighting was over and the Army once again reorganized, the brilliant young *temporary* generals (*i.e.*, of volunteers)—those who did the hard fighting and campaigning and won the war for the Union— with a few exceptions, stepped down to permanent ranks as low as captain and started their upward climb all over again, while the "old regulars"—officers whom, for the most part, no one ever heard of before or since—came out of the Army's woodwork to assume command of the regiments and live out their days memor-

---

[2] During the next four years, these departments were to be arranged and rearranged in an almost bewildering fashion.

izing the *Register*, watching their livers and hoping to "reach the stars" before death or retirement. Regimental seniority *was* the rule. All things being equal, with a clean record and no major professional mistake, Sanford could expect to attain to a lieutenant colonelcy perhaps; more likely, a majority.

In 1861, in expectation of all this, Second Lieutenant Sanford was paid a maximum of $128.83 per month—depending on conditions—not all of which was his. Broken down, this amounted to $53.33 base pay, $36 monthly subsistence (four rations per day at 30c per ration), $16 monthly forage ($8 each for two horses), and $23.50 for one servant (*i.e.*, the pay, subsistence, and clothing of one private soldier). Forage was commuted only when it could not be furnished by the government in kind. Should he by any chance be named regimental adjutant or quartermaster, he would be paid an additional $10 per month. For every five years' service, an officer (generals excluded) received one additional ration per day.

Not too promising, yet Sanford served, in the fullest sense of the word, with a devotion and dedication almost unheard of today. This is evident time and again in *Experiences in Army Life* (as Sanford called his narrative), and when a comrade fell, Sanford was always prompt with praise and mention of his gallantry and skill, if warranted. It all seems somewhat Boy Scoutish today—in short, unbelievable—but Sanford meant it. He was all Army and no fooling about it or about him. One served and took what came his way, survived, and looked ahead. Sanford was tough, physically and psychologically. He had to be to endure four years of war, illness, and privation, plus twenty-five years on the frontier. The fact that he was not a West Pointer, despite his protestations to the contrary, did not help one bit. He made it, although there was doubt in the spring of 1863 when he was struck down with typhoid and malaria. All he seems to have thought about was that he missed the "glorious Gettysburg campaign." He was back on duty as soon as he could walk and back with his regiment as soon as he could persuade higher echelons he was fit. He was, indeed, a soldier.

Sanford was born on 28 June 1842 at 102 Warren Street, New Haven, Connecticut, the son of William Elihu and Margaret Louise

5

(Craney) Sanford. As he mentions in *Experiences*, he prepared for Yale College at William H. Russell's Collegiate and Commercial Institute at 7 Wooster Place in New Haven. He entered Yale with the Class of 1863 but left at the end of his freshman year. For a short time, he was a member of the Class of 1864. While at Yale, he joined the Linonian Society, an undergraduate literary and debating group.[3]

To skip ahead for a moment: in 1883, the Yale Corporation voted to enroll Sanford in the Class of 1863. Such a procedure was not unusual. If a student left Yale before receiving a degree and later distinguished himself in some way, the members of his class could petition the corporation to grant him a degree. Provided the corporation also found him worthy, he was from that time considered a graduate of his original class.[4]

A little more than a year in college was not much preparation or training for a commission in the First Regiment of Dragoons; Sanford was not even graced with the opprobrious cognomen of "ninety-day wonder." He was not alone. There were thousands more or less like him in the Union regiments, especially in the Volunteer Army of the United States. But Sanford was a Regular Army man and he had found a home.

There is no point in retracing Sanford's four years of war; he does that in *Experiences*. We can pick up his story at the very end of the penultimate paragraph when he writes: ". . . I think we left [Parkersburg] about the 20th [of May] on our long journey, and the War of the Rebellion was over." The "we" is the First Regiment of Cavalry (formerly the First Dragoons), and the irony is that his journey has just begun—it will last for the better part of twenty-five years. The War of the Rebellion was over, but San-

---

[3] Founded in 1753, the Linonian Society disbanded in 1871; at the time it possessed a library of approximately 13,000 volumes, which it presented to Yale. For some of the biographical data herein, I am indebted to William K. Wallbridge of Short Hills, New Jersey, son-in-law of Colonel Sanford, who kindly passed on a typescript of Sanford's "Autobiography" found among his papers. It is written in the third person.

[4] Letter from Yale University Library dated 5 July 1963. Although it was an honor to receive this degree, it differed from the usual honorary degree which may be given to persons not connected with the university.

ford's war against the several tribes in the West lay before him; his war was the Army's war, and it would endure almost until the final year of the nineteenth century.

Sanford's memory is vagrant. Actually, the First Cavalry went by rail to Parkersburg, West Virginia, thence by boat to Cincinnati. A day or two layover, and the regiment embarked on boats again and steamed down the Ohio and the Mississippi to Vicksburg, where General Philip Sheridan joined it. A short and pleasant "sail" to New Orleans ensued, the regiment arriving on 2 June 1865.

Sheridan set up his headquarters as commanding general of the Military Division of the Gulf. "It was deemed likely," writes Sanford, "by almost every one at the time, that we should be involved in war with Maximilian's government in Mexico, and not improbably with the French empire."[5] The threat seemed very real then, and Sheridan had been given a command of close to fifty thousand men as a partial consequence. The General quickly sent cavalry divisions to San Antonio and Houston and dispatched infantry units along the Río Grande.

Sanford did not go to Texas with the cavalry. Rather, he and his regiment settled in recently refurbished Jackson Barracks, near the battlefield where Andrew Jackson had defeated General Sir Edward W. Pakenham more than fifty years earlier. Sanford politely refused staff positions in Sheridan's command ("I had had all the staff duty I wanted for a time at least") but managed to wangle assignment to an inspection tour through southern Texas before returning to New Orleans. "It was almost too soon after the great war to settle down to any serious work or study and the ordinary routine duties of garrison life were utterly trivial as compared with the work of the previous four years."[6] Sanford the veteran of line duty was balking at the spit and polish of the peacetime parade ground, and therein he was no different from thousands of combat

[5] Manuscript continuation of *Experiences*. This fragment amounts to fourteen holograph sheets, eight by thirteen inches; it is undated, but was apparently written some years after *Experiences*. The sheets were discovered in late 1966 in the home of William K. Wallbridge.

[6] *Ibid*.

7

soldiers before and since. So dull was life at Jackson Barracks that he even welcomed detail to a general court-martial at Sheridan's headquarters on Magazine Street, six miles from the barracks.

The high point of Sanford's tour of duty in New Orleans was General Winfield Scott's visit. Sheridan and his headquarters staff officers arranged a reception for "Old Fuss and Feathers" in the St. Charles Hotel. As it happened, Sanford was detained by other duties and arrived late. He sent in his card and was ushered, with two other officers, into Scott's presence. What Sanford saw was not the vain and pompous general of former years, but a languid, elderly man (Scott was now seventy-nine) with little time left him in the world, dressed in full uniform, seated on a sofa and propped up among cushions. So weary was he that he did not rise, and he apologized for it. He asked Sanford his regiment. The First Dragoons, replied Sanford, to please the old boy. Scott inquired of the color of the horses in the various troops. Sanford enlightened him.

Scott then turned to one of Sanford's companions, a young First Cavalry lieutenant named John Barry. "And when did you leave West Point, sir?" asked Scott. The officer hesitated and seemed embarrassed. He finally replied that he was a promotion from the ranks. The General propelled himself to his feet and drew himself to his full height. "It does you the more honor, sir," said Scott. He liked this so much that he repeated it, then reached for and shook the lieutenant's hand. "It was a very pretty and very striking scene," remembered Sanford.[7]

By late December, Sanford was contemplating a leave of absence. It had been a long six months, and the young captain looked forward to time with his family in New Haven. It was not to be. His detachment received orders for the Pacific Coast. The sidewheel steamer *George B. McClellan*—a fitting name, for Sanford had been a warm supporter of "Little Mac"—was chartered to carry the regiment to Aspinwall (Colón). From there it would travel by rail across the isthmus to Panamá, thence by Pacific Mail steamer to San Francisco. Shortly after Christmas, 1865, the First Cavalry embarked and began a harrowing journey. Just as the

[7] *Ibid.*

8

vessel weighed anchor, the skipper came down with yellow fever and had to be sent ashore. The first officer assumed command. The *McClellan* was heavily overloaded and, thought Sanford, "in every way unfit for the duty required." Since many of the officers had their wives and families with them, almost six hundred people packed the ship—and this excluded the crew. In an emergency, what boats there were would not have carried a quarter of the total number. "However," says Sanford, "we had to go, and life was considerably cheaper at the conclusion of the great war than it is now-a-days [*i.e.*, the 1890's]; so very little was said about it."[8]

For the first few days, the voyage across the Gulf of Mexico was endurable enough. Then the *McClellan* encountered a "terrific storm" and narrowly escaped a disastrous sinking. Chance commanded for those hours of storm and saw to it that Sanford and his fellows survived.

From here until March, the record is vague, but in that month, Sanford, at the head of Company (Troop) E, First Cavalry, marched from Drum Barracks, near Los Angeles, California, across the desert to Fort Yuma and from there up the Gila River to Fort McDowell, Arizona Territory, where he arrived on 30 May and became part of the garrison commanded by Lieutenant Colonel Clarence E. Bennett, First California Volunteer Cavalry.[9]

On 15 August 1866, Sanford assumed command of Fort Mc-Dowell *vice* Bennett and was to command the post off and on for the next five years while retaining command of Company E. He was also to establish himself, there in the desert in Arizona Territory, as one of the best Indian fighters available. The enemy was the Tonto Apaches and their neighbors, the Yavapais, or Mohave Apaches, deadly and skilled foot soldiers. McDowell was in terra incognita. The road terminated at the post, and no other led from it

[8] *Ibid.* The manuscript breaks off at this point and we are denied Sanford's description of the remainder of the voyage to Aspinwall.

[9] Fort (Camp) McDowell was on the Río Verde, seven miles above its confluence with the Salt River and fifty-two miles north of Maricopa Wells; it had been established on 7 September 1865 by troops of the First California Cavalry under Bennett. The post was named for Brigadier General Irvin McDowell, commanding the Department of California; it was unfinished, rickety, fit for human habitation by the barest of margins. The hospital had neither doors nor window glass.

in any direction except that to Maricopa Wells, on the Overland Stage route. East of the post, not a white man could be found for hundreds of miles, not until the border settlements in New Mexico Territory. And in this mountainous region, interspersed with what Sanford called "beautiful little streams, bordered by lovely valleys" —the perfect Indian paradise—roamed the Apache and other tribes, their only companions (and foes) the wild game. There had been three peace conferences with the Apaches at the post early in August, and even though certain of their demands were acceded to, the negotiations "fell to the ground." On 22 September, an order was issued to go after them.

On 27 September 1866, Sanford led out his first scout against them: ninety-one enlisted men from the First Cavalry and the Fourteenth Infantry and four officers. They marched northeast from McDowell into the Mazatzal Mountains and the Sierra Anchas, west of the Mogollon Rim in central Arizona, and on 3 October found what they were looking for: an Apache *rancheria*. Sanford ordered a charge, and the men swept down and brutally ripped into the Indians, warriors, women, and children alike. Fifteen were killed and two women and seven children taken as captives. The scout returned to the fort on 6 October.[10]

Sanford's was an achievement, for it was the first time the Regular Army had been successful against the Apaches in Arizona Territory. General McDowell praised him officially, and the *Arizona Miner* lauded him unofficially twice in November. Whatever Sanford's guerdon, he had committed the Army to a war with the Apaches which the federal government could not henceforth disavow. Sanford was out again in mid-November, and for the next five years, he is known to have either commanded or participated in twenty-two scouts, resulting in 102 known enemy killed and 34 prisoners.[11] During this period, at intervals, he commanded the

[10] For a much more detailed account of this scout, see my article "Scout Out from Camp McDowell," *Arizoniana,* V (Fall, 1964), 29–47.

[11] The record is incomplete, for Sanford's own manuscript, "Arizona Record Book," does not contain reports for 1867 and 1868, which were lost. Certainly another fifteen to twenty scouts can be added.

post and its many and somewhat incredible details of administration so loved by the military establishment.

There were other nagging but more lethal details. Sanford writes:

For a year or two [after he had assumed command of McDowell] the lives of the members of that garrison was about as full of excitement as usually falls to any one's lot outside the pages of a dime novel. We were occupied in the first place in constructing the post and laying out and working a large farm with which to supply our wants and at the same time repelling constant raids not only on our communications with our supply depots, but on our very houses. No man's life was safe five hundred yards from the garrison by day or five feet from his door by night, and many a poor fellow I can remember who received his final discharge from the service and life together, by the deadly arrow of the Apache.[12]

In 1868, Sanford was granted leave, and he visited his home in New Haven for the first time since his bout with typhoid in 1863. Once again at McDowell, Sanford was active in the field in 1869 and 1870 and into the following year as well, after his quarry, often into country never seen by a white man. We read in his "Arizona Record Book":

Scout, 20 May–8 June 1869:
[4 June] A portion of the command now charged down the cañon, while the remainder endeavored to flank . . . the rancheria. . . . Two large rancherias were discovered . . . one being situated on each side of the stream. The Indians were evidently completely surprised and scattered on all sides, endeavoring to escape up the mountains, and through the cañons and holes. . . . The command pursued . . . in every direction, with great impetuosity and energy—some on horseback and others on foot. . . . After a pursuit and fight of an hour and a half's duration. . . . the number slain . . . was ascertained to have been 20. Four children were made prisoners.

Scout, 9 December–11 December 1869:
[10 December] Passed through a fine rolling country, well grassed,

[12] From an undated manuscript fragment, Sanford's "Papers."

and abounding in game. . . . No fresh Indian signs . . . but as the command was passing over the crest of a hill, we came in sight of a party of Indians travelling in a southerly direction.

A charge was immediately ordered, and executed with the greatest alacrity by the command. The Indians at first attempted to save themselves by flight, and by concealing themselves in the bushes; but, finding that impossible, made what resistance they could. . . .

The fight . . . was not finished until every Indian of the party, eleven (11) in all, were killed.

Scout, 10 May–2 June 1870:

[24 May] In the [Sierra Colorado] country is a stream called by the Apaches—Chivico. I succeeded on the morning of the 24th of May in surprising several large rancherias, killing twenty-two (22) Apaches, taking twelve (12) prisoners, and capturing three (3) horses and three (3) mules. . . . Very large fields of corn and wheat were found. Large quantities of Indian supplies of all kinds were captured and destroyed.

Scout, 21 August 1870:

[21 August] . . . I left the Post [with] twenty (20) enlisted men of "E" Troop, First Cavalry, in pursuit of hostile Apache Indians.

I took a circuit of twenty (20) miles, in an easterly direction, and succeeded in killing one (1) Apache.

The Indian have been about the Post for several nights, and have been getting very bold.

On the night of the 20th inst., they fired arrows into several quarters in the row devoted to Laundresses. . . .

I think the result of this little Expedition will have the effect of making them more cautious in coming about here.

Scout, 8 December–23 December 1870:

[14 December] Marched through an extremely rough mountainous country, crossed several bad canyons, the worst of which was that on the head of the Rio Pinto. . . .

A very heavy rain and snow storm had now set in rendering the traveling extremely bad.

Marched through the Pinal Range the next day [15 December], and the day after [16 December], making poor progress on account of the snow storm, which was blinding in the extreme—the men and animals suffering terribly. . . .

No signs of Apaches . . . in fact, no Apaches could live in such a country at this season of the year. Not even the nearest mountain peaks were visible.

Scout, 8 March–11 (?) March 1871:
[9 March] . . . I struck the trail of the Apaches [who had shot a stage driver] some sixty (60) miles S. W. of this Post. . . . I made immediate pursuit, and had strong hope of coming up with them. . . .

The dust, however, which was terrific, rose in such great clouds as to show the Apaches that they were pursued. . . .

For over thirty (30) miles I followed them at a gallop, with such of the men and horses as were able to keep up. Their advantage in the start, however, was too great to be overcome. . . .

After thirteen (13) consecutive hours in the saddle, having traveled a distance of over seventy (70) miles—the greater part of the time at a gallop—my horses were completely beaten, and scarcely able to move one limb after another. . . .

I regret exceedingly that I was unable to overtake these Indians . . . but fortune seemed to be against us.

We could read on and on this bitter, vicious story. No quarter given or asked; no respite sought, and endured only after man and animal, Indian and soldier, had given out completely. One should not interpret these excerpts to mean that warfare with the Apaches was a constant thing. It was not. Scouts were interspersed with routine and fruitless, mundane duty at the fort and outside it: escorting a paymaster, escorting the district commander, escorting anyone who might require it, trouble calls to settlements and villages, etc. This was Army life on the frontier, so much so, so consistently so, that, as the commanding officer complained in 1869, there was "little time for drills and recreation."

Sanford's grueling campaigning during these years did not go unrecognized; he got his share, as he had in 1866. Some time late in August or early in September, 1869, he received a letter from a longtime supporter, the Honorable Richard C. McCormick, delegate from the Territory of Arizona to the Forty-first United States Congress:

Col—I have heard with much satisfaction of your late success in

13

Indian fighting, and I congratulate you on the gallant service you have rendered, which must add to your already excellent reputation as an officer. I have in conversation with Gen Sherman and the Secretary of War [William W. Belknap] referred in detail to your efficiency, and asked that there be no delay in a favorable consideration of Gen [Edward O. C.] Ord's recommendation of your promotion by Brevet and further I have suggested that a higher promotion or more substantial honor be paid you.[13]

Nothing came of the proposed brevet for Sanford, but it was pleasant hearing from McCormick; he had been governor of the Territory in 1866 and had publicly commended Sanford then. It was good, too, for a career officer to have his man in Washington. Not that this would mean that "P.I." (political influence) would be initialed on his file; simply that a member of Congress knew him. A young officer could do worse.

McCormick's letter of 3 August appears to have begun a desultory correspondence which lasted for a couple of years. The end results were most interesting. At first, the two men exchanged information and ideas about the Territory and the Indians. Sanford wrote McCormick in December, 1869, and McCormick replied on 31 January 1870:

> You are keeping up your reputation as an Indian fighter. I wish you continued success against the Apaches. There is no use talking of treaties with them until they made to feel the power of the military. . . .
>
> I think the new post of which you speak will be a good thing. The only way to do is to establish posts in the heart of the Indian country. The change of the Third & Eighth Cavalry will take place in the Spring. The 3rd has about 150 more men than the 8th, which will be a gain for the Territory.
>
> The most we expect to secure here [in Washington] in the way of new troops is the filling of the companies of the different regiments in the Territory . . . and for economy we hardly expect to secure authority to raise volunteers. . . .
>
> Please continue to write me giving me all interesting information.

13 Sanford's "Papers." The letter was copied on Sanford's monogrammed stationery and attested a "true copy." Brigadier General Ord commanded the Department of California, which embraced the Territory of Arizona.

14

. . . I have so many letters to write that it is impossible to answer them all . . . but I will not entirely forget you. I have sent you papers & will send others.[14]

Sanford wrote on 9 May 1870 (no copy extant), apparently telling McCormick of his success in the field against the Apaches, and McCormick replied on 25 June from Washington:

I hear with great inst. of your successful scouts & the number of Indians you have consigned to reservations from which they make no escape. I am heartily in favor of such reservations—wish they might be extended. Indeed as the whites are encroaching everywhere I think it would be a matter of humanity to transfer all the hostile Indians to happy hunting grounds. . . .

Sherman promises all the recruiting funds to fill up the companies in the Territory at the earliest practicable time, but I fear we shall get no more troops than this addition. . . .

It is now my hope to be in the Territory by the middle of Sept. & I shall probably be a candidate for re-election in-as-much as I have requests to do so from various parts of the Territory. If I take the field I hope I shall have at least the moral support of the military, as I had before.[15]

What is interesting here is not McCormick's simplistic final solution to the "Indian problem"—his differed not a bit from those of scores of his contemporaries, and certainly it reflected his constituents' views. No, what is interesting is that McCormick, with the sure instinct of a politician, has divined who his next opponent may be: none other than Captain George B. Sanford, U.S.A. McCormick very skillfully appeals for his military friend's "moral support." A politician has to know his business.

On 17 September 1870, a group of citizens from Adamsville and the Gila River, Territory of Arizona, held a meeting "for the purpose of Expressing our opinion in regard to a delegate" to represent the Territory in the upcoming elections for the Forty-second Congress.[16] The meeting named a three-man committee—C. S. Adams,

[14] Sanford's "Papers."
[15] *Ibid.*
[16] From a letter-petition to Sanford dated 17 September 1870, Sanford's "Papers."

15

Granvil Wheat, and C. Rice—to nominate a candidate. The trio retired briefly and then returned to inform the meeting that "they had selected as a candidate Col George B. Sanford."[17] In quick time, the nomination was declared unanimous. A petition was drawn up, signed by forty men, in which they pledged themselves to support Sanford if he should get the nomination and if he would consent to run for the office. The petition was forwarded to Sanford at Fort McDowell.

There was no doubt that Sanford would receive the nomination if he wanted it. He was obviously admired and respected by the people of Arizona. It was a crucial moment in his life: he had to choose between a career in the Army or a career in politics. He knew that after a term or two in Washington he would in all likelihood be appointed to an important post in the territorial government, eventually leading to the governorship itself.

The Army won out, of course, but Sanford's decision was not easily arrived at, and for more than a week he struggled with his desires and ambitions in his bachelor quarters at bleak Fort McDowell. A cautious, most ambivalent letter from McCormick (who was at near-by Maricopa Wells), dated 21 September, did not make him any easier in mind:

> I have recd various messages from you and hoped I might meet you here—I will try to visit McDowell in two or three weeks . . . and then to see you—
>
> I am a candidate for re-election with excellent prospects, the opposition being quite unorganized—of course I cannot expect more than your *moral* support; this I hope I shall have—I consider myself fortunate in not having to meet you as a candidate, as I am told there has been a popular wish that I should, or to speak more correctly that you should oppose me.[18]

This is a letter from a worried man.

Mercifully, for both men, Sanford made his decision, and on 27 September, he wrote to McCormick, saying that he had decided to remain in the Army. McCormick was on the hustings, and it was

17 *Ibid.*
18 *Ibid.*

16

several days before the letters caught up with him. He was quick to reply from Florence on 11 October:

> Just as I was leaving Tucson I rec'd your letters. . . . They are in the language and spirit characteristic of your nature and fully meet my expectations.
>
> As I propose to be at McDowell on Friday a m (the 14th) I will not do more at this time than thank you for them and the position you have taken.[19]

McCormick was returned to Congress in November. Sanford was returned to the field, the flurry of political winds blown past him forever.

On 27 March 1871, while out on a scout, Sanford was relieved in the field, effective immediately (of course, it was *later* than the orders by then), and he and his troop were ordered to report to Fort Lapwai, Idaho Territory, Department of the Columbia. Situated in the northwest corner of the Nez Percé Reserve, the fort lay on the Snake River near its junction with the Clearwater River.

Sanford emerged from five years of duty in Arizona Territory unscathed and apparently unshaken in his definition of duty. He left no letters, diaries, or journals in any amount, so we have no way, really, of getting at the man. His official correspondence, of course, reflects nothing of his personal opinions about war against the Indians, nothing of the right or wrong of it. He served with amazing skill. He seems to have had much the same attitude as any professional soldier regarding his enemy: he was out there and he must be disposed of with minimum casualties. If this required maximum effort, then that was the lot of the soldier. It would not do to think on it.

I shall return to this matter later, for Sanford had in fact given it much thought and had decided even while in Arizona that such a struggle was heinous and useless; but he was true to the code of his profession in that he would never discuss official policy while in uniform. Not until 1892 would he utter his thoughts and true feelings.

---

[19] *Ibid.* It is not clear how many letters Sanford wrote. Quite possibly, he sent McCormick a copy of his letter of declination to the people at Adamsville.

17

The change of stations required a good deal of work, and it was not until 6 May 1871 that Sanford arrived in San Diego at the head of his troop, having marched from Fort McDowell. Unknown to him was the death on 5 May, near Camp Crittenden, of Lieutenant Howard B. Cushing, U.S.A., one of Sanford's gallant friends and comrades of the scouts in the desert tracts and rugged mountains. Cushing had attacked and been repulsed by the famed and dreaded Cochise in the Whetstone Mountains.

Two days after his arrival, the *San Diego Bulletin* interviewed Sanford and then published, on 13 May, an informal but pointed encomium:

> Col. Sanford is the hero of nearly two hundred Indian fights since his arrival in Arizona five years ago; and, of what the *Union* said of him, on Sunday morning last [7 May], that he is one of the most gallant and intrepid officers who ever drew a sabre, we unequivocally endorse. All the Territory will miss this thorough officer and gentleman who leaves Arizona with universal good will. . . . He informed us that, upon arriving at San Francisco, if Gen. [George] Crook was to be permitted to sail into the Apache as he did the red man of Idaho, he should make application to return to the Territory and assist in the act of forever ridding that suffering country from the ruthless savage. No officer leaves Arizona with such a splendid reputation as Col. Sanford. But we are selfish enough to desire his return, and with him Gen. Crook. We'll bet on the extermination of the Apache, if the Government will permit these two officers to do their best.[20]

Allowing for exaggeration (the "nearly two hundred Indian fights," for example), this is still quite a comment on Sanford.

He was in San Diego only four days. On Tuesday, 10 May 1871, at 6:00 P.M., he took passage on the steamer *California* for San Francisco, with a stopover at San Pedro. With him was his Troop E, numbering about sixty men. They reported to Benicia Barracks. Here, even though he learned for certain that Crook would be

---

[20] Sanford's "Scrapbook." This valuable repository of data was discovered in the home of William K. Wallbridge in December, 1966. The *Bulletin* story calls Crook a general. During the Civil War, he had served as a major general of volunteers; his rank in 1871 was lieutenant colonel. I have not so far been able to locate the story in the *San Diego Union*.

transferred from the Department of the Columbia to Arizona Territory to replace General George Stoneman, who had been luckless against the Apaches, Sanford decided that he had had enough of Arizona and wisely applied for and was granted a leave of sixty days, dated 18 May 1871.[21] A week later, he requested "an extension of four months" and also asked permission "to go beyond the seas." Both wishes were granted.

Sanford visited in the East and then joined his family in Europe and traveled in Ireland, England, Belgium, France, and Germany. The Franco-Prussian War had recently ended, and Sanford used some of his leave to study the German military machine. On 24 July 1871, from Heidelberg, he wrote the adjutant of the First Cavalry: "I have the honor to request that the leave of absence granted me . . . be further extended six (6) months for the purpose of travelling in Europe." Sanford's colonel, Alvan C. Gillem, his division commander, Major General John M. Schofield, and his department commander, Brigadier General Edward R. S. Canby, all approved the extension. Commented Gillem in his endorsement: "I hope the extension will be granted. An officer of Capt[.] Sanford[']s ability and education can not but be impressed by travel and observation."

No doubt the young captain in Germany had bright hopes, but General William T. Sherman, commanding the Army, turned him down on 20 September with the brusque observation that he had "already received six months['] indulgence." Next day, Adjutant General of the Army Edward D. Townsend notified Sanford of the disapproval, but was more tactful: the extension "has not been favorably considered."[22] Townsend added elsewhere that "the Secretary of War thinks too many officers are abroad—about 20—and has lately refused several new applications."[23] Sanford's leave was due to expire on 25 November, although Army records indicate that

---

[21] Sanford just missed seeing Crook, who departed San Francisco for San Diego, en route to Arizona, on 3 June. See *General George Crook: His Autobiography,* ed. Martin F. Schmitt, 162.

[22] Office of the Adjutant General, Records of the War Department, Record Group No. 94, National Archives.

[23] *Ibid.*

19

it continued until 2 December. However, he must have been present at Fort Lapwai before then, for he signed reports on 29 November 1871.

At this point in his career, Sanford had been in harness about ten and a half years and had held the rank of captain for nine of them. By now he was aware of the "long pull" upward. He had survived the reorganization of the Army called for by the appropriation of 3 March 1869 in which an attached clause required that "there shall be no new commissions, no promotions, and no enlistments in any infantry regiment until the total number of infantry regiments is reduced to twenty-five." The organic act of 28 July 1866 had called for 54,600 enlisted men and 3,036 officers; the 1869 act, 37,000 men and 2,227 officers. True, the ax fell mostly on infantry officers, but others were affected, and by 1872, the Army had pruned its officer lists by more than 700. Many incompetents *et al.* were gone, but so were many of the "very best" officers, Sherman publicly complained, officers "illy qualified to be thrown out of their chosen profession to begin life anew." All enlistments were raised to five years.

The next fifteen to twenty years were crucial to Sanford. A brief preview of them, couched in stripped-down, underplayed, understated service prose, might be informative:

. . . with regiment in Idaho to 24 July 74; on leave to 1 Dec. 74; on recruiting service to 26 Sept. 76; with regiment in Nevada to 5 June 78; in the field, in the Bannock Campaign, to 11 Sept. 78; on leave to 5 Dec. 78; member of a board in Washington, D. C., to 31 March 79; an authorized delay and on leave to 9 Sept. 79; with regiment in Nevada to 2 April 81; on special duty at the Presidio of San Francisco to 6 Sept. 81; commanding battalion in the field in Arizona to 20 Dec. 81; in Nevada to 3 Oct. 82; on leave to 16 March 83; with regiment in Nevada to 26 Sept. 83; at the Presidio of San Francisco to 20 June 84; and at Fort Custer, Montana, to date [18 March 1885].[24]

Now to fill in the details and to note that the record fails to credit Sanford with service in the Nez Percé affair.

[24] *Ibid.* Prepared in Brigadier General Richard C. Drum's office, Adjutant General, 18 March 1885, for the perusal of Lieutenant General Philip H. Sheridan, commanding the Army.

20

Like many forts in the West, Fort Lapwai was dilapidated and scarcely capable of housing decently the cavalry company and the infantry company that made up its garrison of less than a hundred men aggregate. Parsimonious congressional outlays of money were responsible. In 1872, Brigadier Canby spoke plainly about Lapwai: "A new hospital and new officers' quarters will be required if the post is continued. The Indian commissioners have recommended its abandonment and the establishment of a new post."[25] A hospital might cost anywhere from five to ten thousand dollars.

In 1872, Sanford was occupied with what he calls "scouting and reconnoitering expeditions" in the Idaho country; specifically, he was to explore the region north of the Snake River. Earlier in the year, the probings had been interrupted by the proposed transfer of cavalry from the department, but the transfer was deferred and work resumed, one object of which was to locate another point where a post could be established, as suggested by Canby. Sanford led out at least two expeditions, neither of which encountered hostiles, nor were they expected to. From 8 May until 27 May 1872, he covered 361 miles and explored the valleys of the Palouse and Spokane rivers. Another expedition, 31 July through 19 September, covered at least 720 miles and explored the Spokane again, as well as the Coeur d'Alene and St. Joseph's rivers. An excerpt from his report:

August 14th [in the neighborhood of Coeur d'Alene Lake]:

Mosquitoes and gnats exist in multitudes, which I should hardly have considered possible, if I had not witnessed it. The horses were almost frantic and made no attempt to eat, but rushed about through the bushes all night trying to escape from their tormentors. In the morning they were a shocking sight covered with blood and gaunt as skeletons.[26]

Sanford rather proudly noted in his report to Headquarters, Department of the Columbia, dated 21 September, that "I lost no man,

---

[25] "Report," dated 1 October 1872, *Report of the Secretary of War, 1872–1873,* House Exec. Docs., 42nd Cong., 3rd Sess., 71.
[26] Sanford's "Idaho Record Book."

animals or stores during the expedition."[27] He was forced to leave behind one sick animal, but he promised to go to the Coeur d'Alene Jesuit mission and secure it.

Two interludes in Sanford's tour at Lapwai, one which could have been rather nasty and one which could have been boring but turned out to be quite pleasant.

In the fall of 1872, Captain Jack, a Modoc chief, was generally raising fears and troubles by drifting off the reservation and refusing to return. On 29 November, Captain James Jackson, First Cavalry, jumped Jack at Lost River, Oregon. There ensued a fight in which the cavalry suffered one killed and seven wounded in its own ranks, while two citizen volunteers were killed and one wounded. Definitely on the warpath now, Captain Jack holed up in the treacherous lava beds around Tule Lake, just inside the northern California state line on the Forty-second Parallel. It seems ridiculous that Jack never had more than eighty warriors with him —possibly as few as fifty—and yet he put down the U.S. Army in no uncertain terms. The lava beds were almost impenetrable, almost surrealistic in design, almost unbelievable geologically.[28]

On 17 January 1873, 225 regulars under Lieutenant Colonel Frank Wheaton, Twenty-first Infantry, attacked the Modoc caves in the lava beds and in an all-day battle lost 7 killed and 19 wounded; their volunteer allies, 9 killed and 30 wounded. First Cavalry companies were there, but not Sanford, who remained at Fort Lapwai.

Long, frustrating, and useless peace negotiations followed at Tule Lake, capstoned by the murder of the chief peace commis-

[27] *Ibid.* Sanford apparently made other forays into the surrounding countryside, but no record of them is available.

[28] For a helpful article (although weak in the matter of dates), see James Jackson, "The Modoc War—Its Origin, Incidents, and Peculiarities," *The United Service,* VIII (July, 1892), 1–12; see also "Operations of Troops in Modoc Country," Senate Exec. Docs., No. 1, 44th Cong., Special Sess., Vol. II (Report of Colonel Alvan C. Gillem, First Cavalry), and Max L. Heyman, Jr., *Prudent Soldier: A Biography of Major General E. R. S. Canby, 1817–1873,* for background.

The Modocs were few in number. A census in 1873 reported only 100 at the Fort Klamath Agency, Oregon: 42 males and 58 females. There were two other groups in the area. See "Report of the Commissioner of Indian Affairs, 1873," *Report of the Secretary of the Interior, 1873–1874;* House Exec. Docs., 43rd Cong., 1st Sess., 712.

sioner, Brigadier General Edward R. S. Canby, on 11 April in a capital piece of faithlessness by Captain Jack and his warriors. Canby, the only general ever killed by Indians, was succeeded on 14 April by Colonel and Brevet Major General Jefferson C. Davis, who had commanded the Fourteenth Corps under Sherman in the march to the sea.

During the negotiations, Canby had become apprehensive of danger other than that from the lethal Jack. He was there before the Army. They couldn't see him, but he was there. What bothered Canby was the possible effect the peace negotiations, which he regarded as forbearance toward the Modocs, would have on the other tribes in the department. In a telegram to General Sherman dated 14 March 1873, he expressed his fear that such forbearance might be regarded as "weakness" by the Paiutes and the Snakes and provoke them to hostile action. "To guard against this," he told Sherman, "I have ordered Sanford's troops [Company E] from Fort Lapwai to Camp Harney, about which post a large number of Pi-Utes are now gathering."[29] And there in southeastern Oregon, sixty miles south of Cañon City, Sanford sat out the war, which resumed again after Canby's murder, albeit unsuccessfully for a time.

From 11 April through 20 April, forces under Colonel Gillem, First Cavalry, assaulted the lava beds, only to fail. Then on 26 April, the Modocs mauled a scouting party under Captain Evan Thomas, Fourth Artillery, and killed twenty-one men and wounded nineteen. Eventually, however, Colonel Davis (who contemptuously referred to some of the inept privates in his command as "cowardly beef-eaters" who should be made to fight) compelled the surrender of the Modocs, although Captain Jack escaped and was not apprehended until 1 June at Willow Creek, California. He and a handful of his more feared confederates were tried before a military commission on 1 July 1873. It was a foregone conclusion that the commission would sentence all to hang. The commission performed as expected.

---

[29] "War with Modoc Indians in 1872–1873," House Exec. Docs., 43rd Cong., 1st Sess., 71 (Adjutant General's Office, dated 7 January 1874).

While Colonel Davis awaited approval of the sentence, he entertained the same fears about the various tribes in eastern Oregon as had Canby. To calm the settlers, Davis "thought it best to organize as large a force as practicable, and make a tour through the country." Under the command of Majors John Green and Edwin C. Mason, the troops (including Sanford) marched six hundred miles. Reported Davis: "All the tribes throughout the department are now perfectly quiet."[30] Nothing as effective as showing the flag.

On 3 October at Fort Klamath, Oregon, Captain Jack and three other Modoc leaders, bearing the colorful names John Sconchin, Black Jim, and Boston Charley, were hanged, and the Modoc War was over. The fighting had cost the Army eight officers killed and three wounded; thirty-nine enlisted men killed, sixty-one wounded; two Warm Spring Indian scouts killed, two wounded; and, finally, sixteen citizen volunteers killed and one wounded.

Sanford went back to Lapwai. Returns of the Adjutant General's Office show that he commanded the fort for a time in 1873, probably after the Modoc War, but precise dates are unavailable. During part of August and September of that year, Sanford was on detached duty at Sitka, Alaska Territory, part of the Department of the Columbia, as a member of a board of officers convened (under Special Orders No. 109 dated 19 August 1873) to hear various courts-martial. His actual assignment was in San Francisco, where he met Gertrude Minturn of Bristol, Rhode Island, his future wife.

Sanford returned to Fort Lapwai. In mid-June, 1874, Colonel Davis, commanding the department, left his headquarters at Portland, Oregon, for an inspection tour of eastern Washington and northern Idaho territories. At Lapwai, a delegation of citizens complained to him about the conduct of the Indians. Without hesitation, Davis proceeded to Hog Heaven and Paradise Valley with Sanford's cavalry company to look things over and quiet potential trouble. The Indian agent, Monteith, went with them.

We found the Indians there [Davis reports] in considerable numbers

30 *Ibid.*, 112.

24

digging camas-root, hunting, fishing, horse-racing, gambling, insulting the citizens, and in some instances committing trespasses among the farmers, according to their views or whims.[31]

The appearance of the blue uniforms ended the troubles at once, and Davis was satisfied that bloodshed had been prevented. Sanford made a good policeman when one was needed; besides, he had done the same sort of work in Arizona. Davis commented on the unrest:

> The moving cause of this exhibition of ill-nature on the part of the Indians is to be found in the fact that these beautiful and fertile valleys are being rapidly occupied by an industrious and thrifty class of white farmers and stock-raisers. I could discover no other cause.[32]

No comment from Sanford. He had other things on his mind: his engagement and impending marriage. He was in Idaho country until 24 July, when he departed and headed east with a long leave ahead of him. Miss Minturn and Sanford were married on 15 September 1874 in St. Michael's Church at Newport, Rhode Island, by the Reverend George L. Locke.

Sanford's leave expired on 1 December 1874, and the newlyweds were stationed in San Francisco, as choice a post as Sanford could wish for; he served as provost marshal and recruiting officer. He and Gertrude (Gerty to him, all his life) saw a lot of San Francisco, and the couple had two small celebrations in their first year of marriage: he was promoted to major, First Regiment of Cavalry, on 25 June 1875, a longed-for step upward on the promotion ladder, and the Sanfords became parents with the birth of a daughter, Margaret, on 6 August. Altogether, it was pleasant duty.

Such duty is always short, however, and in September of that year, Major Sanford was ordered to command Fort Halleck, Nevada, twelve miles south of Halleck Station on the Central Pa-

---

[31] "Report of Brevet Major General Jefferson C. Davis," dated 1 September 1874, *Report of the Secretary of War, 1874–1875*, House Exec. Docs., 43rd Cong., 2nd Sess., 59. Davis does not mention the tribe by name, but he must be referring to the Nez Percés.

[32] *Ibid.*

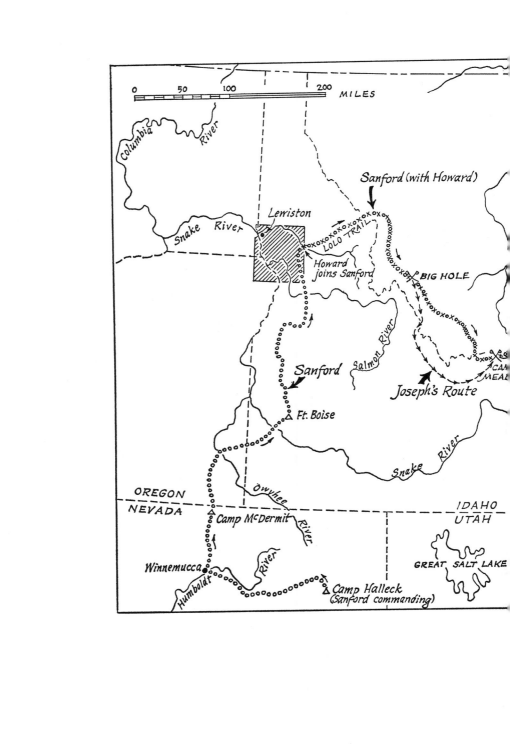

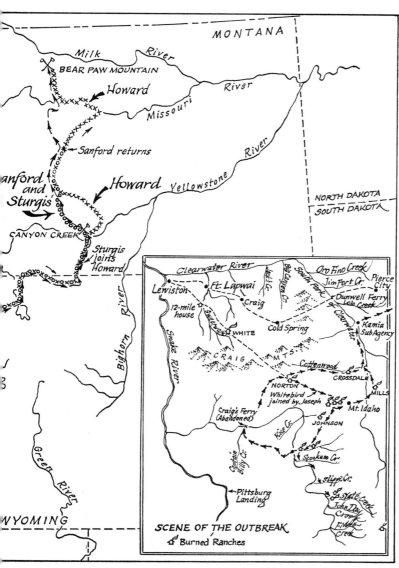

SANFORD'S AND CHIEF JOSEPH'S ROUTES AND THE SCENE
OF THE OUTBREAK OF THE NEZ PERCÉ WAR

cific Railroad. Although Army records indicate that he was with his regiment at Halleck until 5 June 1878, actually Sanford was twice in the field against the hostiles during this tour of duty: in the Nez Percé War in 1877 and in the Bannock War in 1878. But these conflicts were in the future; in 1877, Sanford faced a bleak situation that every officer and enlisted man in the Army faced: no pay and allowances. The Forty-fourth Congress, Second Session, the last under President Grant, had failed to pass H.R. 4691, making appropriations for support of the Army during the fiscal year ending 30 June 1878. It is a long story involving much concern about control of the Army by the President and the Congress; thus failure to pass the appropriations measure is not quite as contemptible as it might seem at first glance. Nevertheless, the bill did not pass before adjournment on 3 March 1877, and the Army was not to be paid. This failure to act was a discredit to the Congress.[33]

Considered by one historian as the "most spectacular Indian outbreak in the history of the Pacific Northwest,"[34] the Nez Percé War featured the incredible and skillful 1,300-mile retreat of the Nez Percés (Pierced Noses) through Idaho Territory and Montana almost to the Canadian border. It was led, at least in concert with other Nez Percé chiefs, by the great and highly respected

[33] H.R. 4691, which would have severely reduced the Army and lowered the pay of certain officers, among other things, was passed by the House on 2 March 1877 and received by the Senate on the same day. The bill was then referred to the Senate Committee on Appropriations. On 3 March 1877, the Senate amended the bill, but the House nonconcurred in the amendments. A committee of conference was appointed at once; it was unable to agree, as was a second committee. Then a third committee was appointed—all this on the final day of the session. The last action on H.R. 4691 came when the House, by a roll call, adhered to its disagreement with the Senate. The yeas totaled 65, nays 43. However, press of time prevented so much as a completion of the roll call! See *Congressional Record Containing the Proceedings and Debates of the 44th Congress, 2d* Session, V, 1886 *passim*.

[34] George W. Fuller, *A History of the Pacific Northwest*, 264. This war has been thoroughly covered in the literature; for example, see in addition Chester A. Fee, *Chief Joseph: The Biography of a Great Indian*, 116–272 (to be used cautiously), and Alvin M. Josephy, Jr., *The Patriot Chiefs*, 313–46, to mention but two sources. Also recommended is Charles E. S. Wood, "Chief Joseph, the Nez Percé," *The Century Magazine*, XXVIII (May, 1884), 135–42, and his "Famous Indians: Portraits of Some Indian Chiefs," *ibid.*, XLVI (July, 1893), 436–45. An interesting article is Mark H. Brown, "Yellowstone Tourists and the Nez Percé," *Montana*, XVI (July, 1966), 30–43. My retelling of the Nez Percé War concentrates on Sanford's role.

Chief Joseph.[35] Ordered to evacuate the Wallowa Valley (regarded by Joseph as his people's ancestral home) in eastern Oregon and come to the reservation in Idaho Territory (where Fort Lapwai was situated) within thirty days, the nontreaty Nez Percés (who, like all Nez Percés, boasted they had never killed a white man) attempted to comply, and then became involved in a series of incidents on the Salmon River in Idaho. War was unavoidable. On 17 June 1877 at White Bird Canyon, the Nez Percés badly defeated and humiliated two First Cavalry units, Companies F and H. The Army lost thirty-four dead, the Indians two wounded. The braves turned Captain and Brevet Colonel David Perry's left flank and forced him to fight his way back to Grangeville.

The war was on, and so was the retreat. It would be a long and arduous pursuit for the Army, commanded by one-armed Brigadier General Oliver O. Howard, a 47-year-old fiercely devout Christian with what can hardly be called a brilliant career behind him. After the debacle on White Bird, Howard sent his aide, Lieutenant Melville C. Wilkinson, to Walla Walla, Washington Territory, to get out some telegrams and begin to assemble the troops of the department in strength in Idaho Territory. Sanford was affected almost at once. On 21 June, he led Company I, First Cavalry, out of Halleck to Winnemucca and Camp McDermit (on the northern border of Nevada) and on to Boise. On 22 June, Company D departed the Presidio. Then Company C joined them at Camp McDermit, and on 30 June 1877, Major George Bliss Sanford led the makeshift battalion north into Idaho. Captain Camillo C. C. Carr had Company I, Captain Henry Wagner Company C.[36]

Howard was worried about the reaction of the Weiser Indians beyond Boise; he decided to interpose a force under Major John Green, First Cavalry, between them and what Howard called the

[35] Much argument centers upon Joseph's actual role or position as leader of the band. Josephy asserts (p. 330) that he sat in the councils but had never been a war chief: "On the march and in the battle Joseph took charge of the old men, women, and children, an assignment of vital importance and sacred trust, while Ollokot and the experienced war chiefs led the young men on guard duty or in combat." This has been disputed.

[36] *Report of the Secretary of War, 1877–1878,* House Exec. Docs. 45th Cong., 2nd Sess., 110. Carr, it will be recalled, had been with Sanford in Arizona.

"renegade" Nez Percés. Captain Charles Bendire's Company K was sent directly from Camp Harney, Oregon, to the Weiser country. He got into position on 29 June. The idea now was for Sanford to effect a junction with Green in order to reinforce the interposition, then march north to join Howard. But troops move slowly, and it was not until 10 July that Green and Sanford were able to shove off from Boise.

The fighting broke out again on the South Fork of the Clearwater River, Idaho Territory, when the Nez Percés, in a vicious two-day battle 11–12 July, fought off Howard (now personally leading in the field), Joseph's forces having previously wiped out a scouting party of ten men under Lieutenant Sevier M. Rains, First Cavalry, on 3 July. Then, on 25 July, Joseph cleverly avoided a trap set by Captain Charles C. Rawn on the Lolo Trail and continued his way toward Montana. Quite some distance behind was General Howard. He had organized the pursuit into two columns, the left under Colonel Frank Wheaton, Second Infantry, the right under Howard himself, with Sanford to command the four-company cavalry battalion; in addition, there would be a reserve column under Major Green. Howard awaited Sanford.

On 28 July, Sanford, with three companies and twenty Bannock scouts under Chief Buffalo Horn, joined the General. There was to be some criticism leveled at Sanford for moving too slowly—somehow, cavalry was always to fly to a spot when needed—but nothing much came of it after Howard pointed out that the unit had averaged about twenty miles a day over very rough country. The next day, 29 July, was spent in moving the cavalry and supplies across South Fork and completing "the preparations" for the push over the Lolo Trail. As commanding officer of the reserves, Major Green was to remain on the river and guard against a return of the hostiles.

On 30 July, the column entered the trail and set out to the east after Chief Joseph. In the clipped language of the military man, Howard discusses progress: "A heavy and continuous rain renders the mountainous trail slippery and exceedingly difficult. The trail runs for the most part through pine forests, with thick underbrush and fallen timber. There are occasional openings."[37] They made sixteen miles that day. But sixteen miles, Howard reasoned, were equivalent to thirty on "a good road and in fair weather." The camp that first night, in a "glade-like opening" in the forest, was named after Sanford.

With Joseph moving eastward and then southeastward into Montana, Colonel John Gibbon, Seventh Infantry, former major general of volunteers, Department of Dakota, moved from Fort Shaw, Montana, to meet him. At Big Hole on 9–10 August, the Nez Percés, at first surprised by Gibbon's force of 163 men and 35 citizen volunteers, rallied and inflicted severe losses upon Gibbon, completely, gallingly, and mercilessly defeating him before leaving the field late that night. The troops suffered 33 dead and 38 wounded (also reported as 40); the Nez Percés sustained at least 30 killed, including two chiefs, Five Wounds and Rainbow. An even more appalling loss resulted from the Army's undeniable skill in killing and wounding women and children, at least 50 of them. Big Hole was not a bright chapter in Army annals. Sanford was not present, nor was any cavalry unit except Company L, Second Cavalry. The battle was otherwise fought by the Seventh Infantry.

The Indians continued their retreat more or less down the southwestern border of Montana, generally in the direction of Yellowstone National Park by way of Targhee Pass, but in reality they were headed for Canada and safety. On 17 August, after a march of twenty-three miles, Howard camped for the night. Then Sanford selected forty troopers who had "horses in the best condition of any in the battalion" and detailed Lieutenant George R. Bacon, First Cavalry, to command them. General Howard sent Bacon out at midnight on an advance scout in the area of Mynhold's Pass, near Henry Lake. Howard's idea was that Bacon might be able to intercept and hinder any Indians who came in that direction. These forty men would be sorely missed in just a matter of hours.

In a brilliant maneuver at Camas Meadows (Creek), Idaho Territory, during the night of 19–20 August, a band of about 40 braves, moving in a military column of fours to deceive Army pickets,

[37] "Report of General O. O. Howard," dated 27 August 1877, *ibid.*, 126.

stole into Howard's camp—by now he was pressing close upon them (with only 100 cavalry and 50 infantry effective); Joseph was tired of this and wanted to set the Army afoot—and ran off with about 150 mules. Second Lieutenant Charles E. S. Wood, Twenty-first Infantry, Howard's acting aide-de-camp, describes the weird night action:

> The mule-herd, successfully stampeded, was flying in a terror momentarily increased by the naked Indians yelling demoniacally at its heels, while Indians in front were shaking the bells stolen from the necks of the lead-animals.

Howard ordered Sanford and his cavalry after them. Wood continues:

> Our cavalry were at the picket line trying to saddle, and at the same time to control, their frightened horses, while the Indians who had remained behind were doing their best to stampede and add to the disappearing mule-herd.[38]

Sanford got his men saddled up, and as soon as it was light, he galloped off in pursuit, at the head of Carr's, Jackson's and Norwood's companies. "The dawn showed the mule-herd far away over the prairie, disappearing toward the hills."[39]

Howard remained temporarily in camp to organize defenses against a possible attack. Sanford managed to "strike" the herd and at first recovered perhaps half of it in the lava beds, but many of the animals, "made wild by the charge and the firing," plunged to the enemy.[40] Control of his men was difficult for Sanford, and without reconnaissance and proper scouting, sad to say, he ran into what amounted to an ambush: hasty defenses thrown up by Joseph in some rocks about eight miles from the camp. Howard reports:

---

[38] Wood, "Chief Joseph," *loc. cit.*, 140. The fact that Sanford, senior cavalry officer, had fortunately ordered the horses to be picketed saved Howard from more woe and tribulation, for it had been Joseph's hope to get the horses as well as the mules. (He did pick up some horses belonging to the citizen volunteers.) After his surrender, Joseph made this comment: "You didn't picket your horses other nights, so I didn't expect it this time." *Ibid.*

[39] *Ibid.* Captain Randolph Norwood, Company L, Second Cavalry.

[40] "Report of Howard," *loc. cit.*, 129.

As Captain Carr, in the advance, charged upon the Indians who were driving the mules, his company received the sudden fire from this position. This checked our onward movement. Norwood and Carr went into position nearly abreast of each other, while Jackson with his company came up on the right. Now the skirmish became quite general.[41]

Sanford's left was turned, and he ordered his men to pull back in order to protect themselves. Almost at once the right (under Jackson) was turned, and now Sanford was in a serious position: he might be cut off entirely from the camp. For once, even with all his combat know-how, he had mismanaged.

Therefore [wrote Howard] he hastened to retire from an untenable position. Captain Norwood began to fulfill the order simultaneously with the rest, when, finding himself pressed too hard to do it with safety, he selected a defensive position and remained, repelling the enemy from every side.[42]

It was quite a fight on all accounts. Norwood was rather cut up by the Nez Percés. Sanford had his hands full and by now had given up any thought of recapturing the forlorn mules.

Just about then, General Howard came charging up with a company of infantry and the remaining company of cavalry (Wagner). He was not happy with what he saw and learned. Norwood, for all good purpose, was cut off. Howard did not lose his temper; he was familiar with bad luck in war.

"What is the matter, Major?" Howard asked, and Sanford gave him his answer.

"But where is Norwood?"

"That," replied Sanford, "is what I am trying to find out."

"Why, you haven't left him?"

"No," Sanford said, "I sent him the order [to retire] at the same time as to Carr, but it seems that he has stopped."

"Well, let us return to him at once."[43]

Together, Howard and Sanford reorganized the line, put the infantry on the right, and moved forward to relieve Norwood, who

41 *Ibid.*
42 *Ibid.*, 129–30.
43 Oliver O. Howard, *Nez Percé Joseph,* 228.

had meanwhile sustained seven men wounded, two mortally. Catching sight of Howard, the Nez Percés quickly withdrew from Norwood's front and went their way toward Yellowstone Park. The Army was back in camp by 3:00 P. M.[44]

Howard was in no condition to push after them; his men and horses were spent. "[He] made a reduction and rearrangement of baggage to suit his crippled pack-train."[45] Then, on the twenty-first and twenty-second, he was on the trail again. Howard wanted to bring Joseph to bay, to fight him, and he hoped, defeat him. On 23 August, he tried once more, but endurance has limits, and Howard reached them. He held up four days at Targhee Pass to let his destitute, sick, bone-beaten men and animals recuperate. They were near Henry Lake.

For twenty-six days, the command had marched continuously, making more than nineteen miles per day on an average. Howard's men needed shoes, overcoats (so cold was it at night that water froze an inch thick in the basins in camp)—everything.[46] Yet it was quite warm during the day. Howard makes an interesting observation on the lot of the Army man in these obscure little byways of history:

> Though under known interpretation of law our campaign against hostile Indians is not recognized as war, yet it has been a severer tax upon the energies of officers and men than any period of the same length of our late civil war, surely some method must be found to encourage and properly reward such gallantry and service hardly ever excelled.[47]

Simply because Howard was delayed did not mean undisputed

---

[44] This brief description ignores some of the details, some of the gallantry, some of the struggle of this pitched battle. On 27 February 1890, Norwood was brevetted major for his "gallant service" here; on 17 August 1896, Jackson was awarded the Congressional Medal of Honor for "most distinguished gallantry." But Sanford, who had endured the same battle, went unmentioned and unnoticed by the Army hierarchy.

[45] Wood, "Chief Joseph," *loc. cit.*, 140.

[46] As of 27 August 1877, when Howard submitted his report from the field, Captain Carr's Company I had ridden 1,256 miles in the saddle, Captain Jackson 1,017. Sanford was in command, and he had ridden the same distances.

[47] "Report of Howard," *loc. cit.*, 131.

passage for Chief Joseph, for a new opponent rose before him: Colonel and Brevet Major General Samuel D. Sturgis, Seventh Cavalry. Sturgis was out there, but Howard was not at all sure where. He tried to communicate with Sturgis and took up the march again after issuing General Field Orders No. 6 (dated 29 August), an old-fashioned "fight talk." Like a good psychologist, Howard baldly (and boldly) noted the hardships and the privations. "The general is not ignorant" or "the general is aware" punctuated his words. And he had praise for his men:

> The march may truthfully be said to have been an incessant "forced march," in which a command, composed partially of foot troops, in thirty-one days gained fifteen days on a body of the best-mounted Indians in the world; but specially may be mentioned the march made by the cavalry command, under Major George B. Sanford, First Cavalry, . . . of more than 70 miles in two days.[48]

No medal winner, no recipient of glory, just a tough, day-by-day soldier—that was Sanford. In truth, so was the entire command, for only two soldiers had deserted since the march commenced. Then Howard threw his strongest pitch:

> The general can only state that he is not unmindful of what his command has done in the face of unusual obstacles. Now that, with scant supplies and burdened with sick, it is plunging into a wilderness, he relies, under God, on that same disciplined spirit which supports the United States soldier in the sharp conflict of war to the death with a savage foe, and sustained him in the suspense, anxiety, and hardship of a protracted campaign—a spirit that looks for its rewards in the conscientious performance of duty.[49]

With such rhetoric tossed at him, who would flag now?

Away they went through Yellowstone Park, quickened and infused with a spirit that only the desperate know, especially now that Howard had found Sturgis and was confident he could block Joseph. But Sturgis was misled by false information and left his position

---

[48] "Supplementary Report of Brigadier General Howard," dated 26 December 1877, *Report of the Secretary of War, 1877–1878,* 619.
[49] *Ibid.*

at Heart Mountain, and Joseph had a clear path into the lower basin of Clarke's Fork. He then swung north. Tricked, Sturgis moved rapidly and by 11 September was within four miles of Howard. Howard went to him, assumed command of both units (he was the senior officer present); the two planned "a series of forced marches" designed to overtake the chieftain. Howard would strengthen Sturgis' command with Sanford's cavalry; Sturgis took fifty cavalrymen, a howitzer battery, and twenty-five scouts. Sturgis had in mind forced marches of fifty to sixty miles a day for three or four days in order to overhaul the elusive Joseph. The next day, 12 September, the command made fifty miles up Clarke's Fork to the north.

On 13 September, Sturgis finally caught the Nez Percés at Canyon Creek, just above the Yellowstone River, and engaged them in a running fight for more than twenty miles. The Army lost three dead and eleven wounded, the Indians many more men and hundreds of ponies. Sanford's command, Company K (such as it was) and detachments of Companies C and I, was in the middle of it and in it again at dawn the next day as Sturgis, still goaded by Joseph's trickery, drove on through the bare and broken country. Overcharged and obsessed, he outdid himself. He covered thirty-seven miles, but his command was spread out over the landscape for ten miles and one-third of it was on foot.

> Captain Bendire's detachment [under Sanford] did not arrive in camp until late at night, with every officer and man on foot. This detachment was so manifestly unable to continue further that I directed Captain Bendire to remain in camp next day.[50]

On 15 September, Sturgis, too, capitulated, his temerariousness now gone: "I do not feel that I would be justified in breaking down my regiment and putting it hors du combat." He was on the Musselshell.

That *was* it for Sanford. Yet on 22 September, he marched north. However, on 27 September, Howard replaced "the exhausted cav-

---

50 "Report of Colonel S. D. Sturgis," no date, *ibid.*, 512.

alry under Major Sanford by the fresher troops" of Sturgis and turned the First Cavalry homeward so that "they might reach their posts before the mountain passes were blocked with snow."[51] This was militarily correct and logical but frustrating to Sanford to have come so far and then miss out in the final confrontation with Joseph.

Colonel and Brevet Brigadier General Nelson A. Miles, Fifth Infantry, well known for his Civil War and Indian campaign services, commanding a force of nearly six hundred regulars, met Joseph at Snake Creek near the Bear Paw Mountains in Montana. Casualties were high on both sides, and both sides dug in. Then on 5 October 1877, Chief Joseph surrendered.[52] So late in the season was it that Howard took his command down the Missouri by steamer to Omaha, then shipped it overland to San Francisco on the Central Pacific.

Was there any praise for Sanford? Yes, indeed. Said Howard:

He commanded the battalion of cavalry during the expedition against the hostile Nez Percés from Kamiah, Idaho, to Judith Basin, Montana. He is commended for his soldierly conduct during the entire campaign, and especially for efficiency and gallantry during a forced march previous to and at the battle of Cañon Creek, near the Yellowstone, 13 September 1877.[53]

And any pay? Any money to meet increased family expenses for Sanford? Relief came that fall, but it came slowly. The Forty-fifth Congress, First Session, met on 15 October 1877. On 2 November, H.R. 902, a new Army appropriations bill, was reported to the House floor from the Committee on Appropriations. It was passed on 12 November. Three days later, the Senate passed it with amendments. Then, at last, after parliamentary maneuvers, final action was taken on 20 November 1877. The Army would be paid. However, Congress refused "to consider reimbursement to officers for

[51] "Supplementary Report of Howard," *loc. cit.*, 628.
[52] Some interesting sidelights can be found in George W. Baird, "General Miles's Indian Campaigns," *The Century Magazine*, XLII (July, 1891), 351–70. Major Baird was subsequently awarded the Medal of Honor for his conduct in action at the Bear Paw Mountains.
[53] Appendix I to "Supplementary Report of Howard," *loc. cit.*, 656.

any interest mulcted from them" by people who lent them money during the freeze.[54]

Sanford and his cavalry were back at Fort Halleck. The garrison was composed of Company I, First Cavalry, Sanford's old comrade, Camillo C. C. Carr, commanding, and Company G, Eighth Infantry, Captain John N. Andrews, commanding. Their stay at Halleck was short. In the early summer of 1878, the Bannock Indians (a branch of the Shoshone, or Snake, tribe), went on the warpath under, ironically, Buffalo Horn, the same chief who led scouts under Sanford in the Nez Percé affair.

The Bannocks had agreed to go to the Fort Hall Reservation in eastern Idaho Territory, but it was their custom to visit Camas Prairie every summer to gather camas (a sweet, edible bulb of the lily family), a principal item of food with them. It was vitally necessary food, too, for the rations doled out to them at Fort Hall Agency, thanks to congressional appropriations, were simply inadequate and provided for a near-starvation diet.[55] However, the influx of settlers had made it less and less possible for the Bannocks to collect their food and exercise what they considered their privilege. As Governor Brayman of Idaho Territory explained from Boise:

> Without exception or doubt [the Bannocks] insist that the "Big Camas Prairie" is theirs by that treaty [*i.e.*, 3 July 1868]. In proof of the sincerity of their belief, it is true that they have each year, during the season for digging camas roots and hunting, resorted in great numbers to and occupied this tract of country. The camas root is to them the equivalent of our potato, and it grows spontaneously in vast quantities on these grounds. . . .
>
> These Indians state that the climate and soil on the Fort Hall reservation are not adapted to the raising of vegetables, and say that Camas

54 R. Ernest Dupuy, *The Compact History of the United States Army*, 157. For the action taken on H.R. 902, see *Congressional Record Containing the Proceedings and Debates of the 45th Congress, 1st Session*, VI, 222 *passim*.

55 For example, for fiscal years 1876, 1877, 1878, and 1879 at the Fort Hall Agency, the appropriations for subsistence were, respectively, $24,000, $14,000, $29,000 and $24,000. With an average of 1,500 Indians and the cost of a full ration about $60 per year per Indian, these appropriations provided for sixteen-, nine-, nineteen-, and sixteen-sixtieths of a ration! See [Garrick Mallery], "The Lessons of the Bannock War," *The Nation*, XXVII (25 July 1878), 52.

Prairie is their garden. . . . To lose Camas Prairie is considered by them the loss of their *only* sure and abundant supply of vegetable food. The increasing wants of our advancing population have for years invited increasing encroachments upon this prairie. Herders crowd upon it with thousands of cattle, destroying the product, and bands of "hogs" that dig up the roots.[56]

The prairie (or meadow) lay between the Fort Hall Reservation and Boise, the Snake River forming its southern boundary.

It is not surprising, then, that General Howard telegraphed Major General McDowell at San Francisco on 30 May:

> Commanding officer [Captain Patrick] Collins, Fort Boise, telegraphs as follows:
>
> "Bannock Indians have been making serious threats and ordering settlers off Big Camas Prairie. Man arrived here this evening reports two settlers shot by Indians this morning. Both wounded . . . 90 miles to where Indians are camped between Big Camas and Snake, in Lava Beds about [forty miles long and six miles wide]."[57]

Collins estimated the number of Indians at 200, well armed and supplied with ammunition, and reported that Buffalo Horn was with them. The still-fresh memory of the Nez Percé uprising was probably what brought a very quick reaction from the Army in the Northwest. There would be more than a half-dozen skirmishes and brushes between the opponents—Sanford would miss all of them— much marching and countermarching, mystifyingly so, but no major action on the scale of the engagements with Joseph.

Sanford was Johnny on the spot. On 1 June, he received a dispatch from Headquarters, Military Division of the Pacific, Department of California, ordering him "to be in readiness to proceed to the scene of expected operations in Idaho with Carr's and Sumner's Companies."[58] At once he began getting Captain Carr's company at Halleck in shape for active field duty.

[56] Letter from Brayman to Howard, commanding the Department of the Columbia, dated 13 June 1878, *Report of the Secretary of War, 1877–1878,* 151.

[57] Appendix to "Report of General McDowell," *ibid.,* 127.

[58] Report from Sanford to the Assistant Adjutant General, Headquarters, Department of the Columbia, dated 16 September 1878, Camp Halleck, Nevada, in Record Group No. 94, National Archives. This report covers the period 1 June– 23 July 1878.

On 3 June, McDowell ordered Sanford to take Companies D and I, First Cavalry, to the Idaho country, and Lieutenant Colonel John C. Kelton, assistant adjutant general to McDowell, so informed Howard at Portland, Oregon. Company D, under Captain Edwin V. Sumner (another comrade from Sanford's days in Virginia), left the Presidio on 4 June for Kelton, Utah Territory, the same day Sanford, with Carr's detachment, departed from Halleck for Kelton on the Central Pacific Railroad. Plans called for Sanford to march the troops (after Sumner's arrival at Kelton) to Camas Prairie "via the Overland Stage Road." Carr and Sanford arrived at Kelton on 5 June, Sumner on 6 June. On 7 June, Sanford marched his command—105 enlisted men, eight officers, and 115 horses—twenty miles to Clear Creek. In a time of plundering, burning, and raiding by the Indians and reports of same, Sanford made his way north into Idaho, covering twenty miles to Raft River on 8 June and twenty-six miles to Birch Creek on the ninth.

Sanford was informed by Pacific Division Headquarters in San Francisco that two companies of the Twelfth Infantry would leave for Camp McDermit, Nevada, that evening and proceed to communicate with him as soon as possible. He was additionally informed of the whereabouts of Captain Reuben F. Bernard, First Cavalry, out of Fort Boise, the first officer to have reached the scene of the outbreak, who was "working" the country south of Camas Prairie in the Bruneau Valley of Owyhee County. Much of the flame of the Bannock uprising was extinguished quite early with the death of Buffalo Horn on 8 June in a skirmish with volunteers under Captain J. B. Harper seven miles from the small settlement of South Mountain, Idaho Territory.

> About this time [*i.e.*, 9 June, reports Sanford] I began to receive constant reports of Indians in all directions and in our immediate vicinity. The Citizens in a complete state of panic were fleeing from their homes towards the railroad, and sowing the most exaggerated reports [throughout the] country.[59]

Sanford was but sixty miles from Kelton, yet he had reports of Indians between him and the railroad point in large numbers; an-

[59] *Ibid.*

other report had three hundred warriors at Goose Creek in his immediate front. The people simply could not remove the fear of another Nez Percé rampage from their minds.

> The ranches throughout the country were almost entirely abandoned and the crops were being destroyed by the large bands of stock roaming over the country, with no one to watch them.[60]

On 10 June, Sanford marched through the Goose Creek country with Sumner's Company D. "No Indians were discovered," Sanford reported, "and no signs of any Indians having been there, appeared."[61] They had made twenty miles that day, their portion in life, and camped at Dog Creek.

Next day, Sanford's command moved twenty-one miles to Desert Station on the Overland Stage Road. Here he encountered delay. He was told that a party of citizens had been murdered some days before at Glenn's Ferry and that some freight wagons were partially destroyed. The local citizens clamored "for assistance to enable [them] to bury the dead and recover the property suppose[d] to be left in the train." Although this seemed reasonable, Sanford first had to act upon an even more urgent matter and forget the dead momentarily (if, in fact, there were any):

> I . . . received earnest appeals from the Overland Stage Company for guards to their stages with the information that the mails would stop running, unless I would furnish protection.[62]

The request—and the threat—seemed proper enough to him, and he accordingly provided guards "for the most exposed stations over a distance of fifty or sixty miles and later on gradually covering the whole road as far as . . . Pendleton, Oregon."[63] His plan was to draw in these guards as fast as he thought them unnecessary. He was subsequently satisfied that his stationing sentries was responsible for saving "much property" as well as the mail service.

These plans made, probably during the night of 11 June, Sanford

[60] *Ibid.*
[61] *Ibid.*
[62] *Ibid.*
[63] *Ibid.*

marched next day to Payne's Ferry, "camping on the right bank of Snake [R]iver."

Howard had departed Portland on 7 June for Boise to direct operations; at Baker on 11 June, with a report on hand that Paiutes had left *their* reservation on the sixth, he heard that Sanford "unaccountably [to Howard] was less than one hundred miles from Kelton tonight." The implied charge of dawdling against Sanford was almost precisely the same thing that had occurred less than a year before during the Nez Percé War. Howard was angry this time. But next day in Boise, he telegraphed General McDowell:

> I was misinformed yesterday about Sanford. He is at this time near Payne's Ferry, guarding the overland stages, and has made good time. Reports rumors from his neighborhood much exaggerated. His movement has protected thousands cattle moving east.[64]

Evidently, Sanford had gotten word to him.

As departmental commander, Howard feared a junction of the Bannocks and the Malheurs (Paiutes) under Winnemucca and Egan, and after a conference with Colonel Cuvier Grover, he was convinced of it. He promulgated his first plan on 12 June: prevent the junction. He informed McDowell in San Francisco that he had

> sent force under Grover, including Sanford, to clear up scattering Indians toward Fort Hall. Please ask commanding officer Fort Hall to work toward Grover to detain the Bannock families reported going to Hall, principally relations those on war-path. I am concentrating against Bannocks and Malheurs, near Sheep Ranch . . . taking charge of this column myself.[65]

Howard supposed the "main body of the Indians" was somewhere in the vicinity of Camas Prairie and the lava beds, was still comparatively small, and would remain so until reinforced by the Malheurs. His best approach to them was from the Sheep Ranch, a station on the stage line, and while he operated from there, he hoped Grover would be able to sweep the others toward Hall and

---

[64] Appendix to "Report of General McDowell," *loc. cit.*, 148.

[65] *Ibid.*, 147. Colonel and Brevet Major General Cuvier Grover commanded the First Cavalry, with headquarters at Fort Walla Walla, Washington Territory.

"soon defeat and capture them."[66] He would have to split his forces, always dangerous in any military operation, but as he observed at a later date:

> Indian warfare, unlike any other, demands that oftentimes the commander shall divide his force to guard exposed settlements, and to meet or head off the force of an enemy who, having no base and nothing but themselves to guard, scatter and come together again at will. This division of command makes it difficult for the commander to secure such action as would be possible if he could be present at or indeed within reach of each exposed point.[67]

At Payne's Ferry on 13 June, Sanford got around to the matter of the sacked train and the dead at Glenn's Ferry. There was also good reason to believe that some Indians were along the Snake River between him and the ferry. He sent Camillo Carr and Company I to that place with orders to cross "if the ferry boat was still there" and join him at King Hill Station. Carr was also instructed to afford protection to the citizens in burying the dead and in rescuing the stock and property "belonging to the train captured at that point."[68] Sanford then proceeded toward King Hill with Sumner's troop, but orders came from Howard to return to Payne's Ferry, which he and Carr did on 14 June.

At Glenn's Ferry, Carr found the partially destroyed train, caught mules running at large, and buried three dead men. (So the local citizens had been right and not rumormongering; there were dead men.) The ferry boat was cut adrift, but Carr brought back to Payne's Ferry the salvageable wagons.

On 15 June, in accordance with instructions received from Colonel Grover, who was now in command of all troops in the vicinity of Boise, Sanford sent all of his transport to Boise: four government wagons and some citizens' wagons "which had been hauling grain." The procedure left Sanford without any "means of moving," as he put it, but he was informed that a pack train would be

---

[66] "Report of General O. O. Howard," dated October, 1878, *Report of the Secretary of War, 1877–1878*, 214.
[67] *Ibid.*, 208.
[68] Report of Sanford, 16 September 1878.

sent to him from Boise. Sanford understood that he was to operate toward Fort Hall.

Another change of plan was in the offing, however, and the Fort Hall sweep never got under way. Having arrived at Sheep Ranch on 14 June, Howard learned on the fifteenth from Sarah Winnemucca, the Paiute spy who had rescued her chieftain father, that the Bannocks and Paiutes had joined. The Indians were now at Jupiter Lake (slightly north of Stein's Mountains in Oregon), more than a hundred miles away, and determined to give battle with a force of at least seven hundred. Howard immediately changed his plan. On 16 June, he ordered three columns to bear on Stein's Mountains. The center column would be under the command of Colonel Grover (turned away from his sweep to Fort Hall) and would consist of Companies D, I, and K, First Cavalry, under Sanford, and Company E, Second Infantry. Howard would be with the right column, under Major Joseph Stewart, which was made up of Bernard's four troops.

On 17 June, Grover directed Sanford to move "as rapidly as possible" to Boise and to recall the wagons he had already released. The delay meant that Sanford would not actually be a part of the center column. The wagons did not reach Payne's Ferry until the evening of 18 June, and it was not until 19 June that Sanford moved over "an exceedingly bad road" for twenty-nine miles to Clover Creek Station. It was a tough march, made the more difficult because he was escorting "a large wagon train of Emigrants on their way to the Columbia [R]iver." On 20 June, his command made twenty-four miles over another "very bad road" to Cold Springs, where the emigrants' train was detached.

Howard's columns were within striking distance of Stein's Mountains on 19 June, but the Indians sighted Bernard and fled, rushing westward, "as only Indians can, for over a hundred miles."[69] Bernard was after them southwest of Camp Harney. On 23 June at Curry Creek (near Silver River, Oregon), the advance under Bernard engaged the hostiles in a bona fide but indecisive cavalry fight in which Egan was wounded in a personal duel with Colonel

[69] Oliver O. Howard, *My Life and Experiences Among Our Hostile Indians*, 397.

Orlando Robbins, chief of scouts. The Indians withdrew, and Howard anticipated they would make "a push" for the Columbia River via the John Day River; the General was determined to pursue them. They moved fast, crossed the John Day River, and headed northeast. Chief Oytes, now the leader after taking over from the wounded Egan, was looking for allies, and he hoped that the Klamaths and Umatillas would join him.

Meanwhile, Sanford arrived at Boise on 23 June and reported to Colonel Grover. Next day, the two departed Boise and headed for the Malheur Agency, moving along very well and efficiently: 31 miles on 24 June, 20 miles on 25 June, crossing the Snake River at McDowell's Ferry. They had to move fast because they were engaged in a game of catchup with Howard and Bernard. They arrived at McDowell's Ranch on Willow Creek (Oregon) 26 June after a march of 34 miles. Both officers drove themselves and their men, and the next day, they covered 40 miles to Clover Creek—just about twice an ordinary day's march. Finally, on 28 June, they reached Malheur Agency, another 25 miles. They had made 150 miles in five days, an amazing feat.

Marching and countermarching is always confusing for friend or enemy, and Grover and Sanford apparently overshot their mark, for on 29 June they backtracked to Clover Creek and on 30 June went into camp on Willow Creek near the village of Malheur, yet another twenty miles. Nearly two hundred miles now in seven days, but they had not so much as sighted a hostile Indian.

On Willow Creek, Colonel Grover relinquished command of the cavalry battalion to Sanford and ordered him "to remain in the vicinity of Malheur City" until further orders and "to forward all information of importance by telegraph and to watch the country towards Burnt [R]iver and Ironsides Mountain."[70] In other words, determine the probability of the Indians' going north. Grover was sent to Walla Walla, Washington Territory, to report to Colonel Frank Wheaton, commanding the District of Clearwater, and take command of the First Cavalry. The cavalry companies in the district and those under Sanford would constitute Grover's command.

[70] Report of Sanford, 16 September 1878.

Sanford was just below Burnt River, a little more than one hundred miles south of Walla Walla. It was imperative that Howard first disperse the Indians and then round them up if at all possible.

On 1 July, Sanford moved his camp five miles, and for the next three days he opened and repaired "the telegraph line which had been broken near Burnt River."[71] On 5 July, he shoved off from Malheur with orders from Howard "to move northward on the Umatilla stage road" pending further instructions from either Wheaton or Grover. Sanford cut through the Powder River Mountains and arrived at Baker, Oregon, on 6 July, after a march of thirty miles in two days. He did not pause, but continued to the North Powder River on the seventh and to La Grande, twenty-seven miles beyond, on the eighth. Grinding down men and horses was Sanford's lot in the Bannock War as it had been in the Nez Percé War. At La Grande, Second Lieutenant Charles A. Williams, Twenty-first Infantry, and a detachment of Nez Percé scouts joined Sanford. Young Williams, only a few years out of the Academy, was en route to Howard's field headquarters.

During this time, General Howard was with Bernard, toiling through the mountains and falling snow, but they were coming on after the Bannocks. Howard's advance met troops from Wheaton's command, but the quarry somehow "chassezed" to the right and escaped battle. Howard was bitterly disappointed,

> but learning that Major Sanford on his way from the Malheur country, had already passed through the Round Valley [*i.e.*, Grande Ronde] and was ascending the Blue Ridge toward the summit just in time to head off the hostiles in that direction, I was yet hopeful of forcing them to a decisive battle.[72]

On 8 July, Howard's troops (Companies A, E, F, G, H, K, L, First Cavalry) closed with the Indians on Birch Creek in the Blue Mountains and drove Egan (at least so thought Howard, but undoubtedly Oytes) from a height which was "steeper than Mission-

---

[71] *Ibid.*

[72] Oliver O. Howard, "A Mountain Chase," *The Overland Monthly*, Second Series, X (September, 1887), 314.

ary Ridge," but the Indians escaped again. The troopers lost five
enlisted men and twenty horses wounded.

The hostiles broke up into small parties and ran in the direction
of the Grande Ronde River in northeastern Oregon. With Howard
in the mountains, Captain Evan Miles, Twenty-first Infantry, near
Camas Meadows (south of the Birch Creek battlefield), and Sanford in the Grande Ronde Valley, Howard saw he had the Indians
potentially trapped within this "triangle." He sent instructions to
Miles "to take up the pursuit" along the Grande Ronde, to Bernard
to form a junction with Miles, and to Sanford "to close in on Miles's
right flank." The three forces were to meet. If the Indians still
escaped, Sanford, in command, was to pursue them. Such an operation would have resulted in the "complete capture" of the hostiles,
except Howard noted, for two unfortunate circumstances: the
interruption of couriers carrying dispatches and the treachery of
supposedly friendly Indians who informed Egan of the traps. Failure or not, certainly Sanford and his comrades gave it the old college try.

Sanford was at Meacham's Station, twenty-five miles from La
Grande.

> Here I received instructions by letter from Hdqrs. Dept. of Columbia
> [writes Sanford] directing me to discontinue my march northward and
> to return to the vicinity of La Grande and watch the passes through
> Grande Ronde Valley towards the Wallowa country.[73]

On 10 July, he marched twenty-five miles to Oro Dell and camped.
He had about 104 troopers and about 20 scouts with him to guard
the passes. It wasn't a very hopeful job. For the next four days,
he sent out various detachments in various directions. One unit,
under First Lieutenant Frazier A. Boutelle and Second Lieutenant
William C. Brown, First Cavalry, marched to Starkey's Ranch on
the Grande Ronde "with orders to scout well over towards the John
Day Valley."[74] Sanford placed another detachment near Pelican
Station; he also dispatched scouts "in all directions to watch the

[73] Report of Sanford, 16 September, 1878.
[74] *Ibid.*

passes through which the hostiles might appear."[75] Sanford was thorough. He communicated with Captain Harry C. Egbert, Twelfth Infantry, at North Powder River and arranged with him to guard those passes in the rear. He could not have done more.

On 13 July, Miles had a brush with Egan (or Oytes; the record is not clear) and sent the Indians flying toward Sanford's front. At this point, the various maneuvers become confusing and open to several interpretations and several critiques. According to Howard, Sanford's force split the hostiles, "part going almost south" toward Malheur and Bakersfield and part going into the neighborhood "of Joseph's old haunts in that immense Wallowa Valley."[76] Howard (at Lewiston, Idaho Territory) felt that Sanford missed an opportunity by not pressing forward "with the utmost vigor," a most peculiar noun to use, particularly when speaking of Sanford. His estimate of the situation is highly debatable,[77] so debatable, in fact, that we must look at Sanford's explanation.

Orders came to him on 14 July to move north again toward the Umatilla Agency and join Captain Miles, "supposed to be in that vicinity." Sanford hurried twenty-five miles to Meacham's Station. That night, he got intelligence which indicated "the presence of a body of Indians" to his front, as well as information about Miles's brush of the day before. He tried to get more:

> I sent scouts with information of my approach to the Agency and attempted to obtain information of the whereabouts of Miles & Forsythe's [sic] columns, but could learn nothing in regard to them.[78]

Finally, after days of marching and maneuvering, Sanford sighted his foe at daybreak on 15 July. A party of hostiles appeared on the road in his front, and his pickets fired on them. Sanford quickly formed a line and sent out skirmishers under Lieutenant Brown. The Indians seemed to be moving in the direction of the

---

[75] *Ibid.*

[76] Oliver O. Howard, "The Back Tracks," *The Overland Monthly,* Second Series, X (December, 1887), 653.

[77] Egan, by the way, was killed on 15 July in a treacherous move by Chief U-ma-pine of the Umatillas.

[78] Report of Sanford, 16 September 1878.

Grande Ronde Valley; however, "some parties also appeared on the old Emigrant road," which lay to Sanford's right and was nearer the Wallowa Valley. Somehow, the skirmishers lost the Indians about eleven o'clock that morning, and despite Howard's view, it was not Sanford's fault. He immediately moved back towards Grande Ronde

> to comply with instructions from Colonel Wheaton directing me to continue to guard the approaches to that Valley and to watch the Daily Wagon road in particular.[79]

Sanford remained near Grande Ronde River on the sixteenth, sending scouts out toward Starkey's Ranch and Sommerville. Indians were reported at the latter place. Deciding that he was too far from the Daily Road to guard it with any effectiveness, on 17 July he moved his command to Campbell's Ranch at the head of Ladd's Cañon and from here put scouts on the road.

With the "beautiful little town" of La Grande (as Howard fondly recalled it) as a center, Sanford worked his cavalry and the Nez Percés outward; Howard complimented him for scouting "the different approaches to that valley to the east and to the southeast, following up every road, trail, and footpath where there was the least recent signs of the presence of Indians."[80] On the eighteenth, some trigger-happy white men fired at Lieutenant Williams' Nez Percé scouts and killed one brave; Williams apprehended the killer and took him into Union, the county seat. Not overlooking any possibility, Sanford sent Lieutenant Boutelle to Granite Lakes in the Powder River Mountains, "where Indians were reported crossing." None were found.[81]

Hunting was not good, and Sanford moved his camp to the North Powder River. He had no more than arrived when he received dispatches telling him that Howard was moving to Ladd's Cañon and that he was to join the General. Sanford came back to Campbell's Ranch and reported. The two officers teamed up now and pushed south into Baker County, moving thirty miles to Granite Lakes on

---

[79] *Ibid.*
[80] Howard, "The Back Tracks," *loc. cit.,* 653.
[81] Report of Sanford, 16 September 1878.

the twenty-first and twenty-one miles to Independence on the twenty-second. They had marched *over* instead of around the Burnt River Mountains. The two leaders were old hands at pursuit, and as they shoved their way through the country, both recalled the futile chase of Joseph the year before in Montana.

On 23 July, they moved another 23 miles to Burnt River Meadows, where they found Forsyth. Sanford reported to him at once and was assigned command of the First Battalion, First Cavalry. "At this point," he writes, "my independent command ceased."[82] They had marched a distance of 774 miles. These were route miles—map miles—and did not include various side marches by detachments and scouting parties. Forsyth was short on supplies and was glad enough to have found Sanford, who generously divided his rations, "running some risk of having his own command go hungry."[83]

They remained in Burnt River Meadows, stocking up on supplies and refurbishing animals and equipment, until 27 July, when they broke camp and marched twenty-five miles to the Malheur Agency. They were joined here by other units. Howard listened to various reports and decided that

> our Indians were no longer moving in any considerable detachments, but had broken up into very small, fragmentary parties, hurrying through the woods and across the lava rocks, which were here very extensive and barren of vegetation.[84]

On 28 July, Howard once again redistributed his pursuing force, but maintained the three-column formation in order to "sweep [the word is his and is not accurate] an extent of country as wide as that of Sherman's march to the sea." Howard had been on that march, and in the difficult Oregon country, his military imagination was working very hard. He called the march "exceedingly rough," and he was not wrong. Once he suffered a bad fall from a mule and barely escaped serious, if not mortal, injury (remember, he had only one arm). But on they went. Howard comments:

[82] *Ibid.* This concludes the report of 16 September 1878. From 23 July until 12 August, Sanford was with Forsyth, but this period is not covered in any of his reports.

[83] Howard, "The Back Tracks, *loc. cit.,* 655.

[84] *Ibid.,* 657.

50

My object was to bring in the Indians as prisoners, and if possible, allay the wild fears of the ranch people and settlers, who never felt sure of protection until they saw the troops.[85]

On 29 July, by way of Malheur Agency, Howard was able to telegraph McDowell:

The crisis of the campaign has certainly passed. The check at the Columbia serves to keep peace north of that river. The Bannocks and Piutes fleeing southward have not fully separated, but divided their trails and run over the roughest mountain country. I am moving my troops so as to pick the hostiles up in detail or drive them to the reservation.[86]

Down the crooked Malheur River they rode and marched. On 31 July, they went due east and observed a partial solar eclipse, which rendered the environs strange and ultrahuman: "For a while everything appeared very much as when the heavens are obscured by the smoke of forest fires, only now the air was pure and the sky was clear."[87] They gained the Owyhee River on 1 August, ascended the high tableland, and found water and bunchgrass for the horses. They made camp by a small lake. Rested, the insatiable Howard took them across a sage prairie until they struck a telegraph line. The civilian operator traveling with him hooked in, and Howard learned what the other columns were up to: driving the Indians before them, pretty much the same as he was doing. The largest column had crossed the Snake.

Sanford was with Colonel Forsyth's column as they marched from the Malheur Agency to Stein's Mountains and beyond to Old Camp C. F. Smith on 3 August. Forsyth detained the command here because of "signal fires in the mountains" and citizens' reports that Indians were hiding up there. Until the seventh, Forsyth sent Sanford and other scouting parties into those mountains and they came back with prisoners. Forsyth then swept the lower country

---

[85] Howard, *My Life and Experiences,* 413.

[86] Appendix to "Report of General McDowell," *loc. cit.,* 179.

[87] Oliver O. Howard, "Close of the Piute and Bannock War," *The Overland Monthly,* Second Series, XI (January, 1888), 101.

to the Flint River, to the Bruneau Valley, up the Snake as far as Payne's Ferry.

On the evening of 12 August, they reached Sinker's Creek in Idaho Territory. Forsyth divided the command. Sanford was ordered to Cold Springs, on the Overland Stage Road, where he was "to take charge of the Depot . . . and scout the country in that vicinity." He was further instructed to "observe the country" toward the Snake and to follow any Indian trails.[88] Captain Bernard proceeded south. Forsyth himself was sent by Howard to Boise to assume temporary charge of all operations south and west of the city.

At 8:45 A.M. on 13 August, Sanford led his battalion out of camp and got on the road. Once again he had an independent command. He had under him eight officers, 130 men, and 122 horses.[89] On the sixteenth, he ran into trouble as he tried to cross the Snake opposite Big Bottoms. Instead of riverworthy boats, he had three most fragile and dangerous craft. One was a "small canoe in very bad condition" and without oars. On the second trip over, it sank, dumping six men, including Lieutenant Parnell and Captain Robbins, and "a load of saddles and arms" into the water. Another boat was dispatched to rescue them. Let Sanford tell the tale now:

> Lt. Parnell and Trumpeter Reilly . . . were rescued in an insensible condition and only returned to consciousness after several hours['] hard work by Dr. Spencer. The other men[,] two of whom were unable to swim, were safely brought to shore by the boats owned by the Frobman brothers (scouts). Capt. Orlando Robbins of the scouts is entitled to great credit for his conduct . . . as he risked his own life, in endeavoring to save others and undoubtedly did save both Lt. Parnell and Reilly by assisting them until the arrival of the boats.[90]

Fortunately, this was the only accident during the passage and the command was across by 6:45 P.M.

[88] Report of Sanford to the Adjutant, First Cavalry, dated 14 September 1878, Camp Halleck, Nevada, in Record Group No. 94, National Archives. This report covers the period 12 August–5 September 1878.

[89] The battalion consisted of Company A, Captain Thomas McGregor; Company I, Captain Camillo C. C. Carr; and Company H, First Lieutenant W. R. Parnell. Also with him was Captain Orlando Robbins and some scouts.

[90] Report of Sanford, 14 September 1878.

52

They arrived at the subsistence depot at Cold Springs on 17 August. Next day, Sanford had the stores moved to his camp downstream. He then rested. He had the horses sent out on grass during the day and fed them hay and grain at night. "Every exertion was made to recuperate them after their exhausting march."[91] Like so many cavalry officers, Sanford, ironically, hated horses and regarded them as "fool animals," but he always took care of them. Between 20 August and 29 August, he ordered "scouts out on the various trails leading from [the] Snake [R]iver to the East, but no fresh Indian signs were seen in any case."[92] Equally active were Bernard, Green, and others, following up, as Howard described their activities, "every road and pathway, and ferreting out every possible hiding place."[93] Such time-consuming, body-wearying, mind-shattering tactics were dictated by the Indians, who scattered, not from fright, but, rather, from a rudimentary grasp of guerrilla warfare.

Pursuant to instructions, on 29 August, Sanford left Captain Carr in command of the depot and then proceeded with Companies A and H to Baker, Oregon, passing through Boise. On 1 September near Boise, Captain William H. Winters, an old comrade from the scouts in Arizona, joined Sanford with Company E, First Cavalry, Sanford's old company and his favorite of them in the First. They moved on to Baker by easy stages.

Then on 5 September 1878, the Bannock War suddenly ended for Sanford: he was granted a leave of absence. The war was over anyway, for Howard's persistency had paid off and about six hundred prisoners were being held at various points. As directed by Howard, Sanford turned the command over to Captain McGregor and rode back to Fort Halleck to write his reports. In this final operation, he had marched 196 miles. Thanks to his careful supervision, not one horse was abandoned subsequent to 13 August, a remarkable achievement. Howard wrote of the campaign in his final report to higher headquarters:

91 *Ibid.*
92 *Ibid.*
93 Howard, "Close of the Piute and Bannock War," *loc. cit.*, 104.

53

[It] has been a hard, long, and expensive one. Many of the troops have marched greater distances than during the Nez Percé war, and in all the services I have been called upon to render the government I have never known officers and soldiers to encounter and overcome greater obstacles. The work has been done, and I hope it is satisfactory to the government and to the people.[94]

The General added a final hope "that this may be the last Indian war that I shall be called upon to wage." Not quite. And it was certainly not Sanford's last campaign.

In a short period of time, Sanford had served in three major Indian uprisings, and yet, as at the end of his Arizona service in 1871—the ravages of time serving to wipe out any trace of his letters, journals, or diaries (memoranda, in other words, revealing personal feelings of the moment)—we know next to nothing of what Major George Bliss Sanford thought of having contributed to "The Battle of Civilization," as General William T. Sherman called it, that twenty or twenty-five years' war *after* the War of the Rebellion. But again we can ask: what effect of the senselessness of it all on him?

There is the story of the Twenty-second Infantry, sent to Chicago in the summer of 1877 to quiet some labor troubles (this was just before the unit was sent into the Nez Percé fracas). One workingman, part of a crowd confronted by the soldiers, called out, "You would not fire on us, would you?" And a private replied calmly, "Not unless the captain ordered it." There is no need to become an Aesop and spell out the moral.

More than one Army officer expressed openly his disgust and his hatred of it all. More often than not, the Regular Army officer admired and respected his foe for the very qualities any professional soldier admires. Years ago, Major Baird wrote:

For every Indian war there is a cause; too often that cause has been

---

[94] "Report of General Howard," October, 1878, *loc. cit.*, 235. R. Ross Arnold, *Indian Wars of Idaho,* 211, asserts that on or about 20 July, Sanford overtook a band of fugitives on Wolf Creek, near the Powder River in eastern Oregon, and in "a sharp skirmish" killed 17 braves, took 25 women and children as prisoners, and captured 600 ponies. I cannot find the slightest trace of this in the records and must reject it.

bad policy, bad faith, bad conduct, or blundering on the part of the whites.[95]

The three campaigns in five years certainly entitled Sanford to a respite. The one month's leave, with permission to apply for an extension of six months, was granted to him in the field; it was dated 3 September.[96] After writing his reports, he left for New York, where, on 27 September, he applied for and received his extension. For three months, Sanford relaxed in the city, a change from the physical and mental deprivations of the western frontier, deprivations that could send a man into enforced (and unwanted) retirement so enfeebling were they at times.

Suddenly he was ordered to temporary duty on the Equipment Board in Washington, D.C. Unwillingly, no doubt, but faithfully, Sanford served until 1 April 1879, when the group was dissolved. Army regulations worked in his favor for once. It was very complicated and General Sherman was forced to make the final decision, but he was granted thirty days' delay and reverted to the unexpired portion of his leave at the expiration of the delay time. It meant an extra month away from the wastes of Nevada and the isolation of Fort Halleck. Sanford was not due back there until 9 September, almost a year to the day of blessed absence.

In the early part of August, the War Department ordered him to report to "the Superintendent, Mounted Recruiting Service, to conduct a detachment of recruits to the Pacific Coast."[97] When this task was completed, he returned to out-of-the-way Halleck and resumed command. He lived in a two-story, multiwindowed Victorian "mansion" that reminds one of a painting by Charles Sheeler. It was a paradox, squatting there amid one-story, roughly built shelters which housed the garrison, the mounts, and the units' offices and which surrounded the rectangular-shaped parade. A sutler at Halleck once told Sanford: "This country is all right for men and cattle, but it's hard on women and horses." Gertrude

[95] "General Miles's Indian Campaigns," *loc. cit.,* 370.
[96] Special Orders No. 109, Department of California, as printed in *Army and Navy Journal,* XVI (28 September 1878), [115].
[97] Special Orders, War Department, dated 12 August 1879, as abstracted in *Army and Navy Journal,* XVII (16 August 1879), [19].

Sanford knew that; she was pregnant. Her second child and second daughter, Gertrude Minturn, was born at the post on 25 January 1880.[98]

Coincidentally, the very next day, 26 January, Governor Charles C. Van Zandt of Rhode Island, nearing the end of his term, wrote a bold and most urgent letter to General Sherman more or less giving him the choice of assigning Sanford as "Executive Officer at Jefferson Barracks, Mo.," or, if this was impracticable, detailing the Major "for duty some place near the East." Van Zandt gave as the reason Mrs. Sanford's ailing health.[99] Now few people dared to write the Lieutenant General in such terms. Sherman replied, politely and firmly, that the best interests of the Army (a marvelous phrase and unarguable) would not be served by such an assignment.

Actually, by its own standards, the Army had been treating Sanford well of late: extended leave and dull but not perilous duty at Halleck. Of course, neither the general commanding the Army nor any other senior officer could explain away the grubby life out in Nevada. Such an explanation was not required of them. Sanford could have complained. But he didn't. It wasn't part of his code. He knew that if an officer were competent and soldierly (as General Howard had called him after the Nez Percé War), not spectacularly or violently heroic, just a solid man, then he must expect to be called upon. It so happened that he had been called to Halleck, almost as if he were a priest, and had duties there: a court-martial eight days before his daughter's birth, a suddenly insane soldier to be dispatched safely to San Francisco and incarceration, a court of inquiry involving two brother officers (certain "accusations or imputations" had been made), and more courts-martial. It was quite dreary. Yet, given a short leave, Sanford returned early and notified the Adjutant General on 19 February 1881:

I have the honor to report that I returned to this post for duty Feb-

[98] She became the wife of William K. Wallbridge. The Sanfords had no other children.

[99] Record Group No. 94, National Archives. Van Zandt (1830–1894) was the thirtieth governor of Rhode Island, 1877–1880. Since he was a native of Newport and an influential man, one can assume that Mrs. Sanford's family connections had been brought to bear.

ruary 18th 1881, and desire to relinquish the unexpired portion of the leave of absence granted . . . January 6th 1881.[100]

There is no record of demurral from the Adjutant General.

Finally, Sanford was removed from the desert. On 21 March 1881, he was ordered to report to the division commander for "temporary duty" as Acting Inspector General,[101] and on 5 April, Headquarters, Military Division of the Pacific, Presidio, San Francisco, issued General Orders No. 4, announcing Sanford as same. Seems simple enough—routine change, and Sanford insists that he *was* Inspector General—but the order prompted much rumbling in the offices and corridors of the bureau-ridden War Department. Adjutant General Drum scribbled on the bottom of the printed order: "Existing orders require the approval of Secretary of War before placing officers on duty as Inspecting Officers." Someone else then wrote: "Shall Gen McDowell be so informed?" He was informed by the Adjutant General in this prodigious display of red tape:

> I am directed by the General of the Army to invite your attention to the act of 23 June, 1874, section 1 . . . which provides that officers of the line "not to exceed four" may be detailed by the *Secretary of War* as acting Assistant Inspector Generals, and to inform you that, as four officers of the line are already detailed by authority of the Secretary of War, another cannot, under the law, be so detailed.
>
> The General further directs me to say that . . . Major Sanford may be assigned to special duty at your Headquarters . . . and then be ordered from time to time, as Special Inspector, to make such inspections as may be required.[102]

All this was undoubtedly correct and according to the book, but it is a fact that Sanford says he was Inspector General. Therefore, Major General McDowell, who had no fear of authority, must have arrived at some satisfactory *modus vivendi* within the regulations —or, more accurately, within the red tape within the regulations.

Sanford had at least one assignment. In late July or early August,

[100] *Ibid.*

[101] Special Orders No. 43, Military Division of the Pacific, as abstracted in *Army and Navy Journal*, XVIII (9 April 1881), 741.

[102] Record Group No. 94, National Archives.

he journeyed over to Fort McDermit, Nevada, and its neighborhood to hold conversations with Chief Natchez and Lee Winnemucca of the Paiute tribe relative to the proposed government plan to return the Paiutes from the Yakima Reservation in Oregon to their home in Nevada. The Paiutes were having a hard time at Yakima—the climate was very damp and cold and the provisions were short, an old story. Sanford talked, conferred, listened. On 9 August, he wrote up his report, couched in cautious language within a cautious viewpoint:

> I am strongly inclined to believe that they [the Paiutes] are in condition to be easily handled. . . . They should be brought together, placed on a reservation, and instructed in farming. . . . They are not a warlike tribe, and not likely to make any trouble again; but at the same time their numbers are large [Sanford estimated about 1,100 to 1,200], and if some occupation is not given to them, their natural vitality must find a vent in some direction, and that direction is likely to be indicated by the citizens themselves in their neighborhood, who are constantly watching for an outbreak and prepared to attribute the worst motives to every action of an Indian and resent it accordingly.[103]

What we have here, in the final sentence, is about as near an opinion from Sanford relative to the Indian as a human being as we are likely to find while he was in service. Sanford was but five months at the Presidio when he was called out into the field again.

There was trouble among the White Mountain Apaches, who were living on Cibecue Creek in the northwestern part of the San Carlos Reservation in Arizona Territory. Here an Indian medicine man named Nocky-del-klin-ne proposed, in return for gifts of horses, blankets, etc., to bring back to life some chiefs who had died not too long before. For two months in the deadly hot summer of 1881, dances were held for this purpose; but then the medicine man announced that the spirits had said they would not (or could not) return to the country "until the whites had left it, and fixed

---

[103] *Report of the Secretary of War, 1882–1883*, House Exec. Docs., 47th Cong., 2nd Sess., 136–37. The chief informant for the Paiutes was Lee Winnemucca, son of the friendly Paiute chief of Bannock War days.

the date of their leaving at the time of the corn harvest."[104] This *was* dangerous. The whites feared that the medicine man was working on the superstitions of the Indians either to bring about an outbreak or to work them up to a state where they would join in any "demonstration" made by the hostiles from New Mexico Territory.

On 13 August, Colonel and Brevet Major General Orlando B. Willcox, commanding, Department of Arizona, telegraphed the renowned Indian campaigner Colonel and Brevet Major General Eugene A. Carr, Sixth Cavalry, commanding Fort Apache, to arrest the medicine man. (Agent Tiffany said arrest him or kill him or both.) Carr set a date, 28 August, to meet Nocky-del-klin-ne, but the arrangement failed. On 29 August, Carr, with Troops D and E, Sixth Cavalry, and a company of Indian scouts (the force totaled six officers, seventy-nine enlisted men, and twenty-three scouts), set out for the medicine man's village on Cibecue Creek and reached it on 30 August. The arrest was made, but the troops were fired on and a "severe fight" developed in which Carr's command lost one officer and four men killed, four men wounded, two mortally. Carr buried his dead and beat it back to Fort Apache the following day. En route, elements of his command fought the Apaches in another skirmish. Then on 1 September, in a rare tactic indeed, the Apaches attacked the fort itself in the afternoon; they were repulsed, but Carr lost an additional four men killed and several wounded, as well as forty-five horses and ten mules killed, wounded, and missing. These three days were rugged for the Sixth Cavalry.

Rumors were disconcertingly wild: Colonel Carr had been exterminated; Fort Apache had been attacked and captured. Apparently, they affected even stolid Major General McDowell, who had been in San Francisco so long he seemed to own his billet. His first reaction was to relieve Sanford from his "special duty" and have him resume command at Halleck (Camillo C. C. Carr had been in command). This was countermanded very shortly—Sanford

[104] "Report of the Commissioner of Indian Affairs, 1881," *Report of the Secretary of the Interior, 1881–1882*, House Exec. Docs., 47th Cong., 1st Sess., 6. Barbara Ann Tyler, "Cochise: Apache War Leader," *Journal of Arizona History*, VI (Spring, 1965), 2–4, gives a good breakdown of the various Apache bands and identifies each.

59

went nowhere—and the word now (3 September) was that the commanding officers at Fort Halleck and Fort McDermit would send companies G and I "at once by rail" to Willcox Station, Arizona Territory, there "to take the field."[105] On 5 September, Captain Reuben F. Bernard's Troop G left McDermit for Arizona. Next day, Carr's Troop I left Halleck. At the same time, Sanford was ordered to Lathrop, California, south of Stockton, to assume command of the two cavalry troops and proceed to Arizona.[106]

Whatever Sanford's mood as he headed out for another campaign —the odds were getting short—it could not have been helped by a current and silly parody of Gilbert and Sullivan, called *The Song of the Apache,* in the weekly *San Francisco News Letter.* One of its jingling verses went:

> *I'm the Terror-of-the-Mountain and the Horror-of-the-Plain!*
> *I'm the Painted-Piebald-Pelican, you bet!*
> *I'm the Scavenger-of-Dead-Men's Bones, the Burrower-of-Brain,*
> *The Dainty-Dusky-Darling of our "set."*

Chorus of Braves:

> *We're the Hair-Scrapers, the Corpse-Drapers,*
> *The Devils-of-the-Pyre and-the-Torch!*
> *When the blood flows fast and free, we dearly love to see*
> *The Paleface wriggle, giggle, squeal, and scorch.*[107]

Two other companies of the First Cavalry were sent down, and other complements came in from the Department of the Missouri. Willcox needed every man he could get. In the whole of his department, he had only 1,184 personnel to guard simultaneously the San Carlos Reservation (4,550 square miles), the settlements, and 382 miles of border from Yuma, on the Colorado River, to New Mexico Territory; 1,184 men "to watch, pursue, head off and

---

[105] *Army and Navy Journal,* XIX (17 September 1881), 137. Willcox Station was on the Southern Pacific Railroad in Cochise County, southeast corner of Arizona.

[106] *Ibid.* Lathrop was on the Southern Pacific Railroad in San Joaquin County.

[107] Reprinted in *Army and Navy Journal,* XIX (17 September 1881), 147. It was signed "T. A. H."

destroy the Apaches, on all sides, celebrated for their fleetness over such an immense range of rough country as Arizona."[108]

Willcox bordered on despair, for not only did he have the White Mountain Apaches to contend with, he also had the even more fearsome Chiricahua Apaches, the most belligerent of them all, the tribe which counted among its leaders over the years such chiefs as Cochise, George, Bonito, and Geronimo. The Chiricahuas broke out of the reservation on the night of 29–30 September 1881. But let's take each outbreak in its place. After the fight at Fort Apache, the White Mountain Indians struck not another blow, amazingly enough. Wrote Willcox:

> The troops were moved to Cibicu country in such a manner and time as to drive the hostiles from their strongholds into the folds of the reservation without a fight. . . . Many of the worst [had] surrendered.[109]

This in a country parts of which consisted of "rocky ridges and canyons," difficult to attack and easy to defend, said to be worse even than the awful Modoc lava beds.

The reason why the Chiricahuas broke out is obscure, but in August, 1882, General Willcox reported one possibility was that the reservation authorities had refused to help them "take out a water ditch"; the two principal chiefs, Juh and Natchez, had twice asked for assistance, only to be turned down. Anyway, they broke out and headed south for the Mexican border and beyond into their favorite wilderness, the Sierra Madres.

On 30 September, General Willcox sent First Lieutenant Gilbert E. Overton and First Lieutenant John N. Glass, Sixth Cavalry, in pursuit; Willcox headed out himself, taking along Sanford and his command of two cavalry companies (Bernard and Carr) to guard forty-seven Apache prisoners who had been in the Cibecue fight on 30 August. Willcox also wanted Sanford available in the southern part of the Territory, which was now without the protection of any cavalry.

[108] "Report of Brevet Major General O. B. Willcox," dated 31 August 1882, *Report of the Secretary of War, 1882–1883*, 147.

[109] "Report of Brevet Major General O. B. Willcox," dated 12 October 1881, *Report of the Secretary of War, 1881–1882*, House Exec. Docs., 47th Cong., 1st Sess., 155.

The first day, 1 October, they made thirty-five miles to Camp Thomas; next day, they moved out towards Camp Grant. Willcox impatiently moved ahead to Cedar Springs. When Sanford was about four miles from the Springs, he received an urgent message to join Willcox—the Chiricahua Apaches had attacked a train near by. Sanford left Carr behind to guard the prisoners and galloped out with Bernard's company to Cedar Springs and beyond, following the trail of the fugitives. Glass and Overton teamed up with him, and Willcox ordered Sanford to "push in."

Five miles south of the Springs, Sanford moved Overton's two companies (A and F, Sixth Cavalry) to the front. They passed the corpses of "several soldiers," only recently slain, about 3:00 P.M. At this moment, Overton was fired on from the front by the Apaches, concealed in the rocks and brush. The Lieutenant deployed as skirmishers (just like the book) and moved forward dismounted. Sanford then directed Bernard, mounted, to the left, and he moved forward deployed. It might have been Camas Meadows for Sanford all over again, but he had control and experience.

The firing became "very rapid"; the cavalrymen edged the Apaches before them, and Bernard's right and Overton's left hooked up. The enemy, never one to fight when at a disadvantage, debouched from his position in the lower rocks and took off for higher ground. "The fighting commenced with great severity," reported Sanford, "from this time until about 9 P.M., the bright moonlight greatly favoring the Indians, who were in shadow themselves, but could see every movement on the side of the troops."[110] Sanford's foes fought hard and with what he called "great boldness and desperation," for they were buying time, in holding their position, in order to remove their stock to safety. On one occasion, about 8:00 P.M., they came down the mountainside and charged Bernard's line, coming within ten feet of it and firing seven volleys in all to bolster their charge. Bernard's men pushed them off, but not without a galling struggle. Just before nine o'clock, Sanford discovered that the Chiricahuas had moved off "in the darkness of

[110] "Report of Major George B. Sanford, 1st Cavalry," dated 5 October 1881, *ibid.*, 146.

the cañons"; he withdrew his command to the plain, bringing along his dead and wounded. He had lost one man killed, three wounded, and fifteen horses killed and wounded—light casualties considering the length and conditions of the battle.

Meanwhile, Willcox, his staff, and the Apache prisoners had taken the Eureka Springs Road and were on their way to Camp Grant. Sanford was anxious for Willcox because reconnaissance had suggested that perhaps the Apaches were also traveling in the same direction. However, Willcox made it safely, as did Sanford by 3:00 A.M. on 3 October. He had marched eighty miles and fought one engagement in two days. He was ill when he came into Grant, and he missed the final brush with the Chiricahuas on the fourth at South Pass in the Dragoon Mountains. By now the Apaches were in full flight. Sanford recovered quickly enough, but did not participate in the pursuit that ranged across the Mexican border until December. Of the Cedar Springs fight, General Willcox wrote:

> Great praise is due Sanford, officers, and men for their gallantry, zeal, and persistent energy, which resulted in such a complete discomfiture of the Chiricahuas that they have not made another stand. Their own killed were concealed or carried off in the night, but bloody clothes dropped on the trails, and the large number of horses and mules found killed on the mountain side (twenty-three in number), proved how severely they must have suffered.[111]

Sanford had other things to do in Arizona Territory besides chasing down Apaches. On 24 October, he was sent to Tucson to consult with the Assistant Adjutant General "in reference to the site of the post of Huachuca."[112] Apparently, Sanford was assigned the job of deciding on a permanent site, and he went down to Huachuca for several days for an on-the-spot inspection. On 14 November, he was relieved and dispatched to Fort Bowie, Arizona Territory, to assume command; he remained there for a little more than six weeks—he was officially relieved on 14 December—and

---

[111] *Ibid.*, 147, Willcox's first endorsement to Sanford's report.
[112] *Army and Navy Journal,* XIX (12 November 1881), 314.

was then directed to rejoin his "proper station," Fort Halleck. He was still at Huachuca on 29 December, thereby missing a Christmas with his family.

At Halleck, Sanford again took up his quiet and dull life, punctuated by service as president of three courts-martial in April, May, and July. Old comrade Camillo Carr was another member.

As he whiled away his days there in the desert, Sanford may have (most likely did) come across an article entitled "Cost of Indian Wars" in the Army officer's "Bible," the *Army and Navy Journal*. It was a fascinating medley of statistics couched in the coldest of language, without comment or opinion. Derived from a recent report of the Secretary of War, the article listed the costs of the various Indian wars during the decade from 1872 to 1882. The Modoc War had cost $335,009; Nez Percé War, $975,082; Bannock War, $567,571; the recent (and continuing) Apache uprising, $43,850. The Sioux War in 1876–77 had been truly expensive: $1,894,361. The total cost "of these active attempts to control the aborigines" was $5,058,821. But this was only a beginning, a modest portion of the whole figure. "The aggregate cost," continued the article, "of all kinds of service by the United States Army west of the Mississippi was for 1872–1882 $205,474,759."[113] Add to this various expenses and the total was $223,891,264 "as the estimate submitted by the Secretary of War of the total cost of troops in the Indian country."[114]

We can get a better idea of the cost if we estimate that the value of the dollar in the 1880's was about five or six times its purchasing power at the time this book was published in early 1969, so figure the Secretary of War was talking about spending well over a billion dollars in something like ten years. And, as the *Journal* pointed out, this was "the cost of troops" and did not account for "the peace offerings, annuities, and other inducements which have been provided at very large expense by the Government."[115] Sherman's conclusion, the *Journal* reported, was that 80 per cent "of

[113] XIX (18 March 1882), 747.
[114] *Ibid.*
[115] *Ibid.*

the expenditures of the annual appropriations has been made on Indian account" from 1872 to 1882.[116]

It is interesting that Sherman construed all of the Army west of the Mississippi (and that was not quite 75 per cent of its total strength) "as either in Indian country or so near as to be incident to their control or observation."[117] Sanford was in an expensive business with operations in a vast territory and with a yearly average force of about 18,500 of 23,700 effective.

In September, 1882, Sanford applied to the Department of California for two months' leave of absence ("to visit my home in New York City"); this was granted, as was an extension of four months. His address would be 16 East Sixty-eighth Street. He had "business of importance" to take care of.

Back again to dreary Halleck. Then on 26 September 1883, he boarded the Central Pacific and journeyed to the Presidio and reported for duty. He was through with Halleck and Nevada forever. Troop I, under Captain Carr, had already taken station there, joining Troop M from San Rafael, California. Sanford assumed command of all of the cavalry.

San Francisco seemed especially charming to the Sanfords that fall. For a time after their arrival, there were no accommodations on the post and the Army rented quarters for them in the city. Duty at the Presidio was almost exclusively drills, training, parades, and guard mounts. Sanford, more accustomed to the rough life of a frontier fort, was somewhat out of his element for a few weeks, but he was too good a trooper to be nonplussed for long. On 2 November, there was a "grand parade" and maneuvers by the cavalry and artillery before more than one thousand spectators. The *Alta California* was able to report to its readers:

> The drill of the regular cavalry came first with a series of evolutions that showed, despite all the taunts so freely flung around, that the United States cavalry is the equal of any in the world. The troop has just been supplied with remounts, and many of the horses were very

116 *Ibid.*
117 *Ibid.*

green, yet they were forced through a series of complicated movements that would bother a circus-rider.[118]

In December, the *Alta California* advised its readers that "the daily battalion drills . . . under Lieut. Col. Sanford make the Presidio unusually attractive. . . . Col. Sanford and his subordinates . . . have been doing admirable work."[119] His subordinates were old hands and old friends: omnipresent Camillo C. C. Carr and Captain Moses Harris. They worked well together and in March they held a full-dress mounted inspection, along with the light artillery battery, in Golden Gate Park. As such formalities go, it was fairly successful but was not repeated because the park was not a suitable area.

Orders for Sanford and the First Cavalry were being processed. On 17 April 1884, Army Headquarters announced that the First and Second Regiments of Cavalry would exchange stations. Troops I and M of the First were slated for Fort Custer, Montana, regimental headquarters. Such complicated troop movements required weeks of preparation, and it was not until the early morning of 20 June that Troops I and M, Major George B. Sanford (recently recovered from a nasty fall from his horse during drills) commanding—115 men, four officers, and 120 horses—marched quietly out of the Presidio and down to Fourth and Townsend Streets and loaded the horses on "the cars." There was little leave-taking. It was going to be a long trip. Officers' furniture and effects were loaded, too, but in those days the government, a model of frugality for all to see, forced the officers to change quarters at their own expense. Fodder, rations, all the standard equipment of the cavalry, were shoved on board. They had a long march ahead of them after detraining, and Sanford had to pack enough with him to make his command independent of outside assistance.

On 23 June, a battalion of the First, Major George G. Huntt in command, left Fort Missoula, Montana, on the march for Helena. On the same day, Sanford entrained his battalion (augmented by

118 *Army and Navy Journal*, XXI (17 November 1883), 309, quoting the *Alta California* of 3 November.
119 *Ibid.* (8 December 1883), 371; no date given for the *Alta California*.

Troop A from Fort Bidwell, California, and Troop K from Fort Klamath, Oregon) at Ogden, Utah Territory. They arrived at Helena on 26 June; Huntt came in on the twenty-ninth. Then on 1 July, the headquarters, staff, band, and Troops D, G, I, K, and M, First Cavalry, commanded by Sanford, mounted and departed Helena for Fort Custer. This makeshift battalion numbered several hundred men and was the largest unit he had commanded since the Civil War. Sanford was on the march for two weeks before arriving at Custer on 15 July. They had covered 132 miles.[120]

Built in 1877 on the high bench at the junction of the Big Horn and Little Big Horn rivers, thirty miles from Custer Station on the Northern Pacific Railroad, Fort Custer was a large and important installation. In the fall of 1884, the garrison numbered approximately 33 officers and 476 enlisted men. Colonel Cuvier Grover, commanding officer of both the fort and the regiment, was ill and would be dead by June. For Sanford, nothing of moment occurred during his truncated tour of duty there other than his unfortunate luck to be entrapped in an old Civil War claim about a horse which he had made use of in Missouri early in '62. It cost him three hundred dollars to settle up.[121]

What was life at a frontier fort in the mid-eighties? Well, the officers' association presented amateur plays, one of which was entitled *Home*. Then there was the Fort Custer Social Club, which gave biweekly dances. Literary and debating clubs met once a week. The local G.A.R. post was active. More active was the I.O.G.T. (International Order of Good Templars); it had going a campaign for total abstinence and claimed 140 members of the garrison. Post Chaplain J. H. Macomber was popular and respected and worked hard on all types of religious services and training. In December, the temperature dropped to 47.5 degrees below zero; nevertheless, on the tenth, the post's officers and ladies performed *Caste* to an admiring audience. There was a "real Christmas tree" that year, and each child was given a basket of candy and an orange. The

---

[120] "Report of Brigadier General Alfred H. Terry," dated 6 October 1884, *Report of the Secretary of War, 1884–1885,* House Exec. Docs., 48th Cong., 2nd Sess., 113. Terry commanded the Department of Dakota.

[121] For details, see n. 69, Chap. I.

enlisted men and civilian employees, having organized a new society known as the Rounders, gave a ball on 22 January, and the post quartermaster thoughtfully provided "sleighs to take the fair ones." They all danced until 4:00 A. M.

This was life at Custer that winter of 1884–85. Considering the dreadful cold, it might have been very disagreeable, but in February, the chinooks, warm and dry, began blowing and the snow melted.

Sanford's friends on the "outside" were busy again. In March, the Honorable Daniel H. Chamberlain of Washington and New York, attorney at law, addressed a letter to recently appointed Secretary of War William C. Endicott on Sanford's behalf, pointing out that the Major had been "on duty on the plains nearly all the time since the War." The fact that Sanford was at Fort Custer did not impress Chamberlain. Far from it. "His family are suffering in health and it would be a great boon to them . . . if he could be given duty at the East." This request was important enough to provoke a first endorsement from the Lieutenant General himself, Philip Sheridan:

> The reasons given herein by Mr. Chamberlain are not, in my judg-ment, legitimate for the assignment of an officer to duty at any particu-lar station.
>
> For the information of the Secretary of War, however, I will say that I have had under consideration the name of Major Sanford for detail as Instructor at the School of Application, Fort Leavenworth, Kansas, when the proper time arrives for making the detail.

This was on 23 March. On 9 April, Endicott answered Chamber-lain's letter, saying ultimately: "I am constrained in the interests of the military service to decline compliance with your request." It was a negative reply meant to sever all discussion, but eleven days later, Chamberlain wrote a second letter, expanding upon and explaining the first, and said emphatically that his request was not to be con-strued as meaning merely and solely some eastern station for Sanford:

> I would like to add that any change which should bring him within the

limits of the older Western States so as to make him more favorably situated with respect to his family, and especially his children, for the purposes of schools, etc, would be all that his friends could ask, and I trust you will permit me to prefer this request.

Chamberlain's name carried weight, as he knew it would (he was a Democrat), in Grover Cleveland's newly installed Democratic administration. Two days later, 22 April 1885, the Adjutant General, Richard C. Drum, informed him that Sanford "has been ordered on duty at the School of Application for Infantry and Cavalry, Fort Leavenworth, Kansas, the first of July, next."[122] General Drum then proceeded to paint a glowing picture of Leavenworth as "one of the most desirable stations in the country—if not the most desirable."[123] He was not exaggerating. Leavenworth had brick buildings and spacious grounds and was the showplace of the Army. And the school, established at Sherman's direction in 1881, was soon to become (after a rough beginning) the bright and shining star in the Army's education program for its officers. A showplace all around, if one chooses to ignore the many problems brought about by cheeseparing congressmen.

The school and the post were commanded by Colonel Thomas H. Ruger, Eighteenth Infantry, about due for promotion to the coveted star of the brigadier general.[124] Leavenworth was also headquarters for the Department of the Missouri, Brigadier General Nelson A. Miles commanding, and its garrison consisted of 73

[122] Special Orders No. 88, Washington, dated 17 April 1885, paragraph 6, assigned Sanford and Major Abraham K. Arnold, Sixth Cavalry, to the school, to report in person on 15 July.

[123] The foregoing correspondence is to be found in Record Group No. 94, National Archives. Daniel H. Chamberlain (1835–1907) was a good man for Sanford to have on his side. A native of West Brookfield, Massachusetts, he was a graduate of Yale, Class of 1862 (thus Sanford's connection). He migrated to South Carolina after the Civil War and was attorney general of the state from 1868 to 1872, the height of corruption during Reconstruction. In 1874, he was elected governor and was renominated in 1876, running against Wade Hampton in a violently conducted campaign. Chamberlain claimed victory and was inaugurated on 7 December 1876, but he withdrew and entered law practice in New York City.

[124] Ruger had served in the Civil War as a brigadier general of volunteers and was a veteran of Sharpsburg, Chancellorsville, Gettysburg, the Atlanta Campaign, the Battle of Franklin, and Sherman's campaign in the Carolinas. He and O. O. Howard were classmates at West Point, class of 1854.

69

officers and 550 enlisted men. The course at the school was two years; an average of 40 officers attended. Apparently sometime in June, Sanford came down from Fort Custer, reported, and was designated senior instructor of cavalry tactics.

Everything looked quite cozy and professional except for one thing (and there was always *something* hovering about Sanford): the unrest of the Cheyennes and the Arapahos in the Indian Territory. In late June, reports of an outbreak by the Cheyennes reached the department. A familiar story, only this time it was the cattlemen who encroached on Indian lands with their herds. Orders were issued and the four troops of cavalry on duty at Leavenworth left there, organized as a battalion, on 8 July 1885 under Sanford's command for duty in the field.[125] There was no combat, none of the epic battles and marches of the Nez Percé campaign. Rather downright prosaic duty in sweltering southern Kansas by what some observers called the finest cavalry unit in the Army: to guard and protect the extensive settlements against "possible incursion by Indians until recalled."[126] An additional duty was to assure that the cattlemen moved their herds from the Indian lands by 4 September as per proclamation by President Cleveland.

Reports coming into the War Department in late August indicated that the cattlemen were actually complying with the proclamation, and Sanford withdrew and marched back to Leavenworth. Precisely at noon, 4 September 1885, he halted his battalion in front of post headquarters and reported his arrival to Colonel Ruger. The last day and night had been tough; heavy rains had lashed the area, and the troops had come the final miles through a nasty storm. But they presented a good appearance to Ruger as he accepted Sanford's salute. Troop B, Third Cavalry, even added a little color to the ceremony: each trooper wore a sunflower in his hat. Ruger

---

[125] Company I, First Cavalry, Captain Camillo C. C. Carr commanding; Company B, Third Cavalry, Captain John B. Johnson; Company L, Fourth Cavalry, Captain Theodore J. Wint; and Company M, Sixth Cavalry, Captain William A. Rafferty.

[126] "Report of Colonel Thomas H. Ruger," *Report of the Secretary of War, 1885–1886,* House Exec. Docs., 49th Cong., 1st Sess., 212.

chose to ignore this larksome uniform discrepancy. And well he could, for Sanford and his officers and men had done a good job. The men knew it, too, and in conversation with a reporter from the *Leavenworth Times*, they said that Sanford had "no peer in the service as a cavalry officer. He was kind to them and showed every consideration due them. They will all swear by Sanford hereafter."[127]

General Miles and Lieutenant General Sheridan made an inspection of the Indian Territory and visited the Cheyenne and Arapaho reservations. Here is Miles's partial account:

> The condition of affairs might rightly be termed a pandemonium. A very large part of the Indian Territory and reservations had been leased, fenced, and to some extent stocked with cattle. The Cheyennes and Arapahoes had been, as far as possible, huddled together in disagreeable and unhealthy camps; they were turbulent, disaffected, and on the verge of open hostilities. Two of their prominent men had been murdered, and they were defiant and utterly beyond the control of their agent or his Indian police.[128]

Such field duty as Sanford's naturally had a disrupting effect on the school, for the officers were assigned to duty at Leavenworth first and at the school second; in other words, the commanding officer of the school, for the most part, had to draw his instructors from the officers on duty at the post. This did not always make for first-class instruction. Colonel Alexander McD. McCook, Sixth Regiment of Infantry, former major general of volunteers, who succeeded Ruger on 13 May 1886, observed in a report:

> Besides the field officers on duty at the school, the instructors are necessarily selected from the officers on duty with the companies composing the garrison, and on account of insufficient quarters for other officers the commandant of the school is limited to his selection to those officers, some of whom, by physical disability and want of proper knowledge, are not competent to teach any subject. Hence he does

---

[127] *Army and Navy Journal*, XXIII (12 September 1885), 122, quoting the newspaper but giving no date.

[128] "Report of Brigadier General Nelson A. Miles," dated 12 September 1885, *Report of the Secretary of War, 1885–1886*, 153. Miles was happy to report that "this condition of affairs was soon changed."

not deem it proper to ask for the intelligent, bright, and progressive officers of our Army to be placed on duty as his assistants.[129]

So behind the façade of the showplace of the Army were some cracks in the walls that could not be plastered over.

Naturally enough, Sanford was valued and desired as an instructor by McCook, and when the Colonel heard an unpleasant rumor, he wrote to the Adjutant General on 4 July 1886:

> A[braham]. K. Arnold, is now Lt. Col: 1st Cav [as of 11 June 1886], Major G. B. Sanford belongs to same Regiment. Should the Dept decide that two Field officers from same Regt: is impracticable—I hope Major Sanford may be retained here. He is cavalry instructor, and a most valuable man for the school—and only reached here last year.[130]

General Drum quieted McCook's fears: it was not "the intention" of the Lieutenant General to relieve either Arnold or Sanford until at least the end of the school year in 1887.

As senior instructor, Sanford taught and supervised a complete curriculum in the Department of Cavalry, including tactics, equitation, field service, practical field exercises, hippology (this encompassed, among other things, the anatomy, physiology, and pathology of the horse), and, as often as possible, clinics under the direction of the veterinary surgeon. The course work also entailed instruction "for the purchase of remounts" in which the student officer was required to examine, weigh, measure, test for age, and inspect for defects and gaits all horses presented by the instructor.

The regimen at Leavenworth was strict. McCook was always a disciplinarian of the first order—indeed, a borderline martinet. Certainly he lived by the book and for the book. During his first year at the post, he issued orders on uniforms ("officers will, on all occasions, wear the prescribed uniform"), against firecrackers, on prohibiting children from going on the parade or drill grounds

---

[129] "Report of Colonel McCook," dated 29 August 1886, *Report of the Secretary of War, 1886–1887*, House Exec. Docs., 49th Cong., 2nd Sess., 211. For a different and highly romanticized view, see Charles King, "The Leavenworth School," *Harper's New Monthly Magazine*, LXXVI (April, 1888), 777–92. Sanford served as a model for one of the illustrations.

[130] Record Group No. 94, National Archives.

during military ceremonies (children were restricted elsewhere under McCook), and against gambling ("the officers' club room is to be closed at 11 o'clock P. M., and gambling thereat with cards for money will not be tolerated"). School was held six days a week, usually from 11:00 A.M. until 3:00 P.M., Saturdays excepted, when it continued until 5:00 P. M. The no-nonsense program was work and study for both the students and the instructors, for McCook demanded that his officers work as hard as the students. Examination periods were in January and June. The students ranged from recent United States Military Academy graduates (which was certainly a commentary on the quality of education at the Point) to mustangs recently up from the ranks. All were lieutenants.

Sanford carried on his other duties with the cavalry when he was not in the classroom. Twice (in 1886 and 1887) he acted as grand marshal of the Memorial Day parade at the post. In the spring of 1887, McCook, who loved pageantry, instituted mounted dress parades; Sanford was in command on two occasions. The cavalry battalion carried what was considered a "beautiful" yellow silk standard bearing the inscription "Cavalry Battalion, Infantry and Cavalry School." The coat of arms was worked by hand. The national colors, also of silk, had the words "U.S. Infantry and Cavalry School" running in embroidered letters across. All units had new guidons. McCook was tireless in his efforts to instill pride.

And he was direct and pointed in reminding officers of their duty at all times. On one occasion, he called attention to Paragraph 813, Infantry Tactics, saying: "A listless and half-avoided performance of the duty required by this paragraph is reprehensibly common and calls for correction. At all roll calls officers superintending must be present at the formation of their troop or company."

Yet McCook was socially inclined, and the post glittered. The Fort Leavenworth correspondent to the *Kansas City Times* once gushed:

Its clubs, libraries, billiard halls, canteens, schools, churches, stores,

73

and theatres crowd upon my imagination, and between regal receptions, fashionable parties, able lectures, excellent theatricals of every kind and a constant round of balls and germans, I know not where to begin. Never, perhaps, has Fort Leavenworth seen a more joyous time. The days of General Pope are still remembered, but that was a family gathering compared with the intellectual and social life of today.[131]

There was a time to play and there was a time to work, and for those officers who could perform well in both endeavors, life was worth living indeed at Leavenworth. Professionals only were wanted because they were required. In the Department of Cavalry, Sanford had under him five assistant instructors and a veterinary surgeon in the 1887–88 academic year. Each had a hand in the cavalry-tactics class held Tuesday through Friday from 2:00 to 3:30 P. M.

To further the spirit of professionalism among the cavalry officers, the United States Cavalry Association was formed in the early fall of 1887. Sanford was one of its organizers and one of its officers.

> The design of the association [wrote the *Army and Navy Journal*] contemplates professional unity and improvement by correspondence and discussion; the reading, translation, and publication of professional essays; and generally, the advancement of the cavalry service.[132]

Sanford was chairman of the publications and correspondence committee, and at an early meeting of the association, he read a paper on "The Mounted Fire Action of Cavalry" with General Wesley Merritt in the chair.[133]

But everything was not always as pleasant. On 30 June 1887, Sanford left Leavenworth on two months' leave. Late in August— the twenty-eighth, to be exact—he left New York City, where he had spent his leave, on the regular express train. He felt he had ample time. However, the train was three hours late getting into

---

[131] *Army and Navy Journal*, XXIV (12 March 1887), 655; no date is given for the *Times*.

[132] XXV (26 November 1887), 340.

[133] This paper was later published in the first number of the *Journal of the United States Cavalry Association*.

Chicago, arriving there about midnight, long after all trains for the West had departed. Sanford no longer had "ample time." He immediately telegraphed the post of his delay and took the first train out of Chicago; nevertheless, he was a day late in reporting. "Unauthorized delay," the Army called it and barely refrained from calling it absence without leave. Sanford wrote a letter of explanation to Sheridan in November. It was fruitless: Sheridan did not consider the explanation "satisfactory." In the view of the Army, Sanford had been overpaid. A stoppage was issued, and Sanford lost $9.72, or one day's pay, galling to an officer as conscientious as he was. This was the second and last time he would be entangled in the system; the first had been the incident involving the horse when he was at Fort Custer.

Much more acceptable and personally gratifying was this letter from an old comrade and friend, Colonel John C. Kelton, Assistant Adjutant General of the Army, dated 6 September 1887:

> I have a son to name, and very much wish to have him baptised with the name Atlee *Sanford.* May I take that liberty and will you kindly consent to be his sponsor in baptism by proxy[?] A long appreciation of your many chivalric qualities convince me that my son with that name will grow up to be a useful Christian gentleman. Hence my request. I am convinced there is much in a name.[134]

There is wonder about a letter like this: wonder that it might ever have been written; wonder that there *were* men of this caliber in the nineteenth century, men so easy to satirize and burlesque at a later time; wonder that such a letter would never, or rarely, be written in our day.

On 9 January 1888, Brigadier General and Mrs. Merritt gave a musical and literary entertainment in their handsome home. There was a selection from *La Traviata,* a second lieutenant played a piano solo, another lieutenant sang *Speed On,* and yet another lieutenant recited *Tam O'Shanter.* It was a grin-and-bear-it evening until Major Sanford arose and read a prepared paper, "Fort Leavenworth in '61." He reminisced of the days he spent there, early in

---

[134] Sanford's "Scrapbook." Kelton was no youngster; he was in his late fifties. He died at the Soldiers' Home in Washington, D.C., 15 July 1893.

the Civil War, as a young second lieutenant in the First Dragoons. It was an entertaining piece, but he took the opportunity to deliver a light jab at some of the guests. He discussed the crowded conditions at Leavenworth because of extra units stationed there:

> It is rather a curious subject for consideration, as showing the great tendency for improvement in the care of officers and men when we consider that though the strength of the garrison at that time was twice as great as at present, the accommodation was certainly fifty per cent less, and yet it was so generally accepted as all right and proper, that I never remember hearing the subject of quarters alluded to even. Probably the lieutenants of today, when they return here in 1915 as, let us say general officers, will wonder how people ever managed to exist in the poor accommodations that they had in 1888.[135]

This was the Sanford's last social affair for quite some time because nine days later, Special Orders No. 14 came through from Army Headquarters, Washington, and assigned Sanford to a board of officers to assemble in Washington on 10 February "to prepare a system of infantry tactics, a system of cavalry tactics, and a system of light artillery tactics for the use of the armies of the United States."[136] Thus was established the rather famous (depending on one's viewpoint) Tactical Board, as it was popularly known, or Army Board for the Revision of Tactics, as it was officially known. There were eight members, including Sanford, who was senior cavalry officer. Senior officer was Lieutenant Colonel John C. Bates, Eighteenth Infantry.[137] It was a prestigious and important assignment as well as a cursed one. The fact that he was a member of the board did not relieve Sanford from Leavenworth or the school. The duty in Washington was detached service.

McCook felt Sanford's loss keenly, and in his annual report to the Adjutant General, he stated what was on his mind:

[135] *Leavenworth Times,* January 15, 1888, in Sanford's "Scrapbook." His paper was so highly regarded that the *Times* printed it with his permission.

[136] Record Group No. 94, National Archives.

[137] The other board members were Captain Edward S. Godfrey, Seventh Cavalry; Major Henry C. Hasbrouck, Fourth Artillery; Captain John C. Gilmore, Twenty-fourth Infantry; Captain Joseph T. Haskell, Twenty-third Infantry; Captain James M. Lancaster, Second Artillery; and First Lieutenant George Andrews, Twenty-fifth Infantry, recorder.

It is . . . requested that the officers on duty at the school as instructors be not detailed away from their assigned duties. During the past year the instructor in charge of the department of the art of war and infantry, also the instructor in charge of the department of cavalry [Sanford], were ordered from the school, one in January, the other in March of same year.

The latter instructor is still absent on a tactical board, and it is not known when he can return.[138]

As the board was preparing to convene in Washington, the *Army and Navy Journal* editorialized:

The Board appointed to revise the Army tactics have a formidable task before them, if they propose to sift all the suggestions for changes and improvement which have been transmitted to the War Department. Upton's Tactics appear to have been peculiarly provocative of these, and there is an accumulation of them sufficient to fill a Saratoga trunk. It will probably require at least a year for the Board to reach any conclusion, unless it should be sufficiently impressed with some one of the complete systems submitted to adopt it in its entirety. Upton's Tactics have held their ground now for twenty-one years.[139]

The tone was anything but encouraging to the board. Room 47 in the north wing of the State, War and Navy Department Building was assigned for the officers' exclusive use. They held their first session there on 14 February 1888, then waited for the files from the Adjutant General's Office in order to proceed with their work.

Sanford and his colleagues had not long to wait before the documents and manuscripts poured in upon them; the amount, the variety, and the worth were a fantasy of paper and officialese. Patiently, the board members shuffled the pages, and just as patiently, the *Army and Navy Journal* watched them and commented

[138] "Report of Colonel Alexander McD. McCook," dated 12 September 1888, *Report of the Secretary of War, 1888–1889,* House Exec. Docs., 50th Cong., 2nd Sess., 197. Sanford was replaced by Captain William A. Rafferty, Sixth Cavalry, who had been out on the Cheyenne scare with him.

[139] XXV (11 February 1888), 570. The tactics of Baron von Steuben had been in use from 1779 to 1812, General Scott's tactics from 1834 to 1855, and General Upton's tactics since 1867. Before his death, Upton had prepared a manuscript revision of his tactics.

from time to time. It was apparent from the very outset that any forward motion would be slow, and it was no help at all when the board was moved to Room 111 on the third floor, west front, of the hideous building. On 26 May 1888, the *Journal* said in another editorial:

> The operations of the Army Board for the Revision of Tactics are, and have been for some time past, confined mainly to the reception and critical examination of the various systems either adopted, or proposed for adoption, by the leading warlike powers of the continent of Europe. From a glance at the quantity of work already accomplished . . . in this particular line, it is not difficult to understand that the task laid before them is of no inconsiderable magnitude.[140]

Into the depressing Washington summer they worked. By 21 July, the *Journal* could report that the board had finished "the tedious, but to them, interesting, task" of reading and digesting the various documents.[141]

That they had done; yes, they had done that. But what else is not clear. Progress was disappointingly slow. Intraservice politics hovered over and around the members as they weighed, decided, and concluded. Each decision was painful, for it meant that some officer, some clique, would be angry or thwarted—or happy and satisfied—because his or their particular concept was or was not acceptable. On 27 October, the *Journal* advised that the board was "well advanced with the important task" and then, in the same breath, reported that it had "made haste slowly."[142] Nothing more was said until March, 1889. By then, Sanford and his fellows had been in session for over a year and had nothing to show for it except rough drafts and notes.

> This Board is still far from completing the important work. . . . The School of the Soldier is pretty well perfected and tolerably good progress has been made in instructions in drill, but much practical work is necessary before even these branches are fully perfected. At least another six months will elapse before their work is finished.[143]

[140] XXV [869].
[141] *Ibid.*, 1039.
[142] XXVI, [161].
[143] *Ibid.* (9 March 1889), 557.

Patently, everyone was getting restless. Something had to be done and Army Headquarters came up with a change of station.

On 23 March, the board was ordered to adjourn its sessions in Washington and to reassemble at Fort Leavenworth on or before 1 April and there complete its work.[144] Its members held their final meeting on the same day, 23 March. Once reassembled in offices provided for it in the city of Leavenworth (to refurbish and make the rooms fit for habitation took several weeks), the board frankly admitted that at least a month's work had been lost. Even the normally (and semiofficially) hopeful *Journal* seemed to mock when it reported in May that the members were doing "actually more hard work than any similar number of officers in the Army."[145]

This unfruitful episode, extending over eighteen long months, ended peculiarly for Sanford, but it cannot be said that his work ended. *Stasis* accurately describes the state of the board that hot, sultry summer in Kansas. Finally, Sanford himself took a hand. From the Planter's House in Leavenworth on 12 August, he wrote a personal letter to the Adjutant General of the Army, his old friend General John C. Kelton, confident of *some* sort of action:

> Genl. McCook is very anxious that I should go to duty at the garrison as soon as possible. He thinks that I can be of use to him at such times as I am not occupied with the Board. Of course he takes it for granted that *that* work must have precedence. I shall be glad to do anything I can, and if it is thought advisable, I will take hold out there. . . .
>
> The artillery have completed their work, and have it about ready to submit. The cavalry is nearly done as far as writing is concerned, but editing will take some little time yet. The infantry are not as far advanced I believe, but I understand are getting along very well. I don[']t know whether "combined operations" of the nature I suggest would lead to any complications or not, but as the Gen'l. is quite interested in the matter, I venture to ask your opinion.[146]

[144] Special Orders No. 68, Washington, Record Group No. 94, National Archives.
[145] XXVI (18 May 1889), 784.
[146] Record Group No. 94, National Archives. Kelton had succeeded Richard C. Drum on 7 June 1889 as Adjutant General.

To help Kelton decide, Sanford mentioned that he was to be promoted to lieutenant colonel "in a week or so." On 29 August, he was informed that, in addition to his duties as a member of the Tactical Board, he would resume his duties at the School of Application for Infantry and Cavalry.[147] By then he was a lieutenant colonel, Ninth Cavalry, *vice* Lieutenant Colonel James S. Brisbin, Ninth Cavalry, promoted to colonel, First Cavalry.

Events were now beginning to crowd together for Sanford after a career of "waiting to be tapped," which was inevitable in such an antiquated and incredibly ineffective system of lineal or regimental promotion, one exceeded only by an even worse system in the United States Navy—if such were possible. For years an officer might molder, literally sleep in a rank; then suddenly, as retirement approached in one form or another, he might then be whipped through the field grades—assuming he attained to them—at a dizzying speed. Or an officer might never make it at all, under any conditions. Neither quite applied to Sanford, but the former is close enough to be illustrative.

Everyone, it seems, disliked the promotion system but did shockingly little to ameliorate its inequities and wrongs. In 1889, General Miles characterized it as "disheartening to the officers of the line who have to remain so long in subordinate positions." He had on hand some fascinating statistics: 110 officers in the same grade they held twenty years earlier; in the infantry, there were 57 captains who had been captains twenty years or more, some of them almost sixty years old; 409 officers who had commissions in the Civil War who were still lieutenants and captains.[148] Let us

---

[147] Letter from Major Thomas Ward, Acting Adjutant General, to Sanford, dated 29 August, Record Group No. 94, National Archives.

[148] "Report of Brigadier General Nelson A. Miles," dated 16 September 1889, *Report of the Secretary of War, 1889–1890,* House Exec. Docs., 51st Cong., 1st Sess., 174. Miles's recommendations for change nevertheless were mild: the three-battalion organization for the infantry (this would allow promotion of fifty of "the most deserving officers in the Army") and promoted for an officer after fifteen years' continuous service in the same rank.

The system had many other problems. To name one, the retired list, excluding the "forty years' service" and "sixty-four years of age" provisions, was limited to

understand that these were not officers who had been passed over for promotion necessarily.

So it was, and Sanford was extraordinarily fortunate to have been promoted to lieutenant colonel on 20 August 1889; but because there was no vacancy in his beloved First Cavalry, with which he had served since 1861, he was transferred to the Ninth Regiment of Cavalry, a Negro unit with white officers. This was not to Sanford's liking, for he was fiercely proud of his regiment and his service. There was nothing at all racial in his feelings.[149]

If Sanford was fortunate in attaining the silver oak leaf, the United States Army was in many ways even more fortunate to have such a skilled, competent, and loyal officer in its ranks. His concept of duty has been noted, and under such an antiquated promotional system almost insanely based on seniority, there was little in the way of inducement for an officer to extend himself one micromillimeter beyond routine duties. Obviously, the system of lineal promotion allowed for many notorious incompetents to reach the Army's higher ranks. Simply put, loyalty and duty—or either one alone—were never rewarded. How the Army escaped chaos and demoralization is not to be analyzed here. In his annual report for 1888–89, Secretary of War William C. Endicott strongly urged examination of officers, a professional examination "as would demonstrate the fitness of a candidate for promotion properly to perform the duties of the grade to which he aspires." There was no such program in the infantry, cavalry, or artillery, although there was some sort of examination, in greater or lesser degree, in the

---

400. Therefore, an incapacitated officer might not be able to retire until someone (or several) on the retired list died. There was always a number of debilitated officers, drawing full pay, rendering no service, awaiting retirement.

149 In the fall of 1879, while stationed at Fort Halleck, Sanford noted an error in the *Official Army Register* for 1880 which showed him to have been commissioned in the First Cavalry on 26 April 1861. He wrote to the Adjutant General's Office and pointed out that he had joined the First Dragoons. If the error was allowed to stand, "I appear as belonging originally to the regiment at present known as the 4th Cavalry." He concluded: "As I am rather proud of my connection with the regiment . . . (the only regiment in which I ever held commission) I should be glad to have the record corrected." Record Group No. 94, National Archives. Negro regiments (with white officers) in the Army since 1869 included the Ninth and Tenth Cavalry and the Twenty-fourth and Twenty-fifth Infantry.

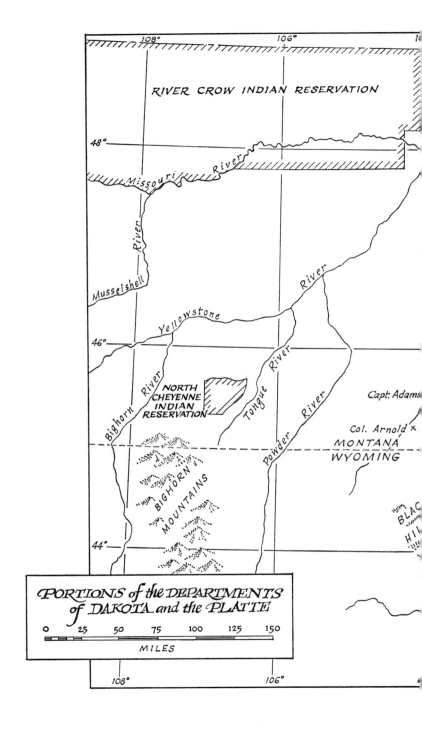

PORTIONS of the DEPARTMENTS
of DAKOTA and the PLATTE

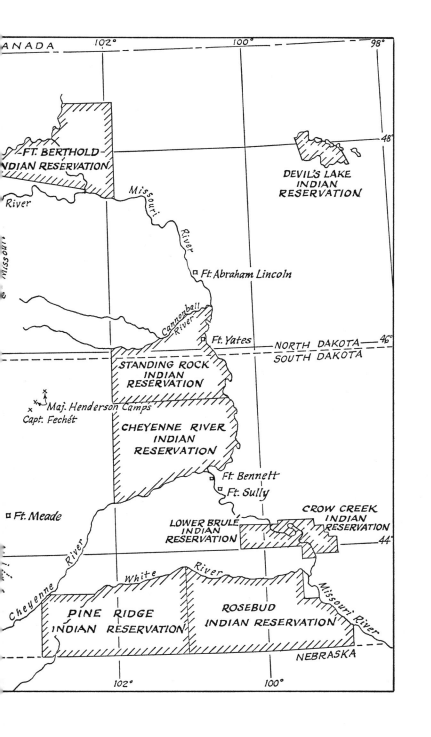

Medical and Ordnance Corps and the Corps of Engineers. Endicott was categorical:

> If he [the officer] gets his promotion and his pay, and his rank and authority through lapse of time, and a perfunctory routine performance of his daily duty without offense, why should he labor and strive for a higher excellence? If he is of better and truer mettle than to be content and indifferent, and does strive and labor and learn, he gets no more than he who is idle and waits. It is the presumption of fitness and superiority, because of seniority, that makes seniority a ground for promotion; but, like all presumptions, it may be rebutted, and, if the man is shown to be unfit, the reason utterly fails.

Sanford's return to the School of Application for Infantry and Cavalry was acknowledged by the *Army and Navy Journal* with an editorial comment that the school and McCook were to be congratulated "in the retention of this officer, whose services in the past have proven most valuable in its advancement and improvement."[150]

He executed his academic chores, served on a board or two, on one abortive court-martial, and on the semiannual examinations. This was the quietest, most uneventful period in George Bliss Sanford's entire Army career. That he served well and faithfully is seen in Colonel McCook's remarks on his efficiency report, dated 1 May 1890: "an advanced student of this profession . . . a most excellent officer in all respects . . . will fill any military detail suitable to his rank with honor to himself and credit to the Service . . . a progressive Military Student . . . Col. Sanford is an accomplished officer and gentleman, a credit to the Army at large . . . conscientious in the discharge of all of his duties."[151] McCook mentioned that Sanford was still a member of the Tactical Board, but this is all that is known of his "service" thereon.

Before the new course of studies began at the school in September, a major personnel change was effected. McCook was promoted to brigadier general on 14 July 1890 and posted to command the Department of Arizona. He was succeeded as commandant by Colo-

---

150 XXVII (14 September 1889), 43.
151 Sanford's "Scrapbook."

nel Edwin F. Townsend, Twelfth Infantry, on 29 August. When school opened, Sanford assumed supervision of the Department of Cavalry (and hippology), although classes in cavalry did not take up until 10 November. Operations continued smoothly through 21 November. Then, on 22 November, Townsend received a telegram from Headquarters, Department of the Missouri, directing that all the cavalry be put "in readiness to take the field against the Indians in the Department of Dakota."[152]

The conflict that was developing has come to be known as the Ghost Dance War because of the fantasy of the dances and of the "Messiah," he who would deliver the wretchedly unhappy Sioux from their fate: insufficient food, crop failures in 1889 and 1890 with a concomitant absence of game, etc., etc. Disaffection was obvious and strong at the Standing Rock Reservation, the Pine Ridge Reservation, the Rosebud Reservation, and the Cheyenne River Reservation, all in western and southwestern South Dakota. Wrote Miles:

> In this condition of affairs, the Indians, realizing the inevitable, and seeing their numbers gradually diminishing, their strength and power weakening, very naturally prayed to their God for some supernatural power to aid them in the restoration of their former independence and the destruction of their enemies.[153]

There came forth, therefore, the Messiah delusion and the ghost dancing, the personation of the Christ who spoke passionately of deliverance. In a public harangue, Short Bull asserted he would "shorten the time for a general uprising" and called on the warriors to assemble in the Bad Lands (Mauvaises Terres) on the White River in November, 1890. He was persuasive, and about 3,000 Indians (a possible 600–800 braves) from the Rosebud and Pine Ridge reservations moved to "that rough, broken country of high buttes, ravines, and impassable gulches."[154] Short Bull, Kicking

---

[152] "Report of Colonel Edwin F. Townsend," dated 1 July 1891, *Report of the Secretary of War, 1891–1892,* House Exec. Docs., 52nd Cong., 1st Sess., 267.

[153] "Report of Major General Nelson A. Miles," dated 14 September 1891, *ibid.,* 140–41.

[154] *Ibid.,* 143.

85

Bear, and the well-known Sitting Bull (the Hunkpapa, not the Oglala) were busy and influential, and the warriors on the Standing Rock and Cheyenne River reservations were ready to join them. A "large amount" of ammunition and arms, especially their favorite Winchester rifles, was obtained. And the ghost dancing went on and on, assuming the character of a craze, gradually working itself out of control. Affairs seemed particularly serious at the Pine Ridge Agency.

On 17 November 1890, Brigadier General John R. Brooke, commanding the Department of the Platte, ordered troops into the area with the objective of preventing the murder of civil agents, the destruction of public property, and protecting the loyal and peaceful Indians, not to ignore the extended white settlements adjacent to the Sioux reservations. To carry out the orders would necessitate involving nearly one-half of the infantry and cavalry from nearly "all parts of the country" west of the Mississippi. And anything that involved the troops in the West often involved Sanford.

Meanwhile, at the infantry and cavalry school, pursuant to the telegram of 22 November, Colonel Townsend had made the required preparations to send out his cavalry, but no orders to move were received. On 24 November, another telegram directed the entire command to be in readiness to take the field. "All this created much disturbance among the instructors and students at the school," Colonel Townsend grumbled.[155] But since no orders to *move* had come, matters began to quiet down, although school "was out," in spirit if not in fact. Then on the evening of 1 December came orders to move the cavalry to South Dakota and two companies of infantry to Fort Riley, Kansas. Sanford's ever present Number One, Captain Camillo C. C. Carr, First Cavalry, was assigned command of the four troops of cavalry (I, First; F, Second; I, Fifth; and C, Ninth). They took the cars at the post railroad and headed for the trouble zone. They were there by 4 December and moved into position at Oelrichs, located west of the Bad Lands in the southwestern corner of South Dakota, just above

155 "Report Townsend," *ibid.,* 267.

the Nebraska line, on the Fremont, Elkhorn and Missouri Valley Railroad.

What of Sanford? He asked the same thing on 1 December in a telegram to the Adjutant General: "Post Commander informs me cavalry from Leavenworth ordered out. Shall I go with them or remain with Board?"[156] Which board is unclear. Sanford was still a member of the Tactical Board, but he was also on two promotion boards. General Kelton took Sanford's duties seriously (probably because of the discontent about promotion policies) and stated in a memorandum to Major General John M. Schofield, commanding the Army, that "it would be difficult to replace him on the Examining Boards."[157] There was no problem with the Tactical Board; that was dead.

On 2 December, Sanford was advised to continue his present duties, but this set not at all well with Major General Miles in Chicago. He needed good men in South Dakota. On 3 December, he wired Kelton: "The services of field officers being very necessary with command I respectfully request that Lieut Col George B. Sanford with cavalry be ordered to join his regiment."[158] Miles was the third-ranking general in the Army; he could get necessary action. Schofield allowed that Sanford could be spared from both the Tactical Board and the school and could go to South Dakota, provided the Secretary of War did not deem his services necessary on the boards of examination. It was a neat bit of maneuvering. The Secretary of War declared that Colonel James F. Wade, Fifth Cavalry, could be detailed on the boards.

The way cleared up ahead, Sanford was informed on 4 December that he was relieved of his duties at Leavenworth and was to proceed "to join the Fort Leavenworth Cavalry Battalion in the field."[159] Sanford shoved off on 6 December. Three days later, he was in command in the field.

Real skill and leadership were demonstrated by the Army command as it set about to place detachments in order to surround the

---

[156] Record Group No. 94, National Archives.
[157] *Ibid.*
[158] *Ibid.*
[159] *Ibid.* Miles was also informed.

Sioux. Miles frankly admitted that, in many aspects, the Army was not prepared; several years of peace and inactivity had impaired the efficiency of the troops. There was a lack of proper equipment for winter warfare, "entirely inadequate" transportation, and too little time, the most important element of all, for it can never be purchased or requisitioned. Yet Miles got his officers and men into their positions. Detachments were dispatched to the Cheyenne River Agency (to restrain the Indians on that reservation and intercept any from Standing Rock); to Forts Bennett and Sully to the east on the Missouri; to Rosebud Agency and Fort Niobrara, Nebraska, to the south; to Pine Ridge Agency and Reservation to the west; and to Sanford at Oelrichs. North of Sanford on the railroad were detachments at Buffalo Gap and Rapid City, South Dakota. Then the perimeter swung east again to units on the South Fork of the Cheyenne, and beyond them was yet another detachment. A small garrison was also stationed at Fort Meade, northwest of Rapid City. (There had not been troop movements like these since the Civil War.) "Most of the force was placed in position between the large hostile camp in the Bad Lands [under Short Bull and Kicking Bear] . . . and the scattered settlers endangered by their presence."[160] Colonel Eugene A. Carr's command at Rapid City was considered "the most liable" to contact the hostiles, and Miles established his temporary headquarters there. Sanford's battalion at Oelrichs apparently was not considered "liable."

When the cavalry departed Leavenworth, there were no instructors left in the Department of Cavalry and all recitations were suspended. The Department of Military Art suffered, too. Townsend testily observed:

The minds of both instructors and students, more or less excited by the events of the day, were in but slight mood for study, and the results necessarily were not as satisfactory as desirable. All this demonstrates [echoing McCook] that instructors at the school should be selected from officers not on duty with any of the companies or troops stationed

160 "Report of Miles," *loc. cit.*, 148; two good maps showing the movements and dispositions of the troops face pp. 155 and 188.

at the post; so that in case of the troops being suddenly called away, the school will not be affected.[161]

Small chance that Generals Brooke or Miles or Schofield cared a jot for Townsend's problems. What was at stake, said Miles, was the imperilment of peace in an area of the United States equal to an empire: Nebraska, the two Dakotas, Montana, Wyoming, Colorado, Idaho, Nevada, and Utah Territory. And this empire was on the verge of being overrun by "a hungry, wild, mad horde of savages." Little wonder that federal, state, and local officials, encouraged by the newspapers, called for aid and protection. Miles, who commanded the Department of the Missouri, designed a plan which would *"anticipate the movements of the hostile Indians and arrest or overpower them in detail before they had time to concentrate in one large body"*[162] and at the same time apprehend their principal leaders: Sitting Bull, Hump, and Big Foot.

After William F. (Buffalo Bill) Cody had been frustrated in his special attempt to take Sitting Bull, General Miles, on 10 December, told Lieutenant Colonel William F. Drum, commanding Fort Yates on the Standing Rock Reservation, to arrest him. Drum arranged for the Cheyenne Indian police to make the actual arrest, supported by troops under Captain Edmond G. Fechét, Eighth Cavalry. On 15 December, about forty police under Bull Head and Shave Head entered Sitting Bull's camp on the Grand River. A brief but violent firefight broke out, and Sitting Bull and seven of his warriors (his son Crow Foot among them) were killed; the police lost Bull Head, Shave Head, and many others killed and wounded. Only Captain Fechét's arrival saved the police from obliteration. As many as fifty of Sitting Bull's followers fled south to Hump and Big Foot, about thirty actually making it.

Next on the Army's list of persons to be removed was Hump, sometime resident of the Cheyenne River Reservation and regarded as "one of the most dangerous Indians" in the country. Strangely enough, though, his removal was accomplished with a minimum of trouble. Captain Ezra P. Ewers, Fifth Infantry, an old acquaint-

[161] "Report of Townsend," *ibid.*, 267.
[162] "Report of Miles," *ibid.*, 145; italics are Miles's.

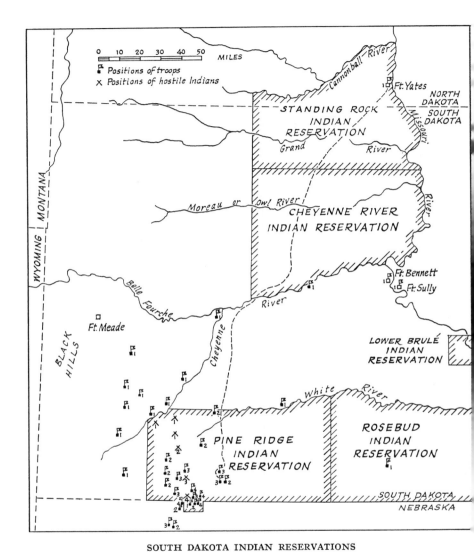

SOUTH DAKOTA INDIAN RESERVATIONS

ance, was brought up from Texas to "communicate" with him. Ewers left Fort Bennett and went sixty miles into the country, met Hump, and persuaded him to come in to Bennett; all but 30 of his band did likewise. The malcontents defected and joined Big Foot's party, swelling his ranks to 116 warriors.

Naturally, Big Foot was now the top name on the Army's (revised) list. On 16 December, Lieutenant Colonel Edwin V. Sumner, Eighth Cavalry, was chosen for the somewhat delicate task of bringing him in. After some maneuvering, conferring, and sparring, Big Foot came into Sumner's camp at Narseilles' Ranch near the Cheyenne River on 21 December 1890, bringing with him 333 Indians, 51 wagons, and a herd of ponies, 38 of them from the Standing Rock Reservation. Sumner's intention was to march the band to Fort Bennett, but on a pretense, Big Foot slipped away toward the Indian rendezvous in the Bad Lands. When General Miles heard of this, he was furious. He notified Sumner: "Your orders were positive, and you have missed your opportunity, but such does not often occur. Endeavor to be more successful next time."[163] It was unfortunate—and stupid. Miles's anger was well founded.

So far, there had been no fighting between the Army and the Indians—precisely what was desired, for Miles and Brooke wanted to avoid conflict and induce as many hostiles as possible to return to the reservations. The troops to the west of the trouble zone (Sanford at Oelrichs was a part) formed a strong cordon which had "the effect to gradually force" the Indians back to the agency. Miles urged the federal authorities to give "some positive assurance" that the government would fulfill its obligations in the understanding with the Sioux. In the Bad Lands, Short Bull and Kicking Bear, with the cordon of troops to nudge them along, broke camp on 27 December and moved to the agency by slow marches. They had left a stronghold which Miles described as "a series of natural fortifications, almost impenetrable."[164] The de-

---

[163] Exhibit H to "Report of Operations Relative to the Sioux Indians in 1890 and 1891," Brigadier General Thomas H. Ruger, *ibid.*, 235.
[164] "Report of Miles," *ibid.*, 150.

tachments under Colonel Carr, Lieutenant Colonel Robert H. Offley, Seventeenth Infantry, and Sanford followed slowly after the Indians but within what they regarded as "communicating and supporting" distance. "In fact," reported Miles, "the fires of the Indians were still burning in their camps behind them when the troops moved in to occupy the same grounds."[165] Sanford and his comrades continued to apply pressure, gentle but firm, and remained instantly ready for conflict if need be. Affairs seemed to be progressing very well.

On 28 December, Major Samuel M. Whitside, Seventh Cavalry, intercepted Big Foot and his band, now about 120 braves and 250 women and children, one and one-half miles west of Porcupine Creek. Whitside demanded their surrender, and Big Foot meekly complied, whereupon the Major moved the Indians seven miles to Wounded Knee Creek. Colonel James W. Forsyth, Seventh Cavalry, was ordered in by General Brooke to support Whitside, and he arrayed against the Sioux 470 regulars and scouts, plus artillery. With Big Foot in hand, the trouble did indeed seem near an end.

The next day, 29 December 1890, at about 9:00 A.M., all hell suddenly broke loose in Big Foot's camp, and when the terrible melee was over at three in the afternoon, the Army had lost 30 killed and 34 wounded, the Indians 145 killed (many of them women and children, some of the victims far from the scene of battle) and 33 wounded. Without doubt, this was the most notorious affair in the bitter annals of Indian wars in the western United States with the possible exception of the incredible Sand Creek (Chivington) Massacre in Colorado during the Civil War. Sadly, too, as Miles truthfully said, the Wounded Knee battle prolonged "the disturbance and made a successful termination more difficult," for Short Bull and Kicking Bear had been scheduled to camp within four miles of the agency on the night of 29 December. Now a general alarm was raised among the hostiles, and by 30 December their camp was greatly augmented and they were very dangerous.

Forsyth exhibited his talent for mismanagement again on 30 December when he got involved in another battle (known as the

165 *Ibid.*

Mission Fight) on White Clay Creek and lost men needlessly (including one officer killed). For this, finally, Forsyth was relieved of his command. That same day, the Indians attacked the Ninth Cavalry's wagon train near Pine Ridge Agency but were repulsed. On 1 January 1891, Captain John B. Kerr, Sixth Cavalry, celebrated the new year by fighting off a surge against the western cordon near the mouth of Little Grass Creek in South Dakota.

It was at this point that Miles moved directly into the conflict to deal with the Indians. He proved to be the master. Armed with funds and assurances from Congress and supported by his troops, who surrounded the Indians and kept pushing at them, he brought them to surrender at Pine Ridge in mid-January.

About ten days before the surrender, Sanford was indirectly involved in the tragic death of 38-year-old First Lieutenant Edward W. Casey, Twenty-second Infantry. On 29 December 1890, Sanford had made camp in the vicinity of the White River and White Clay Creek, where Casey (with his detachment of Cheyenne scouts) joined him. The hostiles were camped eight miles away at No Waters on White Clay Creek. At Sanford's direction, Casey used his scouts to locate and watch the Sioux. On 5 January, General Brooke established his headquarters with Sanford. Two days later, Casey and two Cheyennes left camp and went to the Sioux camp, apparently to speak to the principal chief. Casey never reached the chief. While he was engaged in a conversation with Pete Richard, a halfblood Sioux, and another hostile, Plenty Horses slipped in behind him and shot him in the back of the head, the ball exiting under his right eye. Casey was dead in an instant.

Counting from the day of Sitting Bull's death until the surrender, the war had lasted thirty-two days and had cost the government $1,200,000, or about $40,000 per day.[166]

Sanford and Carr were back at Leavenworth and the School of Application for Infantry and Cavalry by 26 January 1891. During their absence, Colonel Townsend had worked out a new schedule

[166] Fairfax Downey, *Indian-Fighting Army*, 272. See also [J. B. Bishop], "Cost of Our Latest Indian War," *The Nation*, LII (22 January 1891), 63–64. Newspaper correspondents, who are reported to have kept a close account, placed the loss of life to the Indians at about 480.

of studies, and Sanford's cavalry course resumed 24 February and continued until the end of March. "Notwithstanding [the] interruptions the progress of the class was highly commendable," reported Townsend. [167] Sanford remained on duty, as instructor and as a member of an examining board for promotion, until after the examinations, 13 June 1891, when he was granted sixty days' leave with permission to apply for an additional four months.

Sanford spent most or all of his sixty days in his beloved Litchfield, Connecticut, where, on 5 August, he asked for and was granted his extension with notation that at expiration he would proceed "to join his regiment, reporting by letter to his department commander for assignment to a station."[168] This was on 11 August. On the same day, he was succeeded as senior instructor at Leavenworth by Camillo C. C. Carr, now of the Eighth Cavalry, recently promoted to major after twenty-two years as a captain. No more would he have to stand (and serve) in Sanford's shade.[169]

Returned from leave in December, Sanford was ordered to command Fort Robinson, Nebraska, Department of the Platte, and the garrison there, succeeding Lieutenant Colonel Alfred T. Smith, Eighth Infantry. Sanford joined on the twelfth. It was a large fort: six companies of the Ninth Cavalry and two of the Eighth Infantry, totaling 35 officers and 520 enlisted men. However, there were accommodations for only 24 officers and 486 men, so it was crowded on the White River in the winter of 1891–92. It was Leavenworth all over again. Neither Sanford nor his wife were especially pleased.

One field officer's and ten company officers' frame quarters (five double sets) were under construction, as was one infantry barrack (there were nine barracks in use), and $42,397 had been authorized for the work, to include plumbing; but the projects were niggardly funded, a few thousand here and a few thousand there—

---

167 "Report of Townsend," *loc. cit.*, 267. In his own report, Sanford recommended that horses be sent to the school for the student officers to use in their mounted work. He also requested, of all things, a "papier mache model of the horse" similar to one used at West Point.

168 Special Orders No. 184, Record Group No. 94, National Archives.

169 When Carr retired on 3 March 1906, he was a brigadier general.

it was a favorite game of ball with unsympathetic, venal congress-men. In his annual report for 1892, General Brooke was moved to suggest that "the unfinished condition" of the fort called for "prompt action." Robinson did have a sewer system and was fur-nished spring water. Affairs could have been much better for San-ford in his last months in the Army, for he was contemplating retirement.

On 28 May 1892, Sanford was given thirty days' leave. He pleaded "important business" as the reason, and he may well have meant it. Back to Litchfield he went. The long-sought colonelcy was his but for formal administrative procedures. No matter. From Litchfield on 10 June, he addressed a letter to the Adjutant General:

> I have the honor to request that I may be placed upon the retired list of the Army, as soon as I arrive at the grade of Colonel. I am at present the senior lieutenant colonel in the cavalry army & have com-pleted over thirty one (31) years of active service. . . . My reasons for making this request are my own failing health and urgent family affairs needing my personal attention. . . .
>
> Should my most earnest petition be granted, I would further respect-fully request that I may be allowed pending retirement to await orders at my home in Litchfield.[170]

Much more interesting than Sanford's letter was another, written on the same day to the same addressee by Mrs. Sanford, the first time she had directly and personally intervened in her husband's career:

> Col Sanford to-day wrote his application to be placed on the retired list. . . . [H]e asks to be ordered home to await retirement. Will you as a last act to me, do what you can to get this done for us. My husband is far from well, the water at Robinson had a bad effect on both of us. I think we have earned our home, and I should like to enjoy it in peace and quiet *together* for a few years. [W]e left both our children at boarding school when we went to Nebraska, it was very hard, but there was no chance for them out there. . . . Litchfield seems *so* lovely. [W]e only got here yesterday, I went up [the] street this morning,

---

[170] Record Group No. 94, National Archives. There were two vacancies on the retired list. Everything was in order.

and every man woman & child stopped, and seemed glad we were back. Now dear General, this is the last time I shall trouble you. I have always felt so sure of your interest & affection, and I hope you will help us in this. I am sure we shall be happy here. Mr & Mrs Sanford are getting to be very old people, and my husband can be a great help & comfort to them, and I shall not have to be separated from my husband or children in my case. I have to leave my children, as my husband needs me most. With much love for you all,

Gertrude Minturn Sanford[171]

Nothing further need be said on the subject. This letter from a wife who had spent eighteen years in the Army says it all. The Adjutant General granted her (and her husband's) request.

On 19 July 1892, Colonel Eugene A. Carr, Sixth Cavalry, was promoted to brigadier general after thirteen years as colonel. A vacancy was created, and into it moved Sanford, who was promoted, *vice* Carr, to date from 22 July. The oath of office was administered to Sanford in Litchfield on 29 July by George Woodruff, a notary public. Almost simultaneously—the precise method is not known—Sanford was officially retired on 28 July.

Once Carr's promotion became known throughout the Army (which was almost like a private club) but before word of Sanford's retirement had spread (the club was not that private), letters of congratulation came to Sanford, all of them hoping that he would continue in service. "I believe you will like the 6 Cavalry, and will find many excellent officers in it," wrote a major from Fort Reno. An officer at Fort Omaha wished him "all success and pleasure" in his "new regiment and home." Captain James W. Pope, then at Fort Leavenworth, wrote: "I know of no one who would be more likely to reach the stars if you should remain." Said another officer at Fort Clarke, Texas: "I am glad to see that you go to the 6th wh. *I* consider a much better regiment in many ways than the 3rd." A young lieutenant in the Sixth asserted from Jefferson Barracks: "I do not know another field officer whom I could half as gladly welcome as our chief." Finally, Captain John B. Kerr, Sixth

---

[171] *Ibid.* The fact that such a personal letter as this should have been retained in the files is unusual.

Cavalry: "We hope that we may be able to contribute something towards your Star."[172]

Sanford, however, was satisfied with his career. By Army standards, he was still a young man (his plea of poor health cannot really be accepted); he was but one month beyond his fiftieth year, still active, still very much the soldier, hardly superannuated. But he was realistic, too. His chance for "The Star" was slim and would come only after at least thirteen years—and probably fourteen years—in grade. And then enforced retirement almost at once. Yet, ironically, had he remained in the Army, there is no doubt, what with the upcoming Spanish-American War and the various troubles in China and the Philippines, that he would have gathered The Star rather more quickly than anticipated—perhaps even two of them. Many an oldster limped down to Tampa and on to Cuba in '98 in much worse physical and mental shape than would ever befall Sanford.

Sanford purchased what he described as "the old house in Litchfield . . . that once belonged to Governor [Oliver] Wolcott," Secretary of the Treasury under Washington. He enlarged and beautified it with loving care. This would be his home for the remainder of his life, although he would not spend many days in it. He enjoyed travel too much.

It was here, within a year or two of his retirement, that Sanford prepared the manuscript of *Experiences in Army Life* and apparently commenced an extended narrative of his days in the Indian Wars; but as fortune unfortunately would have it, he never progressed beyond a few handwritten pages.[173]

His retirement, which was leisurely and pleasurable as his wife had so sincerely hoped, can be divided into clubs, societies, and travel. He pursued all with near passion.

When the Sons of the Revolution in Connecticut was incorporated on 7 September 1893, Sanford was elected a member of the board of managers. A month later, he was elected to the Phelps Association. On 5 April 1894, the Society of the War of 1812 was

[172] Sanford's "Scrapbook."
[173] See n. 12 *supra*.

instituted in Connecticut and Sanford was elected its first president. In July of that year, he was named vice president general for the state in the General Society of the War of 1812. In November, he was notified of his election as deputy governor, Society of Colonial Wars.

Sanford was a member of the Connecticut Historical Society, the Military Order of the Loyal Legion, and the Society of the Cincinnati (he was, not surprisingly, the president of the Connecticut group). In later years, he was a corresponding member of the National Geographic Society. From 1902 to 1906, he held the office of vice president general in the General Society of the War of 1812.

The cynical will at once jump on such activities as a chapter out of a J. P. Marquand novel. This would be unfair. Sanford was proud of his forebears and he furthered this pride by delving into genealogy and history, for his own benefit and for the benefit of his children. After all, what harm done? His roots were deep and spread widely. Sanfords had been a part of the American idea for a score of decades. Had not the Colonel enlarged that part ever so much with a third of a century of service in the United States Army?

It was this work in his beloved societies and not his military service that finally gained him a place in *Who's Who in America* during the last year of his life. Not as illogical as it seems.

Sanford was a clubber, too: the University in New York City, the Army and Navy in Washington, the Graduates in New Haven, the Anglo-American in Dresden (life member). He was very close to and very intimate with his wife and family, but his years in the Army also gave him a close feeling for the comradeship of men. In every respect, Sanford was a man's man.

In 1896, he was in England, and while there he was granted a pass to the Members' Gallery of the House of Commons. He joined an officers' club. The Sanfords like the country so much they returned, with their daughters, for another stay in May, 1898. The date is interesting. The Spanish-American War was in progress, but it did not tug at the Colonel. He had served once before.

Fellow officers continued to correspond with Sanford. Old memories and battle days are implicit in this letter from First Lieutenant Albert L. Mills, First Cavalry, written from Fort Grant, Arizona Territory:

> I take great pleasure in inclosing . . . a Roster of your old regiment. Many of us still feel you belong to the regiment, and with good grounds, for no officer has contributed more than you to its reputation, and its roster shows you have had longer service with it than any other officer *ever* borne on its rolls.[174]

In November, 1894, Alexander McD. McCook, his chief at the School of Application for Infantry and Cavalry at Leavenworth, was promoted to brigadier general. Sanford sent a telegram of congratulation. McCook acknowledged it and followed with a letter to Miss Gertrude Minturn Sanford:

> None of the hundred telegrams, of the three hundred letters were more appreciated than yours. It almost brought tears to my eyes when your dear letter came—Mrs. McCook was near me when I opened the letter and she was effected [*sic*] the same way. I thank you from the bottom of my heart. You know or remember, how I love children and when they return my affection, as you have done in your good letter, it makes me very happy. It is sweet to be remembered by you Gertrude, and you will always have a warm and loving spot near my old soldierly heart.[175]

The years were closing in. The Colonel's father, William Elihu Sanford, died on 25 May 1895 at the age of eighty-one; his brother, Frederick C., died of pneumonia on 4 January 1901; and his mother, Margaret Craney, died on 5 November 1902. She was eighty-five. Of her ten children, four survived her: George Bliss and his three sisters.

For final effect and final emphasis, even though chronology is wrenched, two incidents will cap this brief biography: one quite ordinary for a clubbable man, but important, shortly after his retirement in 1892; the other, extraordinary but unimportant as such, in 1906.

Sometime in either December, 1892, or January, 1893, Sanford

---

[174] Sanford's "Scrapbook."
[175] *Ibid.*

delivered an address on the American Indian to the Litchfield Scientific Association. It was never published; in fact, it was unknown even to his family until its discovery in late 1966.[176] He expended much effort, plus his usual thoroughness and energy, to make the speech a good one because at last he had a chance to speak out on a subject with which he had been concerned for more than twenty-five years.

Sanford outlined in detail the life and customs of the Pimas and the Apaches; he analyzed Indian warfare; he told two fascinating folkloristic stories; he even evaluated the performance of one of his more distinguished Army contemporaries, Major General Nelson A. Miles, under whom, it will be recalled, he served in the winter of 1890–91. But much more significantly, Sanford unburdened himself about the Indian question and revealed his own attitudes. Military custom and law had prevented his venting any emotions while in uniform. He spoke warmly:

> We read constantly in newspapers . . . the statement that the *government* has been unjust to the Indians; that it has violated treaties, taken their lands by force, made war without cause, and in a hundred ways been guilty of cruelty and bad faith. These statements are accepted by the majority . . . with the greatest complacency as regards *themselves* and with the greatest horror and indignation as regards the Government. As Nathan said to David, "Thou art the man."[177] The United States is a government of the people, by the people, and for the people; and it is the *people* who are guilty of these crimes, if such exist, and it is the people who are responsible for them.

He continued—warmly:

> Army officers . . . in the Western frontier know these statements are true and are witnesses to their truth. Although they see these things . . . they are powerless to interfere. They have less power, in fact, than any other citizens. . . . The last people in the country to desire an Indian

176 Found in a trunk in the home of William K. Wallbridge, Short Hills, N. J. The manuscript consists of fifty-three holograph pages approximately eight inches by twelve and three-eighths inches in size; the writing, in ink, covers one side of the page. The address is untitled. For long excerpts from this paper, see my article " 'Thou Art the Man.' " *Journal of Arizona History*, IX (Spring, 1968), 30–38.

177 Sanford quotes from II Samuel 12:7.

war are the officers, for they know by bitter experience the horror of it. They appreciate its frequent injustice. And they are sure, finally, that there is little honor or glory to be acquired, whatever the exposure and risk, however faithfully the duty may be performed.

And if these words were not clear enough, Sanford became even clearer; now that a dam was broken within him, he would not stop:

It is often said by people . . . that Indian wars are forced upon the country by the ambition of officers desirous of obtaining glory or promotion. Officers know well enough that there is little promotion and less glory to be had; but there is endless toil, exposure, dreadful hardship, and rank ingratitude from the very people whose lives and property they are risking their own to save.

Major General Miles, Sanford told his audience, was "the most ambitious officer" he knew in the Army. However, "but for his cool and judicious conduct" two years earlier in the Sioux uprising, hundreds, perhaps thousands, of lives would have been lost. The Dakotas would have been drenched with blood. He went on:

But no one man or set of men can withstand the influence of the body of the people when they are determined upon any particular course, and it is to the body of the people that we have got to look for justice to the Indians. Until they are educated to the point of acknowledging [the Indians'] right to an equal share in a portion of this continent . . . with the dense masses of overcrowded Europe and Asia, there will be no justice for the Indians or such scant approach to it as is little worth consideration.[178]

Now we know what Sanford had been thinking, what he had been observing, what he had been storing inside himself as he rode the trails and marched across the face of the West. What we may have wondered at after his service in Arizona, after the Nez Percé and Bannock wars, is now clear. It always comes as a shock to discover that not all officers love war, enjoy killing, hanker after the blood of it. The image of the professional soldier so many of us construct is at once all wrong. He can, after all, be a human being. Swiftly

[178] I have regularized spelling, etc. It should be mentioned that the paragraph which dealt with General Miles was marked "Omit" by Sanford.

101

there comes to one a brief but searing insight into just what duty means to the man in uniform who has taken his oath of office.

In the spring of 1906, Colonel and Mrs. Sanford and their daughter Gertrude were vacationing in central California. They looked forward to their upcoming visit to San Francisco and the pleasure of family and friends. The Colonel hadn't seen the city in years.

They put up at the Palace Hotel, famous among San Francisco hostelries since its opening in 1875, in rooms on the third floor. Two stories above them was the Metropolitan Opera Company, in town for its annual visit. On the evening of 17 April, Enrico Caruso sang the role of Don José in *Carmen*. The Sanfords did not attend, but they had a fine evening in the hotel, dining and chatting with some members of the Minturn family. Early in the morning of the 18th—

> Awakened by severe jarring of my bed which adjoined Gerty's and was about two feet distant. . . . Jarring increased every instant, accompanied by tremendous roar[,] the crashing of glass & plaster[,] and falling of all movable objects. Recognized cause at once & motion dying down a little attempted to get out of bed & find Gertrude but was thrown violently back, great blocks of plaster falling over me in all directions.

The great earthquake and fire had begun.

The Colonel looked at his watch. It was 5:12 A.M. He assumed command in a trice. He was never one to lose an opportunity, however small, to lead and to serve. He advised his wife and daughter to dress. He followed his own advice and led them down the stairs (the elevators were out of order):

> People screaming & crying in every direction, notably one man in an adjoining room who was bawling like a great calf. . . . Gerty & Gertrude as cool and unconcerned through out the whole affair as if nothing whatever was the matter.

Sanford went outside, turned up Market Street, then up Montgomery to observe the destruction and to reconnoiter the area. Fires were starting, and he saw that they would have to debouch the Palace and find safety. They climbed up to their rooms and packed.

102

"I took the opportunity to shave . . . not knowing when I would get another chance," wrote the Colonel. They got their trunks to the street, commandeered "a market wagon with a crazy looking horse," loaded the baggage, and set out for the Presidio, where Sanford's brother-in-law, Lieutenant Colonel Alexander B. Dyer, was stationed.

> The roar of the flames was terrific & the whole scene too awful to describe. We travelled slowly up Sutter st. stopping almost every hundred yards to rest as our bags were very heavy. Men[,] women and children laden with all sorts of impedimenta were working in the same direction.

They entered the Presidio gates at 4:00 P.M. and settled in the empty Dyer cottage (he had just been assigned to duty at the Presidio). The post quartermaster sent them some supplies, and they were "pretty comfortable" during their short "tour of duty" there. On the morning of 21 April, they managed to reach the Union Ferry Building at the foot of Market Street, where they boarded the ferry for Oakland. That afternoon, a special train took them and scores of other refugees to Fresno. "This I had judged to be a good place to wait until we could get our belongings together, get a little rest and make arrangements about going home."[179] On 27 April, the Sanfords boarded a Santa Fe Pullman car and headed for the East Coast. They were in Drawing Room No. 13.

Sanford had been a heavy smoker from early manhood—cigars and pipes—and the habit finally took its toll. On 30 April 1908, he entered New York Hospital in New York City, and Mrs. Sanford also took a room in order to be with him. There was not much hope. On Memorial Day, George M. Woodruff, chairman of the Memorial Day meeting in Litchfield and the notary who had sworn him in as colonel, sent Sanford a telegram: "The assembled men, women, and children of Litchfield, send love to the gallant man

---

[179] They rested at the Hughes Hotel, and it was on twenty-three sheets of the hotel's stationery that the Colonel wrote out an account of the earthquake and their experiences, calling it "Notes on a Strenuous Week." This is the source of the information included here.

who led Phil Sheridan onto the firing line at Cedar Creek." Their sentiment was nice even if their history was incorrect, but nothing would have helped.

On 13 July, in the afternoon, Sanford died at the age of sixty-eight, having endured agony and discomfort without so much as a whimper. The cause of death was cancer of the tongue. The funeral was held in Litchfield on 15 July, and he was buried in Litchfield Cemetery.[180] The *Enquirer* ran a long and appreciative obituary, ending it with these lines from Bayard Taylor's *The Song of the Camp:*

> *Sleep soldiers! still in honored rest*
> *Your truth and valor wearing:*
> *The bravest are the tenderest,—*
> *The loving are the daring.*

A prose antiphon to this verse is this letter to Sanford from his grandfather when he was a "pup" and homesick second lieutenant at Carlisle Barracks, Pennsylvania, in 1861 before he left for Missouri:

New Haven   May 22. 1861

Dear George   the position & rank which you hold is a very high one for a young man—but few attain to it—it therefore behooves you to devote all your attention—thoughts & energies to qualify yourself for the place—think of this till you have fully perfected yourself to perform the duties of your station—it is a profession for life—an honorable one & whether you will retain it or not depend on you—on your good conduct and qualifications for the Post—fit yourself for it by close application to the study & practical use of arms, let nothing divert your attention till you are a proficient in the art & can maintain a standing equal to any of your comrades. You may be called at a moments warning & a want of that knowledge which will enable you to perform the duties required of you by your superiors to the satisfaction of your self & those with whom you act may win your prospects for life. Write & let me know what progress you have already made—the time you spend in the study of cavalry Tactics—in sword exercise—in the use of the Horse—& in short—the division of time & how the

---

180 Obituary, *New York Times,* July 14, 1908, p. 5.

whole is employed. As I said before, all depends on your good conduct—never take the first wrong step and you will be safe.[181]

What I have presented here is a bare biographical record, a selection of moments, a minimal introduction to the person of Colonel George Bliss Sanford, U.S.A., a man who served his country in what is still regarded in many circles as literally a holy war, then served his branch of service in what is still regarded in many circles as barbarism unadorned by any cause whatsoever, concomitantly serving his inclination (the professional soldier) for thirty-one years, making his way through the maze, building his reputation in competition with brilliant leaders and fraudulent duds, consolidating his place, amidst familiar and unfamiliar scenes and persons, in a very special cosmos in the latter half of the nineteenth century, only to slip, if not plunge, into obscurity, then into oblivion in the crowded years of the twentieth century. He remains enigmatic, partially, perhaps wholly, because of the way he chose to spend his last years: a sudden retirement from almost a third of a century of sustained routine and sudden violence to the sedate life of the traveling New England gentleman who dabbled in history, genealogy, and clubs, seeking no fame and shunning acclaim as if he were perfectly aware that none would be his anyway, since, after all, he was only a colonel.

Nevertheless, it is improper that he has been allowed to become forgotten, to have been dropped from our history and by our history, and it is my hope, even though I am very much aware of the gaps in the record, that this Introduction and edition of his *Experiences in Army Life* will return him to his place in the sun, if only for a brief moment. Crook, Miles, Custer, Sheridan, and Sherman, to call out loud and clear but a few names from the roster in Sanford's career, are secure in their niches in history. They will never be dropped. But what of Sanford? What of those men who served with him? There are many. They, too, must be regarded: James Jackson, Reuben Bernard, William H. Winters, Camillo C. C. Carr, Albert G. Forse, Charles Bendire, Randolph Norwood, John Green.

[181] Sanford's "Scrapbook."

There are many, many others. I sound out these names only because they were in the West. I ignore scores of men who were with Sanford in Missouri, in Virginia, whom the reader will meet very shortly.

The manuscript of *Experiences* which came into my possession for editing was one long chapter with frequent exhaustingly long paragraphs. Sanford's spelling was for the most part acceptable except for proper nouns, *e.g.*, patronyms and geographical place names. His punctuation was at times irregular enough to obscure meaning or render reading very difficult. I therefore divided the manuscript into ten chapters, shortened many of the paragraphs considerably by subdividing them, regularized the spelling and punctuation, and silently corrected obvious errors of fact or style, although there are a few exceptions to these general rules. I did all this to make his story the more presentable. What I hope was common sense was my guide. In no way did I change his meaning or his data, nor did I tamper at any time with the context.

I assumed that Sanford wrote *Experiences* shortly after his retirement, probably in 1893 and 1894. I also assumed that he worked from notes, orders, correspondence (official and otherwise), and other memorabilia, the serious and unfortunate loss of his "Notebooks" during the Civil War sadly acknowledged. None of his working material seems to have survived. His memory was unusually good, but I further assumed that when it did fail or confuse him, he turned to the official records. After all, thirty years is a long time, and memory does fade; on the other hand, a soldier's memory is a good deal sharper, through training, than the average civilian's.

The final result of Sanford's labors in the 1890's is something less than autobiography, something more than memoirs, very little of reminiscences. It is a record of heroism in all its ramifications, intense enough and sustained enough that the reader must be infected with it, despite, perhaps, his distaste for war, his abhorrence of violence. The story does not merely recount the specter of charging horsemen and sabers brandished and clashed as foes met on a field; it also recalls the endless hours in the saddle, terrible

106

to mind and body, the rain, the diseases, the bivouacs, the aggregation of which can, after a time, break the toughest of men.

Amazingly enough, Sanford manages to tell his story in *Experiences* from the point of view of the boy barely in his twenties, nevertheless a man because of maturation by combat, the American boy-man, although he was in his fifties when he wrote. There was within him, strongly so, very much of this boy-man throughout his career; in any competent and successful officer there must operate actively (and hyperactively at times) Donald Dareall, Eagle Scout.

In *Experiences*, Sanford implies himself. Never does he dwell on himself and thereby provoke the charge of braggadocio. After a spell of more than thirty years, it was inevitable that a kind of glow would pervade the work, if for nothing else than the war of the Rebellion *was* the experience of the nineteenth century. Rarely does Sanford criticize or castigate his superiors or his peers, Secretary of War Edwin McMasters Stanton excepted. For the most part he praises, and supports those he admired: McClellan, for example, or, more logically, Sheridan and Sherman.

A few years ago, Russell F. Weigley had this to say about the books written by the war veterans:

> A by-product of final victory was a tendency of Union memoirists to be uncritical of anything in the Union war effort save the mistakes of their personal rivals. . . . Civil War memoirs tend to be descriptive narratives, not critical analyses seeking to capitalize the war experience for guidance in future wars.[182]

Sanford *was* uncritical, and he was too junior in rank during the war to concern himself with carping criticism of his rivals. *Experiences* is a descriptive narrative, one which occasionally tries to make plain the military lessons learned by the cavalry. And cavalry was Sanford's *raison d'être*.

We must return now to the spring of 1861 when Sanford, a lad in his nineteenth year, not yet detached from home and parents, was commissioned a second lieutenant in the First Regiment of Dra-

---

[182] *Towards an American Army: Military Thought from Washington to Marshall,* 83.

goons, the oldest cavalry regiment in the Army, a regiment proud of its record, which went back to the Battle of Withlacoochie River, 27 February 1836, in the Florida War and was to come forward to include the campaigns in South Vietnam.

· EXPERIENCES IN ARMY LIFE ·

Of Colonel George B. Sanford, U.S.A., Retired,
Lately Colonel, Sixth Cavalry, U.S.A.

·CHAPTER I·

THE RESIGNATION OF MANY OFFICERS of the regular army during the winter of 1860–61, owing to the passage or impending passage of secession ordinances by the legislatures of their respective States, resulted in making many vacancies in the ranks of the commissioned officers of the U.S. Army which the Cadet Corps at the Military Academy was quite inadequate to fill. I was at this time in my eighteenth year, quite small for my age, and undeveloped, but with an excellent constitution, as from my earliest youth I had been fond of the open air and devoted to all out door sports and athletic exercises of every kind. Many of the games of the present day, such as tennis, golf and the improved forms of base-ball and foot-ball, were then comparatively unknown or at least little practiced, but their places were of course filled by others.

During the trout fishing season every spare hour I had at my disposal was devoted to that—to me—most fascinating of pursuits, and for many miles about New Haven, I have explored every promising looking stream, obtaining many fish and more pleasure, and laying up a stock of health and strength which stood me in good stead a few years later. During the summer months rowing, sailing, and swimming in the harbor were the principal amusements. Of the latter sport I was extremely fond and became very proficient. One swim, which was quite famous among the boys of my age and time, and which brought me a good deal of reputation, was from Benedicts Wharf to Long Wharf and back without stopping. In the rough water of the Bay this was a good deal of an achievement for a boy of fourteen or indeed of a considerably greater age, and was so regarded by my comrades. My schoolmate and *fidus Achates*[1] Thomas B. Kirby was the only other boy who ever accomplished it as far as I know. On another occasion, we two swam across Lake Saltonstall and back to our starting point without resting, not so much of a feat, in fact, but considered remarkable at the time, from the superstition which prevailed among the boys, in reference to the supposed bottomless depth of that pretty sheet of water. In the Autumn months, hare and hounds, foot-ball, base-ball, etc. came in—in all of which I took great delight and held high rank among my comrades, most of whom during my boyhood were my seniors in age.

This outdoor life kept me in splendid physical condition, so that when in response to an application to the War Department for a commission in the regular army I received the appointment of Second Lieutenant in the 1st Regiment of Dragoons on the 26th of April, 1861,[2] I was eminently fitted to withstand the hardships and exposure of many subsequent years. My father had always hoped to obtain for me a commission in the army, and had made several efforts in that direction, but prior to the great Civil War, entrance into the service except through the avenue of the Military Academy at West Point was exceedingly difficult. A cadetship at the Academy resulting in a commission on graduation after four years of hard study, was considered as a great prize and was eagerly sought for, but among the multitude of applicants there were necessarily many disappointed ones. The appointments rested in the hands of the members of Congress from the various districts, and one of these, the Hon. Samuel Arnold, of the Second Congressional District of Connecticut, had at one time promised to appoint me.[3]

[1] Vergil's *Aeneid:* faithful Achates, trusty friend. Kirby did not, however, attend Yale.

[2] The First Regiment of Dragoons was organized by Act of Congress, 2 March 1833; its designation as First Regiment of Cavalry was changed by Act of Congress, 3 August 1861. Sanford's formal acceptance of commission is dated 2 May 1861. He was eight weeks shy of his nineteenth birthday.

[3] Samuel Arnold (1806–1868), banker and businessman from Haddam, Connecticut, and a Democrat, represented the Second District for one term only in the Thirty-fifth Congress, 4 March 1857–3 March 1859.

For some reason or other, however, he did not do so, but gave the appointment to his nephew, who graduated at the Academy during the War, near the head of his class, and became a Second Lieutenant of Ordnance some time after I had received my promotion through the various grades to a Captaincy in the Cavalry.[4] On the whole I think I had the best of it. My assignment to the 1st Dragoons was accompanied by an order directing me to report to Major-General Wool, commanding the Department of the East, Headquarters in New York City, for further instructions;[5] so about the 1st of May I proceeded to New York and reported at Headquarters as directed. I had no interview with Gen. Wool in person, but was received by his Adjutant-General, Col. H. L. Scott, who was a son-in-law of Lieut. Genl. Winfield Scott, the Commanding General of the Army.[6]

Colonel Scott was exceedingly curt in his manner, bordering on discourtesy I thought, in his reception of me, and I obtained a first impression of army life which was by no means favorable and which I have certainly never forgotten. It was a matter of small importance, and possibly the majority of young men would have never given it another thought, but I was a shy and rather sensitive lad, and was a good deal hurt at his manner. I had an exaggerated idea of the importance of a West Point education, and was

[4] Congressman Arnold's choice was not bad. His nephew, Isaac Arnold, Jr., was graduated from the United States Military Academy (henceforth designated USMA) in 1862, thirteenth in a class of twenty-eight. When Sanford was writing his memoirs, Arnold was a major in the Ordnance Department.

[5] The Department of the East comprised the country east of the Mississippi River.

Entering the U.S. Army as a captain, Thirteenth Infantry, on 14 April 1812, John E. Wool (1784–1869) rose to brigadier general by 1841 and was brevetted major general, dated 23 February 1847. He was retired on 1 August 1863 with the rank of major general. In the *Official Army Register* for 1861, Wool is the senior of four brigadier generals, ranked only by Major General Winfield Scott. On 24 January 1854, Wool was given the thanks of Congress and presented with a sword for his services at Buena Vista in the Mexican War.

[6] Henry L. Scott, USMA, Class of 1833, General Scott's son-in-law, was carried in the *Official Register* in 1861 as the senior captain, Fourth Regiment of Infantry, aide-de-camp to General Scott, and ex officio lieutenant colonel since 7 March 1855. Scott retired on 30 October 1861 as inspector general with the rank of colonel. In that same year, he published his authoritative *Military Dictionary*. See n. 32 *infra*.

painfully conscious of the fact that I was not a graduate of the Military Academy. There was then, and for many years afterwards, an impression among civilians that an officer appointed to the army from civil life, or still more from the ranks, was looked down upon by the West Point men and that he necessarily had a very hard time in his intercourse with them.

Let me say here once for all, that after an experience of more than thirty years in the regular service, I am fully prepared to testify to the fact that there is not one particle of foundation for any such charge. If a man attends to his business and shows an adaptation for it, he will receive courteous treatment and assistance from his comrades whether he is a graduate of the Academy or not, but if he is a trifler or worthless fellow he will get scant ceremony wherever he hails from. In the latter case, I fully believe that the West Point graduate would have less consideration shown him than a representative of either of the other classes mentioned, for the very reason that it would be presumed that his previous experience should have taught him better.

This episode had one excellent effect however for in all my long service during over twenty-five years of which I was in positions of command, I was exceedingly careful never to hurt the feelings of any young man reporting to me for duty, whether officer or soldier. My knowledge of the customs of service or the art of war in its scientific sense at the period of my entry into the service was naturally almost nothing. With reference to infantry drill, however, and the manual of arms I was rather unusually well posted. For several years of my boyhood I had been a student of Gen. Wm. H. Russell's Military Institute in New Haven.[7] The school was organized as a battalion of infantry and divided into four companies, and I had served in all the various grades of corporal, sergeant, 1st sergeant, lieutenant and finally Captain of "C" Company. Our drill instructor was 1st Lieut. Lyman Bissell of the 9th Infantry,

[7] Sanford has recalled the Collegiate and Commercial Institute in New Haven where he prepared for Yale. It was located at 7 Wooster Place, and William H. Russell, M.D., was the principal. Prior to about 1845, Russell had conducted a boys' school on East Water Street. See *Patten's New Haven Directory, for the Year 1840, 1844–1845, and 1845–1846.*

a veteran of the Mexican War and afterward of the Rebellion.[8] Under his excellent instruction and supervision I became quite proficient in the duties of the various positions mentioned, as far as pertained to drill. Of logistics, strategy or tactics in its proper sense, I of course knew nothing.

By direction of Gen. Wool I was ordered to report for duty at the U.S. Cavalry Depot then at Carlisle Barracks, Penna.,[9] and after providing myself with the proper uniform and equipment of my rank, I proceeded to that station via Philadelphia and Harrisburg. My father accompanied me on this trip and on reaching Harrisburg we found it would be necessary to remain all night, as there was no train to Carlisle until the next morning. We stopped at the United States Hotel near the depot, a wretched place, and I have a vivid recollection of the miserable night I spent there,— the rain pattering against the windows and on the roof, the locomotives shrieking and wailing in the adjoining yard, and a noisy crowd of "intending" volunteers getting up their enthusiasm by copious libations, in the hotel bar-room. I realized then for the first time I think that a great break had come in my life, and that I was leaving home and friends probably forever. I slept little if any and arose in the morning with anything but cheerful anticipations as to my future career. My father's intention was to accompany me to the Barracks and introduce me to the Commanding Officer and then return at once to New Haven, so that I expected to sever the last link that bound me to my early life in a very few hours. As it turned out, however, he was made so very welcome by the genial old soldier who commanded the post, and his charming and always lovely wife, that he remained several days at the Barracks. When I pulled up my window shade that morning, there was little or nothing inviting to see—a dull drizzling rain was falling, and a heavy fog mingled with soot obscured the view. Trains were back-

---

[8] A native of Connecticut, Lyman Bissell (d. 1888) was appointed first lieutenant, Ninth Regiment of Infantry, 9 April 1847; captain, 8 September 1847. Disbanded 26 August 1848, Bissell was appointed first lieutenant in the Ninth on 3 March 1855. When he retired on 31 December 1870, he was a major.

[9] About 110 miles west of Philadelphia, Carlisle Barracks was garrisoned by recruits. Sanford was ordered there on 6 May 1861.

115

ing and filling along the railroad tracks, the train men were splashing about through the puddles, and everything looked mournful and wretched. Nearly opposite stood another railroad hotel, a rather poorer looking establishment, than the one we were in, apparently. I don't see now that there is anything particularly funny in the name "Bombgardner Hotel" which was painted across the front in great black letters on a white ground, but at that moment it seemed to me supremely ridiculous, and I burst into a hearty laugh. It was probably a nervous reaction, but it did me good, cleared the mental atmosphere, and broke up one of the worst fits of homesickness I ever remember to have experienced. My father who had just come into my room said nothing. I fancy he understood the case, and we at once went down to breakfast, and afterwards took the train for Carlisle, which we reached by ten A.M., and drove out to the garrison. It was at that time a very pretty place, with many pretty houses, standing among beautiful trees in grassy lawns, and surrounded by flowers and shrubs. The guard house at the entrance to the post was a quaint old structure built as I was afterwards told, by the Hessian prisoners who were confined there during the Revolutionary War, by Gen. Washington's orders. We went at once to the Post Headquarters, where I reported for duty to the Commanding Officer, Major Lawrence Pike Graham of the 2nd Dragoons.

My second experience in reporting for orders was very different from the first. "Old Pike," as he was affectionately called, though by no means an old man at that time, was a thorough gentleman of the old Virginia school—tall and dignified in bearing, and with exceedingly courtly manners. He was an eminently handsome soldier, and the model of a dashing dragoon. He had been highly distinguished in the Florida and Mexican campaigns, notably at the battles of Palo Alto and Resaca de la Palma for which he received the brevet of Major. The hardship and exposure of twenty-five years of army life in malarial climate, had so told upon his vigorous frame that he was unable to perform much active service during the Rebellion, though he served for a short time as Brig. Genl. of Volunteers in the Army of the Potomac. He would un-

116

doubtedly have risen much higher, had his health not failed. In 1870 he was placed upon the retired list of the army, being at the time Colonel of the 4th Cavalry and a Bvt. Brig. Genl. U.S. Army.[10] In addition to the regular garrison of the Post there were at this time at Carlisle Barracks several troops of the 2nd (now 5th) Cavalry under command of Maj. George H. Thomas[11] of that regiment. They had arrived only a few days before from Texas where they had been serving in campaigns against the Kiowas, Comanches and Apaches, up to the time that State was dragged into the secession whirlpool and its garrison treacherously surrendered to the Rebels by the Department Commander Gen. David E. Twiggs.[12] Major Thomas was a Virginian, and like Graham thoroughly loyal to the Union. I was so fortunate as to become well acquainted with him during the few weeks of his stay at the Barracks, principally owing to the fact that his wife was then visiting in my native place (New Haven) and knew many of my friends and relatives there. General Thomas, as he soon became, was a man of reserved manners and great personal dignity, but of kindly and gentle disposition. Of course I did not realize at that

[10] Sanford is generally correct in his data on Lawrence Pike Graham (1815–1905). On 31 August 1861, Graham was appointed brigadier general of volunteers; on 1 October 1861, he was promoted lieutenant colonel, Fifth Cavalry. his permanent rank. He had entered service as a second lieutenant, Second Dragoons, in 1837 and had been promoted major 14 June 1858.

[11] To become one of the great generals in the Civil War, George H. Thomas (1816–1870), USMA, Class of 1840, was appointed second lieutenant in the Third Regiment of Artillery. On 17 August 1861, he was made a brigadier general of volunteers.

[12] On 18 February 1861, Brevet Major General David E. Twiggs, United States Army (henceforth designated USA), commanding the Department of Texas, formally surrendered United States military posts in his department. At the time, Twiggs was one of four brigadier generals in the Army, second in rank and junior to General Wool (see n. 5 *supra*), and recipient of a sword for his gallantry and good conduct in storming Monterrey in the Mexican War. In mid-January, Twiggs had asked to be relieved and, in fact, was so relieved on 28 January 1861. He received the orders on 15 February. On 1 March 1861, by order of President Buchanan, Twiggs was dismissed from the Army "for his treachery to the flag of his country." Even though he was seventy-one years old, he was appointed major general in the Confederate Army. He died on 15 July, 1862.

Companies A and F, Second Regiment of Cavalry, came from Fort Mason; Company B, Camp Colorado; Company C, Fort Inge; Companies D and H, Camp Cooper; Company E, Camp Hudson; Company G, Camp on the Río Grande; Company I, Camp Ives; and Company K, Camp Wood—all posts in the Department of Texas.

117

time to how great a height he was to rise in the terrible conflict then impending, but I remember distinctly that I did feel whenever I spoke to him that I was speaking to a great man. Not long after my arrival the troops under his command were ordered to the vicinity of Harpers Ferry on the Potomac and I well remember that as they rode out of the garrison I was performing my first tour as officer of the guard and turned out the guard to salute as they marched by. Richard W. Johnson, who afterwards became a Major-General of Volunteers, was one of the Captains.[13] Chas. J. Whiting was another,[14] and among the lieutenants were Royall and McLean who soon after had the desperate fight with their former regimental comrade Fitzhugh Lee, at Old Church, Va., in which Royall was desperately wounded by sabre cuts in the head, and McLean was killed.[15]

In May, 1861 I received orders to accompany a detachment of recruits en route to the West, and to join my Company "D" 1st Dragoons at Fort Breckinridge, New Mexico.[16] This post was

[13] Richard W. Johnson (1827–1897), a native of Kentucky, had been promoted captain on 1 December 1856 and was appointed brigadier general of volunteers 1861. He was retired from the army with the rank of major general on 12 October 1867.

[14] Senior to Johnson in rank was Charles J. Whiting, whose captaincy dated 3 March 1855. He was promoted major on 17 July 1862 and dismissed from the Army on 5 November 1863. He was restored, however, on 2 August 1866 as major, Third Regiment of Cavalry, with same date of rank.

[15] William B. Royall, William McLean, and Fitzhugh Lee (1935–1905), the latter Robert E. Lee's nephew and Confederate general, were fellow officers in the Second Regiment of Cavalry, later designated as Fifth Regiment of Cavalry by Act of Congress, 3 August 1861. McLean, then a captain, died on 13 April 1863.

[16] In the Department of New Mexico, Fort Breckinridge at the beginning of the war was garrisoned by elements of the First Regiment of Dragoons and Eighth Regiment of Infantry; it was soon abandoned. Had Sanford ever reached this department, there is a very good chance he would never have served in the East during the war.

Companies D and G, First Regiment of Cavalry, took part in the battle at Valverde, New Mexico, on 21 February 1862.

Fort Breckinridge (originally Fort Arivaypa), named for the vice president under Buchanan, was destroyed by fire shortly after the beginning of the Civil War and was abandoned. In 1862, it was rebuilt and named Fort Stanford, but was abandoned that same year. These two forts were at the mouth of the San Pedro River. In 1865, California troops "established a new site at the junction of the Arivaypa [Aravaipa] and San Pedro Rivers" and called it Camp Grant. This was removed to the foot of Mount Graham in Graham County, Arizona, in 1872. Sanford is incorrectly referring to it as the same place. See Bruce Grant, *American Forts, Yesterday and Today*, 332.

118

afterwards designated as Fort Grant, and was situated at the mouth of the Arivaypa Canon near the junction of the Arivaypa and San Pedro rivers, in the territory now known as Arizona. I little thought then that it would be eight long years before I reached that post, though I was well aware that the journey was a long and difficult one. The detachment to which I was assigned was under the command of Capt. Washington L. Elliott of the Mounted Rifles (now the 3rd Cavalry) and consisted of recruits for his own regiment and for the 1st and 2nd Dragoons, about two hundred and fifty men and some eight or ten officers in all. Elliott rose to the rank of Major-General of Volunteers during the war, and retired from active service as Colonel of the 3rd Cavalry about 1878.[17] Another officer was 1st Lieut. and Bvt. Captain Gordon Granger of the Mounted Rifles, who also became a Major-General of volunteers and commanded the 4th Army Corps in the Chattanooga campaign.[18] Both were excellent officers. My especial companion was a young officer of the 2nd Dragoons named Canfield, who was several years older than myself and who knew something of military customs, owing to having been for a short time a cadet at the Military Academy at West Point. He took a fancy to me and helped me a good deal in getting acquainted with the various unwritten laws of service which are so hard for a beginner to acquire, for the reason that older soldiers take it for granted you ought to know them instinctively. Two years later, on the 9th of June, 1863, Canfield was shot dead, while gallantly leading his troop in the splendid charge of the 2nd Cavalry at Beverly Ford, Virginia.[19]

[17] Washington L. Elliott (1825–1888) had entered service on 27 May 1846 and was promoted captain in the Regiment of Mounted Riflemen, a unit that saw service only in the West, on 20 July 1854. Appointed brigadier general of volunteers on 11 June 1862, he became chief of cavalry of the Army of Virginia. His retirement date was 20 March 1879; he held the rank of colonel, Third Regiment of Cavalry, formerly the Mounted Riflemen but whose designation had been changed by Act of Congress, 3 August 1861.

[18] A USMA graduate, Class of 1845, Gordon Granger (1822–1876) was to be promoted captain on 5 May 1861. He had been brevetted for service in the Mexican War on 13 September 1847. He was appointed brigadier general of volunteers 5 April 1862 and major general of volunteers 17 September 1862. He served with distinction at both Chickamauga and Chattanooga.

[19] Charles W. Canfield had been a USMA cadet from 1 July 1853 to 26 April 1854. He was appointed second lieutenant, Second Regiment of Dragoons, 26 April

119

Our command marched from the Barracks to the railway station at Carlisle, escorted by the officers and troops of the garrison, the band playing "The Girl I Left Behind Me" according to established custom. At this time no one apparently believed that the war would last more than a few months, and it was supposed that we who were going to the far West would see nothing of it. We got off in good order amid the cheers and good-byes of the garrison. I remember especially an old grey-headed Sergeant, who was evidently a veteran of the Florida and Mexican Wars, jumping on to the step just as the cars were starting and asking to shake my hand, as he could not bear to see so young a boy going off to the wars. He realized what was before me much better than I did, and it made his honest old heart ache to think of it. Railway travel was slow in those days, and it was three days before we reached St. Louis, Mo. On arrival there we learned that the city was in a state of great excitement and that it was not at all unlikely that we should have trouble with the mob. I was officer of the guard that day, and received orders from Capt. Elliott to march my guard about one hundred yards in rear of the command along the levee to the steamboat on which we were to take passage to Hannibal, Mo. When I got my men off the cars I found that the crowd had closed in, in rear of the command, and I had considerable difficulty in forcing a passage. We were armed with sabres only, and in the temper the crowd were in at the time we did not present a very formidable appearance. However we had some friends among them apparently, for one young man pressed forward and handed me an orange, saying, "Take that my boy, you look tired and heated." The majority however were hostile enough and we heard frequent allusions to "Lincoln's hirelings," "Hessians," etc. After reaching the steamboat we soon got under way, and sailed up the river.

I was greatly pleased with this part of the journey which was indeed a perfectly novel experience to me. The magnificent river, and the wildness of the country along the banks, as compared to that which I was accustomed to in the East, greatly interested and

---

1861 and first lieutenant 14 May 1861; his regiment was designated Second Regiment of Cavalry on 3 August 1861.

excited me. We steamed along all night and as it happened to be a beautiful evening. I spent most of it on the deck, admiring the scenery and thinking a good deal of the wonderful change in my life which had so suddenly occurred. At Hannibal we once more took the cars and started across the State of Missouri for St. Joseph, or St. Jo. as it is usually called, then a very thriving "river" town on the Missouri River.[20] During the greater part of this trip we were passing through an almost hostile section and heard constant rumors that the track would be torn up ahead of us—that we would be attacked at such a place, and so on. However nothing of note occurred except that at the little town of Breckenridge we saw what purported to be the *Rebel flag* flying from a recently erected staff. It was the first one any of us had seen I suppose, and I know it inspired me with very singular sensations. Here then was actual defiance of the Government. I thought of course that we should be disembarked and ordered to charge down the street and seize the hated emblem; but nothing of the kind occurred, and the older officers seemed to take it as a matter of course. The only one whom I heard express any special indignation was a young fellow of the Rifles named Henry, who had just been graduated from the Military Academy, and was very eager to "get at those fellows." Six months later he was on the staff of the Rebel General J. E. B. Stuart, and did gallant service in the Confederate army throughout the War. There were many such instances, some of which I will mention hereafter.[21]

In due course of time we arrived at St. Jo. and embarked on the steamer *A. J. Majors* for Fort Leavenworth, which we reached one morning early in June, 1861, and landed near the present Missouri Pacific railway station. At that time there was no railway of course and the post fronted, like the river towns, toward the river, the levee being the main business street. We marched up the hill and formed on the parade ground in front of the Commanding

[20] On the Hannibal & St. Joseph Railroad, which passed through such towns and hamlets as Palmyra, Hunnewell, Macon City, Brookfield, and Osborn.

[21] The officer in question here was Second Lieutenant Mathias W. Henry, USMA, Class of 1861. He served in the artillery, Confederate States Army (henceforth designated CSA).

Officer's office, which was then in the building now known as "Thomas Hall." Capt. Delos B. Sacket of the 1st (now 4th) Cavalry was the commanding officer at the time, but left for the East a few days later. He was a very distinguished officer and afterwards became the Inspector-General of the U. S. Army.[22] Capt. Elliott after bringing us to a "rest" went to the office and for the next hour or so we remained awaiting instructions. During this time I looked with interest at my new surroundings. Fort Leavenworth was then a frontier post, built in the form of a rectangle, with the soldiers' barracks on one of the long sides, the officers' quarters opposite, the Commanding Officer's house on the North end with the staff and other officers near by, and at the South end were the stables; the sutler's store, quartermaster buildings and business quarters generally were near the Levee. The parade ground enclosed by the quarters and barracks was a beautiful rolling lawn shaded by immense oaks, elms, black walnuts and lindens. There were many other varieties of trees, twenty-eight I think I counted some thirty years later when stationed there as an instructor in the Infantry and Cavalry School.[23] Many officers of the garrison came up and introduced themselves while we were waiting, and among them I recognized the insignia of all the arms of the service and with most pleasure the deep orange of the Dragoons of which I myself belonged. Finally we received our instructions, and marched to a little valley about a mile northwest of the post, where we were ordered to go into camp, and where for the first time I saw a camp pitched by soldiers. Our men being many of them recruits, needed a good deal of instruction in the complicated process (as it seemed to me) of pitching tents, but

22 It would appear that Delos B. Sacket was recently promoted major in the First Regiment of Cavalry, dating from 31 January 1861; he had entered the Army as a brevet second lieutenant, Second Regiment of Dragoons, 1 July 1845. He was named brigadier general, Inspector General of the Army, on 2 January 1881.

Until lately, Fort Leavenworth, Department of the West, had been commanded by Captain and Brevet Lieutenant Colonel Horace Brooks, Second Regiment of Artillery; the fort was garrisoned, at least till the outbreak of war, by elements of the First and Second Artillery.

23 Sanford was senior instructor of cavalry tactics, School of Application for Infantry and Cavalry, from June, 1885, to August, 1891, with service in Washington, D.C., and in the field in 1888–89 and 1890–91.

there were many old hands among them, and long before sundown everything was completed, and my first military camp was an accomplished fact.

We expected of course to remain for a few days only to fit out for our long march across the Plains. Horses were to be purchased, transportation obtained, rations and forage drawn and everything put in order for a three months' journey through a country destitute of everything but grass and water. The principal work in this respect lay upon the shoulders of the Commandant and his staff, but the rest of us found ample occupation in the almost incessant drill which went on at intervals from morning until night.

After a few days rumors began to fly about that perhaps we might be needed nearer at home than in the country West of the Rocky Mountains; that the Rebels were organizing in Missouri; that the Liberty Arsenal had been captured;[24] that there was a camp of the enemy at Independence and that Fort Leavenworth itself might be attacked. Suddenly came notice that Kansas City, Mo. twenty-six miles distant, was threatened and that we were to go to the rescue, and go we did on the steamer *Iatan* down the river. On arriving we found quite a command assembled under command of Maj. W. E. Prince of the 2nd Infantry, and at once our force began to take on the semblance of an army.[25] Pickets were thrown out in the direction of the supposed hostile section, and the cavalry made frequent reconnaissances. The earliest in which I took part was an expedition to Liberty, Mo., a small town on the left bank of the Missouri River in which was situated an U.S. Arsenal.[26] This had been seized by the Rebels, and a com-

[24] It had, in fact, been seized; see below.

[25] Sanford is doubly in error here. William E. Prince was still a captain and a the First Regiment of Infantry. He had entered the Army as a second lieutenant, First Regiment, 1 August 1838 and was breveted captain for service in the Mexican War. His promotion to major was dated 23 November 1861, Third Regiment of Infantry. Elsewhere, Sanford says that during this period, he himself was attached to "a company of Rifle Recruits," *i.e.,* recruits for the Regiment of Mounted Riflemen.

[26] A chronological account of the events in Arkansas, Indian Territory, and Missouri in the late winter and early spring of 1861 may be of help here: 8 February, U.S. arsenal at Little Rock seized; *ca* 12 February, U.S. ordnance stores at Napoleon, Arkansas, seized; 16 April, Fort Washita, Indian Territory, abandoned; 18 April, U.S. subsistence stores at Pine Bluff, Arkansas, seized; 20 April, U.S.

mand was supposed to be organizing there for the purpose of attacking the post of Fort Leavenworth. We crossed the river in ferry boats and at early dawn approached the village under cover of a dense land fog. Major Prince had made his dispositions well, and by the time we were discovered the enemy's outposts had been captured, and his camp surrounded. A few shots were fired, but as well as I remember now no one on either side was injured, and in a few moments white flags were thrown out, and the enemy gave up. A large flag pole near the camp I remember, was cut down and the flag floating from it taken. The enemy were gathered together and the oath of allegiance administered, after which they were released, and our command went into camp rejoicing. I have no doubt that every man of them joined the Confederate army later; but that was the way things were done in those days. On the whole I don't know that anyone could have blamed our commander reasonably, for his leniency to them. It was by no means certain at that time that there would be any actual war and the policy of the authorities at Washington seemed to be decidedly one of conciliation. For some time after this expedition we remained in camp near Kansas City, drilling and preparing for an expedition to southwestern Missouri. A rebel force from Texas under the well-known Ben McCulloch was reported as advancing to the assistance of Gen. Sterling Price who was preparing to invade Missouri from Arkansas.[27] Gen. Lyon of the U.S. Army was advancing from St. Louis to resist Price, and our forces under command of Maj. Sturgis of the 4th Cavalry were to march southward and form a junction with him. Our command was composed of four troops, of the 1st

---

arsenal at Liberty, Missouri, seized; 4 May, U.S. ordnance stores at Kansas City, Missouri, seized. At Liberty, the Secessionists got their hands on 1,500 arms and a few cannon. The arsenal was northeast of Kansas City, about fifteen miles overland.

27 Ben McCulloch (1811–1862), as a colonel in the Texas State Troops, had received Major General Twiggs's surrender at San Antonio, Texas (*supra,* p. 117; he was commissioned brigadier general in the CSA on 11 May 1861 and was instrumental, with General Sterling Price, CSA, in the Confederate effort at Wilson's Creek (*infra,* pp. 130 ff.), where he was in chief command. He was an experienced frontiersman.

Sterling Price (1809–1867) was named to command, as major general, the Missouri State Guard in May, 1861; he had been colonel and brigadier general of volunteers in the Mexican War and governor of Missouri.

124

(now 4th) Cavalry, one troop of the 2nd Dragoons, a battalion each of the 1st and 2nd Infantry, a battery of artillery and two regiments of Kansas Volunteers.[28]

The Kansas Volunteers were a peculiar organization; brimful of patriotism and inured to hard service, and a rough life, they were utterly lacking in discipline and in many respects difficult to manage. The officers except in the higher grades were of the same class as the men, and all hands seemed to regard the expedition in the light of a foray on their ancient enemy—the State of Missouri. For more than six years continual hostilities had been breaking out between the free state men in Kansas and the pro-slavery element in Missouri,—or as they were generally called, the jay-hawkers and the border-ruffians. Between the two I fancy there was little to choose in point of vindictiveness. Each had bitter wrongs to avenge and neither was slow in visiting condign punishment on the other's territory. Now that we were regularly encamped in Missouri, with an apparently irresistible force, the Kansas men seemed to think they had a perfect right to treat the inhabitants as conquered enemies, and levy on their property indiscriminately. If this had been allowed to go on, a perfect reign of terror would shortly have existed in the State and neither age nor sex would have been safe for a moment. The regular troops would have soon become demoralized by the example of their comrades, and the condition of Missouri would shortly have equalled that of France in the days of the Free Companies. Major Sturgis' orders therefore were very stringent against all forms of riot and plunder, and in the neighborhood of the camps were well

[28] Nathaniel Lyon (1818–1861), who was to command and be killed at Wilson's Creek, Missouri, 10 August 1861, was a graduate of USMA, Class of 1841. He was brevetted captain for service in the Mexican War and was also wounded. He had been appointed brigadier general of volunteers 17 May 1861.

A graduate of USMA, Class of 1846, Samuel D. Sturgis (1822–1889) was a major in the First Regiment of Cavalry, not yet the Fourth, to date from 3 May 1861. He had been in command of Fort Smith, Arkansas; after the defection of some of his officers, Sturgis marched his command to Fort Leavenworth, having evacuated Fort Smith. In March, 1862, Sturgis was appointed brigadier general of volunteers, to date from 10 August 1861, the day of Wilson's Creek.

It is possible to reconstruct partially this command: Companies B, C, and D, First Regiment of Infantry; Companies B and E, Second Regiment of Infantry; Company C, Second Regiment of Dragoons; and the First and Second Kansas.

125

observed; but soon from a little distance reports began to come in of robbery and insult.

One morning I recollect that a man was brought in who had been taken by a guard in the act of plundering a house. It was determined that summary justice should be dealt out to him, so by direction of Capt. Gordon Granger, who was acting as Adjutant-General for Maj. Sturgis, two long lines of men were formed, facing each other, each man armed with a switch or stick. The lines stretched toward the Kansas or Kaw river, as it is generally called, and the victim was started at one end and told to run the gauntlet. I can see the poor wretch's face now as he stood there pale and desperate. A first he could scarcely move, but in a moment he sprang into a run, and went flying down between the ranks amid the shower of blows from either side. I do not believe the physical punishment was very severe, but he must have been nearly frightened to death. When he reached the line of high bluffs overlooking the Kaw he hesitated a moment; but Captain Granger seized a rifle from a sergeant standing by my side, and sent a bullet over his head. With a wild cry he threw his hands up over his head, dashed over the bank and disappeared. Of course Granger did not intend to hit him, but it seemed to me cold-blooded work.

Soon after this episode we moved south on our march to join Gen. Lyon. I think it must have been early in July when we were encamped near the pretty village of Clinton that I saw another instance of the way justice was meted out in those days.[29] This time affairs were conducted in a more regular manner. Two men of the Volunteers had been tried by Court Martial for robbing a house, and were sentenced to a certain number of lashes on the bare back in the presence of the whole command. We were drawn up in a hollow square, the criminals were brought to the centre, and the sentence of the Court read to them. Then they were tied up to the spare wheel of a caisson and the lashes vigorously administered by the drummers, the military surgeon standing by. I do not remember that either uttered a sound, but I do recollect the "swish" of the lash and the sickening sight of the first blood that spurted up.

29 Clinton was the county seat of Clinton County, southeast of Kansas City.

After that I saw no more of the punishment and was glad to get back to my tent when we were dismissed. These punishments seemed dreadfully cruel to me at the time, and gave me a sort of disgust for the whole business; but I can understand now that they were necessary and doubtless prevented the perpetration of more dreadful crimes.

About this time it was determined, as there was very little probability of our detachment ever joining the posts and regiments to which they had been assigned, that the enlisted men should be turned over to the command of infantry officers, and the cavalry officers assigned to the troops of the 4th Cavalry which were with the expedition. I was attached to "D" company which was under the command of Capt. W. L. Elliott afterwards Bvt. Maj. Gen. Elliott. This I liked much better than doing duty with the recruits, who were all on foot. We now began to do a good deal of scouting and reconnaissance work, more I suspect for practice than because there was any expectation of finding signs of the enemy. After crossing the Grand river and the Osage however, we got occasional rumors of their whereabouts, and soon came the reports of Gen. Sigel's "tremendous battle" of Carthage.[30] I suspect it was the very smallest specimen of a skirmish, but at that time every incident was magnified to an unlimited extent. Late in July our forces made their expected junction with Gens. Lyon and Sigel in the vicinity of Springfield, Mo. and in a day or two moved south by the old stage road in hopes to attack Gen. Price before he had been joined by McCulloch.

In this expectation Gen. Lyon was disappointed as at Dug Spring on the 2nd of August, 1861, we ran up against the advance of the enemy and obtained sufficient information to show that the junction had already been made. As this was the first actual engagement in which I took part I have always retained the memory of it with

---

[30] Franz Sigel (1824–1902), a native of Germany with but nine years' residence in the United States, was a brigadier general of volunteers as of 7 August 1861, to rank from 17 May 1861 (same date as General Lyon), and major general as of 21 March 1862. He was still a colonel here and at Wilson's Creek. There is little point to examining Sanford's irony about the skirmish at Carthage, Missouri, 5 July 1861. Yet the engagement did have political significance.

127

greater distinctness than that of many much more important encounters. It was a bright beautiful morning as we were moving
along quietly through a lovely wooded country, when we first
caught sight of a few mounted men at some distance in our front.
Capt. Elliott's troop was in advance and I had charge of the advance guard which was some distance in front of the main body.
As soon as it seemed probable that the enemy was in sight, I sent
word back to Capt. Elliott and he rode forward to examine into the
situation. The troop to which I was now attached had only a few
weeks before been commanded by a Capt. McIntosh, who had resigned his commission and joined the Confederate army. As we
rode nearer the people in advance, who were now intently watching
us through glasses, one of the men in my troop suddenly called
out "My God, boys, that's Capt. McIntosh." It was a curious coincidence that in their first encounter this troop and their old Captain, who had been very much liked by his men, should have run
up against each other.[31]

Capt. Elliott now ordered a set of fours to dismount and fire at
the party ahead, as they evidently did not intend to allow us to
approach them.[32] This was done, and the bullets whistled about
the limbs of the trees over their heads. I do not believe the men
would have tried to hit their old Captain. At all events they did not,
and after taking off his hat and bowing low towards us, he and his
party cantered off.

Our main body was now coming up, and deploying skirmishers
to the front and on the flanks, we moved on and before long developed a considerable force in front. The artillery was then brought

[31] Graduated from USMA at the foot of his class, 1849, James McQ. McIntosh
(1828–1862) was a captain in the First Regiment of Cavalry when he resigned from
the Army on 7 May 1861. During the engagement at Dug Spring, McIntosh officially
served as assistant adjutant general (rank of captain) to McCulloch, to date from
29 July 1861. Yet at Wilson's Creek he was a colonel, commanding the Second
Arkansas Mounted Riflemen, McCulloch's Brigade. Both McIntosh and McCulloch,
brigadier generals, were killed on 7 March 1862 in the Battle of Pea Ridge (Elkhorn
Tavern), Arkansas. See n. 28, Chap. VII.

[32] That is, four men abreast. Sanford's unit was marching in a column of sets
of fours, approved cavalry tactics. "Marching columns to be by file, twos, fours,
or platoons; by fours and platoons in preference when the ground permits." Henry
L. Scott, *Military Dictionary*, 156.

into action, and for the first time I listened to the roar of the guns which for the next four years was to be so familiar a sound. Our line of battle was formed in rear of the cavalry and then we were drawn off toward the flanks as the whole body advanced. The fighting was quite sharp for some time, but the enemy steadily fell back as we advanced, and at one time a very gallant charge was made by a party of "C" troop 1st (4th) Cavalry under Lieut. Kelly.[33] He mistook the trumpet call to halt for the signal to charge and dashed into the enemy's lines completely routing them at that point, though nearly all his own men were killed or wounded. The rest of "C" troop under Capt. Stanley afterwards Maj. Gen. Stanley and my own troop both under command of Capt. Elliott then moved to the front in support, and the enemy fell back.[34] The contest was soon after terminated by darkness. One fine young fellow named Roys, a corporal of Capt. Stanley's troop, was desperately wounded, after behaving in the most gallant manner. His horse was shot under him, with no less than fourteen balls. Corporal Roys afterwards received a commission as 2nd Lieut. in the regular cavalry for his magnificent conduct on this occasion.[35]

Our bivouac this night was a very exciting one, and I certainly slept little. With others I visited the hospital tent and talked to such of the wounded as were able to converse, and later sat by the camp fire discussing the events of the day and the prospects for the morrow. Daylight soon came and with it the order to move.

[33] Michael J. Kelly, a native of Ireland, was appointed second lieutenant in the First Cavalry (Fourth) and 8 May 1861, first lieutenant 17 July 1862. He died in 1867.

[34] Only recently a captain (16 March 1861), David S. Stanley (1828–1902) was graduated from USMA, Class of 1852, and served in the West until the outbreak of war. He was appointed brigadier general of volunteers 28 September 1861. Stanley was awarded the Medal of Honor for distinguished bravery at the Battle of Franklin (Tennessee), 30 November 1864.

[35] William H. Powell, *List of Officers of the Army of the United States . . . 1779 to 1900*, 565, tells this young man's story very well: "ROYS, ELBRIDGE G. Priv., Corpl. and Sergt. Troop B, 1st Cav. (4th), 2 Dec., 1856, to 17 Sept., 1862. 2nd Lieut. 4th Cav., 17 July 1862. 1st Lieut., 1 Dec., 1863. Killed 2 April 1865, in action near Selma, Ala."

Reported Union losses at Dug Springs were four killed and five or six wounded. Henceforth, the following abbreviations will be used for casualties: killed in action, KIA; wounded in action, WIA; missing in action, MIA; prisoners of war, POW.

The cavalry went at once to the front and soon found the enemy with whom we had a skirmish at a place called McCulloch's Station. This affair gave the opportunity for our main body and trains to move back toward Springfield,[36] and we followed shortly afterward. For the next few days our little army lay in the vicinity of that pretty village, eagerly hoping for the arrival of the re-enforcements from St. Louis which had been promised to Gen. Lyon by Gen. Frémont.[37] But they never came, and eventually Lyon decided to attack the combined forces of Price and McCulloch at Wilson's Creek, ten miles south, in the desperate hope of being able to surprise them and deal them a heavy blow under cover of which we could withdraw towards St. Louis sufficiently far to await re-enforcements and supplies without danger. On the evening of the 9th of August, accordingly, he moved his command out in two columns, one body under Gen. Sigel aiming to move around the enemy's right flank, the other under Lyon in person to attack the enemy in front as soon as the sound of Sigel's guns were heard in their rear.[38] The manoeuvre was well planned and well carried out, with the exception that our force was too small as compared with the enemy's to risk division. Sigel made his attack successfully, completely outflanking the enemy's right, and getting possession of their camp; then his men turned their attention to plundering

[36] Springfield is in Greene County, as is Wilson's Creek, the site of the battle.

[37] John C. Frémont (1813–1890), presidential candidate in 1856 and one of the more controversial men in the war, had been appointed a major general in the Regular Army to rank from 14 May 1861, the same date as Major General George B. McClellan, an act which made both men senior major generals by 1863. On 25 July 1861, Frémont had assumed command of the Department of the West, which embraced Illinois "and the States and Territories west of the Mississippi River and on this side of the Rocky Mountains, including New Mexico." *The War of the Rebellion: A Compilation of the Official Records of the Union and Confederate Armies,* Series I, Vol. III, p. 390 (henceforth designated *OR*). By 9 November 1861, a week after Frémont had been relieved, the state of Missouri, at least, was merged into the newly established Department of the Missouri. Frémont reappears later in Sanford's narrative.

[38] There is a good map of the battle in *Atlas to Accompany the Official Records of the Union and Confederate Armies,* III, Pl. CXXXV. General Lyon had perhaps a few more than 5,000 effective troops, the Confederates almost 13,000; thus Lyon was outnumbered two and one-half to one. For a good article, see Jared C. Lobdell, "Nathaniel Lyon and the Battle of Wilson's Creek," *Bulletin of the Missouri Historical Society,* XVII (October, 1960), 3–15.

130

the tents and trains and ceased to be in any respect available for purposes of attack or defense. The enemy who had many good officers among them were not slow to remark and take advantage of this condition of affairs, and about the time that Gen. Lyon's forces under himself and Sturgis were moving to the attack, they rallied their troops and swept down on Sigel, capturing his battery and completely destroying his column. The only part of it that appeared again as an organized body was "C" troop of the 2nd Dragoons under Lieut. C. E. Farrand, which re-took one of Sigel's guns and brought it back to Springfield, covering at the same time the retreat of his routed column.[39] I myself saw Farrand, with his troop and the recaptured gun, riding down the road, and a non-commissioned officer of the troop carrying a captured Confederate flag. Gen. Sigel also I saw with a few members of his staff and orderlies, but his men were straggling over the country in every direction, and no other organized body from his column marched into Springfield, as far as I saw or heard.[40]

After Sigel's command had been repulsed, the enemy turned his united strength upon the column of Lyon and Sturgis which up to that time had been perfectly successful, and begun to offer a very stout resistance. Many of our leading officers were shot down and the men began to run short of ammunition. Lyon who had already been slightly wounded and had his horse shot under him, went to the front and determined to make a last attempt to break the lines of the enemy. He called on the men of the 1st Missouri to follow him, and as they sprang forward at the word he fell dead. The enemy at about the same time began to fall back, and the contest gradually ceased on either side. Gen. Lyon's body was placed in an ambulance and carried to the field hospital where it

[39] Charles E. Farrand, USMA, Class of 1857, apparently had a temporary command in the battle; he wrote and signed a report as second lieutenant, First Infantry, commanding Company C, Second Regiment of Dragoons. And a very junior second lieutenant he was. He was later captured by the Confederates, but escaped at Corinth. His subsequent career was utterly undistinguished, and he was mustered out in 1871. Sanford's story about the recaptured artillery piece can be verified in *OR*, III, 90–92.

[40] Severe as Sanford's comments about Sigel are, they are mild compared to those of his other fellow officers on the field that day. See *OR*, III, 93–98.

was taken out, but afterwards replaced and taken to Springfield. Maj. Sturgis after consulting the senior officers present concluded to retire and brought the remnant of the command back to the village in a perfectly orderly manner.[41] The battle, as far as the fighting went, was undoubtedly a drawn one; but as we were the attacking force and withdrew without accomplishing our object, the moral effect of a victory of course remained with the enemy. Neither side held the field at the close of the affair. My own troop was sent to regain the body of Gen. Lyon, which was erroneously reported to have been abandoned at the field hospital, and no enemy was visible anywhere when we rode on to the field. Of actual fighting in this battle I saw nothing, as my command was on picket duty except during our expedition just mentioned.[42] After ascertaining the facts in reference to our unfortunate commander, Capt. Elliott returned to Springfield with the troop, and we were undoubtedly the last body of Union troops who were in the vicinity of the battle ground. I am certain that there were no Rebels there when we left. Our camp that night near the Court House at Springfield was not a very cheerful one. Gen. Lyon's body was brought in and buried temporarily in the orchard of Mr. Phelps' fine place near the village. It now lies within a few miles of where I am writing in Connecticut.[43]

Maj. Sturgis and the senior officers of the army discussed the problem of our future course that evening, and decided that we

[41] After Lyon's death, Sturgis, who had commanded the First Brigade, assumed over-all command.

[42] For the record, Company D, First Regiment of Cavalry, sustained one wounded and three missing in action at the battle; see *OR*, III, 72. Sanford's unit was one of several unattached organizations in the battle; others included the First Iowa Infantry, Wright's and Switzler's Missouri Home Guard Cavalry, and the Missouri Pioneers. Aggregate casualties for Lyon's command, Army of the West, were: KIA, 223; WIA, 721; MIA, 291; total 1,235. Allan Nevins, *Frémont: Pathfinder of the West*, 488, says: "Within its limits, it was one of the fiercest encounters of the Civil War."

[43] John S. Phelps, governor of Missouri, 1876–80. On 24 December 1861, the thanks of the U.S. Congress were extended to Lyon and his officers and men; the joint resolution spoke of "the eminent and patriotic service" of Lyon and also referred to the battle's being at Springfield. In fact, the battle is known under three names: Oak Hills (the Confederate name), Springfield, or Wilson's Creek. At his death, Lyon was listed in the *Official Register* as a captain, Second Regiment of Infantry, sixth in a list of ten.

should fall back, and soon after midnight the retreat began. My troop was detailed in the rear guard and did not leave until after daylight, and I well remember the appearance of the town, and the few scattering citizens who saw our exit. The Confederates were expected to arrive every moment, though in reality I do not think they made their appearance for some time after we left. We rode out quietly with our skirmishers deployed, but with no sign of the enemy, and took the road toward St. Louis. It was a pretty country through which we marched, rolling hills and beautiful woods, and our camp on the Gasconade I especially remember as strikingly beautiful. We brought up finally at Rolla, Mo., to which point a railroad line extended and where we obtained supplies in plenty.[44]

Soon after our arrival a flag of truce appeared brought by Major Emmet McDonald, a young officer of the Confederate service, well known to many of our people.[45] He was a St. Louis man, well known to all Missourians either personally or by reputation. Many of the German troops of the 1st Missouri were very much incensed against him, and threats were made that he would not be allowed to return to his command. However I was detailed to escort him back as far as should seem to be necessary and rode out one morning with a detachment for that purpose. He had a carriage and pair of horses with a coachman and servant, and at his suggestion I lent my horse to his Negro boy and took a seat beside him in the carriage, after passing our pickets. We travelled some fifty miles back to the road that our army had retreated upon, and I certainly enjoyed the trip at the time, but it cost me my fine horse in the end, as the Major's boy rode him hard and watered him carelessly, which resulted in his being badly foundered and of course ruined. I got

[44] Rolla was the county seat of Phelps County and terminal point of the South Pacific Railroad to Pacific City, thence to St. Louis. Sanford's marches formed a large V: from Kansas City to Springfield to St. Louis.

[45] Spelled as Emmett MacDonald in *OR*, III, where he is cited for service in the engagement at Carthage, Missouri, 5 July 1861, and in the siege of Lexington, Missouri, 13–20 September 1861, as a captain of the Missouri State Guard. In *List of Staff Officers of the Confederate States Army, 1861–1865*, 109, his name is spelled McDonald and he is listed as volunteer aide-de-camp to Colonel Richard H. Weightman, First Brigade, Missouri State Guard; same to Brigadier General Nicholas B. Pearce, August, 1861. Later, he served as colonel, commanding McDonald's Cavalry Regiment, Missouri.

McDonald safely through, however, to his own lines, and then returned to our army with my escort.

Soon after this episode the troops with which I was serving were ordered to St. Louis and on arriving there took station at Benton Barracks—at the old Fair Grounds. This post was at that time a depot for the reception and instruction of recruits, and new regiments were coming in in large numbers. After a short term of service there, I was ordered to report at Gen. Frémont's Headquarters in the city for duty as Mustering and Disbursing officer of the Department.[46]

Gen. Frémont's office was in the Brant mansion on Chouteau Avenue, and everything in its surroundings was very elegant.[47] After reporting for duty and being assigned to an office, I settled down to work for some time having my quarters at the Planters' House. My duties during the day kept me very busy, but terminated at night fall, and after that I had ample opportunity for seeing something of the city. Almost at once I met a classmate of Yale, named Wm. G. McRee, a son of an old army officer.[48] He was a Southerner and of course a Confederate sympathizer, but at that time the lines were not so closely drawn as they were afterwards, and it made little difference. Another acquaintance I made while living at the Planters' House, and of a very different kind, was that of Philip H. Sheridan.[49] He had recently been promoted from a Lieutenancy in the 4th Infantry to a Captaincy in the 13th Infantry then being recruited in St. Louis, and of which Wm. T.

46 That is, the Department of the West.
47 The residence of Colonel J. B. Brant.
48 *A History of the Class of 1863 of Yale College* lists William G. McRee as a nongraduate, whereabouts unknown. His father appears to have been Major Samuel McRee, USA (d. 15 July 1849). He was born in St. Louis on 22 July 1841 and was formerly in the Class of 1862. He left Yale at the end of the first semester, freshman year, and went into real estate business in St. Louis.
49 Certainly one of the great captains in the Civil War, Philip H. Sheridan (1831–1888) at the time was languishing in Missouri, his career scarcely promising. Graduated from USMA, Class of 1853, he was appointed brevet second lieutenant, First Regiment of Infantry, in the West; he was promoted second lieutenant, Fourth Regiment of Infantry, 22 November 1854; first lieutenant 1 March 1861; and captain, Thirteenth Regiment of Infantry, 14 May 1861. Finally, on 25 May 1862, he was named colonel, Second Michigan Cavalry. Sheridan figures prominently in Sanford's subsequent narrative. See pp. 221 ff.

Sherman was the Colonel.[50] Neither Sherman nor Sheridan, how-ever, was on duty with the regiment, the former being a Brigadier-General of Volunteers, and the latter on duty inspecting accounts in the Department. In this connection Capt. Sheridan did me a great favor, which probably saved me from endless trouble. My duties as Mustering and Disbursing officer included the payment of all accounts for collecting, drilling and organizing the volunteer regiments, and some of them were very large.[51] The instructions for auditing these were exceedingly indefinite, and I was often at a loss to what ones should be paid and what rejected. One for an exceedingly large sum was offered by a Major Corwin, a relative of the famous Senator "Tom" Corwin.[52] I was in great doubt about this account, but finally drew the check for a certain portion of

[50] Nor was the career of William T. Sherman (1820–1891) any too promising in the early fall of 1861. After graduation from USMA, Class of 1840, which included George H. Thomas, Sherman served in the Mexican War (he was brevetted) and resigned from the Army on 6 September 1853. He was a captain. Prior to the war, Sherman was, in a word, unsuccessful in his endeavors, which included a stint as the superintendent of what is now Louisiana State University, 1859–61. On 14 May 1861, he was appointed colonel of the Thirteenth Regiment of Infantry, organized by direction of the President 4 May 1861 but not confirmed by Congress until 29 July 1861. Sherman served at First Bull Run, where he commanded a brigade in General Daniel Tyler's division, which lost heavily in the battle. On 7 August 1861, he was appointed brigadier general of volunteers, the seventh ranking officer in this grade. Sent to Kentucky, Sherman was ultimately relieved by General Don Carlos Buell and went to St. Louis.

[51] Sanford is quoting from *Revised United States Army Regulations of 1861* on the duties of mustering and disbursing officers. In more detail, *Regulations* stated: "They will disburse the fund 'for collecting, drilling, and organizing volunteers.' They will make requisitions for funds monthly upon the Adjutant General . . . This fund is intended for the payment of all expenses that may be incurred therefor, as well as for the reimbursement to individuals of such amounts as have been already justly and actually expended by them in raising troops that have been, or may be, received into the service of the United States."

[52] Probably Major C. J. Corwin (1824–1904), who had worked on newspapers in New York City and Sandusky, Ohio, before he came to Missouri in 1854 and took over the *Jefferson City Examiner*. From 1856 to 1860, he was state printer but had many friends on the other side of the political fence. "During the Civil War he was faithful to his Southern friends, but maintained his status as a State Rights Union man." From an undated newspaper clipping, Archives, Missouri Historical Society, courtesy of Mrs. Lovelle H. Felt.

Thomas Corwin (1794–1865) was a most influential man: representative (1831–1840, 1859–1861) and senator (1845–1850) from Ohio, governor of Ohio (1840–1842), Secretary of the Treasury under Fillmore, (1850–1853), and minister to Mexico (22 March 1861–1 September 1864).

it, amounting to over five thousand ($5,000) dollars I think. On that same evening Sheridan came up to my room in the hotel, and after some conversation broached the subject of my duties and suggesting the probable difficulty so young an officer would have in untangling their intricacies, offered his assistance in any doubtful cases. I was very thankful and at once stated the case in question that day. After careful examination, he advised me to withdraw the check or stop its payment, which I was able to do, as it had been issued after banking hours so that it had not been cashed. I have now, and had then, no idea that there was any intent of fraud in the matter, but the account was undoubtedly irregular, and had it been paid would have been disallowed by the Auditors at Washington, and might have cost me infinite trouble. Sheridan then suggested that any doubtful accounts should be held over and submitted to him and that he would be glad to advise me each day as to what should be paid and what rejected. It is only since I have grown older that I have fully realized how fortunate I was in meeting this great soldier and noble man at that time, and receiving the benefit of his counsel and assistance. After this I often asked his advice and never failed to receive kindly help.

About the end of the year (1861) I was instructed to report to Col. B. L. E. Bonneville of the Army, at Benton Barracks as Adjutant, in addition to my other duties. Col. Bonneville was a very old officer, having entered the service after graduating at the Military Academy in 1815. He was a Frenchman by birth and had passed a great part of his life in the Rocky Mountains. For several years he was given up for dead, and his name dropped from the Army Register. After his return to civilization he had no difficulty in procuring his reinstatement and Washington Irving wrote an account of his adventures during his long absence in the far West.[53]

[53] Data on Benjamin L. E. Bonneville (1796–1878) are confusing. *The Official Army Register* for 1863 lists him as having been retired for incapacity on 9 September 1861, yet he was on active duty throughout most of the war as commanding officer at Benton Barracks in St. Louis. He had served in the Mexican War (after his explorations), had been brevetted, and had been wounded at Churubusco. In 1861, before the outbreak of war, he was colonel, Third Regiment of Infantry, and had been since 3 February 1855; he commanded the garrison at Fort Clark, Texas, Department of Texas. He was fifth in relative rank among the ten infantry colonels

Col. Bonneville was a most genial and courteous gentleman and was always delighted to talk of his thrilling adventures among the Northern Indians. I greatly enjoyed my short service with him. While on duty with Col. Bonneville I was one day invited to dine with him at Gen. W. T. Sherman's, who was also stationed at Benton Barracks in general charge of affairs there.[54] It was not a large party, and I only remember besides Gen. Sherman, himself, a Gen. Strong, Col. Bonneville and Maj. Curtiss, Asst. Adj. Gen. of Volunteers.[55] Gen. Sherman was at this time under a certain cloud, owing to the utterly unjust and untrue stories which had been circulated in regard to his mental condition. The fact that he had by his great ability and experience grasped the situation to so much greater an extent than many of the statesmen and general officers of the period, had led to his being pronounced crazy by men who never had a tithe of his capacity or a conception of his immense brain power. At this time he was in a sense *shelved*, and had it not been for the great influence of his distinguished brother, the late Secretary of the Treasury and Senator from Ohio, it is more than likely that he would have been driven from the service in disgust.[56]

in the Army. His status when Sanford reported is not clear: he was not yet commanding Benton Barracks; however, units of the Third Infantry he had commanded in Texas were in the East. Bonneville was dropped from the Army list on 31 May 1834 but reinstated 19 April 1836. In 1850, Washington Irving published an account of his explorations entitled *The Adventures of Captain Bonneville, U.S.A., in the Rocky Mountains and the Far West.*

[54] On 23 December 1861, Sherman was assigned to command the "camp of instruction and post of Benton Barracks." William T. Sherman, *Memoirs,* I, 246.

[55] William K. Strong (1805–1867), recently commissioned a brigadier general of volunteers and to succeed Sherman in command of Benton Barracks, St. Louis.

I cannot positively identify "Maj. Curtiss," but he may have been Henry Z. Curtis, assistant adjutant general with rank of captain, to date from 26 November 1861; with rank of major, 28 April 1862. Killed in action at Baxter Springs, 5 October 1863, he was the son of Brigadier General Samuel R. Curtis (1805–1866), USMA, Class of 1831.

[56] Sanford's allusion is to Senator John Sherman (1823–1900). His other reference to Sherman's mental condition is best summed up by Ezra J. Warner, *Generals in Blue,* pp. 442–43: "At this stage of the war [Sherman was then in Kentucky to assist in holding the state] Sherman's volatile temperament was strained by the insufficiencies of the volunteers, the ingrained knowledge that the war was not going to be a picnic, and the constant probing of news correspondents into affairs which he deemed to be the exclusive province of the military. Outraged reporters portrayed him as a visionary, unstable and even mentally deranged."

During the dinner the incident occurred which has always made it a memorable affair to me—as indeed it was the turning point in his career. A telegraphic despatch was brought in, which he opened and read, and laying it down on the table with emphasis said, "Well gentlemen, I am ordered to the front."[57] To the best of my recollection he started for Paducah, Kentucky, the next day, and assumed command of the division with which he performed such valiant service at Shiloh. Nothing more was ever heard of his mental incapacity, though one more unsuccessful attempt was made to ruin him by the equally undeserved stigma of disloyalty, just at the close of the war.

It is remarkable that the man combining the greatest intellect with the most thorough-going patriotism of any of our leaders, civil or military, should have been at different times charged with mental and political unsoundness during the Rebellion.

During my tour of duty in St. Louis, I met many officers who afterwards rose to high positions during the Civil War. Gen. J. C. Frémont was in command when I was first assigned to duty, and I remember well the Headquarters at the Brant mansion on Chouteau Avenue, guarded by the famous body guard under command of Major Zagonyi.[58] Gen. Frémont was at that time an exceedingly handsome man, in the prime of life, courteous in manner, but with an air of hauteur scarcely suited to the conditions obtaining in our country. He was surrounded by a personal staff consisting principally of foreign officers, generally of Polish or Hungarian blood. As few of them spoke the English language fluently, access to the General was exceedingly difficult and many officers, especially plain business men who had entered the volunteer service, were repelled by what they naturally believed to be the inten-

---

[57] Sherman's orders, from Major General H. W. Halleck, were dated 13 February 1862, so this dinner must have been that night. Sherman, *Memoirs,* I, 249.

[58] Major Charles Zagonyi, commanding the well-known Frémont's Body Guard (Zagonyi Guard), composed of Missouri cavalry. The battalion was organized in August, 1861, at Cincinnati and St. Louis to serve three years. It was mustered out of service on 30 November 1861. Official records show the letters "a. w. m." after Zagonyi's name: "appointed and waiting muster into United States Service."

tionally haughty manners of his following. As adjutants general he had, however, two excellent officers—Capts. Kelton and Mc- Keever,—the former of whom has since risen to the position of Brig. General and Adjt. Genl. of the U.S. Army and the latter is the senior Colonel in the Adjt. General's Department.[59] To both I was then and have been indebted for many kind offices for which I am and have been sincerely grateful. Gen. Frémont, in addition to the foreign element, which surrounded him, was attended by numbers of his old California associates, some of whom bore any- thing but a savory reputation, and in a large measure contributed to his early downfall. Among these was "Baron" Steinberger of San Francisco, a contractor for army supplies, who had been quite famous in the early mining days in San Francisco.[60]

The enormous expenditures under Frémont's administration and the "shady" character of many of the men who fastened on to him soon led to his relief from command. I do not believe for one moment that he was personally cognizant of any wrong doing in the affairs of his Department, but he had fallen into the clutches of a set of harpies who kept him in ignorance of the rascality they were carrying on for their own benefit. He took command of his forces in the field late in the Fall and made a futile attempt to bring Price to battle in the neighborhood of Springfield, Mo. Gen. Halleck succeeded him in command of the Division at St. Louis, and after it was demonstrated that Price would not accept battle in south- west Missouri, Gen. David Hunter relieved him from command

[59] John C. Kelton, USMA, Class of 1851, late of the Sixth Infantry, was assistant adjutant general, headquarters, Department of the West, and served as adjutant general on General Henry W. Halleck's staff in Washington, 1862–65. Chauncey McKeever, USMA, Class of 1849, late of the Third Artillery, also was assistant adjutant general at Frémont's headquarters.

[60] A well-known beef and army supplies speculator in San Francisco in the early 1850's who did fabulously well and once boasted of five million dollars' worth of debts. He had originally moved from St. Louis to San Francisco. He was as dis- honest as he was handsome and striking in appearance. By 1861, he was bankrupt and followed Frémont to St. Louis, where he died in a hospital. Sanford's account of his last days differ from others more widely accepted in which the Baron figures as a kind of shuffling derelict. See Edward Bosque, *Memoirs, passim,* and Sherman, *Memoirs,* I, *passim.*

of the Army in the field.[61] Gen. Halleck with whom I came into frequent contact in St. Louis was an officer of great intellectual force, and of whom great things were expected, but owing to circumstances, little was realized. His one field campaign—from Shiloh to Corinth—led to no battle, and though greatly outnumbering his enemy, he allowed him to escape practically uninjured. His later career was entirely in Washington, where while nominally in command of all the armies of the United States, he was actually a mere clerk for the all-powerful War Secretary, Edwin M. Stanton. After the war was over he commanded the Military Division of the Pacific, where I again came under his command.[62]

Early in the winter of 1861-2 Gen. Halleck directed me to report to Gen. David Hunter at Fort Leavenworth, Kansas, to muster in some regiments of volunteers in his Department.[63] I accordingly left St. Louis with my clerk, a young Englishman named Gibson and proceeded to Leavenworth via St. Joseph, Mo. On reporting to Gen. Hunter at the Post I was directed by him to proceed to West Point, Mo. and muster in two regiments of volunteers which had been organized at that point. There was no

[61] The situation in Missouri *was* confusing in 1861, and Sanford's comments do not help matters any. That Frémont had been inept in his "pursuit" of General Price (Frémont had more than 38,000 men under his command) was certainly the opinion of Brigadier General Lorenzo Thomas, Adjutant General of the Army, in a stinging report to Secretary of War Simon Cameron dated 21 October 1861. See *OR*, III, 540–49. Three days later, 24 October, Major General David Hunter, who commanded the First Division in Frémont's army, was ordered to supersede Frémont. On 2 November, Hunter formally relieved Frémont near Springfield; the latter bade farewell to his forces and left for St. Louis and eventually the East. On 19 November, Major General Henry W. Halleck, USA, assumed command of the Department of the Missouri. On 29 March 1862, Frémont assumed command of the Mountain Department but was quickly relieved (27 June 1862). He resigned from the Army on 4 June 1864.

[62] Many historians and military men have commented, as does Sanford, on Henry W. Halleck (1815–1872) as a strange combination of success (outside the Army) and failure (inside the Army). Graduated from USMA in 1839, he served until 1854, when he resigned (he was a captain) and embarked on an amazingly successful career in California. On 19 August 1861, he was appointed a major general in the Regular Army, ranked only by Scott, McClellan, and Frémont. From 23 July 1862 until 9 March 1864, he was commander-in-chief of the Army, succeeded by Grant.

[63] By now there had been additional administrative changes in Missouri, etc. On 9 November 1861, the Department of Kansas was constituted, and on 20 November 1861, General Hunter, with headquarters at Fort Leavenworth, assumed command of the department.

means of communication available except by wagon road, and as I could get no transportation from the government, I determined to hire horses for myself and clerk and make the journey on horseback.[64] Gen. Hunter informed me that a volunteer officer who was well acquainted with the country would escort me over a portion of the road which was supposed to be unsafe, owing to the frequent raids of Quantrill's Guerillas, who at that time were particularly bold.[65] Gibson and I proceeded to Kansas City where we were to meet the escort, which in due time appeared, and I found to consist of a detachment of five men under command of Capt. John Brown, a son of the famous Free State leader, who had been hung at Charlestown, Va. two years before, for his attempt to raise a Negro insurrection at Harpers Ferry. It occurred to me that my chances for personal safety were not especially increased by the presence of Capt. Brown, in case we should happen to fall into the clutches of Quantrill's people. However, orders are orders, and we left Kansas City one bright cold morning in January in good health and spirits.

I found Capt. Brown an exceedingly interesting companion, rather reserved at first, like most men who have passed through such terrible experiences as he had encountered, during the border troubles in Kansas and Missouri.[66] We met with no special adventures until we came to the canon of the Little Blue river where one of our scouts who were riding in advance returned and reported that he had seen mounted men on the flanks of the canon.[67]

[64] The word "hire" is central to a rankling and unpleasant incident in Sanford's later career centering about a horse used during this journey. It is not clear here whether Sanford means that he determined to hire horses from Leavenworth to Kansas City only or at various points along his ride. See n. 69 *infra*.

[65] Kansas and Missouri infantry units were actively seeking out William Clarke Quantrill (1837–1865) in the winter of 1861–62, but they were unsuccessful. On 21 August 1863, Quantrill swooped down on Lawrence, Kansas, and massacred more than 150 people. He died in a military hospital in Louisville, Kentucky, in May, 1865.

[66] John Brown, Jr. (b. 1821), who had experienced so much in Kansas with his father, seems here to be rational enough, although he suffered periodically from mental derangement. Brown commanded a company, in the Seventh Kansas Cavalry, from Ashtabula County, Ohio. "The members of this company were all fanatical abolitionists," writes Albert Castel in "Kansas Jayhawking Raids into Western Missouri in 1861," *Missouri Historical Review,* LIV (October, 1959), 6.

[67] Sanford and Brown have been riding eastward; they had already crossed the Big Blue River. Both the Big Blue and Little Blue flow in a northerly direction into the Missouri.

Capt. Brown had evidently expected this, for he had been saving his horses up to this time, but then he determined to make a run for it and dash through the canon. We accordingly dismounted for a moment and tightened our saddles, and then started on a sharp gallop down the road. His theory as he afterwards explained, was that the men who had been seen were scouts who would notify their leader of our presence, but that by a sudden dash we could get through and on to the plains before the main body were prepared to resist us. After reaching the plains he said that there was little or no danger of an attack on a party of our size. As we galloped up the canon we increased our speed and succeeded in reaching and crossing the stream before the Guerrillas appeared, but as we went up the bank on the opposite side they appeared in the hills and fired a few shots which we returned, with no apparent effect. Getting out in the open country the pursuit soon ceased, as he had predicted, and we rode along quietly during the rest of the day.

On the second day's journey we came into the lines of our own people and Captain Brown and his party bade us good-bye, as he was under orders to report to his own regiment of Kansas Cavalry, which was stationed in that vicinity. Gibson and I made our way alone in the direction of West Point, riding through a very pretty prairie country, and quite enjoying the trip, despite the intensely cold weather. I think it was on the third day that we descried a body of mounted men a short distance in advance, who instantly rode up and surrounded us, at the same time ordering us to surrender. The attack was so sudden that there would have been no opportunity for resistance, even had I contemplated it, but as I was assured that our own troops held all the country in that vicinity, I had never given the matter a thought. The party consisted of about twenty men under command of a lieutenant, and at first I was in considerable doubt as to which side they belonged. They were rough looking young fellows, well mounted and armed, but with no indications of the service to which they belonged. As both Gibson and I were in citizen dress, we were as much of a mystery to them as they to us. The officer in command was inclined to believe we were spies and indicated his opinion pretty plainly, coupling with it the statement that if we did not confess he would hang us to the first tree. I showed him my orders and explained the circumstances, but he said that he had been at Fort Leavenworth and "he knew none of them regular officers would have been sent down into that country without a good four horse ambulance and a strong escort." He concluded, however, to dispense with the hanging for the present, and take me to the Headquarters of his regiment where he assured me that "the Colonel and the boys" would make short work of me if I was guilty. When I learned that the "Colonel" was the celebrated Jennison so famous for his desperate deeds during the Kansas troubles years before, I was inclined to agree with him and to think that perhaps he would hang us up first and investigate the matter afterward.[68]

We were soon ordered to fall in to the column and with a trooper on either side of us we marched along all day reaching the camp about dusk. This I learned was in the vicinity of a small village called Morristown. Col. Jennison was absent with a portion of the command on a scout, but the officer in charge of the camp seemed to be a good-natured easy-going sort of fellow, and rather inclined to believe my account of myself. He took me over to the Colonel's quarters, where we found Mrs. Jennison, the Colonel's wife, and

---

[68] Charles R. Jennison, who had led a Free Soil band before the war and was called one of the boldest Jayhawkers (another was James Montgomery; the most notorious was Marshall Cleveland), was in command of the Seventh Kansas Cavalry at this time. In the summer of 1861, he led raids into western Missouri. He was a bona fide colonel of U.S. volunteers. He was regarded with suspicion by many Union officers—General Halleck cited him specifically as having "turned against us many thousands who were formerly Union men." *OR,* VIII, 819. On the other hand, General Sterling Price, commanding the Missouri State Guard, complained to General Ben McCulloch on 6 December 1861 that men like Jennison, supported by Union forces, "are not only desolating the country, but are committing the most barbarous outrages," etc. *Ibid.,* 702.

Shortly before Sanford was apprehended, Jennison had received orders to proceed to West Point, Missouri, and "if possible, protect the frontier of Kansas from incursions of the rebel bands now in that neighborhood." *Ibid.,* 423. It is ironic to see that Sanford was "captured" by Brown's own regimental commander.

"The jayhawkers' professed objective was the abolition of slavery and the repression of proslavery settlers. Actually . . . their main interest and motivation was plunder and excitement." Albert Castel, "The Jayhawkers and Copperheads of Kansas," *Civil War History,* V (September, 1959), 288.

after a talk with her it was decided that Gibson and I should be retained in an honorable sort of captivity until Col. Jennison's return. Mrs. Jennison, who was a plain, hard-featured country woman, was occupying a little board house, which had two or three rooms in it, and one of these was placed at our disposal, and she kindly invited us to take our meals with her. A sentry was placed at our door and we were advised to make no attempt to leave the house as the "boys" were a little doubtful about our character, and *might* "cut up rough" if they took the notion. We did not require more than a hint in this direction, and accordingly kept pretty quiet until Col. Jennison's return, which occurred within a few days. I found him a perfect type of the border Free State man of those days. He was a lightly-built active looking man of perhaps thirty-five years, of rather less than medium height and without an ounce of superfluous flesh about him. He looked as hard as iron. He had brown hair, a thin pointed beard, rather a high narrow forehead and cold, glittering, grey eyes. His whole face and manner expressed indomitable resolution, but was so filled with hatred of the "border ruffians" as the Missourians were called, as to be exceedingly disagreeable. He was, however, an intelligent man in his way, and a very short examination satisfied him that my story was perfectly straightforward. More in order to satisfy his men than from any doubt in his own mind, evidently, he decided to keep us in camp until he could ascertain from Dept. Head Quarters whether we were what we represented ourselves to be. The sentry over our door was withdrawn, but we were required to give our parole not to leave the immediate vicinity of his quarters, which indeed it would have been decidedly unsafe to do under the circumstances.

A few days later despatches from Fort Leavenworth completely relieved us from all suspicion, and by the same mail I received orders to return via Kansas City to my station, the troops which I was to muster having been ordered to another point. We left camp soon after in a driving snow storm and to add to our discomfort I soon found that my horse was going lame. During my captivity Jennison's bold troopers had saved their own steeds to some extent by making use of him, and the poor brute had been completely used up. Eventually I had to leave him at a farm house with instructions to send him to Kansas City as soon as he could travel, and as no other animal could be procured, Gibson and I had to depend on his horse to get us through.[69] To accomplish this one of us would ride on in advance four or five miles, dismount, and tie the horse, and go ahead on foot. The other when he came up, mounted and rode on until he overtook and passed the other, to dismount and tie up in his turn. In this way we worked our way along until we reached the banks of the Big Blue river, which we found swollen by the rain and snow and in anything but inviting condition to cross. We were not sure whether it was fordable under

[69] Did Sanford pay for this horse? No, he did not. Was it merely lent to him? (*Cf.* his statement about hiring horses, p. 141). This is brought up now because of a letter, dated 20 September 1884, sent to the War Department by one Miguel Salazar, attorney at law in Las Vegas, New Mexico, on behalf of his client, one John Friedsam. Salazar asserted that in 1862, in Kansas City, Sanford "obtained a valuable horse from Mr. John Friedsam under the promise and assurance" that as soon as Sanford reached Harrisonville, Missouri, he would either return the horse or its value "which was at the time $200." Salazar points out that the horse was never returned, that some years later, Sanford met Friedsam and promised to pay the amount with interest. "Of course the money was never sent," Salazar continues. Sanford refused to answer letters (seeking $300) on the matter. It is obvious, feels Salazar, that Sanford never intended to pay for the horse. "He is criminally liable for obtaining the horse under false pretenses. Besides he has proved himself to be the most ungrateful and consummate rascal living; because at the time he got the horse ... he was not only stranger in the city but to Mr. Friedsam as well; had no money and was in great need of a horse." Salazar seeks prompt action and consideration of the case; in other words, force Sanford to pay his debt.

Eventually the letter reached Sanford at Fort Custer, Montana, for explanation —this at the direction of Lieutenant General Sheridan, commanding the U.S. Army. Sanford replied on 20 October: "From Kansas City, Missouri no transportation was procurable to my next point .... A horse was offered to me at Kansas City which I was of course to return on the completion of my journey." But, as stated in the text above, the horse was used by Jennison's men. "On my return trip I found the animal so lame that I was obliged to leave him at a ranch or farm house some distance from Kansas City. The farmer promised to take good care of the animal and return him to his owner as soon as he recovered."

Sanford was then almost immediately ordered to his regiment in the East. He recalled some correspondence at the time, but heard nothing more and assumed that "the Quartermaster Dept. had settled it." He admitted receiving letters demanding $300 and having consulted senior officers on the matter. Sanford said he was willing to pay "the amount claimed if I am wrong," but he did not feel he should be "held responsible for the loss of an animal injured by no fault of my own, in the service of the U.S." Lieutenant General Sheridan thought otherwise and on 10 November 1884 directed Sanford to pay for the horse at once. On 24 November 1884, Sanford forwarded a check for $300 from Fort Custer.

145

the circumstances and we *were* sure that Gibson could not swim a stroke, so it was settled that I should get across on foot by wading or swimming, and he should follow me on horseback. We had little or nothing to eat for some time, and we were pretty well worn out with toil and exposure, but it was absolutely necessary for us to cross and find food and shelter, which we knew could be had on the other bank. The water was like ice and I had to swim, but we made the passage safely, and soon afterwards came across an old German, who like most of his compatriots was fortunately for us a Union man. I think his care and that of his wife in all probability saved my life, as I was in a severe chill when I reached his house, followed in the night by a high fever; and if I had been obliged to sleep out, as was by no means unlikely, I should have certainly been very ill. However, as it was, everything was done to make us comfortable, and the next day I was all right again; and as the old farmer agreed to hitch up his team and drive us to Kansas City our troubles were all over. We then returned to St. Louis and I resumed my duties as mustering officer at the Department Headquarters.

·CHAPTER II·

Eᴀʀʟʏ ɪɴ Fᴇʙʀᴜᴀʀʏ, 1862, I heard that my regiment had arrived, by sea from California, in the East, and that Headquarters were then at Washington with the Army of the Potomac.[1] I accordingly looked anxiously for orders to join, which were soon received and about the middle of the month I reported to the commanding officer at Camp Sprague, Washington, D.C., out on 7th St. N.W. I had by this time been promoted 1st Lieutenant of "K" troop commanded by Capt. Benj. F. Davis of Alabama.[2] Capt. Davis was a handsome man of about twenty-eight years. He was a graduate of the Military Academy of the class of 1854, and had served with the regiment in Arizona and New Mexico, gaining some reputation for his gallantry in action with the Apaches. Although born

[1] It had been quite a task to gather the First Regiment of Cavalry (less Companies D and G at Fort Craig, New Mexico) together, for they were pretty well spread out about the Department of the Pacific in the fall of 1861. In that year, the regiment's permanent stations were Fort Walla Walla, Washington Territory; Fort Dalles, Oregon; Fort Crook, California; and Fort Tejon, California. As early as 9 September 1861, General Scott had ordered all regular troops in the department, except four artillery companies, to come by steam to New York. But this would take a number of weeks. Companies A and F departed San Francisco on 30 November; Companies H and I, 11 December; Companies C and E, 21 December. The journey was made via the Isthmus of Panamá, which was traversed by railroad from Panamá to Aspinwall, thence to New York. Arrival dates are unavailable. *OR, I*, Pt. 1, *passim*.

[2] Benjamin Franklin "Grimes" Davis, USMA, Class of 1854, was a classmate of J. E. B. Stuart. He was wounded in the Apache engagements in 1857, promoted captain 30 July 1861. He had a brief stint as a lieutenant colonel in the First California Cavalry, 19 August–1 November 1861, when he resigned to return east with his regiment. When he was killed at Beverly Ford with the Eighth New York, he was thirty-one years old. *Cf.* a similar discussion of Davis, pp. 175–76.

Sanford's promotion to first lieutenant was dated 31 July 1861.

and brought up in the South, he was as loyal as he was brave, and nothing but his early death prevented him from reaching very high rank in the service. He obtained the colonelcy of the 8th N.Y. Cavalry and was shot dead at the head of his regiment in a cavalry charge at Beverly Ford, Va. on the 9th of June, 1863. To Captain Davis more than to any other one officer I was, and am, indebted for whatever I afterwards became in the service. He was a thorough officer, and as far as I can remember, never missed an opportunity to impart the instruction that I required. As long as he remained with the troop, he required me to study and recite to him daily, both in camp at Camp Sprague, and afterwards during the Peninsula campaign. On the march he taught me to notice the character of the country, the advantages of positions for attack and defense, sites for camp etc. At a halt he would practice with me in the sabre exercise, and give me instruction in posting pickets and sending out scouts. In a word he kept me "on the jump" as some of the young fellows said, and I had a good deal of chaffing to undergo on account of my constant instruction. If I did not fully appreciate his kindness at the time, I certainly have since, and thanked him for it; but even then I had a dim perception of the fact that instruction in the mysteries of my profession was likely to be more useful than in those of draw poker, which some of the other youngsters were obtaining.

Maj. Geo. A. H. Blake was at this period the senior Major and in command of the regiment. Fauntleroy, the Colonel, had sent in his resignation and joined the Confederacy and Ben Beall the Lieut. Colonel soon retired from disability resulting from long and arduous service, so that Blake became our Colonel.[3] He was one of the old time frontier officers, rough in his manner, but a gentle-

[3] Thomas T. Fauntleroy (d. 12 September 1883) was appointed colonel, First Regiment of Dragoons, 25 July 1850. He resigned from the Army 13 May 1861 and served as brigadier general, Virginia Volunteers, CSA, 1861–65.

On 15 November 1861, Brigadier General George Wright, commanding the Department of the Pacific, ordered Colonel Benjamin L. Beall (rank dated from 13 May 1861) to transfer command of the First Regiment of Cavalry to Lieutenant Colonel George A. H. Blake. Beall retired 15 February 1862; he died on 16 August 1863. Blake had been promoted the same day as Beall and was a veteran of fifteen years' service. He had been brevetted for gallantry in the Mexican War. About the time Sanford is referring to, 15 February 1862, Blake was promoted colonel.

148

man at heart. Besides Capt. Davis, the principal officers were Wm. T. Magruder, Reno, Carr, McKee, Baker and Kellogg.[4] Among the younger were Allen, Fisher, Pleasonton, Hunt, Ogden and Dunkelberger.[5] Our life was the usual routine of camp—drill and recitation in tactics, stable duty and parade. In the evening we were allowed to go in town, and usually went to the theatre. Occasionally we had a review and inspection by some high official. In the latter part of March, Gen. McClellan[6] moved the Army of

[4] Marcus A. Reno, USMA, Class of 1857; captain, 12 November 1861. Milton T. Carr, USMA, Class of 1854; captain, 31 May 1861; wholly retired, 29 December 1863. Samuel McKee, USMA, Class of 1858; captain, 14 November 1861; killed at Cold Harbor, 3 June 1864, age twenty-nine. Eugene M. Baker, USMA, Class of 1859; captain, 16 January 1862; two brevets for wartime service. Josiah H. Kellogg, USMA, Class of 1860; captain, 20 May 1862.

Reno, of course, is familiar for his much disputed role in the Battle of the Little Big Horn and for the fact that he was dismissed from the Army on 1 April 1880; he was to receive four brevets for gallant and meritorious service during the war.

Less well known but indeed more fascinating is William T. Magruder, USMA, Class of 1850, about whom Sanford inexplicably says nothing. A captain since 8 January 1861, Magruder finally resigned from the U.S. Army on I October 1862 and joined the Confederate service. As a captain, CSA, he was killed at Gettysburg on 3 July 1863 at the age of thirty-seven.

[5] Robert Allen, Jr.; first lieutenant, 29 December 1861; killed at Gaines' Mill, Virginia, 27 June 1862. Caesar R. Fisher; second lieutenant, 12 November 1861; died of wounds received at Ashby's Gap, Virginia, 21 June 1863. Augustus Pleasonton received his second lieutenancy the same day as Sanford, 26 April 1861; he was wholly retired 13 August 1862. Not too long before, James C. Hunt, had joined the First Cavalry as a second lieutenant, having transferred from the First New Jersey Cavalry. Frederick C. Ogden; second lieutenant, 21 November 1861; killed in action, 11 June 1864, at Trevilian Station, Virginia. Isaac Dunkelberger, too, had received his commission as a second lieutenant on the same day as Sanford. Ogden appears subsequently in the narrative. It is interesting to note the absence of USMA graduates among the lieutenants and the high casualty rate.

[6] George B. McClellan (1826–1885), still a center of controversy with regard to his military worth, had been graduated from USMA, Class of 1846; he was No. 2 in the standing. Twice brevetted for "gallant and meritorious conduct" in the Mexican War, he resigned in 1857 after about eleven years' service. But with the outbreak of war, he returned to service, first as a major general in the Ohio Volunteers. Then he was appointed a major general in the Regular Army, to date from 14 May 1861, outranked only by Lieutenant General Winfield Scott. On 20 August 1861, McClellan assumed command of the Army of the Potomac; on 1 November 1861, he superseded Scott in command of the Armies of the United States—achievements of a man not quite thirty-five years of age. He was relieved from command of the Army on 11 March 1862.

Getting under way was the Peninsular Campaign in Virginia, 17 March–2 September 1862. This is no place to go into detail about the strategy, etc.; however, in a report dated 19 March 1862, McClellan himself outlined the campaign: "The proposed plan of campaign is to assume Fort Monroe as the first base of operations,

the Potomac out towards Manassas, the Confederates falling back as we advanced. I was much interested in going over the country between the Potomac and the Rappahannock and especially in the battlefield of Bull Run. The squadron to which I belonged reported to Gen. McClellan as escort, and rode with him over the field.[7] Gen. McDowell accompanied the Commander, and pointed out the various positions occupied.[8] McClellan had a large and brilliant staff, among whom I noticed with much interest the Princes of the House of Orléans,—the Comte de Paris, his brother the young Duc de Chartres, and their uncle the Prince de Joinville.[9] De Chartres was a very handsome young man of about my own age, full of life and very zealous in the performance of his duties as aide de camp. I met him frequently during the campaign which followed, and

---

taking the line of Yorktown and West Point upon Richmond as the line of operations, Richmond being the objective point. It is assumed that the fall of Richmond involves that of Norfolk and the whole of Virginia; also that we shall fight a decisive battle between West Point and Richmond." He anticipated and planned a siege and reduction of Yorktown and Gloucester; in all probability, this would delay the campaign for some weeks, *OR*, V, 57, 58.

[7] Sanford's unit was a part of the Cavalry Reserve, Army of the Potomac, commanded by Brigadier General Philip St. George Cooke (see p. 151): Emory's Brigade (Fifth and Sixth Regiments of Cavalry; Sixth Pennsylvania Cavalry), Blake's Brigade (First Regiment of Cavalry and Eighth Pennsylvania Cavalry), and Barker's Squadron (Illinois Cavalry).

[8] Irvin McDowell (1818–1885), Class of 1838, served (and was brevetted) with the artillery in the Mexican War. At the outbreak of the Civil War, he was only a brevet major assistant adjutant general in Washington. However, on 14 May 1861, he was commissioned a brigadier general in the Regular Army and was in command at First Manassas. On 25 July 1861, he was relieved as commanding general of the Army of the Potomac, but then on 14 March 1862, he was appointed a major general of volunteers and given command of the First Corps, Army of the Potomac. The unit was later detached to defend Washington, D.C., and McDowell did not participate in the Peninsular Campaign.

[9] Captain Louis Philippe d'Orléans, Comte de Paris; his younger brother, Captain Robert d'Orléans, Duc de Chartres. Their uncle, Prince de Joinville, "while not formally a member of the staff, constantly was with McClellan during the Peninsular Campaign, and often rendered important services." William S. Myers, *Study in Personality: General George Brinton McClellan*, 217. Comte de Paris later published the highly regarded *History of the Civil War in America*. McClellan himself wrote: "They were borne on the army register as Louis Philippe d'Orléans and Robert d'Orléans, additional aides-de-camp in the regular army, with the rank of captain, and were assigned to the staff of the Major-General commanding the Army of the Potomac. The Prince de Joinville accepted no rank, and simply accompanied headquarters." See "The Princes of the House of Orléans," *The Century Magazine*, XXVII (February, 1884), 616.

accompanied him in several expeditions. We saw nothing of the enemy on this advance except a few small bodies of cavalry which withdrew without resistance. In the works about Manassas I saw several of the Quaker guns, as they were called, which had been placed in the intrenchments for the purpose of deceiving our scouts. They were simply logs of wood, mounted on cart wheels and painted to imitate cannon.[10] I don't see what particular use they were as far as deception was concerned, because the intrenchments themselves of course would be supposed to contain cannon, and if spies actually found their way in to them, they would certainly not be deceived by the wooden logs. Nevertheless the newspaper correspondents made a great time over them, and McClellan was held up to derision for having been terrified by a lot of imitation guns.

Some of the cavalry was sent in advance as far as the Rappahannock river, and after their report as to the retreat of the Rebels had been received, our forces moved slowly back to the Potomac. The weather was perfectly dreadful, and the mud seemingly bottomless. My brigade camped near Alexandria, where we lay for some days in a perfect swamp, the men shivering in their tents and the horses at the picket lines. Drill was out of the question, and it was almost out of the question to keep the animals supplied with forage and the men with rations, even though we were within sight of the Capitol. It was a bitter foretaste of the sufferings and privation that we were to go through for three long years, but which was to make of our raw volunteers a compact body of veteran soldiers, such as have been rarely equalled, and never excelled.

Gen. Philip St. George Cooke, lately Colonel of the 2nd Dragoons, was in command of our brigade, and was a cavalry officer of great merit. He was a Virginian and oddly enough a near relative of Gen. Jeb. Stuart who afterwards rose to great distinction as the commander of the Confederate Horse.[11]

[10] Also known as "Quakers"; they were wooden guns.
[11] Philip St. George Cooke (1809–1895), USMA, Class of 1827. A Colonel (14 June 1858) in the Second Regiment of Dragoons at the outbreak of war, he was promoted brigadier general in the Regular Army 12 November 1861; he also held a brigadier generalcy in the volunteers, same date of rank, for about two weeks. Gen-

I happened to be a witness of rather a good joke which happened to Gen. Cooke while we lay in this camp. The General had an orderly, an old trooper of the 2nd Dragoons, to whom he was much attached, and who had been with him in his campaigns on the Plains for many years. One morning the General wanted something to read and he told his orderly to ride over to Washington and buy the *Strange Story*, Bulwer's novel, which had just been published.[12] The orderly rode off and toward evening returned with a choice selection of yellow covered literature, among which I recollect *Claude Duval, Sixteen String Jack* etc. Of course Gen. Cooke was raging, and demanded an explanation. "Well sir," said the poor fellow, "the General told me to get a strange story and them was the strangest I could find." Allusions to strange stories were current in camp for some days.

As rapidly as possible the army was shipped to Hampton Roads. My own troop went on a schooner down the Potomac and round by Old Point, landing near Fortress Monroe about the 2nd of May.[13] The battle between the *Monitor* and the *Merrimac* had recently taken place, and the latter was then in the Elizabeth river undergoing repairs.[14] The *Monitor* with a large fleet of men of war lay in the Roads. Among them I remember the *Galena*, the *Nantucket* [*sic*], *Roanoke*, and an English man of war, the *Jason*.[15] There were also French and other foreign war vessels and the immense transport fleet, so that it was a grand sight. Sewell's Point, at the mouth of the Elizabeth River was protected by Confederate batteries mounting heavy guns, as was also Pig Point farther west. These batteries were in plain sight from Fort Monroe, and the

eral J. E. B. Stuart, CSA, was Cooke's son-in-law; Cooke's own son, John Rogers Cooke (1833–1891), served as a brigadier general in the Confederate Army; he resigned the U.S. Army 30 May 1861.

[12] *A Strange Story* (London, 1862) was published in two volumes.

[13] This is an obvious error; the date should read "April." On 2 April, McClellan and his staff arrived at Fort Monroe aboard the steamer *Commodore*.

[14] The fight between USS *Monitor* and CSS *Virginia* (*Merrimac*) on 9 March 1862, the first ironclad naval engagement in the world.

[15] USS *Galena*, third rate, 738 tons, screw steamer, with six guns and a crew of 150; USS *Naugatuck*, fourth rate, 192 tons, screw steamer (Sanford erroneously refers to USS *Nantucket*); USS *Roanoke*, first rate, 3,425 tons, screw frigate, with 44 guns and a crew of 347.

former was within long range of our fortification on the Rip Raps.[16] Occasional compliments in the shape of ten inch shells passed between the two and added liveliness to the scene. Twice I saw the *Merrimac* come down the Elizabeth river and out into the Roads, bidding defiance to our fleet. She was accompanied by two or three small gunboats and reminded me of a medieval knight in armor riding down the lists, followed by his squires, to challenge the opposing forces. As far as I could see, nobody seemed particularly anxious to pick up the gage so gallantly thrown down.[17] One occasion which I well remember was when our whole fleet of iron clads, wooden steamers and sailing ships, attacked the Pig Point batteries. It was a magnificent sight, to me, for I had never before seen men of war in action. I suppose now that it was simply a reconnaissance or demonstration.[18] At all events as soon as the *Merrimac* poked her nose out of the Elizabeth River, our whole fleet came slowly back, the little *Monitor* covering the rear, and occasionally sending one of her immense shells towards the *Merrimac*, like a little terrier retreating a big mastiff, but snarling and showing his teeth as he goes. I could not see why they did not fight, at the time, but of course with our great fleet of transports lying in the Roads and more coming all the time, it was not the policy of the authorities to take any risks.

On the other hand, judging from subsequent events, it would seem to have been the policy of the Confederates to have taken

[16] The preceding geographical names can be found in a contemporary map of Hampton Roads and adjacent shores. Old Point is Old Point Comfort, on which Fort Monroe was situated. Sewell's Point is south of and across the Roads from Fort Monroe. Pig Point is at the mouth of the Nansemond River. Rip Raps, out in the Roads, is the site of Fort Calhoun.

[17] Early in the morning of 11 April 1862, CSS *Virginia (Merrimac),* accompanied by CSS *Jamestown* and CSS *Raleigh,* rounded Sewell's Point and made her second appearance in the Roads. *Jamestown* and *Raleigh* working under *Virginia's* guns, captured three Union transports—brig *Marcus* (Stockton, New Jersey), brig *Saboah* (Providence), and schooner *Catherine T. Dix* (Accomac)—almost within "gunshot of the *Monitor.*" See *Official Records of the Union and Confederate Navies in the War of the Rebellion,* Series I, Vol. VII, p. 223 (henceforth designated *ORN*).

[18] Sanford's chronology is confusing. He is apparently referring to the bombardment of Sewell's Point on 8 May 1862 by USS *Monitor,* USS *Dacotah,* USS *Naugatuck,* USS *Seminole,* and USS *Susquehanna.* I can find no data on such an attack on Pig Point.

almost any chances and at least let their ship go down fighting, as the *Cumberland* had done, instead of blowing her up ingloriously a few weeks later.[19]

As soon as our troops were disembarked and the transportation put in order, the army commenced moving up the Peninsula and shortly came up against the Confederate lines at Yorktown. This was classic ground, and the old works used by the British, and French and Americans, in the Revolutionary War were still visible. Every one supposed that we would attack at once, and there is little doubt that if we had done so, we should have broken their lines, but Gen. McClellan decided against it, and we accordingly settled down to regular siege operations.[20] In this business the mounted force of course had little part, but we were kept fully occupied just the same in escorting supply trains up to the army. I suppose there are no worse roads on the planet than those dreadful quagmires through which we forced those wagons.

Our camp, when we were lucky enough to be in it, was at Cheeseman's Landing, on the York river, and I can testify to the good quality of the Cheeseman Creek oysters, which we picked up in great quantities during our stay. Picket, escort and scouting duty occupied us until the Fourth of May when it was suddenly announced that the Rebels had evacuated Yorktown and were in retreat up the Peninsula. Orders to follow in pursuit were at once given, and in a few hours the army was in motion. On that day and the next their rear guard was overtaken at Williamsburg, and after some light cavalry skirmishing, the battle at Williamsburg took place in which the Rebels were defeated, though owing to

[19] CSS *Virginia* rammed and sank USS *Cumberland,* a 24-gun, 1,726-ton sloop of war, during the afternoon of 8 March 1862. On 10 May 1862, Union forces occupied Norfolk Navy Yard after Confederate forces had fired and evacuated it. Denied a base and drawing too much water to operate up the James River, CSS *Virginia* was blown up by her crew off Craney Island, in the Elizabeth River, on 11 May 1862 to prevent her capture. USS *Monitor* herself went down on 31 December 1862 off Cape Hatteras.

[20] The siege endured from 5 April until 4 May 1862, when Union troops occupied the town. The First Regiment of Cavalry, Blake's Brigade, Cavalry Reserve (Cooke), was attached to the Fourth Army Corps, commanded by Brigade General Erasmus D. Keyes, Army of the Potomac. Yorktown was about twenty-four miles from Fort Monroe.

various causes the most potent of which was the absence of any directing power on the field, but little was accomplished.[21]

The pursuit from this point to the Chickahominy was slow and cautious and the army settled down on the latter stream to another siege,—this time of the City of Richmond itself, which was but five miles distant from our lines. The cavalry brigade to which my regiment was attached was principally occupied in picket duty on the right of the army in the neighborhood of Old Church and points on the Totopotomoy Creek.[22] On the 26th of June my squadron under command of Capt. Wm. T. Magruder was on this duty, when Stonewall Jackson's command struck the right of our line, and driving back the troops of Gen. McCall's division, practically isolated us from the army.[23] Magruder was apparently in considerable doubt as to what course to pursue, and for that day and the next he solved the question by not doing anything at all. Why we were not gathered in by the enemy is more than I could understand then, or, for that matter, now, except that they were not bothering their heads much about stray cavalry squadrons. At all events we were completely cut off from the Army of the Potomac by any direct route and could have reached our command only by a circuit involving several days travel. We could of course receive no orders from any source and accordingly remained at Old Church while the sounds of the great battle of Gaines' Mill were echoing in our ears.[24] A portion of our regiment was engaged there and took part in a charge on the Texas troops under Gen. Hood in which Lieut. Robert Allen of our regiment was mortally wounded.[25]

[21] Skirmishes between Union and Confederate forces, in which the First Cavalry was engaged, occurred on 4 May; next day, 5 May, the Battle of Williamsburg was fought. The role of the First Cavalry in this affair is not at all clear. Williamsburg is twelve miles west of Yorktown.

[22] Fifteen to twenty miles northeast of Richmond.

[23] In the passages which follow, Sanford is referring to the Seven Days' Battles, 25 June–1 July 1862. Brigadier General George A. McCall commanded the Third Division, Fifth Army Corps, at Mechanicsville on 26 June; he was captured on 30 June. The other principal battles during this period were Gaines' Mill, 27 June, and Malvern Hill, 1 July. At sixty, McCall (1802–1868) was almost an old man. He was paroled 18 August 1862.

[24] At Gaines' Mill, Union forces sustained more than 6,800 casualties.

[25] See n. 5 *supra*.

155

On the day after that battle Magruder finally decided to withdraw towards the Pamunkey river where we knew our depot of supplies was, and it was quite time too, as a few hours more would have resulted in our capture by the Confederate cavalry under Stuart. Our squadron consisted of two troops, "E" and "K" of the 1st Cavalry, numbering in all about eighty men. We moved at first towards the Chickahominy and if we had reached it, I suppose we should have ridden right into the Rebel lines. Fortunately for us however we ran into a large column of cavalry consisting of various troops of different regiments which like our own had been engaged in picketing on the right of the army and had been cut off by Jackson's advance. These troops had been gathered up by Gen. W. H. Emory and under his command were proceeding to White House landing on the Pamunkey river.[26] Of course we were gathered in with the rest and moved on to the White House where we camped that night.

The next morning we made another attempt by Gen. Geo. Stoneman's orders (who had joined and taken command), to open up communication with the army by way of Bottom's Bridge.[27] My troop was deployed as skirmishers and we got up in sight of the bridge, but found it was destroyed, and the enemy appeared in our front in considerable force. Neither side was quite sure as to who the other was, and we manoeuvred a little to find out.

Gen. Frank Patterson of our army, who had been home recovering from a wound received some time before, rode with me for

[26] William H. Emory (1811–1887), USMA, Class of 1831, resigned from the Army in 1836 but re-entered in 1838. By the outbreak of war, he was a lieutenant colonel, Sixth Regiment of Cavalry, after another reappointment following a second resignation. Emory was appointed brigadier general of volunteers on 25 March 1862. He commanded the other brigade in General Cooke's Cavalry Reserve (see n. 20 *supra*.) Emory next figures in the narrative on p. 288.

The Pamunkey flows into the York River; White House was on the Richmond and York River Railroad.

[27] George Stoneman (1822–1894), USMA, Class of 1846, was promoted major, First (Fourth) Regiment of Cavalry, on 9 May 1861. By 13 August 1861, he was a brigadier general of volunteers. At the time of the Seven Days' Battles, he was chief of cavalry, Army of the Potomac. Despite what Sanford's narrative may suggest, the Army of the Potomac actually regarded Stoneman as engaged in operations, 26 June–2 July, which culminated in the destruction of Federal stores at White House, Virginia, twenty-two miles from Richmond.

some time, hoping to get a chance to get through and rejoin his command.[28] When he saw the Rebels throw out their skirmish line and ride out in our front, he said to me, "Well you fellows are going to have a cavalry fight here in just about five minutes and as it is none of my business, I will bid you 'Good Morning.' " Of course he did not propose to be mixed up in any small affair like that. The fight, however, did not come off. The enemy showed little disposition to attack, and Capt. Magruder probably had orders simply to find out whether the bridge was held by the enemy or not, for he soon withdrew our skirmish line, and fell back to Tunstall's Station[29] and then as the enemy did not follow us at all, he moved to White House and reported the state of affairs.

That evening all the supplies at the depot were loaded on vessels and sent down the river to Fort Monroe, except such as we were unable to transport. Then the torch was applied to all the store houses, and in the blaze of the burning buildings, with Stuart's artillery thundering in our rear, we began our night march down the Peninsula.[30] It was a dreadful scene of disorder and destruction, for the road was crowded with sutler's wagons, and our own trains, including many wagons which could not be sent by the river. The troops behaved well, of course, but orders required that there should be no delay, and if a wagon broke down or stalled, the team was at once taken out and the wagon abandoned to the enemy. As the road was dreadfully cut up and very rough in places, this was constantly occurring, and an immense amount of property was de-

[28] Francis E. Patterson (1821–1862), a veteran of the Mexican War, Regular Army officer, and late colonel, Seventeenth Pennsylvania Infantry. Patterson was appointed brigadier general of volunteers, to date from 11 April 1862, and before his illness on 1 June had commanded the Third Brigade, Hooker's Division, Third Corps (Heintzelman). He died 22 November.

[29] A station on the Richmond and York River Railroad west of White House.

[30] On 18–19 June. In the Pamunkey River, USS *Marblehead* (Lieutenant Somerville Nicholson, United States Navy [henceforth designated USN]) and USS *Chocura* (Lieutenant Thomas H. Patterson, USN), both four guns and 507 tons, supported the Army withdrawal from White House. "At 4:15 all the commissary stores on shore were set on fire, with the adjoining buildings. Several explosions occurred at different times. At 4:30 White House, with its adjoining buildings, was fired." *ORN*, VII, 718. Colonel Henry S. Lansing, Seventeenth New York Volunteers, whose unit was evacuated by the *Marblehead*, noted: "The conflagration was magnificent, but sad; it lighted up the whole country, and prevented the enemy from coming near the shore, as they could be seen." *OR*, XI, Pt. 2, 333.

stroyed or abandoned. Gen. Emory fully expected an attack but none was made and we reached our lines at Williamsburg and moved thence to Yorktown and Fortress Monroe without further incident. From there we took passage on transports up the James River to Harrison's Landing, and rejoined the Army of the Potomac which had reached there via the Chickahominy swamp, and was encamped in a semi-circle from Harrison's Landing where the right rested, to Haxall's Landing where the left lay.[31]

Our regiment lay near the Headquarters of the army, and we at once commenced picket duty, in connection with the other regiments of our division. We were usually out three days and two nights and then lay in camp about the same length of time. The duty was exciting and on the whole agreeable. The enemy's pickets were near and scouting parties from either side frequently came in contact with the other, so that we were kept constantly on the watch and in readiness for an attack.

During a part of the time I was on picket on the ground on which the battle of Malvern Hill had been fought not many days before. One day while sitting on the grass eating my luncheon with my squadron commander Captain Magruder, he spoke of many of his old comrades in the service before the war, and among others talked a good deal of an artillery lieutenant named Wyman who had had rather a wild career in the service, ending with his resignation a short time before the war. On the outbreak of hostilities, however, in 1861, he had returned from Europe where he was travelling, and received the commission of Colonel in a regiment of Mass. volunteers. I had known something of his career, which was indeed quite notorious, and was considerably interested in the conversation, when a volunteer soldier strolled up to us, and in the free and easy manner which obtained among them at that early period, said "Cap., do you know where you are sitting?" Magruder,

[31] After the Battle of Malvern Hill, Flag Officer Louis M. Goldsborough's fleet in the James covered McClellan's withdrawal to Harrison's Landing, "chosen by McClellan at Commodore J. Rodgers' recommendation because it was so situated that gunboats could protect both flanks of his army." Naval History Division, Office of the Chief of Naval Operations, "Civil War Naval Chronology, 1861–1865, Part II, 1862," 75. Harrison's Landing was on the other side of the Peninsula, southwest of White House.

who was a most rigid martinet, was evidently about to order the man about his business, but struck by his manner, which was perfectly respectful and very earnest, I asked him what he meant by his question. He replied that the trench by which we were sitting had contained the body of his Colonel, Powell T. Wyman, of the Mass. Vols., killed at the battle of Malvern Hill and that he with a detachment from the regiment had just disinterred the body, and taken it to an ambulance to send it home. It was a singular coincidence to say the least.[32]

Shortly after midnight July 31–Aug. 1, we were treated to a spectacular performance by the enemy which was quite exciting while it lasted. Our army was camped along the left bank of the James river, and the right bank, up to that time, had not been occupied either by our own or the enemy's forces. On that evening a force of Rebel cavalry and some horse batteries came down under cover of the darkness to the Cole house at Coggins Point on the right bank, which is directly opposite Harrison's Landing. When the whole army was supposed to be buried in the soundest slumbers, they suddenly began a tremendous cannonade, which stirred everybody up in short order. Not much damage was done, considering the fair target we made, our loss being reported at about ten killed and fifteen wounded; but there was a good deal of scurrying round both on land and water, and a good many amusing episodes. Some batteries on our side soon opened in reply, and in a few moments the gun boats in the neighborhood steamed up and commenced shelling the woods vigorously. The enemy were silenced almost immediately, but the gun boats kept up the racket for a long time and the sight of their immense shells flying over the beautiful river made the scene a most martial and inspiriting one.[33]

[32] Powell T. Wyman, USMA, Class of 1850, classmate of Magruder, served as a lieutenant in the artillery until his resignation from the Army on 13 July 1860. On 5 August 1861, he was appointed colonel of the Sixteenth Massachusetts Volunteers. Records indicate that he was killed in action at Glendale, Virginia, on 30 June 1862. He was thirty-four.

[33] *OR* calls this action "Attack on Union camps and shipping between Shirley and Harrison's Landing, Virginia." Firing began about 12:30 A.M. The Confederates had set up approximately forty artillery pieces, including long-range and siege guns. Two Union transports were sunk. USS *Cimarron* (Commander Maxwell Woodhull, USN), an 860-ton side-wheel gunboat with ten guns, fought back with her nine-inch 100-Parrott, and howitzers.

Gen. McClellan sent a force across the next morning and took possession of the country in the neighborhood, and we heard no more of our friends in that vicinity.

Early in August it began to be rumored that the Army of the Potomac would be withdrawn from the James river to the vicinity of Washington. The feeling throughout the army itself was bitterly opposed to this plan, as it was believed that we would have little difficulty in pushing the enemy back across White Oak Swamp to the vicinity of Richmond. Everyone also realized that going back to Washington simply meant giving up all that we had gained by three months' hard work and starting out all over again. It was understood too that Gen. McClellan was strongly adverse to the operation and his opinion had then as always immense weight with his army. Indeed no commander which this army had from the beginning to the end of the war ever exercised one-tenth of the personal influence on the feelings or affections of his men that McClellan did, and looked at in the light of results after an interval of thirty years, I feel sure that no one deserved that affection more. That he made mistakes is granted; but so did his successors. Certainly the morale of the army at the end of the Peninsula and Antietam campaigns was infinitely better than at any other time during the war up to its very close. Even the useless massacre of Fredericksburg and the blundering disaster at Chancellorsville failed to destroy it; and it was not until the best and bravest of its soldiers had been swept away in the bloody business of Cold Harbor that the Army of the Potomac began to lose heart. After that affair it fought stolidly and well, as it had always done, but the earnest, hopeful spirit was gone, and duty was performed in a perfunctory sort of way, as unlike the cheerful response to orders of its early campaigns as daylight is to darkness.

But to return to Harrison's Landing and the life there, pending the decision as to what was to be our future plan.

When not on picket duty we were not kept particularly busy, as our horses being badly run down by the hardships of the previous campaign, it was not deemed advisable to keep them under the saddle more than was absolutely necessary. An additional rea-

160

son was the health of the soldiers, which had been greatly injured by the long sojourn in the pestilential swamps bordering the Chickahominy and James rivers, so that it was unsafe to expose them to the intense heat of the sun when it could be avoided. As a consequence, we had a good deal of time at our disposal, which I passed generally in reading or in riding about the country. This was very interesting to me, as it afforded me an opportunity of seeing something of a state of society of which I knew nothing, except from hearsay or from books, and which has now entirely ceased to exist. I allude of course to the life on the great plantations owned by the rich slaveholders.

At that period of the war and more especially in the Potomac Army while under McClellan's command, it was not the policy of the government to interfere with the citizens of the Southern States when they were not actually aiding the enemy, and while their slaves were not actually forbidden to enter our lines, it was well understood in that army that they were not wanted. The result was that on most of those noble estates, life went on very much as it did before the attack on Fort Sumter, and the opportunity of observing it even superficially was one of which I eagerly availed myself.

One of the finest of these beautiful places was "Shirley" belonging to the Carters, among the most distinguished of the old Virginia families. It was situated on the James river on the left bank and not very far below City Point.[34] It was between our lines and the enemy's and exposed of course to the depredations of marauders from either army. Mr. Hill Carter the proprietor must have been at that time not far from sixty years of age, a thorough gentleman of the old school, loyal to his State, but quite willing to live at peace with our people provided they would allow him to occupy his property. Gen. McClellan was determined that the rights of property owners should be respected, as long as they remained quiet and obedient to the laws, directed that an officer should be sent up there to examine the condition of affairs and report as to

[34] And below the Union camp at Harrison's Landing; City Point was on the right bank of the James at the mouth of the Appomattox River.

their appearance. I was accordingly ordered up on this duty, and Lieut. Sumner of my regiment—now Lt. Colonel of the 8th Cavalry (1893)—offered to accompany me.[35] We were struck, as we entered the park surrounding the house, by the extreme beauty of its situation, and especially by the noble trees which lined the avenues and were dotted over the landscape. The house itself was a fine old mansion of brick, with wide porches and an immense number of rambling wings and outbuildings. Close by was an older building, looking centuries old indeed, in complete ruin, and of course unoccupied. The walls were covered with ivy and the whole was romantic in the extreme. Mr. Carter informed me later that it was built in the early part of the 17th century by one of his ancestors, of brick brought from England. As it became ruinous with age, a new house had been built, and the old one stripped of anything that would decay or was unsightly, was preserved as a relic of the old time.

Mr. Carter received us with great courtesy and introduced us to the ladies of his family, who were polite but reserved, and I thought seemed singularly anxious. At first I attributed this only to embarrassment at meeting those whom they of course regarded as the enemies of their country, but later I found they had a much more serious cause of disturbance. We were shown over the grounds and a portion of the estate, which extended for miles along the river. Afterwards we were invited to dinner, which was elegantly served, and a most delightful change from the rough comforts of camp life, to which we were accustomed. I ascertained from Mr. Carter that he was occasionally visited by small parties of our soldiers and that as a rule they were civil enough in their manner, and quite willing to pay for any supplies they took. But of course it kept the family in a state of anxiety and he would be very glad if Gen. McClellan would furnish him with a small guard for the purpose of

---

[35] Edwin V. Sumner, son of General Edwin V. (see n. 4, Chap. IV), was commissioned a second lieutenant, First Regiment of Cavalry, 5 August 1861; promoted first lieutenant, 12 November 1861; captain, 23 September 1863. On 8 September 1864, he was appointed colonel, Seventh New York Cavalry (also called First Battalion, Mounted Rifles). Sumner was promoted brigadier general, USA, 27 March 1899.

protection. He was quite willing to promise that they should be exempt from any molestation by the enemy, and that he would himself live at peace with the Government; but he said nothing about taking the oath of allegiance and indeed did not attempt to conceal the fact that he considered his first duty as due to his State.

After dinner he excused himself for a few moments, first inviting us to smoke our cigars in a beautiful glass enclosed porch overlooking a noble stretch of grass and woodland bordered by the beautiful waters of the James. Sumner and I were deeply impressed with the beauty of the scene and were commenting on it with enthusiastic admiration when a door opened, and a young man not much older than ourselves, but dressed in the full uniform of an officer of the Confederate army appeared. He looked very pale and weak and was evidently taken by surprise at seeing us. For a moment he seemed about to withdraw, but changing his mind, came forward and apologized for disturbing us, disclaiming any knowledge of our presence. He went on to say that we must pardon him for not attempting to entertain us, as we could see that he was weak and wounded, and he would leave us to ourselves. Then bowing to us both, he went back as he had come. Sumner and I were struck dumb with astonishment. Here was a situation. Ought we to arrest this man—evidently an officer of the enemy—and take him back with us to camp? That would seem the first thing to do; but on the other hand, we were these people's guests, had been kindly entertained by them, and were to a certain extent prevented by the claims of hospitality. The gentleman was evidently a son of the family, who had been wounded in one of the recent battles and had returned to his home for the care and treatment which would be given to him there. I for one was entirely determined to let the matter alone, at all events until I could get advice from my Colonel, and Sumner agreed with me. In a few moments Mr. Carter returned, but made no allusion to what happened. Indeed I am satisfied that he had no knowledge of what had occurred. Of course we said nothing, and shortly afterward we bade him good-bye, and returned to our camp. I had no doubt, after thinking it over, that the young officer hearing his father leave the room after dinner, supposed we had accompanied him out into the grounds, and had accordingly gone into the smoking room where he found us, supposing he would be safe from observation. I felt bound to report the matter to my commanding officer, but was very glad that he did not think it necessary to carry it any farther. Probably the young fellow returned to his command very soon.[36] At all events I never heard anything more of him, though a safe guard was sent to Mr. Carter's place as he had requested.

About the middle of August my squadron was ordered on picket for the usual three days tour. Nothing of any special interest occurred on the first or second day, but on the morning of the third, our relief which should have made its appearance early in the morning failed to appear. As our rations and forage were all gone, of course this was not very pleasant. We thought little of it, however, until Lieut. Nichols, who had gone out before daylight to visit the line of videttes, returned with the startling information that the videttes of the cavalry on our right and left, with whom we had connected previously, had disappeared, and that our line was "in the air."[37] My squadron commander at this time was Capt. Eugene M. Baker, a young officer of unusual abilities and of great courage.[38] He realized of course that something serious had happened, and that for some reason or other we had not been notified. He was determined, however, not to leave his post without knowing something more definitely about the situation. He accordingly took immediate measures for our own better protection, drawing in our vidette line nearer to the reserve, and posting them in such a manner that we would have early information of an attack or advance from any direction. He then sent an officer with a detachment to our left, to reconnoitre the country towards Malvern and Haxall,

36 This officer cannot be identified.

37 John H. Nichols had served as first lieutenant, Eighty-first New York Volunteers, from 21 December 1861 to 31 January 1862. Since he was appointed second lieutenant, First Regiment of Cavalry, 14 July 1862 and first lieutenant 12 August 1862, he must have just joined Baker's company. Nichols was killed 12 June 1864 in the Battle of Trevilian Station, Virginia. He appears later in the narrative.

38 See n. 4 *supra.*

and another small party under my command to the right for the same purpose.[39]

As our previous preparations had taken some time, it was nearly dusk before I started and quite dark in the thick woods a short time after I had left camp. I had two men with me,—the troop farrier named Hurley, and the trumpeter, Chatland. Both were old dragoons and courageous and powerful men, trained by long service against the Indian tribes on the Plains and in the Rocky Mountains. We rode mile after mile in silence keeping a general southerly course, and passing through an abandoned camp which we knew must have been that of the cavalry on our right, on the previous day. This squadron I knew was Capt. Irvin Gregg's of the 6th Cavalry of our brigade.[40] Hurley and Chatland, with the hunter's craft acquired in their long experience in the Indian country, soon picked up the trail, which led off the main road through some country by-paths. It was slow work at first, but finally we came out on a tolerably well marked road, and could get along more rapidly. I had no means of knowing, of course, whether the force that had passed along was our own falling back, or that of a party of the enemy which had driven them in. In a few moments, however, a hurried challenge accompanied, not followed, by the report of a carbine and the whiz of a bullet so close to my ear that it seemed as if it drew blood, gave us something else to think about. We drew sabres at the instant and dashed forward after the vidette, who fell back at full gallop. I did not doubt of course for an instant that it was a pursuing party of the enemy, but concluded to stir up their picket at all events and find out something about them. The reserve of some five or six men was soon reached, but to our surprise, instead of receiving a volley, we were halted and a young officer rode toward

[39] Haxall was downriver from Shirley, due north, and Malvern Hill, north of Haxall, was four to five miles from Harrison's Landing.

[40] John Irvin Gregg was something of an old soldier, having served briefly as an enlisted man, then an officer, in the Mexican War before being disbanded 14 August 1848. He was appointed captain in the Sixth Regiment of Cavalry on 14 May 1861. He also served as colonel, Sixteenth Pennsylvania Cavalry, from 14 November 1862. After the war, he served for thirteen years as colonel, Eighth Regiment of Cavalry. He died in 1891.

us waving his hat, and making signs not to fire. I then found it was Gregg's squadron, and in a few moments we were escorted down the road to his reserve, where we were warmly welcomed. I then found that Gregg knew no more of the situation than we did, except that he had received orders on the previous evening to fall back to his present position, and await further instructions. He had been informed that the videttes of the other squadrons would be relieved also, and was astonished not to be able to communicate with us, as he had been trying to do during the day. We agreed that if no orders were received, it would be absolutely necessary to fall back next morning, as we had simply nothing at all to eat for men or animals.

With this information I returned to Capt. Baker, whom I reached about midnight or soon after, finding him quite anxious. The officer sent out to the left had returned shortly before, without having found any of our people, but had run into a small party of the enemy, with whom he had exchanged a few shots. Baker ordered the command to saddle and stood to horse the remainder of the night, and at an hour or so before daylight, he drew in his pickets and moved back toward the camp at Harrison's Landing. My troop was in advance during this movement and Baker directed me to exercise great care in approaching the intrenchments as there was considerable doubt in his mind as to what we should find there. I accordingly moved rapidly forward until I knew that we were not far from the lines, and then brought the troop to a walk, and went to the front myself with Lieut. Myers of my troop and one soldier.[41] Soon we came in sight of the works which encircled the immense camp of the Army of the Potomac, extending in a great semi-circle for many miles from the river below to the river above Harrison's Landing.

In the dim morning light everything looked weird and sepulchral.

41 Edward Myers, a native of Germany, served five years as enlisted man (private through first sergeant) in the First Regiment of Dragoons and First Regiment of Cavalry. Commissioned a second lieutenant on 17 July 1862, he served with distinction throughout the war and was thrice brevetted for "gallant and meritorious service." He was a captain in the Seventh Regiment of Cavalry when he died on 11 July 1871.

No smoke arose from the camps, and no trumpet or bugle calls or tap of drum could be heard though it was just the time when reveille should be sounding and the air be filled with the hum and bustle attending the arousing from their slumbers of an army of a hundred thousand men. At intervals along the intrenchments we could dimly discern in the faint light of dawn the motionless forms of the sentinels, and occasionally catch a glimpse of the black muzzle of a cannon peeping through an embrasure. "My God, are they all dead?" said Mr. Myers to me in a half whisper; and at the same moment I noticed on the face of the soldier behind us the same awestruck expression which I have little doubt was visible on our own. Just then Capt. Baker rode up and joined us. Cheery and bright as usual, he called out to me "Well, what sort of fellows are those in front?" I was pretty well satisfied by this time as to what was up, and putting spurs to my horse, rode forward with my orderly. As I expected, no challenge came from the sentinels, and when we got close up, it was plain that they were what the soldiers term "Dummies," as were the guns they carried and the cannon in the works. In a word, the Army of the Potomac had vanished utterly, leaving no trace of their present whereabouts.

It was by no means a pleasant condition of affairs. We had nothing at all to eat ourselves, but fortunately we found some grain and hay for the horses among the abandoned camps, and were able to give them a good meal. Then we rode to the river, passing through the abandoned camps of Sumner's army corps, and watered our horses in the James. Here we found a few cattle, one of which Baker ordered killed and butchered, and we got a rough sort of breakfast. He had taken up a good position and thrown out pickets, and now calling his officers together, stated his intention of remaining where he was for at least twenty-four hours longer, unless sooner relieved or driven away by the enemy. He said, what was indeed evident to all, that the army had undoubtedly fallen back down the river toward Fortress Monroe; that they were probably in the neighborhood of the mouth of the Chickahominy, and that it was of infinite importance that the knowledge of their retreat should be kept from the enemy until

167

that stream could be bridged and crossed.[42] We were in no danger of starvation as long as we could get beef, and we knew that there was some cavalry to our right in the same situation that we were, and no doubt there were other squadrons to our left. Whether we had been abandoned intentionally, the authorities thinking it safer not to divulge the retreat until the last moment, and trusting to our good luck and good judgment to get us out of the scrape; or whether we had been accidentally forgotten, or our orders had failed to reach us, was a matter of doubt. In any event our duty was plain, and he proposed to perform it. In the meantime he sent out scouts to endeavor to find the position of any of our forces, and to watch any approach of the enemy, and the rest of the command threw themselves on the ground by their horses, the bridles in their hands, ready to mount at a moment's warning.

It was about the hottest day I ever remember in my life, and as the sun rose high in the heavens, a plague of flies rose from the abandoned camps, which I verily believe has not been equalled since the Egyptians suffered from the same pest. The myriads that had been swarming over that immense camp now seemed to concentrate on our little command, and men and horses were driven nearly wild. It seemed as if the horses would be bitten to death, and it was hardly possible to keep them from stampeding in a body. The men covered them with cast off grain sacks, overcoats and blankets, and beat them with switches and boughs. A poor cow which had been abandoned by some headquarters mess, actually succumbed to the torments and died before our eyes. Fortunately as the day lengthened a breeze sprung up and relieved us in a measure, but I have never seen anything like it in my life,

42 Difficult as it is to believe, the withdrawal was apparently accomplished without the knowledge of Captain Baker, his officers, and men. On 14–15 August 1862, the Third and Fifth Army Corps moved from Harrison's Landing to Aquia Creek, and from 14 to 19 August, Union cavalry covered the movement of the Army of the Potomac from Harrison's Landing to Williamsburg. Captain Baker's lack of knowledge is especially odd in that the First Regiment of Cavalry, as a part of the Second Cavalry Brigade, Brigadier General Alfred Pleasonton commanding, participated in the operations. On 15 August, USS *Galena*, USS *Port Royal*, and USS *Satellite*, James River Flotilla, covered the withdrawal of the left wing of McClellan's army from Harrison's Landing over the Chickahominy. See "Civil War Naval Chronology, Part II, 1862," 91.

though in after years I was exposed to dreadful annoyance in the hot deserts of Southern California and Arizona.

Late in the afternoon one of our scouting parties returned from the extreme left, having succeeded in communicating with some cavalry in that direction. The Commanding Officer soon appeared himself, and as he was a field officer, Major Huey of the 8th Pa. Cavalry, he assumed command of all the troops in the neighborhood and established communication throughout.[43] We turned out to be quite a body altogether, five or six squadrons, I think, and we held the line of the intrenchments until nightfall, when the enemy began to push us all along the line. We did not give at all, however, until after dark, when the videttes were silently withdrawn, and we took the river along the James toward Fortress Monroe. Between midnight and dawn on the 18th of August, we reached the Chickahominy and found the rear guard of the Army on the Southern bank. Everything was across except ourselves, and the engineers with their officers, were already beginning to take up the long lines of pontoons which stretched from bank to bank. As we rode across, the planks were taken up, and before ten o'clock every soldier was across and communication by that route with Richmond was severed.

We soon found our regiment which with the rest of the cavalry was covering the retreat of the army, and were warmly welcomed, as our comrades had about concluded we were "booked for the Libby"[44]—in other words, all taken prisoners. We were tired and hungry, worn out with anxiety and loss of sleep, but an abundance of hot coffee and a hearty meal soon set us to rights, and in a few hours we were as well as ever. But we never found out why we were left in ignorance of the retreat of the army.[45]

[43] Major Pennock Huey, Eighth Pennsylvania Cavalry, was cited by Brigadier General Pleasonton for "important services" in this maneuver. *OR*, XI, Pt. 2, 966. He attained to the rank of colonel.

[44] The Confederate prison at Richmond.

[45] The Peninsular Campaign was a failure and at an end, except for the embarkation of the troops at Newport News, Yorktown, and Fort Monroe.

·CHAPTER III·

Fᴙᴏᴍ ᴛʜɪꜱ ᴘᴏɪɴᴛ we moved to Fortress Monroe without incident, the various divisions being shipped from that point by water, some to Aquia Creek, whence they proceeded to the Rappahannock and eventually joined Pope's "Army of Virginia," others to Alexandria on the southern bank of the Potomac. We were directed to the latter point which we reached about the 2nd or 3rd of September. As we landed at the wharf an ambulance was driven down, which we were told contained the body of Major General Philip Kearny, who had just been killed at the battle of Chantilly, September 1, 1862. Gen. Kearny had been a captain in my regiment during the Mexican War and lost an arm at the battle of the City of Mexico.[1] Corporal Sugden of my troop had been in his troop ("F") in that war, and was detailed to accompany his body to his home in New Jersey. Kearny was a gallant soldier and would have undoubtedly risen to the very high command had his life been spared.

Nothing but bad news met us at this time. We heard of defeat after defeat, and Pope's campaign was considered by everyone with whom we talked a dreadful failure. His army was then approaching Washington and he himself arrived on the 3rd. His troops were ordered to report to Gen. McClellan for duty, and were at once

[1] Philip Kearney (1815–1862), a graduate of Columbia, was appointed second lieutenant, First Regiment of Dragoons, 8 March 1837. Wealthy and widely traveled, Kearny saw action in Algiers in 1840, in Mexico, was brevetted major, and lost an arm. He resigned from the Army 9 October 1851. In 1859, he served in Napoleon III's army in the Italian War. His appointment as brigadier general of volunteers dated from 17 May 1861; major general, 4 July 1862. At Chantilly, he made a mistake which cost him his life: he rode into the Confederate lines.

merged into the Army of the Potomac, and the "Virginia" army ceased to exist under that name.[2] The condition of this force, thus made up of heterogeneous elements, was exceedingly bad. McClellan's old divisions were disheartened by the coolness with which they were treated by the authorities and by a portion of the public press, and greatly incensed at the slights to their favorite, McClellan.

Pope's old command were badly demoralized on the other hand by the rough handling they had received and the ease with which their leaders had been out-manoeuvred by Lee and Jackson. In addition the feeling between the components of the two armies was by no means cordial. McClellan's assignment to the command of the whole force, however, produced an immediate good effect. With his wonderful capacity for organization and singular magnetic power over the feelings of the individual soldiers, a new spirit seemed to spring up at once, and the feeling of hopefulness and confidence that prevailed among the troops during the march through Maryland, was perhaps as strong as at any time during the war. One thing that undoubtedly tended to the re-establishment of a good morale was the fact that the army was for the first time in its history campaigning in a friendly country, and the people themselves seemed overjoyed to welcome us. The country too was beautiful,—well watered, well timbered, and well adapted to camping purposes. No large bodies of troops had passed through it, and it was literally flowing with milk and honey, or at all events their

2 Dreadful indeed had been Pope's campaign with the Army of Virginia (nominally all Union forces in the East except McClellan's Peninsula troops), the capstone of which—if such is possible—was Second Manassas, 29–30 August 1862. When Pope arrived, General James Longstreet, CSA, his classmate at West Point, was literally panting at his heels. Thus the sad end of the Campaign in northern Virginia.

John Pope (1822–1892) had good credentials (family, marriage, politics) and indeed a fair enough record in the West in 1862 at Madrid and Island No. 10. A graduate of USMA, Class of 1842, he served in the Mexican War (two brevets) and with the Topographical Engineers until the Civil War. He was appointed brigadier general of volunteers on 17 May 1861; major general of volunteers, 21 March 1862; brigadier general in the Regular Army, 14 July 1862.

On 5 September 1862, the Army of Virginia and the Army of the Potomac were consolidated; Pope was relieved and ordered to report to the Secretary of War. He was ultimately exiled to the Department of the Northwest (*i.e.*, Minnesota, etc.). The consolidated force, the Army of the Potomac, was commanded by McClellan.

171

equivalents. The Union sentiment seemed to be universal, and if there were any Secessionists in the population they kept well out of sight.[3]

The movement of the army into Maryland began almost with the return of Pope's troops from Manassas and their junction with the soldiers returning from the Peninsula.[4] The cavalry were thrown out to the front of Washington south of the Potomac and engaged in frequent skirmishes with the mounted force of the enemy while the infantry and artillery were crossing the Potomac and massing north of that river. During one of these combats in the vicinity of Falls Church, in the first week of September,[5] my regiment was engaged in supporting a battery of the horse artillery, in action with one of the enemy's batteries. A threatened advance of Stuart's cavalry necessitating a counter-advance on our part, our commander led the regiment at a gallop through the orchard and garden of a neighboring farm house. In this orchard were a large number of bee-hives, some of which were knocked over by the shells of the Rebel battery, and the infuriated insects at once turned their attention to the galloping horsemen who were passing through their territory. My squadron had the luck to get into the thick of it. The bullets of the enemy's skirmishers were flying about thickly, and to this I attributed the unusual confusion among the horses as we passed through the orchard, not knowing at the moment of the ridiculous cause of the excitement. While endeavoring to restore order in the ranks, however, I received a sharp shock on the side of my head where the forage cap pressed against my hair, and supposed of course that I was wounded, but in a few seconds the cause was apparent, and the excitement among the horses and men quickly accounted for. Our rush to get out of the neighborhood of

[3] Diametrically opposed to this statement is one made by General J. E. B. Stuart shortly after his cavalry had crossed the Potomac River into Maryland (see p. 173): "The reception of our troops in Maryland was attended with the greatest demonstration of joy, and the hope of enabling the inhabitants to throw off the tyrant's yoke stirred every Southern heart." *OR,* XIX, Pt. 1, 815.

[4] Indeed, three campaigns merge here in the first week of September, 1862: the recently completed Peninsular Campaign, the recently completed Campaign in Northern Virginia, and the Maryland Campaign, now under way, which was to last until 20 September 1862.

[5] There were skirmishes at Falls Church, Virginia, 3–4 September.

the fiery little warriors thoroughly impressed the enemy who withdrew in short order. Not many of the soldiers were wounded by the enemy in that charge, but comparatively few escaped something to remember the Falls Church affair, and for some time after it made more talk than many a more serious action.

It soon appeared that Lee's army was withdrawing from our front and moving up the Potomoc, apparently for the invasion of Maryland. We were accordingly drawn back across the Potomac and then moved up the river to watch the fords where the enemy might attempt to cross. Their cavalry under Stuart had already entered Maryland and we had almost daily skirmishes with them, but no general action occurred.[6] About the tenth of September the 1st Cavalry was ordered to report to Maj. Gen. Wm. B. Franklin, commanding the Sixth Army Corps, and remained with him until the Battle of Antietam.[7] Franklin had charge of the left of our army at this time and was moving for Crampton's Gap in the South Mountain with the hope of being able to force that pass and proceed rapidly down Pleasant Valley to the Potomac in time to relieve the garrison of Harpers Ferry which was besieged by Jackson and McLaws.[8] It was necessary, however, to preserve general continuity with the other corps of the army, and for some reason the march seemed to be unreasonably delayed. We finally approached

[6] As a matter of fact, the Army of Northern Virginia crossed the Potomac River by the fords near Leesburg, 5–6 September 1862, and marched to Frederick, Maryland, where Lee divided his army. Stuart's cavalry, made up of Hampton's Brigade and Fitzhugh Lee's Brigade, crossed over into Maryland on 5 September. See n. 3 *supra*.

[7] William B. Franklin (1823–1903), USMA, Class of 1843 (Grant's class, but Franklin stood No. 1, Grant No. 21). He had attained the rank of captain in the regular establishment in 1857 and had served in the Mexican War (brevetted), the Topographical Engineers, and in Washington, D.C. On 14 May 1861, he was named colonel of the newly established (4 May) Twelfth Regiment of Infantry; within three days, he was a brigadier general of volunteers. He was appointed major general of volunteers on 4 July 1862. After Fredericksburg, Franklin's career waned, so much so that he resigned the Army on 15 March 1866.

The Sixth Army Corps consisted of the First Division (Major General Henry W. Slocum) and the Second Division (Major General William F. Smith), each having three brigades. The First Regiment of Cavalry was represented by Companies B, C, H, and I, Captain Marcus A. Reno commanding.

[8] South Mountain Range—hills, really—cresting at about 1,000 or 1,100 feet, ran due north and south from the north bank of the Potomac over into Pennsylvania. Lee's army, less the six divisions at Harpers Ferry, lay behind the barrier of hills.

173

the Gap on the morning of September 14. My squadron happened to have the lead this morning, and my own troop was detached in advance.

We struck the enemy's outposts soon after daylight near the village of Burkittsville and pushed them across the stream at a gallop.[9] Finding them in force altogether too great for my small party, I withdrew to the north side of the stream and reported the facts. Gen. Franklin then sent Newton's brigade of Slocum's division forward and supported it by Bartlett's and Torbert's brigade.[10] The enemy held a stone wall at the foot of the pass, and had artillery placed commanding the road. It appeared to be and was a very strong position, but as soon as the lines were formed the troops moved forward to the attack with great spirit and carried the stone wall. From this point our whole force pushed up the mountain and about sun-down reached the crest, capturing one piece of artillery and many prisoners. The cavalry pursued until dark, and then went into camp, the enemy likewise camping in Pleasant Valley a short distance in advance.[11] At the same time the right wing and centre were heavily engaged at Turner's Gap, and the whole crest was carried the same evening. Gen. Jesse L. Reno, commanding the 9th Corps, was killed in this battle.[12] I had known him at Fort Leavenworth in the Summer of 1861, when he

[9] A series of battles and skirmishes was fought on 13 and 14 September. On 13 September, skirmishes occurred at Catoctin Mountain, Middletown, Jefferson, and South Mountain, Maryland; on 14 September, the Battles of South Mountain (Boonsborough, Boonsborough Gap, or Turner's Pass) and Crampton's Pass, Maryland, were fought. *OR, XIX*, Pt. 1, 157.

[10] Brigadier General John Newton (1822–1895) commanded the Third Brigade; Colonel Joseph J. Bartlett (1834–1893; colonel, Twenty-seventh New York Volunteers), Second Brigade; Colonel Alfred T. A. Torbert, First Brigade. All were in Slocum's First Division. Although Sanford does not mention it, General Smith's Second Division was also engaged in the battle. For Torbert, see p. 224 *passim*. Bartlett was appointed brigadier general of volunteers 4 October 1862.

[11] Franklin had won a decisive victory at Crampton's Gap; Pleasant Valley was on the other (western) side of the hills. Brigadier General Howell Cobb, CSA, commanded the Confederate forces in the battle .

[12] Major General Jesse L. Reno (b. 1823), USMA, Class of 1846, classmate of Generals Thomas J. Jackson and George E. Pickett, CSA, and General George B. McClellan, USA. Reno was killed 14 September 1862 at Fox's Gap, South Mountain, just south of Turner's Gap and six miles north of the action at Crampton's Gap. The successful South Mountain battles had cost the Army of the Potomac 438 KIA and a total of 2,346 casualties.

was on duty as a Captain of Ordnance in command of the Arsenal at that point, and I was very sorry to hear of his death.

The morning of the 15th opened with a dense fog which entirely concealed all signs of the enemy in our front, but reconnaissances by our cavalry soon disclosed the fact of their presence. Signal guns were fired to give notice to the garrison of Harpers Ferry, but a few miles distant, that assistance was at hand, and the command was already moving forward when the cessation of all firing from that direction satisfied every mind that we were too late. As it turned out, Col. Miles (Dixon S. Miles), who was in command, gave directions for the surrender about 8 o'clock that morning.[13] Perhaps fortunately for him, he was killed by one of the last cannon shots fired, just before the surrender was consummated.[14] The evening previous to the surrender Colonel Miles had given permission to the cavalry, some two thousand in number, to attempt to cut their way through the enemy's lines, and join the army of the Potomac. This they did without difficulty, capturing en route the entire ammunition train of Longstreet's army corps.

Capt. Benjamin F. Davis of my troop, who had recently been appointed Colonel of the 8th New York Cavalry, was in command of this force and received great praise for his conduct.[15] The President appointed him Major by brevet in the regular army, and we

[13] Harpers Ferry was besieged from 12 to 15 September by Jackson's Corps (Major General Thomas J. Jackson, CSA), Army of Northern Virginia (General Robert E. Lee). The surrender prompted an investigation of the affair by the Harpers Ferry Military Commission, 25 September–8 November 1862, Major General David Hunter, president. See n. 63, Chap. 1.

[14] Colonel Dixon S. Miles, Second Regiment of Infantry, was killed, as a matter of fact, after the white flag had been displayed along the Union lines.

[15] Davis held the rank of lieutenant colonel with the Eighth New York Cavalry. On 23 September 1862, General McClellan, in a dispatch from his headquarters, spoke of Davis' "conspicuous conduct ... in the management of the withdrawal of the cavalry from Harpers Ferry" and recommended him for "the brevet of major." *OR,* XIX Pt. 1, 802. And the conduct had been conspicuous. On the night of 14 September, Davis led out the entire Union cavalry force: his Eighth New York, Twelfth Illinois, and First Rhode Island. Somehow, he got past Major General Lafayette McLaws' two divisions and proceeded to friendly lines. En route, he captured Longstreet's 97-wagon reserve ammunition train and its 600 guards. See Robert D. Hoffsommer, "Jackson's Capture of Harpers Ferry," *Civil War Times Illustrated,* I (August 1962), 13, and John W. Mies, "Breakout at Harpers Ferry," *Civil War History,* II (June, 1956), 13–28. In the subsequent discussion, Sanford seems to forget that he has already spoken of Davis; see pp. 147–48.

all thought and hoped that he would be appointed a Brigadier General of Volunteers, but he was not, and a few months later he was shot dead in the great cavalry battle at Beverly Ford, 9th June, 1863. Davis was born in Alabama and appointed to the Military Academy from Mississippi, and I believe was a distant relative of Jefferson Davis. This hurt him of course with Secretary Stanton, who apparently could not understand that any Southern officer of the Regular Army could possibly be true to the Government. In my opinion no more truly loyal men or finer soldiers held commissions in our army than George H. Thomas, John Buford, and Benjamin F. Davis. In their different spheres each did noble service, and each suffered from the petty spite and malignant meanness of men who could not comprehend their greatness of spirit, but who thoroughly dreaded their exceptional ability.

During the afternoon of the 15th we advanced down Pleasant Valley, McLaws' division of the enemy occasionally forming line to resist us and then falling back as we deployed. The Rebel cavalry covered their retreat, and their long columns on the right hand side of the Valley for a time moved on almost parallel lines with ours on the left.[16] Occasionally a battery on either side would gallop into line, unlimber and throw a few shells. It was a beautiful and inspiriting sight, but nightfall put an end to it, and we went into camp without any very serious fighting.

The next morning, daylight came with a fog so dense that it was difficult to see anything ten yards off. We were soon under way with orders to join the main body of the army which was coming into line in front of Sharpsburg on Antietam Creek. This point was reached in the forenoon of the 17th in the same dense fog as on the previous day, and which indeed prevailed every morning during this part of the campaign. As we came down the Sharpsburg pike the thunder of the guns along the Antietam seemed to shake the very earth. It was a magnificent sight that met our eyes, as the fog lifted, and the whole of the two great armies of the Potomac and Northern Virginia locked in deadly strife, were exposed to view. Franklin's corps moved into action across the Antietam at

[16] The Confederate cavalry was commanded by Stuart.

once, in front of the Dunkard Church. My regiment still remained with this command but shortly afterwards was ordered to report to Gen. McClellan and was placed in position near his Headquarters on the crest of the hill overlooking Sharpsburg. From this point of vantage a magnificent view of the whole field was obtained, except where woods intervened.[17]

The Rebel army was commanded by the famous Gen. R. E. Lee in person and was said to number over one hundred thousand men, although we know now that our secret service people very considerably over-estimated it. However it was a very large and very gallant force, flushed with victory, and with the prestige of having beaten or repulsed everything with which it had come in contact.[18] It was well equipped in all respects, for at this time the Rebels had not begun to suffer from the effects of the blockade as they did a little later, and it was commanded by as able a body of trained and accomplished officers as ever led soldiers. On our own side the Army of the Potomac was, as always, ready to do its duty to the utmost extent of its power, and though the previous phases of the year's fighting had not been fortunate, everyone felt that it was not the fault of the army, but the fortune of war, and the fact that McClellan was in command again, gave renewed confidence and spirit to many who had been disappointed or discouraged with the recall from the Peninsula, and the events of the Pope Campaign.[19] It was well understood that a defeat of the army at that time would result in the almost certain capture of Washington by the enemy and the recognition of the Confederacy by France and England. That this contingency was ever present to Gen. McClellan's mind cannot be doubted and unfortunately for his personal glory, though as I think fortunately for the country, it prevented him from pressing the enemy as vigorously as he might have done in different

[17] McClellan's headquarters was the Philip Pry house, northeast of Sharpsburg across Antietam Creek and just off the Boonsboro Pike. The First Cavalry was officially assigned the duty of quartermaster's guard at McClellan's general headquarters.

[18] During the battle, Lee had available approximately 41,000 men.

[19] The Army of the Potomac at Sharpsburg (Antietam) numbered about 87,000 men.

circumstances. As it was the battle was a very terrible one, and the losses on either side tremendous.[20]

During the forenoon and middle of the day our attack was principally confined to attempts to crush the enemy's left in the neighborhood of the Dunkard Church. Mansfield, Hooker and Franklin in turn dashed their forces against the enemy's lines. The first was killed and the second desperately wounded and carried from the field and though the enemy was forced to give ground repeatedly he as continually returned to the attack so that the slaughter along this part of the field was terrific.[21] McClellan's plan evidently was to crush or weaken this part of their line to such an extent that our left under Burnside would have a comparatively easy task in breaking their right which it was supposed would be depleted by calls for assistance from their left. If this had been successful Burnside would have gained possession of Sharpsburg and the road to the Shepherdstown ford across the Potomac and the Rebel army would have been crowded back against that river with no facilities for crossing, and would have been obliged to disperse or surrender. But unfortunately for McClellan the attacks were not nearly enough simultaneous to properly effect this project.

The battle on our right had been practically fought to a standstill before Gen. Burnside had been able to carry the bridge over the Antietam, in his front, and effect a crossing.[22] When he did succeed in this effort, it was quite late in the afternoon and though his troops made a great gallant advance and actually got possession

20 Antietam has been called the bloodiest day in the Civil War. The Army of the Potomac sustained more than 12,000 casualties, the Army of Northern Virginia more than 10,000. A breakdown of Union losses reveals 139 officers and 1,969 enlisted men, a total of 2,108, KIA; 474 officers and 9,075 enlisted men, a total of 9,549, WIA; and seven officers and 746 enlisted men, a total of 753, POW or MIA. *OR*, XIX, Pt. 1, 204.

21 Major General Joseph K. F. Mansfield (b. 1803), USMA, Class of 1822, commanded the Twelfth Army Corps, formerly the Second Corps, Army of Virginia; its designation was changed on 12 September 1862. Mansfield was wounded during the battle and died the next day. Major General Joseph Hooker (1814–1879), USMA, Class of 1837, commanded the First Army Corps, formerly the Third Corps, Army of Virginia; its designation was changed on 12 September 1862.

22 During the battle, Major General Ambrose E. Burnside (1824–1881), USMA, Class of 1847, commanded his own Ninth Army Corps (immediate command of Brigadier General Jacob D. Cox), on the left and Hooker's First Corps.

CAPTAIN GEORGE B. SANFORD, FIRST CAVALRY, U.S.A., 1865

CAPTAIN GEORGE B. SANFORD, FIRST CAVALRY, U.S.A., 1866

BRIGADIER GENERAL WILLIAM WOODS AVERELL, U.S.A. (1832–1900)

MAJOR GENERAL GEORGE ARMSTRONG CUSTER, U.S.A. (1839–1876)

COLONEL ALEXANDER C. M. PENNINGTON, U.S.A.

MAJOR GENERAL ALFRED PLEASONTON, U.S.A. (1824–1897)

MAJOR GENERAL PHILIP H. SHERIDAN, U.S.A. (1831–1888)

BRIGADIER GENERAL ALFRED T. A. TORBERT, U.S.A. (1833–1880)

MAJOR GENERAL JAMES H. WILSON, U.S.A. (1837–1925)

SEATED, LEFT TO RIGHT: BRIGADIER GENERAL WESLEY MERRITT, U.S.A., BRIGADIER GENERAL DAVID MC MURTRIE GREGG, U.S.A., MAJOR GENERAL PHILIP H. SHERIDAN, U.S.A., COLONEL JAMES H. WILSON, U.S.A., BRIGA- DIER GENERAL ALFRED T. A. TORBERT, U.S.A. (THE OFFICER STANDING IS NOT IDENTIFIED)

LIEUTENANT GENERAL JUBAL A. EARLY, C.S.A. (1816–1894)

MAJOR GENERAL FITZHUGH LEE, C.S.A. (1835–1905)

MAJOR GENERAL WILLIAM H. FITZHUGH LEE (ROONEY LEE), C.S.A.
(1837–1891)

COLONEL JOHN S. MOSBY, C.S.A. (1833–1916)

LIEUTENANT GENERAL THOMAS L. ROSSER, C.S.A. (1836–1910)

COOK COLLECTION, VALENTINE MUSEUM,
RICHMOND, VIRGINIA

MAJOR GENERAL JAMES E. B. (JEB) STUART, C.S.A. (1833–1864)

of the outskirts of the Village of Sharpsburg they were met at this point by fresh troops just arriving from Harpers Ferry and thereby brought to a stand.[23] Had Burnside's advance occurred two hours earlier, it would seem that nothing could have saved the Army of Northern Virginia. They would have been cut in half by the interposition of Burnside's command between their right and left wings and their position would have been a desperate one and as it looks now, even hopeless. As it was the arrival of these troops from Harpers Ferry was only a temporary relief. McClellan had in reserve Porter's magnificent 5th Corps which could have been moved directly on Sharpsburg and most undoubtedly have utterly destroyed the Rebel centre, but it was the only reserve at hand, and he did not deem it proper to run the risk of losing all he had gained in the attempt to accomplish more. As it was, he had been successful, for the Rebel campaign was at an end. The Capitol was saved from capture without question and the moral condition of the two contending forces completely reversed.

Seventeen days earlier he had taken hold of a beaten, discouraged and disorganized force in full retreat before a rapidly advancing army flushed with victory. This force he had organized and equipped at the same time moving so as to keep them between the enemy and Washington. He had then thrown them against the invader in the full tide of his success and beaten him to a standstill. He might have accomplished far more and not improbably have brought the war to a successful issue then and there. Grant would probably have done so, but the risk was great and failure would very likely have been fatal. He pursued the course which to him seemed most judicious, and in the light of following events I believe most wisely. Had the Rebel army of Northern Virginia been destroyed in the Autumn of 1862, one of two events would in all probability have occurred; either of which would have resulted in great damage to our cause, and indeed to the interests of the whole human race:

1. The rebellious faction might have been overthrown from

[23] The troops just arriving from Harpers Ferry were under command of Major General Ambrose P. Hill, CSA.

179

within and the States of the Confederacy have voluntarily returned to their allegiance. Had they offered to do so, there was a powerful party in the North ready to receive them with open arms and practically without conditions. Slavery would have been accepted on the same footing that it had rested before the War. Mr. Lincoln himself had publicly proclaimed his desire and determination to save the Union with slavery or without, but at any rate to save it. This feeling obtained among the immense mass of the population and peace with honor would have been gladly hailed at that time, by all except the advanced Radicals. That this could have been a permanent peace we know now would have been impossible, but it did not appear so then. The Government had existed half Slave and half Free for many years, and might for many more. The War had begun to tell heavily on all classes and overtures from a beaten but still powerful enemy would have been cordially welcomed. That such a peace would have been more detrimental to the country than many years of war will scarcely, now, be denied by anyone. That it would have been broken by another and undoubtedly still more terrible conflict before many years cannot be reasonably doubted. From these disasters we were spared by a further prolongation of the war, which though terrible enough in the ruin and destruction it caused, settled forever the question as to the existence of human slavery on this Continent.

2. The Confederate Government might have abandoned Virginia and drawing its forces together in the interior, have carried on for many years a warfare more or less partisan in its nature, which would have caused infinitely more damage to our institutions, and tended more directly to retard the progress of the Race at large than any combination of circumstances that could have happened. The history of our own Central and South American Republics, is an object lesson in point and renders it entirely unnecessary to quote European precedents for this statement. That either of these two contingencies was influencing Gen. McClellan, I of course, do not mean to intimate. He was a soldier of the Government and as loyal to his trust as any man in the country, soldier or citizen. He be-

lieved that he would be risking the safety of the country by further movements at the time, and therefore he held his hand.

The two armies camped on the battle field and confronted each other the next day. The loss on either side was fearful. In scarcely any battle since has it been greater in proportion to the number engaged, for unlike most of the great battles of our war, it was fought entirely in the open, with no earth-works, or artificial defenses of any description. The Union Army had captured a few pieces of artillery and a few standards, and had gained a few miles of ground. But its great victory was in the complete and utter collapse of the invasion. That was at an end and the Rebels were once more thrown on the defensive. Both armies passed the day in recuperating from the strain of the previous day's conflict, attending to the wounded and burying the dead. I rode over a considerable portion of the field with other officers of my regiment, and even now after so many years, and after the experience of so many other desperate conflicts, can hardly think of the scene without horror. It was the only battle field I have ever seen, which actually I could not look at without being unmanned.

There were some very singular as well as dreadful sights. In one place I saw a soldier, apparently in the act of crossing a high rail fence (stake and rider fences, they are called in that country). His singular position and the fact that he did not move during the minutes I was approaching induced me to ride closer. Soon I found that he had been shot dead; his gun lay by the side of the fence; the bullet had struck him just as his body was at poise, and there he stayed motionless, until the burial parties found him many hours afterward. Many soldiers are probably still living, as I write, who can remember this incident.

Another, and more painful sight I saw the next day near the Dunkard Church. A soldier lay on his back by the side of the road within fifty yards of the Church, to all appearance, stone dead. In his hand was an empty can which had once held tomatoes, or fruit. As we rode up I saw the hand holding the can, gradually and slowly rise from the elbow until the forearm had reached a perpendicular position, and then as gradually and slowly fall to the ground. It was a sight to remember, when one thinks that that young boy had been lying there when I saw him nearly forty-eight hours. We were fortunately able to procure him attention very shortly, but the surgeon who came up told me that the poor fellow was practically dead, and in all probability had been completely unconscious since the bullet had pierced his brain two days before. Many wounded were still lying about the field at this time, owing to the fact that the pickets of both armies had occupied the ground until within a few hours, and no truce had been declared. The hospital corps were now at work however and it was but a short time before all were attended to.

On the morning of the 19th a strong cavalry column was sent out on the Shepherdstown road to envelop the enemy. My regiment happened to be in the advance and on approaching the ford across the Potomac, we were greeted by a tremendous cannonade, which compelled us to deploy to the right of the road. The country was very heavily timbered and the crash of the shells through the branches was terrific. Immense branches were constantly falling, and the horses were greatly excited. The reconnaissance soon developed the fact that the enemy were still in great force on the opposite side of the river. Eight batteries of about six guns each were soon in full play on their side, to which our one horse battery replied as well as it was able. It was evident however that it was quite out of the question for our small command to force a crossing, and the cavalry was accordingly withdrawn about noon.

In the evening Gen. FitzJohn Porter with the 5th Corps got control of some fords and threw a force across the river which early in the morning of the 20th attempted to advance.[24] Within a few

[24] It is obvious, of course, that Sanford is a McClellan man. This probably accounts for his light treatment of the fact that McClellan did not so much as stir after Lee subsequent to the events of 18 September. That night (18–19 September), Lee took his forces across the Potomac at Blackford's Ford, near Shepherdstown, West Virginia.

What Sanford is describing is a skirmish between Confederate and Union forces at the same ford (also known as Boteler's and Shepherdstown). The First Cavalry rode out with units of Brigadier General Alfred Pleasonton's Cavalry Division, Army of the Potomac. Attached were batteries of the U.S. Second Regiment of Artillery. Pleasonton reported that same day: "On arriving near the river on the turnpike,

miles of the Potomac they were met by an overwhelming force of the enemy and driven back across the river, losing quite heavily in the affair. For nearly two months after this action, the two armies lay opposite each other with the river between them, recuperating their strength for another trial.

Our camps were in the beautiful section of Maryland known as Pleasant Valley, and certainly no country could be more appropriately named. The climate was perfect, the camps clean and bright with good water and shade, and the country people friendly and hospitable. The difference between this part of the campaign and the dreadful experience on the Chickahominy and the James was very marked and will certainly never be forgotten by the participants. The troops generally were kept busy at drill, but the cavalry were fully occupied in picketing and scouting. Several sharp affairs occurred between our cavalry under Pleasonton and the Confederate cavalry under the famous leader Gen. J. E. B. Stuart, or "Jeb. Stuart" as he was generally called. This brilliant soldier was a graduate of the military academy at West Point, and had been a Lieutenant in our cavalry service up to 1861. He was of course well known to many of our officers, who had served with him on the Plains.[25]

About the First of October we had quite a lively action between the two opposing cavalry commands, in front of the village of Charlestown, Virginia.[26] As it was only intended as a reconnaissance, we returned to our camp in Pleasant Valley at its conclusion. About the same time or a little later, Gen. Stuart crossed the Po-

---

the enemy's batteries opened a heavy fire from several positions below Shepherdstown, covering Blackford's Ford. Gibson's, Tidball's, and Robertson's batteries replied with such effect that the enemy drew off the greater part of his guns. This cannonade lasted about two hours, when, a part of Porter's corps coming up, my command was relieved from this position, and withdrew to camp." *OR,* XIX Pt. 1, 212. See n. 2, Chap. IV.

[25] James Ewell Brown Stuart (b. 1833), USMA, Class of 1854, was commissioned a brevet second lieutenant, Regiment of Mounted Riflemen, 1 July 1854; promoted second lieutenant, 31 October 1854. He transferred to the First (Fourth) Regiment of Cavalry, 3 March 1855, when it was organized by Act of Congress. By 22 April 1861, Stuart was a captain, but he resigned the Army 14 May 1861.

[26] Sanford is referring to the reconnaissance from Bolivar Heights toward Charlestown, West Virginia (properly, Charles Town), on 6 October 1862.

tomac with a large body of cavalry, and passed entirely around our army, destroying a considerable amount of material and stores, and taking from the farmers a great number of horses with which to remount his cavalry. Our mounted force pursued him with great energy and overtook the rear guard just as it was re-crossing the Potomac, but was unable to bring him to bay.[27]

A good deal of dissatisfaction against McClellan resulted from this movement of Stuart's, and much unfavorable comment as to the apparent weakness of our cavalry force. The fact was that this arm of the service was not understood or well handled during the first two years of the war, and with the exception of the small body of regular cavalry it was almost entirely untrained. Gen. Scott had little confidence in its ability, or experience in handling it, and from the first had deprecated its use. Recognizing the great length of time required to train men and animals for this service and apparently believing that the war would be of but short duration, he considered it as on the whole advisable to confine its use within the smallest limits possible. He distributed the few volunteer regiments at first raised among the various infantry commands where they were used by the brigade commanders almost exclusively for orderly and escort duty. The small body of regulars with a few regiments of specially selected volunteers were brigaded, but even these troops were kept pretty well in reserve at army Headquarters. The campaign of the Peninsula, which was conducted principally in a densely wooded country, interspersed with swamps and deep sluggish streams, entirely unadapted to cavalry operations, tended still more to discourage its employment, and it was not until the Spring of 1863 when the necessity for a large and well trained mounted force had been long apparent, that Gen. Joseph Hooker,

---

[27] This was General Stuart's spectacular raid (reminiscent of his equally spectacular raids against Pope's Army of Virginia earlier that summer) to Chambersburg, Pennsylvania. At daylight on 10 October 1862, Stuart, with about 1,800 men and four guns, crossed the Potomac at McCoy's Ford (between Williamsport and Hancock), captured Chambersburg on the Cumberland Valley Railroad, and tried to destroy a bridge but could not because it was constructed of iron. McClellan was convinced that Stuart would never escape, but he did, avoiding Pleasonton's cavalry, and crossed the Potomac again at White's Ford on 12 October. He had with him some 1,200 Federal mounts and had lost two men POW and one man WIA.

then commanding the Army of the Potomac, was able to put in the field a splendid body of horsemen organized into two divisions and a strong reserve, all under one corps commander. From that time the history of the corps is brilliant in the extreme, and more than made up for the mortifications and discouragements of its early career.

After the fight at Charlestown in the early days of November,[28] my regiment procured a large accession of recruits from the volunteer service. The regular regiments were at this time extremely weak owing to the expiration of the term of service of the old soldiers and the great difficulty of re-enlisting the men. The sergeants and even the corporals as their terms expired took their discharges and went off to their homes where new regiments of volunteers were being raised, and where with their soldierly appearance, and the experience derived from their five or ten years' training in the cavalry service on the western plains, they were almost certain to get commissions as Lieutenants, almost for the asking. Even the private troopers from their knowledge of the drill and the excellent horsemanship they displayed were practically sure of warrants as sergeants and corporals. Of course in the end this worked well for the Government, as it distributed the traditions of soldiership and discipline so well imbued in the regulars throughout the mass, and undoubtedly contributed much more largely than has ever been acknowledged to the magnificent condition of the corps in later years. Its immediate effect however was to practically reduce the regular cavalry regiments to mere skeletons, and this evil Gen. McClellan with his usual foresight and exceptional talent for organization set himself to work to remedy. This he did by a general order issued from Headquarters of the Army of the natural ignorance as to the many little details of camp life, which was common to nearly all of the officers of the service at first, resulted in discomforts and even real hardships to the men of their commands, which familiarity with the customs of the service at length obviated.

All these matters were of course well managed in the ranks of

[28] This must be an error for October.

the regulars, where long habit had rendered the life so familiar that everything seemed to run without effort, and with the regularity of clock-work. The camps were well policed, the rations ample and well cooked, the clothing on hand where wanted and always properly fitted by the regimental tailors. These and many other matters, trifling in themselves, but which taken together make up the life of the soldier, and include the difference between what he regards as comfort and misery, were very apparent to the volunteers when camped in the vicinity of regular troops of any arm of the service. As a natural result, when the order was issued applicants swarmed into our camps.

My regiment at this time was attached to Gen. McClellan's Headquarters and had naturally a splendid opportunity to pick its men. I was assigned to the duty of recruiting officer by regimental order, and in the course of six weeks was able to fill up the ranks of the command with as fine a lot of soldiers as I have ever seen. As the candidates were so numerous, I took none but good horsemen and young fine looking men of American birth and ancestry as a rule, and who appeared to be of good character and habits. Nobly they did their duty for the next three years—though not many of them were left at the expiration of the time.

186

·CHAPTER IV·

Towards the last of the month the long looked for marching orders were received, and the movement into Virginia began.[1] The army was really at this time in high spirits. They had passed through a victorious campaign and had been reorganized and equipped while resting in a beautiful and healthy section of the country. All this tended to influence for good the morale of the army, and I have never seen it better than when the long columns crossed the river at Berlin and swung southward towards Richmond. The Rebel army was known to be on our right flank, in the Shenandoah Valley, with the long line of the Blue Ridge between us and them.

Pleasonton with the cavalry was watching the passes, and almost daily skirmishing with the Rebel horsemen under Stuart.[2] Our road was clear towards Richmond, for which we had the shorter line; or by turning sharply westward we had a good chance to cut the Rebel army in two and perhaps destroy a part of it before the remainder could come to its assistance. Certainly the chances never looked more favorable for a rapid and successful campaign and a

[1] On 26 October 1862 at Berlin, Maryland, the Army of the Potomac began crossing the Potomac River; by 2 November, the Army, less Major General Henry Slocum's Twelfth Corps, was across. The route lay south toward Warrenton, Virginia, on the east side of the Blue Ridge.

[2] Alfred Pleasonton (1824–1897), USMA, Class of 1844, commanded the Cavalry Division, Army of the Potomac. He had served in the Mexican War and was brevetted. In 1861, he was a captain in the Second Regiment of Dragoons. He was appointed brigadier general of volunteers on 16 July 1862; major general of volunteers, 22 June 1863. Nevertheless, his career was not successful, and when the U.S. Army was reorganized in 1866, his prospects did not satisfy him and he resigned in 1868. See n. 24, Chap. V.

sudden ending to the rebellion. That Gen. McClellan fully expected to beat Lee is certain, and also that the army had implicit confidence in his success; but we were doomed to a sudden and most unexpected disappointment. My regiment, as I have said, was still performing escort duty at McClellan's Headquarters, and we were camped in the immediate neighborhood of the Headquarters' tents.

On the 7th a light snow fell so that on the morning of the next day the ground was quite covered. Soon after reveille that morning and while expecting the order to move, an aide de camp brought the news that Gen. McClellan had been relieved, and ordered to his home, and that Burnside was to command the army. It was a wretched morning greeting, and a very miserable body of men who received it.[3]

Our camp at this time was at Rectortown, but the whole army was en route for Warrenton where McClellan's plan had been to concentrate it, with a view to battle. Gen. Burnside, who was now in command, carried out McClellan's purpose up to the time we reached Warrenton, but thereafter his movements were entirely different.[4] Gen. McClellan accompanied the army to Warrenton,

[3] On 5 November 1862, President Lincoln sent out the following order: "It is ordered that Major-General McClellan be relieved from the command of the Army of the Potomac, and that Major-General Burnside take the command of that army." The order further provided that General Fitz John Porter be relieved from command of his corps and replaced by Hooker. OR, XIX, Pt. 2, 545. Formal relief was accomplished on 7 November. Burnside was unwilling to accept the command, but did so anyway. Perhaps never was such an incompetent general officer placed in command of such a powerful force, now numbering approximately 142,000 men. Burnside had command of the Ninth Corps prior to his promotion. McClellan addressed his men on 7 November (Sanford is alluding to this): "I cannot express the love and gratitude I bear to you. As an army, you have grown up under my care. In you I have never found doubt or coldness. The battles you have fought under my command will proudly live in our nation's history." Ibid., 551.

[4] Organization as well as movements. On 10 November, Hooker replaced Porter in command of the Fifth Corps. Then, four days later, 14 November, the Army of the Potomac was organized into three grand divisions, each division possessing two corps of three divisions each, with artillery and cavalry brigade (or division). Major General Edwin V. Sumner (1797–1863) commanded the Right Grand Division; Major General Joseph Hooker, Center Grand Division; and Major General William B. Franklin, Left Grand Division. Sumner had been promoted brigadier general, 16 March 1861, in the Regular Army, vice Brigadier General Twiggs, dismissed 1 March 1861; see n. 11, Chap. I.

and there on the 10th took his leave of the organization he had built up and which he loved so well, and the next day returned to his home in Trenton, New Jersey. It was his last military command, and so his great qualities were lost to the cause. That he was a great soldier and a truly loyal patriot few will now deny, but at that time partisan feeling was bitter to a degree which seems almost beyond belief. That there were many men—and high in position too—who would far rather have seen the army defeated under another general than victorious under McClellan, many believed at the time and believe still. That the President himself meant fairly by him is doubtless true; but he was influenced by men whose motives were far different. Of the feeling of the army in the matter there can be no question; those who saw that leave taking will never forget it. Had Gen. McClellan been other than the noble gentleman and single hearted lover of his country than he was, there might and very likely would have been dreadful work in the next few days— horrors which one shudders to think of, and which would have changed the future of the world.

From Warrenton we turned to the south-east and moved down to the Rappahannock, reaching Falmouth opposite Fredericksburg on our arrival,[5] but it would have been easy enough to drive them away and take possession of Marye's Heights at that time. To be sure, the bridge had been destroyed, and, owing to some mistake or neglect which has never been explained, the pontoon train which was to have met us from Washington, failed to arrive until after Lee's whole army had reached the position and commenced fortifying Marye's Heights. It was one more blunder for which nobody seems to have been responsible. If Washington city had been one thousand miles off the Army of the Potomac would have got on better than it did, from the beginning to the end of the war. As it was, we lay in front of Fredericksburg for nearly a month and watched the rebels throw up their enormous works in plain view and almost within gun-shot. The city itself was only held by their pickets and a small body of sharpshooters.

[5] Sumner's Right Grand Division reached Falmouth on 17 November; by 20 November, the Army of the Potomac itself was in the vicinity of Fredericksburg.

Army Headquarters, to which my regiment was still attached, was encamped a short distance north west of the Phillips House. This fine mansion, afterwards accidentally destroyed by fire, was the Headquarters of Gen. E. V. Sumner, and commanded a magnificent view of the city and the Rebel lines.[6] I used to ride over there daily and watch the "Johnnies," as we called them, working on their fortifications, and wonder if it could be possible that we were to attack such a position. In reality, no one believed that we would do so. The expectation was that a demonstration would be made there, but the real attack would be on one of the flanks and in the nature of a surprise. However, on the 11th of December the engineers threw a pontoon bridge across the river directly opposite the city, losing very heavily in the operation, as also did the 19th and 20th Massachusetts and 7th Michigan regiments which covered the movement and drove off the Rebel sharpshooters.[7]

The next day was occupied in getting the army across both there and farther down the river, where the left wing under Gen. Franklin had thrown bridges across.[8] The usual skirmishing between the advanced parties was going on of course all the time, and prior to the capture of the city itself a tremendous bombardment occurred under the direction of Gen. Hunt, the Chief of Artillery.[9] About one hundred and fifty guns were in position along the left bank, firing on the city. At one time during the bombardment I was sent with a message which required me to pass along the line of these batteries. I was riding in company with Lieut. W. S. Worth, an

[6] First Regiment of Cavalry, Captain Marcus A. Reno, was assigned duty as escort, etc., to General Burnside. Sanford is confused about his houses. The Phillips House, a little over a mile east of the Rappahannock, was Burnside's headquarters. The Lacy House, much closer to the river, was Sumner's headquarters.

[7] Sanford is referring to the two pontoon bridges thrown across the river directly in front of Sumner's headquarters.

[8] Three bridges were constructed across the river for Franklin's Left Grand Division, also on 11 December.

[9] Henry Jackson Hunt (1819–1889), USMA, Class of 1839, two brevets in the Mexican War. At the outbreak of the war, Hunt was a captain (28 September 1852) in the Second Regiment of Artillery and had served as a member of the board (the others were Captain William F. Barry, Second Artillery, and Captain William H. French, First Artillery) which revised the Army's light artillery tactics. Hunt was appointed brigadier general of volunteers on 15 September 1862 after his service at Antietam.

aide de camp to Gen. Hunt, and as we were both of us well acquainted with many of the young officers of the artillery, we
stopped occasionally to speak to them and watch the effect of the
shots.[10] Directly in range of several of the batteries was a church
with a tall spire on which was a clock-dial. This was naturally an
irresistible object for some of the youngsters to aim at, when they
thought none of their superiors were especially on the lookout as
to what was going on. Worth and I were quite ready for any fun
that was going, and with two or three of our artillery friends were
in a wild state of excitement, and bets running high as to which
could put a shell through the clock face first, when we chanced to
look up, and there was Gen. Hunt glowering down on us. It didn't
take us very long to get on about our business, and we fully expected to hear from it later, but we never did. The old General was
as kindhearted a soul as ever lived and had been a boy himself
and had not forgotten it.[11]

On the 13th the attack in force took place.[12] French's division
and Hancock's supported by Howard's made the attempt early in
the day, all under the direction of General Couch.[13] Later they were
reenforced by the Grand Division of Gen. Joseph Hooker, and all
joined in the terrible conflict, while Franklin with the left wing
of the army was attacking lower down the river. Just as Hancock's
command was going into action I met that great soldier and had
the pleasure of a few kindly words from him. He had the royal
faculty (which Gen. McClellan possessed also and in a greater
degree than any man I ever knew) of never forgetting a face or a

[10] First Lieutenant William S. Worth, Eighth Regiment of Infantry; he had
been commissioned the same day as Sanford.

[11] General Hunt was precisely three months past his forty-third birthday.

[12] Opposing the Army of the Potomac was Lee's Army of Northern Virginia,
not quite 92,000 strong, organized in two corps commanded by Lieutenant Generals
James Longstreet and Thomas J. Jackson, as well as Stuart's cavalry and Brigadier
General William N. Pendleton's reserve artillery.

[13] A few words on the organization of Sumner's Right Grand Division. Major
General Darius N. Couch (1822–1897), USMA, Class of 1846, commanded the
Second Army Corps. His three division commanders were Brigadier General Win-
field S. Hancock (1824–1886), USMA, Class of 1844, First Division; Brigadier Gen-
eral Oliver O. Howard (1830–1909), USMA, Class of 1854, Second Division; and
Brigadier General William H. French (1815–1881), USMA, Class of 1837, Third
Division.

name. It was always a pleasure to carry a message to General Hancock, or even to meet him. You were sure of a pleasant greeting and kindly treatment. If any descendant of mine in the next century who comes across these lines should happen to have served as a Cavalry Aide de Camp, he will appreciate the full bearing of this remark. There are all kinds of Generals, as indeed there are of Aides de Camp, but the McClellan and Hancock type are not too numerous.

I have no intention of describing battles, and certainly not this one of Fredericksburg. It was a horrible business, relieved only by the wonderful gallantry of the men and officers. I think perhaps it was the most desperate piece of fighting in the war, as from the first men realized the utter futility of the attempt. It was simply to go up and be killed without even the hope that finally the position would be taken. My part in the battle was limited to that of a spectator, pretty much, save for some aide de camp work. There was no opportunity to use cavalry at all, and our part was simply to wait orders. Gen. Geo. D. Bayard commanding one of our brigades and one of the most promising young cavalry officers in the army, was killed by a shell. He was a Captain in the 4th Cavalry and Brig. Gen. of Vols.[14]

The Phillips House was used as Army Headquarters during the battle and was of course a most picturesque and interesting place. I was in and out of there every half hour or so, when not engaged in carrying despatches. Gen. Burnside and Gen. Sumner were together most of the time, and I well remember their anxious and excited manner about three o'clock in the afternoon of the 13th, when Hooker's Grand Division began crossing. Gen. Sumner was apparently intensely anxious to cross the river and join his own command, the Right Grand Division, which had been fighting all day under the immediate direction of Gen. Couch. Burnside, however, would not permit this, and I saw him run down the steps of the Phillips House, when Sumner, with the assistance of his

[14] George D. Bayard (1835–1862), USMA, Class of 1856, commanded the Cavalry Brigade in General Franklin's Left Grand Division. Bayard was appointed brigadier general of volunteers on 28 April 1862. He was wounded on 13 December and died the next day, four days before his twenty-seventh birthday.

orderly, was endeavoring to mount his horse, and say to him, "General, you will remember you are not to cross the river." I was sitting on the steps at the time, not three feet distant. Gen. Sumner was quite old, and feeble from illness, and it was understood that he should not take any active part; but he evidently was very restive under the restriction.

Gen. Hooker's manner was very different. He was frequently on the porch, and about the house during these terrible days, and his whole appearance and manner of talking indicated disapproval and almost insubordination. As is well known, Gen. Burnside issued an order after the battle, dismissing Hooker from the service, but it was not approved by the President, and Burnside on his own application was then relieved from the command. This however did not occur for some six weeks later than the time of which I am writing.

After Hooker's renewal of the attack on the evening of the 13th which was as unsuccessful as the previous ones of Couch and Franklin, the armies lay on the ground, living and dead together, all night.[15] It was bitterly cold of course, and many were frozen. All the next day, Sunday, and Monday the 15th the armies lay in the same position, but Monday night our forces recrossed without molestation from the enemy.[16] For a month nothing was done. Then about the 20th of January, Gen. Burnside attempted another movement toward his extreme right, intending to cross the river and turn Lee's left, but the weather had grown very warm and a tremendous rainfall had caused the very bottom to drop out of the roads. Wagons were mired down in every direction—batteries of artillery stuck in the mud, and the pontoon train, indispensable for bridging the river, could no more be moved than the pyramids

[15] Union losses in the battle were as follows: 1,284 KIA; 9,600 WIA; 1,769 MIA or POW; total; 12,653. *OR*, XXI, 142. Confederate losses are always a problem in accuracy. *Ibid.*, 562, reports a total of 4,201 casualties, yet another source suggests the total was 5,309, etc. Suffice to say, it was a bloody, vicious, unpleasant battle, and Sanford was lucky that the cavalry was out of it. To say that Burnside's generalship was inept is but to torture the English language.

[16] Yet this retreat across the river, during a storm, was so skillfully done—even the bridges were taken up and carried away—in the darkness that the Confederates did not know about it until the next day. The Army of the Potomac had escaped. It went into winter quarters on Stafford Heights.

of Egypt. The jovial Rebels on picket at the fords, seeing the plight we were in, kindly volunteered to "come over and help us." The conditions favorable to a surprise were evidently not present. Then the Army of the Potomac dragged itself back to its old camps.[17] Burnside was relieved and Hooker placed in command of the army.[18]

Our new commander took hold of the reins with a firm hand, and the army, if not united in believing his nomination to the position the best that could have been made, was at least ready and anxious to obey his orders, and to do its whole part in the solution of the problem all were called upon to face. Almost at once prospects seemed to brighten. Many changes were made in the Corps and Division commands and the Grand Division organization was broken up.[19] Good clean camps were selected for many of the brigades, and a thorough system of drill, inspection and review at once went into operation. The cavalry in particular which had been scattered among the different corps and divisions, neglected and overworked by useless picket and orderly duty, was organized into compact brigades and divisions, remounted and carefully drilled and equipped. That corps certainly owes to Gen. Hooker a debt of gratitude, which it would be difficult to repay. From the date of its reorganization by him until the close of the war, its career was constantly growing more and more glorious, until at the end of the rebellion nothing could stand before the rush of its squadrons. Maj. Gen. George Stoneman was placed in command

[17] This was the infamous "Mud March," 20–24 January 1863. The idea was to cross Rappahannock at Bank's Ford; this was reached, but a "violent rain-storm" on the night of the twentieth made everything impossible. Burnside's tenure of command was now short.

[18] On 26 January 1863, Major General Joseph Hooker, USA, superseded Major General Ambrose E. Burnside in command of the Army of the Potomac. Hooker made many changes in personnel, but the Burnside organization of the Army was short lived.

[19] On 5 February 1863, the grand divisions of the Army of the Potomac were abolished in favor of a corps arrangement: Major General John F. Reynolds, First Corps; Major General Darius N. Couch, Second; Major General Daniel E. Sickles, Third; Major General George G. Meade, Fifth; Major General John Sedgwick, Sixth; Major General William F. Smith, Ninth; Major General Franz Sigel, Eleventh; Major General Henry W. Slocum, Twelfth; and Brigadier General George Stoneman to command the Cavalry Corps.

194

of the corps; Gens. Pleasonton, Averell and D. McM. Gregg of the divisions.[20] The regular cavalry regiments 1st, 2nd, 5th and 6th, and the 6th Pennsylvania were organized into a Reserve under the gallant Gen. John Buford.[21] The months of January, February and a part of March were devoted to constant and careful drill, and the improvement in the appearance and feeling of the troops was manifest to all.

Early in March Hooker determined to beat up the quarters of the enemy for the purpose of finding out what he was doing and for this purpose sent Averell with his own division and the reserve cavalry brigade on an expedition up the river.[22] We crossed the Rappahannock at Kelly's Ford on the morning of the 17th of March, the 1st Rhode Island cavalry carrying the crossing in a very gallant manner, and capturing a number of prisoners. The Rebel cavalry was encountered drawn up in line of battle about two miles back from the river, and the action at once began. The Rebels were commanded by Gen. Stuart and fought gallantly as usual, but were steadily driven back.[23]

Several gallant charges were made in which my regiment took

[20] William W. Averell (1832–1900), USMA, Class of 1855, served in the West with the Regiment of Mounted Riflemen and was wounded in 1858. He had service as colonel, Third Pennsylvania Cavalry, before he was appointed brigadier general of volunteers on 26 September 1862. Shortly after the war was over, Averell resigned the Army.

David McM. Gregg (1833–1916), USMA, Class of 1855, a classmate of Averell, was commissioned a brevet second lieutenant in the First Regiment of Dragoons, an outfit he served with until the war. He had service as colonel, Eighth Pennsylvania Cavalry. His brigadier generalcy came on 29 November 1862. After a most capable and distinguished record in action, Gregg inexplicably resigned the Army on 3 February 1865.

For Stoneman, see n. 27, Chap. II; for Pleasonton, n. 2, *supra*.

[21] The official title given Buford's outfit was the Regular Reserve Cavalry Brigade.

[22] Units involved include Colonel Alfred N. Duffie's First Brigade, Averell's Division (Fourth New York, Sixth Ohio, and First Rhode Island), Colonel John B. McIntosh's Second Brigade (Third Pennsylvania, Fourth Pennsylvania, and Sixteenth Pennsylvania), and Captain Reno's group from the Reserve Brigade (First and Fifth Regiments of Cavalry). Artillery was the New York Light, Sixth Battery.

[23] Field commander of the Confederates at Kelly's Ford was Brigadier General Fitzhugh Lee, CSA, commanding the Cavalry Brigade, Army of Northern Virginia. Units included the First, Second, Third, Fourth, and Fifth Regiments, Virginia, Cavalry, plus a battery. General Stuart was present on the field, but as an adviser; Fitz Lee ran the show. Averell and Lee were personal friends, had been since West Point days.

195

part, resulting in the withdrawal of the enemy's force to a position some miles back from the river, where an enemy command was encamped. Gen. Averell about this time gave me a personal order to support Capt. Bramhall's battery of the 6th N.Y. Artillery which was threatened by a considerable Rebel force of cavalry, and was at the same time engaged in a hot artillery duel with a battery of the enemy.[24] By careful manoeuvres of my squadron, the demonstration of the enemy was foiled, and I succeeded in bringing off the battery entire. Averell and his Adjutant General, Maj. Rumsey, were kind enough to both compliment me on my success in this rather delicate operation. Having fully accomplished the object for which we were sent across the river, we withdrew without difficulty and returned to our camps.[25] Shortly after this expedition, President Lincoln visited the army and spent some days in consultation with his officers.[26] A grand review was ordered for his benefit, and I well remember it as one of the most magnificent spectacles of the war. The President appeared on horseback, attended by Gen. Hooker and a brilliant staff. Mr. Lincoln wore his customary dress —black frock coat with quite long tails which flapped behind him as he passed at a gallop—black trousers and high silk hat. He rode with very long stirrups, and had an excellent seat in the saddle, though his tall, gaunt figure, and odd costume gave him a singular appearance. What he thought of the army I have never heard, but General Couch tells me an interesting anecdote showing the far reaching grasp of his mind. As Couch's corps were passing in review, he turned to that General and said, "What do you suppose is going to become of all those men when the war is over?" Gen. Couch remarks that it seemed quite encouraging to him that some one in authority believed that the war would "be over" at some

24 Walter M. Bramhall, Sixth Independent Battery, Light Artillery (Veteran), had enrolled 15 June 1861 to serve three years; however, he resigned 16 February 1863.

25 Both sides claim victory. Union losses amounted to six KIA, 50 WIA, and 22 MIA. Confederate losses were 11 KIA, 88 WIA, and 34 POW. Interesting are the figures given by Lee on his horses: 71 killed, twelve captured, and eighty-seven wounded. Such statistics were usually not kept by Northern cavalry officers. They give a brief glimpse into the daily life of a cavalryman. Lee had been knocked about —the first time Union cavalry could make such a claim—and departed the field.

26 Lincoln had departed Washington on 4 April to visit Hooker's headquarters at Falmouth.

196

time or other. It did not so seem to many of us, I know, from personal experience.

From this time up to the middle of April, the cavalry were occupied in preparing for the Spring campaign, which opened as far as we were concerned, on the 13th of April. We then abandoned our winter camp near Falmouth, Va., and moved up the Rappahannock toward Kelly's Ford.[27] On the 14th we made a demonstration in front of that ford, for the purpose of drawing the attention of the enemy to that point. This operation was under the direction of Gen. John Buford, commanding the Reserve Brigade, and was completely successful, as was the case with all matters confided to that distinguished officer. The enemy who were watching the various fords on the river, were all massed at this place, and the fords above laid open to the occupation of the troops under Gen. Averell, which were sent to take possession of them. We remained in front of the ford all day, skirmishing with the enemy, and occasionally engaging in an artillery duel.[28]

From the 15th to the 29th we manoeuvred along the river, the brigade engaging in several small affairs with the enemy, and experiencing a great deal of discomfort from the weather. The rain fell almost constantly during the whole time and the country was like a sea.[29] We marched all day in the rain and lay down at night in the mud in our wet clothes, often unable to get even a cup of coffee owing to the impossibility of making fires with the wet wood. In fact from the 15th of April until the 8th of May I doubt whether my clothes were ever dry, and this exposure added to the dreadful

[27] On 13 April, Stoneman took his force of approximately 9,900 men, four horse artillery batteries (22 three-inch rifled guns), plus wagons and pack mules from winter quarters. "The main object of the expedition was to cross the Rappahannock at or above the railroad bridges at Rappahannock Station, and, avoiding any large infantry commands, make its way to some point near Saxton's Junction, on the Pamunkey River, to cut off all communication between the rebel Army of Northern Virginia and Richmond, by destroying telegraphs, railroad bridges, and culverts, and tearing up the track." *OR*, XXV, Pt. 1, 1068.

[28] On 14 April, Stoneman made demonstrations (feints at crossing the river) at Beverly Ford, Kelly's Ford, and the railroad bridge in the area. The Confederates were commanded by Brigadier General William Henry Fitzhugh "Rooney" Lee, CSA, the general's second son.

[29] Clarification is needed here. During the night of 14 April, a severe rainstorm, to endure for close to thirty-six hours, hit the area and so flooded the Rappahannock that Stoneman could not get across. In fact, he did not cross for two weeks.

malarial poisoning of the Chickahominy swamps in the previous summer, told on me very seriously soon after, as will be seen.

On the 29th of April the Reserve Brigade crossed the Rappahannock at Kelly's Ford in advance of the Cavalry Corps and the Stoneman Raid began.[30] My squadron, consisting of my own troop and Lieut. Hunt's,[31] had the advance of the brigade, and just after dark in the evening, struck the enemy's pickets near Stevensburg. Their challenge and my reply of "Friends to the Union" was followed by a volley which lit up the road, at that point passing through dense woods. I ordered a charge at once, and dashed through the slight obstructions they had placed across the road, driving them out of sight and off the road.[32] We captured a few prisoners of the 5th Va. Cavalry, and found that they had been looking for a column of their own cavalry to approach in that direction which led to a slight hesitation on their part, and probably saved us from heavy loss. At all events we were on them before they had a chance to make up their minds. We went into camp at this point, the pickets repulsing an attempt made by the enemy later in the evening to regain the position. The next day we advanced to the Rapidan and crossed at Morton's Ford, capturing an officer and troop of cavalry.[33] Reconnaissances were sent up and down the river, and considerable skirmishing took place.

On this day our supply train was sent to join Gen. Slocum's infantry division, to be guarded by that command until we rejoined the army. We were allowed only to take such provisions as the men

[30] "The [Calvary] Corps did not reach the river until near 8 a. m. on the 29th. Arriving at the river, we found but one ford within the limits prescribed in our instructions which could be passed over, and that not by pack-mules or artillery. By dint of great exertion we succeeded in getting all over the river by 5 p. m." Stoneman's report of the raid, dated 13 May 1863, *OR,* XXV, Pt. 1, 1058.

[31] First Lieutenant James C. Hunt, First Regiment of Cavalry.

[32] This occurred about four miles beyond the crossing at Kelly's Ford. Once across the river, Stoneman divided his force. Averell, with his division, the Second, Davis' First Brigade (Pleasonton's Division), and Captain John C. Tidball's Battery A, Second Artillery, was to push toward Culpeper Court House. Stoneman, with Gregg's Third Division, Buford's Reserve Brigade, and artillery under Captain James M. Robertson, was to head for Stevensburg.

[33] Buford's Brigade had first attempted a crossing at Mitchell's Ford, but it was found "impracticable." The main body of Stoneman's cavalry crossed at Raccoon Ford.

could carry on their horses for themselves, and to the officers of each squadron was allowed one pack mule to carry their food and a suit of extra clothing and blankets. Through some carelessness my pack mule went off with the supply train, so that during the remainder of the expedition I had to depend on charity for supplies. However, I got on well enough as far as food was concerned, but I missed a change of clothing greatly. Unfortunately I had placed my overcoat on the pack mule, not wishing to burden my horse unnecessarily, so that I had nothing to resist the weather except my light cavalry jacket and trousers, to ride in by day, and not even a blanket when I lay down at night. As it turned out, we didn't lie down very much on this trip, so it didn't matter a great deal.

My orderly at this time was a young trumpeter named John Powers, who was attached to me closely for the next ten years, and for whom I grew to have a great respect. This boy could not have been more than fourteen years old when he joined me at Camp Allen from Carlisle Barracks. Although rated as a trumpeter he was never able to sound the calls, but made up for his deficiency by his usefulness in other respects. He was the best "forager" I have ever seen, and no matter how short the supplies were, his horse and mine were pretty sure to have plenty, and his saddle bags always contained a supply of corn pone and fried chicken. He was so small for his age that during his first year of service he was unable to mount from the ground, but would climb up the side of his horse like a cat. He rode a pony for the first few months, but in one of the cavalry fights after Gettysburg the poor brute was struck in the belly by a bursting shell and absolutely disembowelled. The same projectile badly wounded the boy in the leg, and feeling the pain and seeing the horse's entrails hanging down, he cried out that he was shot through the bowels. Some of the men, who were all very fond of him, took him off his horse, and he was sent to hospital, where he soon recovered, but he had to submit to a good deal of chaff for a long time afterwards. There never was a braver little fellow in the service, and the men were all proud of him; but they had to have their fun.

After crossing the Rapidan, the command was divided into numerous detachments which were sent in various directions. My regiment with the Reserve Brigade camped on the south side of the North Anna river on the 1st of May, and on the next morning dashed into Louisa Court House on the Virginia Central Railroad, and proceeded to destroy the track.[34] Gregg's Division were engaged in the same work and met with some resistance from the enemy, one of his regiments, the 1st Maine Cavalry, losing twenty-five or thirty men.[35] Captain Lord with the 1st Cavalry was then sent to Tolersville, and from there to Frederickshall Station, with instructions to destroy as much track as possible.[36] At the latter point a large tobacco warehouse was destroyed, and the men were allowed to help themselves to all the tobacco they wanted. We also burned Carr's bridge over the North Anna river, driving off the enemy's guard at that point, and capturing several prisoners.[37] Thence we pushed on to Thompson's Crossroads, on the South Anna, where we found Gen. Stoneman and a portion of the command. Shortly before reaching this point the 5th U.S. Cavalry was attacked by a brigade under Gen. Fitzhugh Lee, who was formerly a Lieutenant in that regiment. Captain Harrison, commanding the 5th, made a gallant defense, and succeeded in saving his command, though he lost two officers and about thirty-five men.[38] Two brigades under Gen. Kilpatrick and Col. Davis were sent from here towards Richmond by different routes. Both rode

[34] In all, some eighteen miles of track, etc., were devastated.

[35] Captain Benjamin F. Tucker, First Maine Cavalry, of Colonel Judson Kilpatrick's First Brigade.

[36] Richard S. C. Lord, USMA, Class of 1856, Fitzhugh Lee's class. Lord had been a captain since 26 October 1861. He died in 1866; he was thirty-four. Fredericks Hall was about twelve miles from Louisa Court House.

[37] Carr's Bridge was important. It was on "the main road leading from Spottsylvania to Goochland, on the James River, and is one of the principal highways." OR, XXV, Pt. 1, 1060.

[38] James E. Harrison had been in the cavalry since 1856. His force numbered less than 100—a most determined stand! Harrison was dead by late 1867. Lieutenant Wesley Owens, USMA, Class of 1856, who really had a singularly mediocre record in the war, was captured in this engagement. He, too, died in 1867. Temple Buford, a recently commissioned second lieutenant, was also captured. He was out of the Army by 1864.

Sanford is confused regarding which Lee was in command of the Confederates. At Shannon's Cross Roads, Brigadier General Rooney Lee was in charge.

around that city creating much excitement, and doing considerable damage. They eventually reached our lines on the Peninsula near Yorktown. On the 5th the whole command was united at Yanceyville on the South Anna, with the exception of the commands of Kilpatrick and Davis, which were not expected to return.

Gen. Stoneman now had reason to expect information and orders from Gen. Hooker and the Army of the Potomac.[39] We knew that they had probably been engaged all this time in a great battle, and that if they had been successful we should have begun to see or hear something of the retreating Rebels. In fact, the General's instructions had said plainly that in six days from the time we started, we would be in communication with the main body. On the contrary, we saw nothing of our own people, but in every direction that we turned, we came across parties of the enemy. We were entirely out of rations and had been living on the country for some days. Of course this means of supply was too uncertain to depend on much longer, and in addition both men and horses were nearly exhausted by the incessant work. Consequently the General determined to move back toward the Rappahannock and endeavor to open up communication with the Army. To do this, he knew would be much more difficult than it had been to penetrate the enemy's lines in the first place. They had been watching our movements for a whole week, and been gathering their forces together to overwhelm us on our return. In addition, though luckily we did not know it, Hooker's army had been out-manoeuvred and repulsed, and were now back in their old camps on the north side of the river.

It seems now as if there should have been no escape for our little force, which by casualties and detachments was now reduced to about two thousand men. In order to deceive the enemy and throw them off the scent, if possible, Stoneman ordered Gen. Buford to take a picked force, composed of the best men and horses from his

[39] Three months after relieving Burnside, during which the Army of the Potomac was stationary, General Hooker got it marching again on 27 April, concentrated it at Chancellorsville on 30 April to the rear of Lee's army. This is the Chancellorsville Campaign, 2–4 May, when Lee, with a little more than 60,000 men, defeated Hooker's army of more than 133,000. Casualties for both sides totaled 30,000.

Stoneman's absence from the Army of the Potomac—he was its "eyes"—is regarded as a contributing factor in the Federal defeat.

201

brigade, and move straight for Gordonsville on the Virginia Central R.R. It was known that this point was garrisoned by a large force of Rebel infantry, and as it was a very important point, it was taken for granted that if it was threatened the enemy would concentrate all his available cavalry in that neighborhood. This would give Gen. Stoneman and our main body an opportunity to push straight for the Rapidan, and if that stream was fordable to cross it and make for the Rappahannock. In the meantime, Buford was to depend on his own skill and address to slip through the enemy and get back to the command.

It was a forlorn hope, but it was the only thing left us, and Buford was the man of all others to be entrusted with such an undertaking. He accordingly selected about six hundred and fifty of his best mounted men, and officers, and leaving the rest with the main body, we started early on the 5th for Gordonsville.[40] At Louisa Court House we found the enemy had replaced the telegraph wires which we had destroyed some days before. These were again destroyed, the post office was seized and some valuable information obtained. We then marched rapidly down the railroad toward Gordonsville, reaching Trevilian Station, which we captured, about night fall. Here a large amount of arms, ammunition and rations were destroyed, the railroad torn up and the water tanks burned. When within two miles of Gordonsville, we found a large force of infantry and artillery in our front, and it looked very much as if our time had come. I little thought then that thirteen months later I was to be engaged in a terrible battle at this very spot, but so it was.

Fortunately for us the night was intensely dark, and the rain as usual falling heavily. Orders were issued to preserve perfect quiet, no pipes were to be lit, and no loud talking permitted. Then we left the road, and turned north through the fields, passing within a few hundred yards of the Rebel camp fires. They never suspected our presence apparently, and about daylight we struck the North

[40] "At Flemmings' Cross-Roads [Shannon's] all of the strong horses of the brigade were selected, 646 in number, and the command started to Gordonsville." Buford's report, dated 15 May 1863, *OR,* XXV, Pt. 1, 1089.

Anna river.[41] It was very high, and we were obliged to swim our horses. The rear guard found even that impossible on account of the rapidity of the current, but rafts were built, and all got safely across.[42] About two o'clock the next morning (the 7th) we reached the Rapidan and joining Stoneman's column we crossed that stream by daylight of the 7th.[43] The rain still continued and the men were so worn out with cold, hunger and fatigue that it was almost impossible to keep them in the ranks. Whole regiments moved along sound asleep on their horses. Time and again I saw men swept from their horses by low branches of trees, which the horses walked under while their riders were asleep. In fact this very thing happened in my own case and in addition I got a severe wound which nearly put out my eye, from the projecting limb of a tree.

On the 7th we began to get the news from the country people of the defeat of Gen. Hooker at Chancellorsville, and the retreat of our Army. It looked then as if we would certainly be unable to cross the Rappahannock. In the condition both men and horses were in, we could have scarcely resisted an energetic attack, but there was no grumbling or discontent, and I am satisfied that we should have been a hard mouthful to digest. Some time in the night of the 7th we reached Kelly's Ford on the Rappahannock and found it "*swimming*" and the current very swift. Of course nothing could be done until daylight, so we stood to horse all night, and with the first streak of dawn, began the really perilous passage. Few doubted that with the rising of the sun, Stuart with his horsemen would be upon us in force, and every precaution was taken to guard against surprise. No attack was made, however, and as we ascertained later, the enemy were quite as badly used up as we were. Our erratic movements had puzzled them, and kept their columns

[41] The north side of the North Anna River, near Orange Springs.

[42] "The water in the North Anna was rising fast when the head of the column struck it, and before the rear of my short column passed it was swimming. The rear guard found it impassable, and crossed it on rafts," Buford's report, *loc. cit.*

[43] Over Raccoon Ford; Buford's Brigade was across the Rapidan by 4 A.M. "The men had been almost constantly in the saddle for two nights and a day, and we were all wet, cold, tired, and hungry. The horses were unsaddled and fed with what little forage we had on hand; the men permitted to build fires and cook whatever meat and meal they might still possess, and to rest until 10 a. m., when we again started for Kelly's Ford." Stoneman's report, *ibid.,* 1063.

hurrying from point to point so that what with the fatigue and the dreadful condition of the roads, and the weather, they failed to appear as soon as we expected. Most of the horses swam well, and carried their riders safely over. A few were carried away by the stream, and swept down the river, but were nearly all rescued by men posted below on good horses. Finally only one man and six horses were drowned in the passage. A raft was improvised for the ammunition and the guns were absolutely hauled through under water by their own teams, swimming ahead of them. This sounds like a "tale for the marines," but it is a fact, as many witnesses can affirm. Of course it is not probable that all the horses were swimming at one time for any great distance; but certainly all had to swim, or drown.[44]

That night we moved to Bealeton Station on the Orange & Alexandria Railroad where we got forage for the horses and rations for the men. Then we settled down to the routine work of picket and escort duty for the next three weeks, and attempted to get our horses into condition for the campaign which we knew would shortly recommence. Our loss in horses on the Stoneman raid was terrible.[45] In no other expedition during the war was it as great, and this was owing primarily to bad management on the part of men and officers. This may seem a strong statement after what I have said in reference to the weather, the condition of the roads and the incessant marching required; but it is based on the experience gained in later years, and I am satisfied that it is quite within bounds. The fact is that from the commanding general down, we were all new at the business of "raiding" and in consequence made

[44] General Stoneman estimated that the command had to swim about twenty yards, a "cheering fact" to him. The crossing occupied most of the day, 8 May.

[45] Pleasonton, who was at Chancellorsville during the raid, estimated a loss of 8,000 mounts! This seems high. However, Buford's brigade alone abandoned 365 horses, and most horses abandoned were killed. Lieutenant Colonel Charles G. Sawtelle, USA, chief quartermaster, Cavalry Corps, estimated the loss at 1,000 from abandonment. The raid accomplished little of military importance. In his report of 13 May, Stoneman argued: "Not one of the least valuable among other results of this expedition is the influence it has had upon the cavalry arm of the service, both in showing us what we are able to accomplish if we but have the opportunity and in convincing the country that it has not spent its men and money in vain in our organization." *OR*, XXV, Pt. 1, 1064.

many errors, which were subsequently corrected. The principal fault committed was in the treatment of the animals when not marching. Gen. Stoneman evidently considered that as we were far within the enemy's lines and entirely cut off from all assistance from our own army, that it was necessary to remain in constant readiness to meet attack, and therefore kept the horses saddled night and day, and the men under arms during the whole expedition almost. In fact we may be said never to have "camped" during the whole time that we were south of the Rappahannock river. When not marching the whole command was practically on picket, expecting an attack every moment. The result of course was broken down horses and exhausted men.[46] By a proper system of patrols and outposts, the command would have been actually safer than it was in the way it was managed, and all the horses not actually on duty would have been resting or grazing and recruiting their energies, and the men would have obtained their natural sleep, instead of dozing on their horses, and by that means still more contributing to the injury of their [the horses'] backs, already in a dreadful condition from being kept under the saddle for such a length of time.

My own mount during this raid was a very beautiful chestnut stallion—"Prince." I bought him in 1862 from Captain McKee of my regiment, and rode him until the end of the war, and never had a finer charger.[47] He was of Morgan blood and like all of that stock a smooth and quick walker and trotter. His one blemish was a trick that he had at times of getting sulky under fire, and refusing to move. This was awkward at times, and on one occasion, as will be seen later, decidedly dangerous. However, it only happened occasionally, and his merits in other respects were so great that I was obliged to overlook it. He was a great favorite in the regiment, and for that matter was known throughout the brigade.

---

[46] Discussing the condition of the horses, Lieutenant Colonel Sawtelle said on 26 May that, since the raid, many of the animals had suffered from "a disease known as 'mud-fever,' and a very large proportion have sore backs." He agreed with Sanford that one cause was defective McClellan saddles, "being made too narrow across the withers of the horse." *Ibid.*, 1069.

[47] For McKee, see n. 4, Chap. II.

Even the enemy came to know Prince, and contributed their meed of admiration. At a later date than the time of which I am now speaking, my regiment was entrusted for some months with the duty of picketing a long stretch of the river, where the ground for some distance was perfectly level. The opposite bank was occupied by a division of the enemy, regularly in camp with earthworks, abatis, &c. No picket firing, of course, was expected, as our outposts were within one hundred yards of each other, and it would have been simply murder. I used to trot down this long stretch and the "Johnnies" would collect on the bank on their side, which overlooked ours greatly, and call to me to "let the little fellow out" and applaud his performance heartily. Prince seemed to thoroughly appreciate this, and I have never known him to do finer work than along that piece of land by Corbin's Neck on the Rapidan river.

During the latter part of May and early in June I experienced a severe attack of chills and fever. The doctors succeeded in breaking up the chills, but a low fever continued which they could do nothing to abate. I struggled against it with all my might for I could not bear to give up at what I felt sure was the beginning of a very active campaign. But resistance was of no use, and early in June I was sent to hospital in Washington. The surgeons there diagnosed my case as one of typho-malaria, and evidently thought that there was little chance of my recovery. At all events, they concluded my only opportunity would be from that afforded by home care and nursing, and accordingly packed me off to New Haven. By this time I was really more dead than alive, and have no recollection of the journey until I found myself driving up to my own door. Just before reaching the house, I saw my mother and my cousin Helen McGregor, now the wife of Gen. N. B. Sweitzer of the army,[48] and stopped the carriage. I can remember the terror depicted in my mother's face when she saw me, and the exclamation of my cousin. From that time on I have no recollection of anything, but wild nightmare-like dreams for an indefinite period. I know, however, that for days and weeks I lay at the very verge of the grave, and that under Providence, I owe my life to the unremitting care and

[48] See n. 4, Chap. V, for Sweitzer.

206

skill of my cousin, Dr. Leonard J. Sanford, and the patient nursing of my mother and eldest sister.[49] During this terrible illness, my regiment was engaged in the glorious Gettysburg campaign, and as always, behaved with distinguished gallantry. I was detailed as soon as I was able to walk out, to report to Gen. Lewis Cass Hunt, commanding the Draft Rendezvous at New Haven as Aide de Camp; but I prevailed on this officer to let me attempt to join my regiment, though greatly against his judgment.[50] However, I succeeded in getting permission to join, and found the brigade at Camp Buford on the Potomac river, a few miles below the City of Washington, where they were being remounted and equipped.[51]

[49] A physician highly esteemed in New Haven, Connecticut, in later years of the nineteenth century. See Rollin G. Osterweis, *Three Centuries of New Haven 1638–1938*, 342. He was born in 1833, was graduated from Jefferson Medical College in Philadelphia, and in 1863 was appointed professor of anatomy and physiology in Yale, a post he was to hold for the remainder of his life.

[50] Lewis Cass Hunt (1824–1886), USMA, Class of 1847, had served in the Mexican War and was a captain in the 4th Regiment of Infantry on the eve of the war. He was wounded seriously at Seven Pines in 1862; on 29 November 1862, he was appointed brigadier general of volunteers. When Sanford reported to him, Hunt held the permanent rank of major, Fourteenth Regiment of Infantry, dated 8 June 1863.

[51] The Reserve Brigade was at the Cavalry Depot from 12 August to 11 October 1863.

·CHAPTER V·

The City of Washington in September, 1863, was a very remarkable place, and in all probability its like will never be seen again within the limits of the United States. To begin with, it was a fortress, and a very strong one. Entirely surrounding the city was a chain of forts, connected by lines of earthworks mounted with the most powerful guns at that time in use. A strong permanent garrison with a completely equipped train of artillery, the proper proportion of cavalry and an efficient working staff, constituted in itself quite a formidable army, always in readiness to man the works, or if necessary to take the field. The streets were swarming with officers and soldiers, the hotels were crowded day and night, the theatres reaped a golden harvest, and money, in the form of "greenbacks," as the treasury notes were called, seemed to be a drug in the market. Congress was practically in permanent session, and the galleries were constantly filled by soldiers from all parts of the country, attracted by the—to them—novel proceedings.

The City itself was in a transition state from its overgrown Southern village condition of 1860 to the beautiful capital of twenty years later. The streets, now so beautifully paved with asphalt, were then quagmires of the most frightful description. I have actually seen army wagons mired down and abandoned on Pennsylvania Avenue, near Willard's Hotel. I have seen regiments of cavalry ploughing through the mud near the present site of the British Embassy on Connecticut Avenue with the mud up to the horses' hocks. In summer great clouds of dust filled the air, and the heat was almost insupportable.

No one seeing the city for the first time now, can imagine the fearful condition of things existing then. Willard's Hotel and the Ebbitt House were the great centres of attraction, and from dawn to midnight were filled with a restless, whirling crowd of officers, contractors, politicians and curiosity seekers from every country on the face of the globe.[1] Other hotels there were in numbers too great to mention, but those two were preeminently "Headquarters" —the former for the citizen element, the latter for the Army and Navy and out of one, into the other and back again, the crowd seemed to gravitate day and night. It was bedlam and pandemonium rolled together. Business or curiosity took me over to the City occasionally during our few weeks' stay at Camp Buford, but I was always glad when I could get away from it and across the Eastern Branch and back to our quiet camp under the beautiful trees near the river.

My first independent command of a body of troops larger than a squadron occurred about this time. A large herd of beef cattle and a heavy train of supplies was ordered through to the army which was at this time lying in the vicinity of Warrenton Junction and along the Rappahannock. A detail of one or two squadrons from each of the five regiments in the Reserve Brigade was ordered to escort them, and I was selected by our new Brigadier (Gen. Wesley Merritt) to command them. Merritt was a captain in the 2nd Cavalry, who had just been appointed Brig. General, and assigned to the brigade vice the gallant Buford who took command of the 1st Division of Cavalry in which from this time on our brigade was included.[2] I was not a little proud of this duty, though

[1] The Willard Hotel was at Fourteenth Street.

[2] Wesley Merritt (1834–1910), USMA, Class of 1860, was commissioned a brevet second lieutenant in the Second Regiment of Dragoons on 1 July 1860. He had been appointed brigadier general of volunteers on 29 June 1863 and had served at Gettysburg. He will figure strongly in the narrative now that he has been introduced. His postwar career was most successful, and when he was retired in 1900, he was a major general, having served on command levels in the West, in departments, as superintendent, USMA, and in the Philippines during the Spanish-American War. See p. 225.

a good deal frightened at the responsibility so suddenly placed upon me. It was no holiday business by any means. The ubiquitous Mosby with his band of partisan rangers kept the whole country between the army and Washington in a state of terror, and it was on his account that so strong a guard was necessary.[3] We made the march, however, in perfect safety, owing, I have no doubt, to the excellent officers in my command, and the thorough discipline and good conduct of the troops. Mosby's men, who half the time wore our uniform and were constantly in our camps, and about them, kept him informed as to the character and disposition of the forces in his neighborhood. If they were careless, indifferent, negligent in the performance of guard duty, or straggling about the country on private foraging expeditions, he was down on them like a whirlwind; but a command which attended to business was pretty apt to be let alone. The fact was there was plenty of plunder to be had without the trouble of fighting for it, and though he and his men were quite ready to fight when it was necessary, they were by no means foolish enough to run their heads against stone walls, without an object.

After turning over my convoy to the proper officers at Headquarters, I returned with my command to Camp Buford, and reported to my regiment for duty. We were actively engaged for the next few weeks remounting and reorganizing the regiment, which had become greatly depleted in horses and men by the casualties of the late campaign. Captain N. B. Sweitzer of our regiment, who had been for the two preceding years Lt. Col. and A.D.C. to Maj. Gen. McClellan, at this time joined and took command.[4] He was

3 Mosby will be treated later; see pp. 260 ff.

4 Nelson B. Sweitzer (1829–1898), USMA, Class of 1853—other members were Sheridan, McPherson, Sill, and Schofield—was commissioned a brevet second lieutenant in the Second Regiment of Dragoons and 1 July 1853; on 7 May 1861, he was promoted captain in the First Regiment of Dragoons. His service as aide-de-camp extended from 2 October 1861 to 31 March 1863. He was one of McClellan's favorite aides and was usually selected by McClellan when "hard riding was required." His record during the war brought him five brevets. He was appointed colonel, Sixteenth New York Cavalry, on 12 November 1864 and served in this capacity until 17 August 1865. Sweitzer retired as colonel, Second Regiment of Cavalry, in 1888. Elsewhere (*cf.* p. 206), Sanford refers to Sweitzer as "general"; this was brevet brigadier general, to date from 13 March 1865.

an officer of much intelligence, and great promise, but owing to his intimate connection with Gen. McClellan had fallen into great disfavor at the War Department, and more especially with the all-powerful Secretary—Edwin M. Stanton. Repeated offers of colonelcies were made to him, by the Governors of States, as his capacity was widely known, but Mr. Stanton would never authorize his appointment. In fact it was not until just before the close of the Rebellion that he was allowed to accept the colonelcy of the 16th New York Cavalry—too late to accomplish anything of importance for his own promotion, though it is true that a detachment from his command succeeded in bringing to bay and killing John Wilkes Booth, the assassin of President Lincoln. Sweitzer soon brought our regiment into fine shape. A capital mount was secured, each battalion of four troops receiving horses of one color. One battalion was bay, one black, and one chestnut. The trumpeters and band rode grey horses and made a fine appearance, though I am utterly opposed to the reception of white or grey horses in cavalry regiments on account of the conspicuousness of the color. As far as the band is concerned it does not make much difference, for as a rule they are not brought under fire; but the trumpeters are constantly exposed, and as they always accompany the Colonel and captains, they indicate the positions of those officers at once to the enemy, who are thus enabled to pick them off by their sharpshooters.

While we were lying at Camp Buford a curious incident occurred in connection with the Secretary of War, Mr. Stanton, which we suspected contributed materially to intensify the dislike for the regular troops and their officers, which he was known to entertain. The Secretary was driving in the vicinity of our brigade camps one afternoon in an open carriage, when he met an officer on horseback, coming from Washington. This gentleman, who was well known and very popular in our brigade, though disposed to be rather wild in his habits, did not belong to one of the regular cavalry, but to the volunteer regiment attached to the brigade—the 6th Pennsylvania Cavalry. He was personally unknown to the Secretary of War; but on meeting, the Captain thought he recognized in the

211

Secretary an acquaintance between whom and himself there happened to be some ill-feeling. It is probable that Captain T. had been dining rather too freely. At all events, he addressed Mr. Stanton by his supposed friend's name, and on the Secretary resenting in his well known haughty manner the advance, hot words passed. The Secretary ordered the captain to his quarters in arrest—told him he was the Secretary of War and demanded his name. Capt. T. laughed in derision at the statement that he was the Secretary, and riding close to the carriage seized Mr. Stanton by the luxuriant beard which he wore at the time, and gave it a violent tug, and also slapped his face. Then he rode off leaving the Secretary in a frightful rage. Mr. Stanton fortunately did not think of coming to Brigade Headquarters, but returned to the War Department, and sent an aide de camp to inspect the brigade at once, and to bring the officer described to his office. Long before the A.D.C. reached camp the whole story was out, and everyone expected the skies to fall. Capt. T. was hurried off at once on some manufactured piece of duty which took him out of sight for a day or two. The brigade was thoroughly inspected, but no officer at all answering the description could be found in the regular regiments—which indeed was not strange. The Lancers (6th Pa. Cavalry) which had not been indicated by the Secretary received rather a perfunctory examination, and the aide was able to return with the report that no gentleman at all answering the description could be found. Our stay was short after this occurrence, and the offending and badly-scared Captain was kept well out of sight while we did remain.[5]

On the 11th of October, 1863, we marched from Camp Buford to rejoin our division in the Army of the Potomac.[6] Owing to the temporary absence of Gen. Merritt, Capt. Sweitzer commanded

[5] The officer cannot be identified.

[6] Still commanded by Major General George G. Meade (1815–1872), USMA, Class of 1835, who resigned the Army in 1836 but re-entered in 1842 as a second lieutenant in the Corps of Topographical Engineers, with which he served until war began; by then he was a captain. He was appointed brigadier general of volunteers on 31 August 1861; major general of volunteers, 29 November 1862. At Fredericksburg, he had commanded the Third Division, Reynolds' First Corps, in Franklin's Left Grand Division. Meade succeeded General Hooker as commanding general of the Army of the Potomac on 28 June 1863 and led it at Gettysburg.

the brigade and Capt. Reno the regiment. We reached the army Oct. 13th, and immediately took part in the fighting consequent on Gen. Lee's advance toward Washington in what is generally known as the "Bristoe" campaign.[7] From the 14th to the 18th of October we were engaged in scouting and reconnoitering in front of the army in the vicinity of Bull Run, Centerville and Manassas Junction, and were daily engaged with the enemy's cavalry. On the 19th we reached Catlett's Station, and drove off a small body of the enemy.[8] In this movement my squadron made a very pretty charge through the little hamlet of Cedarville. Gen. Lee at length drew off behind the Rappahannock and our forces moved forward at the same time and took position along the river.[9] Constant skirmishing and manoeuvering continued until Gen. Meade thought he saw a favorable opening for an advance in the direction of Mine Run and the army accordingly moved to that point. The part of the cavalry in this expedition was confined to protecting the trains, the densely wooded nature of the country not admitting of any extended movements. Gen. Meade failed to discover any weak point in Gen. Lee's line, and drew off without attacking, and the two armies went into winter quarters in December along the line of the Rapidan, the enemy holding the south and we the north bank of that stream.[10]

My brigade was stationed near Mitchell's Station on the Orange and Alexandria Railroad, and the Headquarters of the Division were in the village of Culpeper Court House. Gen. Wesley Merritt had temporarily succeeded to the command of the Division, owing to the severe illness of Gen. Buford, and Col. Alfred Gibbs of the 1st New York Dragoons (and Captain 3rd U.S. Cavalry) had com-

[7] The Bristoe Campaign, 9–22 October 1863, was a no-decision, no-results maneuver for both the Army of the Potomac and the Army of Northern Virginia. Lee tried to outflank Meade, withdrew, and established his army on line of the Rappahannock on 18 October.

[8] OR, XXIX, Pt. 1, 1054, acknowledges that a skirmish took place at Catlett's Station, Virginia, but laconically notes "no circumstantial reports on file."

[9] The Bristoe Campaign, in terms of the numbers of men and equipments involved, was light; yet the Army of Northern Virginia sustained 205 KIA and 1,176 WIA, and the Army of the Potomac, for roughly the same period, sustained 136 KIA, 733 WIA, and 1,423 captured or missing, the last a rather high figure. *Ibid.*, 226, 414.

[10] The Mine Run (Virginia) Campaign, 26 November–2 December 1863.

mand of the Reserve Brigade. Buford, who had been constantly in active service since the beginning of the war, had at length given way under the strain, and had gone to Washington on sick leave, and soon after we heard that his disease had developed into the low type of typhoid fever at that time so prevalent. Early in December I happened to be in Washington for a day or two on business, and received a message from Gen. Buford saying he would like to see me. I called on him at once at his quarters on H Street, near the War Department, and found him very ill. Gen. Stoneman occupied the house with him, and was doing everything for his comfort, but it was evident that he was a very sick man, and I who had so lately recovered from this same dreadful disease, felt very anxious about him. However he seemed bright and cheerful—said he had been anxious to see an officer of the Reserve Brigade as he had a message to send to the command. He then asked me if we were aware that he had been offered a command in the West, and on my replying that the fact was certainly not generally known, he said, "Well it is true. I have been offered the command of all the cavalry in the West (Sherman's Army) and I have replied that I will accept it on one condition, viz: that I may be allowed to take with me my own brigade" (the Regular Cavalry or Reserve Brigade). "Now I want you to give this news to the Brigade, and have it understood that I wish no promotion that will separate me from them." He then sent some personal messages to Gen. Merritt and other officers, and then Gen. Stoneman motioned to me that I must say good-bye. I did so, and for the last time. He died on the 16th of December, 1863.[11] Had he lived, I have no doubt that he would have risen very high. We certainly had no cavalry officer to equal him, and I doubt whether he had many superiors in any respect. It was to him, above all others, that the country owes its

[11] General Buford had contracted typhoid fever during the recent campaigns along the Rappahannock River. Buford (b. 1826), USMA, Class of 1848, saw a good deal of service in the West before the war. By 1861, he was junior captain in the Second Regiment of Dragoons. In November of that year, he was promoted major and assistant inspector general, Inspector General's Department. Appointed brigadier general of volunteers (to rank from 27 July 1862), he was seriously wounded at Second Manassas, performed well at Gettysburg, and was promoted major general of volunteers (to rank from 1 July 1863) on his deathbed.

thanks for the selection of Gettysburg as the battle ground on which the armies of the Potomac and Northern Virginia were to contend. The Comte de Paris in his splendid work *The Civil War in America* says: "Knowing that Reynolds was within supporting distance of him, he boldly resolved to risk everything in order to allow the latter time to reach Gettysburg in advance of the Confederate army. This first inspiration of a cavalry officer and a true soldier decided in every respect the fate of the campaign. It was Buford who selected the battle field where the two armies were about to measure their strength."[12]

Gen. Buford was graduated at the Military Academy in 1848, and served in the 1st and 2nd Dragoons on the Plains, until 1861. In 1861 he was promoted Major and Assistant Inspector General in the Regular Army. In 1862 he was appointed Brig. Gen. of Volunteers. He was born in Kentucky in 1825, and his family, as was so frequently the case in the border States, was greatly divided on the question of secession.[13] Gen. Buford, however, was so thoroughly loyal a soldier as lived, but had to suffer, like so many others, for the sins of his relatives. The War Secretary never trusted him, and his promotion came slowly and was given grudgingly. It is most painful to think that his commission as Major General of Volunteers only reached him on the day of his death, and that Mr. Stanton positively refused to allow it to be issued until assured that he was dying. Gen. Stoneman who was deeply attached to him, brought it to his bedside and gave it to him with some expressions of hopefulness, but Buford simply said "Too late," and died. He had the respect and esteem of every man in the army, and the cavalry loved him as a father.

As soon as the brigade reached Mitchell's Station and had established its line of pickets along the Rapidan, the men went to work to make themselves comfortable for the winter. As the country was quite heavily wooded, large details were made to fell trees and huts were erected after the fashion of the log cabins of fron-

[12] Comte de Paris, *History of the Civil War in America,* III, 544–45.
[13] Brigadier General Abraham Buford, CSA (1820–1884), was a cousin, and Brigadier Napoleon Bonaparte Buford, USA (1807–1883), was a half-brother.

215

tiersmen. The picket lines on which the horses stood were "corduroyed" and walks made about the camps. As soon as the horses and men were comfortable, schools were established for the officers and non-commissioned officers and regular drills commenced. Capt. Sweitzer, who was in command of the 1st Cavalry at this time, was a most excellent disciplinarian and organizer, and the regiment at once began to show the effect of his judicious control. The drill and instruction of men and officers was under charge of Capt. Samuel McKee, who was perhaps the best drill officer I have ever known. His early death at Cold Harbor a few months later cut short a most promising career and deprived the regiment of one of the finest and best loved officers who ever followed its colors.

Early in the winter I received an order to report at the Headquarters of the 1st Cavalry Division for special duty, and on repairing to Culpeper Court House for that purpose, was placed on duty as Provost Marshal of the Division, on the staff of Gen. Merritt.[14] I was sorry to leave my comrades in the regiment, but received the assurance of Gen. Merritt that if I desired I could return to the regiment at the beginning of the next campaign. The Adjutant General of the Division was Capt. Theodore C. Bacon, of New Haven, a boy with whom I had been intimate at school, and afterwards a classmate at Yale College.[15] This fact tended greatly to reconcile me to the change in my surroundings, and I shortly found myself quite comfortable in my new situation. I found Headquarters established in a very pretty house in the centre of the village; the officers were quartered in the various rooms, and all lived together at the mess. The Headquarters of other Divisions and Brigades were near by, and as many ladies and gentlemen from the North visited their friends, during the winter, we had a very gay time. Balls and parties, theatrical entertainments and horse races alternated with drills and reviews and an occasional scouting expedition to keep us occupied and happy. My duty as

14 Sanford was also aide-de-camp.

15 Theodore C. Bacon (1842–1878), nongraduate of the Class of 1863, Yale, had seen service with volunteer Connecticut and New York regiments before he was appointed assistant adjutant general on 9 September 1862. He resigned on 13 February 1864.

Provost Marshal was not particularly onerous and consisted principally in examining deserters from the enemy and receiving the reports of scouts and spies.

One piece of work however was of a more serious nature, and gave me a disgust for the office of Provost Marshal, which would have probably resulted in my asking to be relieved, had not other circumstances occurred by which I was transferred to a more agreeable position. The draft order of 1863 had brought into the ranks many conscripts who were dissatisfied with their lot, and many "bounty jumpers," as they were called, who had enlisted from no sense of patriotic duty, but merely to obtain the large amount of money offered by the different States and cities. These men were constantly deserting themselves and inducing others to do so, and stringent measures had to be taken to abrogate the evil. Courts-Martial were urged to inflict the maximum penalty for the crime, and one of these cases occurring about this time in our Division, I found myself by virtue of my office, obliged to take charge of the execution of a soldier who had been condemned to be "shot to death by musketry." I don't know whether the poor fellow felt much worse about it than I did. If he did, he certainly felt pretty bad. All the arrangements were made, however, but on the night previous to the date specified, telegraphic instructions were received from President Lincoln commuting the sentence to imprisonment for a specified term. It has been said that Mr. Lincoln erred greatly on the side of leniency in these cases, and very likely the statement is true; but I must acknowledge that I have always been grateful to him in this particular case.

Very soon after this occurrence, my old friend Bacon was obliged to tender his resignation owing to the state of his health at the time, and I was selected by Gen. Merritt to fill the vacancy as Asst. Adjt. General of the 1st Cavalry Division. This was very much pleasanter for me. I liked the work, and more especially the inside view it gave me of affairs pertaining to the army. A line officer serving with his regiment in war really knows less about what is going on in some respects than a civilian five hundred miles away from the army. The latter has access to all the newspapers, and hears matters discussed on the street and in the clubs. The young officer goes his daily round of duty, takes his tour of the guard or picket service, and occasionally is under fire; but outside of the small circle of his regimental intimates or brigade acquaintances he sees little and hears less. He is cut off from the newspapers until they are almost out of date; but old as they are, they always contain matter of interest to him, for his own opportunities for acquiring information are of the scantiest. Even in battles in which he has been engaged he rarely knows much outside of the fortunes of his own brigade. The staff officer and especially the officers of the corps or division staff in the cavalry have infinitely greater opportunities for becoming acquainted with the work of the army. Their commands are usually stretched over nearly the whole theatre of operations, and though the duties are necessarily harder, the interest is so great that the aide de camp is well repaid for his extra work. I do not mean by any means that a young officer should despise troop duty or seek detached service away from his regiment. His first and greatest fealty is due to his own regiment and he should make his position there a solid one before he even thinks of staff work; but having accomplished that object, a certain amount of staff service tends to broaden his views, enlarge his knowledge of his profession and enables him to come in contact with the older and more distinguished officers of the service. During my own tour on the staff of the 1st Cavalry Division and afterwards on the staff of the Cavalry Corps I had the good fortune to become well acquainted with all of the great corps and division commanders of the Potomac except two or three. Gen. John F. Reynolds, who was killed at Gettysburg, was I think the only officer of that army who rose to high place, whom I never remember to have met. Gens. Grant and Meade I saw often, and knew perfectly well by sight, but was brought into personal contact with them on but a few occasions, and can claim no acquaintance. The same is the case with Gen. Hooker. But McDowell, McClellan, Burnside, Hancock, Franklin, Sheridan, Buford, Stoneman, Howard and many others of the Potomac Army, as well as Thomas, Sherman and Schofield of the Western armies, I knew long and well.

218

Early in February, 1864, there were rumors of an intended raid by the enemy down the Shenandoah Valley, and our division was sent under Gen. Merritt to feel the enemy's line in the direction of the Blue Ridge, and ascertain whether their cavalry was still present. This movement led to some lively skirmishes in the neighborhood of Barnett's Ford on the Rapidan, in one of which Capt. Joseph P. Ash of the 5th Cavalry was wounded.[16] His wound was not particularly serious and he soon recovered but the incident illustrates the singular fatality which seemed to attend some men while others—equally exposed—were rarely or never touched. Ash had already been wounded six or seven times during the war, and was eventually killed at one of the battles in the Wilderness three months later.[17] On each of the occasions last mentioned I happened to be very near him when he was wounded and on the last I stood by his side when he died. He was scarcely more than a boy in years, but gave promise of becoming a very brilliant soldier. He was a singularly handsome young fellow, and one of the finest horsemen I ever saw. After our return from Barnett's Ford the larger portion of the command settled down in their old camps, and the usual routine work of a winter camp was again taken up. As the Spring opened however reconnaissances and scouting expeditions became more frequent, as did also inspections and reviews of the various brigades and divisions.

Early in March, 1864, Lieut. Gen. U. S. Grant was placed in command of all the armies of the United States and made his Headquarters with the Army of the Potomac for the purpose of personally directing the movements of that army, the most important of all under his command.[18] This did not relieve Gen. Meade from

[16] Sanford is referring to the Demonstration on the Rapidan, 6–7 February 1864; there was an engagement at Morton's Ford, skirmishes at Barnett's and Culpeper fords, Virginia. General Wesley Merritt's report of the skirmish at Barnett's lists fifteen casualties: three KIA and twelve WIA. *OR,* XXXIII, 139–40. The only officer wounded at Barnett's was Joseph P. Ash. His captaincy dated from 25 September 1863, and he held a brevet of major for service at Warrenton, Virginia, in 1862.

[17] Killed in action 8 May 1864 in or near Todd's Tavern, Virginia; brevetted lieutenant colonel for "conspicuous gallantry" at Battle of Spotsylvania, Virginia, 8 May 1864.

[18] On 12 March 1864, Lieutenant General Grant was assigned to command the Armies of the United States; Major General H. W. Halleck was chief of staff.

his command at all, but Grant of course to a certain extent over-shadowed him.[19] Many changes were made in the various corps and division commands and two of the corps—the 1st and 3rd—were abolished, and their troops consolidated with the 2nd, 5th and 6th corps, which, with the cavalry corps and the artillery, thereafter composed the Army of the Potomac proper.[20]

Under this arrangement Maj. Gen. Winfield S. Hancock commanded the 2nd Corps, Maj. Gen. G. K. Warren the 5th Corps, and Maj. Gen. John Sedgwick the 6th Corps. Maj. Gen. P. H. Sheridan was assigned to the Cavalry Corps in place of Gen. Alfred Pleasonton, who was relieved, and Gen. Henry J. Hunt commanded the Artillery.[21]

Gen. A. T. A. Torbert was assigned to the command of the 1st Cavalry Division and Gen. Wesley Merritt, who had been temporarily commanding it since Gen. Buford's illness and death, went back to the command of the Reserve Brigade.[22]

[19] And overshadow Meade he did, although Meade remained in command (almost in a technical sense) of the Army of the Potomac. Even more awkward was the fact that on 13 April 1864, Major General Burnside resumed command of the Ninth Army Corps, not an integral part of Meade's army but assigned to operate with it. The situation was awkward in that Burnside outranked Meade, although he was only a corps commander.

[20] On 23 March 1864, the First Army Corps was abolished and its troop assigned to the Fifth Army Corps; on 24 March, the Third Army Corps was abolished and its troops assigned to the Second and Sixth Army Corps.

[21] General Hancock had formerly commanded a division (the First) in the Second Army Corps; see n. 13, Chap. IV. Gouverneur K. Warren (1830–1882), USMA, Class of 1850, had been appointed brigadier general of volunteers on 26 September 1862; major general of volunteers, to rank from 3 May 1863. John Sedgwick (1813–1864), USMA, 1837, brigadier general of volunteers, 31 August 1861; major general of volunteers, 4 July 1862; he was badly wounded during the Peninsular Campaign and was killed at Spotsylvania 9 May 1864.

On 25 March 1864, Brigadier General David McM. Gregg, USA, superseded Major General Alfred Pleasonton as temporary commander of the Cavalry Corps, Army of the Potomac; then on 4 April 1864, Major General Sheridan (see n. 49, Chap. I) was assigned the Cavalry Corps command. He had established his reputation in the West—at Perryville, Murfreesboro, Chickamauga, and Missionary Ridge—but as a general of infantry divisions, not cavalry. On 13 September 1862, he had been promoted brigadier general of volunteers (to rank from 1 July 1862); major general of volunteers, 31 December 1862 (to rank same date).

[22] The Cavalry Corps (approximately 12,424 men in 32 regiments) was reorganized as follows: *First Division,* Brigadier General Alfred T. A. Torbert; First Brigade (the so-called Michigan Brigade), Brigadier General George A. Custer; Second Brigade, Colonel Thomas C. Devin; Reserve Brigade, Brigadier General Wesley

Gen. Torbert was good enough to invite me to retain my position as Asst. Adjt. General of the Division, and to say that he had received the most satisfactory accounts of me from Gen. Merritt, but I had determined from the time I took a staff position that I would return to my regiment as soon as the active work of the campaign began, and on explaining this to Gen. Torbert, he accepted my excuses, but said that later in the summer he should probably require my services. With this understanding I bade good-bye to my staff comrades and rejoined my regiment at Mitchell's Station. I was glad to be with them again and they seemed to be glad to have me. After all there is nothing like the comradeship that exists in a good regiment, that has long served together, where every officer and soldier feels a personal interest in every other. The ranks were full and the regiment had been drilling hard all winter and showed it. The men were trim and as hard as nails and looked "fit" in every respect. The horses were perhaps a little low in flesh from the severity of the outpost duty, but looked strong and active. Sweitzer was in command with Lieut. Fred C. Ogden as his adjutant, and some twenty officers were present for duty.

Soon after joining the regiment the whole corps was ordered to parade for review and inspection by our new chief Gen. Philip H. Sheridan. The day appointed was a beautiful one, and the display was magnificent. The strength of the corps at the time was about twenty thousand men, of which twelve thousand were reported as present for duty, equipped.[23] Sheridan, when he took command, was personally known to but few officers of the corps. He was

Merritt. *Second Division,* Brigadier General David McM. Gregg; First Brigade, Brigadier General Henry E. Davies, Jr.; Second Brigade, Colonel John Irvin Gregg. *Third Division,* Brigadier General James H. Wilson; First Brigade, Colonel Timothy M. Bryan, Jr., Eighteenth Pennsylvania Cavalry; Second Brigade, Colonel George H. Chapman, Third Indiana Cavalry. Twelve batteries of horse artillery were attached.

[23] Sheridan arrived at the headquarters of the Cavalry Corps on 5 April 1864 and issued orders "assuming command" on 6 April. He retained most of Pleasonton's staff officers. Sheridan estimated the strength of his corps during the review to be about 12,000 officers and men "with the same number of horses in passable trim." As a matter of fact, Sheridan was unhappy about the shape of the mounts—"thin and very much worn down by excessive and, it seemed to me, unnecessary picket duty." Philip H. Sheridan, *Personal Memoirs,* I, 353.

graduated at the Military Academy about eight years before, and assigned to the infantry arm of the service. Prior to the breaking out of the Rebellion he had been stationed most of the time on the Pacific coast, principally in Washington Territory, and had acquired an excellent reputation by his conduct in the Indian War in that section. Although an infantry officer he had been for a long time attached to the 1st Dragoons for duty, and had developed great fondness for the cavalry service. When the Rebellion broke out, he obtained command of a Michigan Cavalry regiment with which he performed excellent service, and was soon promoted Brig. Gen. and afterwards Maj. Gen. of Volunteers. His conduct at Chickamauga and Missionary Ridge, gained for him so much credit with Gen. Grant, that he obtained his assignment to the command of the Cavalry of the Army of the Potomac, in place of Gen. Alfred Pleasonton, who had commanded the corps with great ability and success, but who had unfortunately had some difficulty with Gen. Meade which rendered it impossible for them to work together.[24] Sheridan was at this time about thirty-three years of age, a short, stocky man of dark complexion, and rather saturnine expression when in repose.[25] In action, however, or when specially interested in any subject, his eyes fairly blazed and the whole man seemed to expand mentally and physically. His influence on his men was like an electric shock, and he was the only commander I have ever met whose personal appearance in the field was an immediate and positive stimulus to battle—a stimulus strong enough to turn beaten and disorganized masses into a victorious army. Many of our generals were more warmly loved by the soldiers; McClellan and Thomas, Buford and Sedgwick are instances; some perhaps ranked

[24] Pleasontown had opposed General Judson Kilpatrick's unsuccessful expedition against Richmond, 28 February–4 March 1864, among other things. Relieved on 25 March, Pleasonton was exiled to St. Louis, where he reported for duty to Major General William S. Rosecrans, commanding the Department of the Missouri. *OR*, XXXIII, 732. See n. 2, Chap. IV.

Sheridan and Meade were having their differences over the question of tactical employment of cavalry. Sheridan has some interesting things to say about this in his *Personal Memoirs*, I, 353–57, 368–69.

[25] Sheridan was short—about five feet, three inches—but he was not stocky; in April, 1864, he weighed little more than 115 pounds. The campaign in the West had been rugged and exhausting.

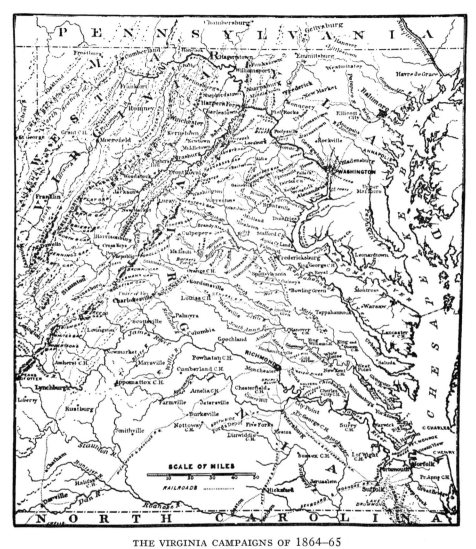

THE VIRGINIA CAMPAIGNS OF 1864–65

FROM JOHNSON AND BUELL (EDS.), *Battles and Leaders of the Civil War,* IV, 494

higher in their esteem as able soldiers, as Grant, Sherman, Mc-
Pherson and Meade; but none, to the best of my belief, carried
such a convincing air of success to the minds of his men, or could
get the last drop of strength out of their bodies, when an effort was
demanded, in the style of Philip H. Sheridan. They simply believed he was going to win, and every man apparently was determined to be on hand and see him do it. It was the sort of influence
that Lord Dundee seems to have exercised over the Scotch High-
landers, and it is the sort of influence that, added to super-eminent
abilities, made a Napoleon.[26]

Torbert, our Division commander, was a young man of perhaps
thirty-two. He had been a classmate of Sheridan's at the Academy,
and it was supposed that Sheridan's wishes had influenced the
authorities in transferring him from the command of an infantry
brigade to that of the 1st Cavalry Division, to be exchanged some
six months later for the command of the Cavalry Corps. He was a
handsome, dashing fellow, at this time, a beautiful horseman, and
as brave as a lion; but his abilities were hardly equal to such large
commands. Personally I was very much attached to him, as indeed
were all who knew him. He resigned from the service at the close
of the war,—dissatisfied—and justly so I think—at his failure to
obtain promotion. About 1878 or '80 he was drowned in the wreck
of a steamship off the coast of Florida. Being an excellent swimmer
he made his way safely through the surf to the shore, but in his
strenuous efforts to save a drowning companion, he became exhausted, and could not be resuscitated. It was exactly what might
have been expected of him.[27]

[26] John Graham of Claverhouse, First Viscount Dundee (1648–1689), who, as
James II's general, defeated Mackay in the pass of Killicrankie on 27 July 1689
but who was killed just at the moment of victory.
[27] Alfred Thomas A. Torbert (b. 1833), USMA, Class of 1855 (Sheridan was in
the Class of 1853, after a suspension of one year from the Academy), was commissioned a brevet second lieutenant in the Second Regiment of Infantry. He served
in the South and West before the war. On 16 September 1861, he was appointed
colonel, First New Jersey Volunteers; on 25 September 1861, he was promoted
captain, Fifth Regiment of Infantry, his permanent rank in the Regular Army. He
was promoted brigadier general of volunteers on 25 November 1862. Brevetted six
times during the war, he somehow failed to be included in the "new" postwar Army
except as a captain. He resigned 31 October 1866, having been mustered out of the

Gen. Wesley Merritt of the Reserve Brigade was a young man of perhaps twenty-five or six years—tall, slender, and intellectual-looking. He had a constitution of iron, and underneath a rather passive demeanor concealed a fiery ambition. He was and is, I am glad to say, a successful and very able soldier, and well deserves the high rank he now holds in the regular army of the United States. My connection with him as a staff officer and line officer was long and intimate, and extended with intervals over a period of thirty years, terminated only with my retirement from active service.[28]

The 1st Brigade of the Division was commanded by Gen. Geo. A. Custer, Merritt's life-long rival. He was even younger than Merritt in age and probably one of the youngest men who ever bore the commission of a general in the United States service. He was a graduate of the Military Academy of the Class of 1861, and at this time a Captain in the 5th U. S. Cavalry and Brig. Genl. of Volunteers. He was scarcely more than a boy in years, but was a man of tremendous energy and immense physical power. His great height and striking countenance made him a very imposing figure. His blue eyes, blond moustache and great mass of blond curling hair falling almost to his waist gave him the appearance of one of the Vikings of old, and his fancy for startling effects was still further indicated by his dress, which I remember about this time to have consisted of an immensely broad "slouch" hat, a black velvet jacket heavily trimmed with gold lace, riding breeches of the same, and immensely long cavalry boots. He wore also (though at a later period, I think) a long cross-hilted sword quite four feet in length, and which would have taken two hands to wield—bearing a motto in Spanish "Draw me not without cause—Sheathe me not without honor." This he had captured somewhere, and I suppose its curious old medieval look had taken his fancy. One thing I have forgotten and that perhaps the most conspicuous article of his apparel—around his neck, loosely knotted, he generally wore a long flowing ribbon or cravat of brilliant red cashmere or silk.

Volunteer Service on 15 January. Torbert was drowned in the wreck of SS *Vera Cruz* off the east coast of Florida on 29 August 1880. He was forty-seven. See n. 10, Chap. III.

[28] For Merritt, see p. 209.

This streamed behind him as he rode, and made him a marked man a mile away. This afterwards became the tacitly acknowledged badge of his command, and toward the end of the war was said to be worn by every officer and man in the 3rd Cavalry Division, which he then commanded.

Although this all sounds a little farcical and was at all events scarcely in good taste, it would be a great mistake to suppose that Custer was a braggadocio or anything of the kind. In the first place he was but a boy in years and feelings when the war commenced, and full of youthful extravagances. He had been brought up in a little Western country village and had seen little or nothing of life until his graduation from the Military Academy simultaneously with the beginning of the war opened for him a career of wonderful brilliancy and made him the recipient of such boundless adulation as would certainly have turned a weaker head. Custer was a man of boundless confidence in himself and great faith in his lucky star. This faith eventually cost him his own life and the lives of several troops of his regiment (the 7th Cavalry of which he was Lt. Col. Commanding) in the famous "Massacre of the Little Big Horn," June 25th, 1876. He was perfectly reckless in his contempt of danger and seemed to take infinite pleasure in exposing himself in the most unnecessary manner. Notwithstanding this, to the best of my recollection, he was never wounded until the day of his death.[29]

29 To add a few details to Sanford's sketch, George A. Custer (1839–1876) was graduated last in the Class of 1861, USMA, a class largely distinguished by the fact that eight of its thirty-four members died in wartime service and four had resigned four to six months before graduation. One of the legendary figures in the war, Custer was a first lieutenant (dated 17 July 1862) in the Fifth Regiment of Cavalry in the *Official Army Register* when, on 29 June 1863, he was commissioned a brigadier general of volunteers through the efforts of General Pleasonton, on whose staff Custer was serving. His wartime service was most spectacular and he was appointed major general of volunteers on 15 April 1865. By this time, he was a captain in the regular establishment (8 May 1864). After the war, he was appointed lieutenant colonel, to rank from 28 July 1866, the same day on which the Seventh Regiment of Cavalry was organized by Act of Congress. When he was killed at Little Big Horn, he was not yet thirty-seven.

·CHAPTER VI·

O N THE 4TH OF MAY, 1864 the Army of the Potomac made the crossing of the Rapidan without any serious resistance from the enemy, and moved out from the river with the intention of turning Lee's right flank. Lee however was not to be taken by surprise, and early on the morning of the 5th of May met our columns face to face and commenced the sanguinary struggle which practically continued until we drew off from the front of his lines at Cold Harbor about six weeks later.[1] The 1st Cavalry Division was employed in guarding the immense wagon trains of the army during the crossing and on the 5th of May.[2] During the latter day, as also on the 6th, the two armies were heavily engaged; and the sound of the musketry exceeded in intensity anything to which I have ever listened before or since,—owing to the density of the timber —especially the undergrowth—but little artillery was employed during the greater portion of the time, and for the same reason but little of the fighting was visible from any one point. It is probable that many of the men engaged on each side never got sight of

[1] Under way is the Campaign from the Rapidan to the James River, Virginia, 4 May—12 June 1864, Grant's first concerted move after his assumption of command. The campaign (sometimes called the Grand Campaign) had two objectives: Lee's Army of Northern Virginia and Richmond, Virginia.

[2] Torbert's First Division was assigned by General Meade to stay in the rear and guard the Rapidan fords and the wagon trains crossing them. Such duty was Meade's conception of the proper use of cavalry. Says Sheridan: "After detailing the various detachments which I was obliged to supply for escorts and other mounted duty, I crossed the river with an effective force of about 10,000 troopers." *Personal Memoirs,* I, 357.

half a dozen of their opponents at any one time.[3] Nevertheless the contest was at close quarters and the losses enormous; but on the evening of the 6th Grant was obliged to acknowledge his failure to push Lee aside from his position in our immediate front, and to take refuge in a flank movement to our left. This began on the 7th of May, and the 1st Cavalry Division led the advance towards Spotsylvania Court House by the Todd's Tavern Road.

In front of the Tavern we encountered the Confederate cavalry under Stuart, and soon after mid-day became severely engaged. The battle lasted until some time after dark, and resulted only in our gaining a mile or so of ground. In my own regiment, the 1st Cavalry, we lost six officers wounded out of about eighteen,[4] engaged, and in many of the regiments of the Division the loss was almost as heavy. After the fighting ceased we lay down on the ground, just where we stood, and sought what rest we could get preparatory to the renewal of the contest at dawn.[5] By three o'clock in the morning we were aroused with orders to push on at all costs, and the attempt was made, but we had certainly not advanced a mile, and daylight had scarcely broken, when we were again as heavily engaged as on the previous evening. For perhaps an hour or more we managed to make some slight progress, but then by the increasing weight of the fire it became evident that Stuart had been re-enforced by the Confederate Infantry, and our advance came practically to a standstill. The men behaved magnificently, however,

---

[3] Reference here is to the Battle of the Wilderness, including engagements at Parker's Store, Craig's Meeting-House, the Brock Road, Todd's Tavern (which Sanford is about to discuss), the Furnaces, etc., 5–7 May 1864. Union forces, numbering more than 118,000 men, sustained 15,387 casualties; Confederate forces, numbering more than 61,000, sustained 11,400 casualties.

[4] Wounded were Captain Edwin V. Sumner, Jr.; First Lieutenants James A. Hall, William T. Pennock, Reuban F. Bernard; and Second Lieutenants Robert J. Ward and Camillo C. C. Carr.

[5] Sanford indicates confusion about the dates. This affray at Todd's Tavern took place on 6 and 7 May 1864; "dawn" refers to the morning of 8 May, and Sanford reports the continuation of the action at Todd's Tavern, near Spotsylvania Court House. That evening, Sheridan sent a report to Major General Andrew A. Humphreys, Chief of Staff, Army of the Potomac: "The cavalry made a very handsome fight here this afternoon.... They had constructed barricades and rifle-pits, which we charged and captured. I had only four brigades engaged .... They all behaved splendidly." *OR*, XXXVI, Pt. 1, 776.

as they had done on the previous day, and did not lose one inch of ground. Warren's 5th Corps was following us closely, and the Corps Commander, who had no great love for cavalry, became considerably incensed at our failure to clear his road more rapidly. At last he received instructions to push to the front himself and open the way. The gallant 5th Corps came up in good style as usual —Gen. Robinson's division in the lead—and evidently expected to push the enemy's light troops out of the way in short order. In a very few moments, in fact before they had reached the fighting line of our cavalry at all, they were thrown into great disorder and Gen. Robinson lost a leg.[6] They were soon reformed however and stood bravely up to their work all day, but the battle ended where it began, some three miles from Spotsylvania.

In the confusion consequent on the break of the infantry, Capt. Ash of the 5th Cavalry, of whom I have before spoken, rode out among their men to endeavor to restore order, and to assist their officers in leading them into position in the cavalry skirmish line. I happened to be talking with him at the moment, and it seemed scarcely more than two minutes when his orderly rode back and reported to Gen. Merritt, "Captain Ash is killed, sir."[7] As it turned out, he was not, for when some few moments later he was brought back by some soldiers it was evident that he still breathed. He appeared however to be entirely unconscious as the surgeon cut open his blouse and shirt to examine the wound. After a glance, he said in response to my inquiry and before he had turned away from his work, "There is no hope whatever." Ash was lying on his back, his head reclining on one side and his eyes closed. At the

[6] John C. Robinson (1817–1897) was an "old Army man," for he was commissioned a second lieutenant, Fifth Regiment of Infantry, on 27 October 1839. He had been promoted brigadier general of volunteers to rank from 28 April 1862. He retired from the Army on 6 May 1869 and was promoted to major general.

[7] Ash was the only officer killed in the First Division. General Merritt had succeeded Torbert as commanding general, First Division, on 7 May because of the latter's illness. Colonel Alfred Gibbs, Nineteenth New York Cavalry (First Dragoons), succeeded Merritt as Reserve Brigade commander. Torbert assumed command again on 26 May.

Alfred Gibbs (1823–1868), USMA, Class of 1846, had been captured in 1861 in New Mexico and was not exchanged for more than a year. His future service in the Battle of Cedar Creek would bring him promotion to brigadier general.

remark of the surgeon, he half raised his head, opened his eyes wide, and said, "Let me die quietly, then," closed his eyes and was dead. His regiment buried him on the ground where he lay, and I do not know whether his body was ever removed. He was as gallant a soldier as fell during the War of the Rebellion, and had he lived would I believe, have risen to very high rank. Gen. Merritt, in his official report of the battle, says: "He died nobly in the discharge of a most important duty; a heroic, patriotic, intrepid cavalry officer, a noble martyr in his country's service."[8]

As soon as the 5th Corps had gotten into position our Cavalry were relieved and moved to Silver's plantation where we rested and got something to eat for ourselves and our horses. Our regiment lost thirty-nine men and six officers in the two engagements, besides a number of horses.[9]

At half-past four next morning, May 9th, the whole corps, Gen. Sheridan commanding, started to ride around the right flank of Gen. Lee's army and fight the Rebel cavalry, after which, if successful, we were to destroy the enemy's communications with Richmond, and then to move South to the James River and procure supplies from Gen. Butler's command, known to be in the vicinity of Bermuda Hundred on the South side of the James. This expedition is usually spoken of as Gen. Sheridan's "first raid."[10] In fact the word "raid," as used in this connection, is an entire misnomer. The raid expeditions of the Civil War were generally composed of comparatively small bodies of light troops, intended to make sudden dashes upon the enemy's communications to destroy as much property as possible, and to get back to their own command without loss. As a rule, no wagons accompanied the expeditions, and scarcely any artillery, as conflicts with the enemy were in the nature of the case avoided rather than sought; the troops were expected to subsist on the products of the country and to destroy what they

---

[8] *OR,* XXXVI, Pt. 1, 812.

[9] *Ibid.,* 128, lists the following casualties for the 6–8 May battles: First Cavalry— eight KIA, 34 WIA, and three MIA; total for the Reserve Brigade—34 KIA, 121 WIA, and 43 MIA.

[10] Sheridan's Richmond Raid, or the Expedition from Todd's Tavern to the James River, 9–24 May 1864.

could not use, and to effect this purpose they were as widely dispersed as was consistent with safety.

Gen. Sheridan, on the contrary, started with his whole cavalry corps fully equipped for a campaign.[11] His principal motive was to get outside the sphere occupied by the enemy's foot troops, where he might meet the opposing cavalry in open country and test the question of superiority once for all on a fair field. In pretty much all the cavalry actions of the war prior to this time one side or the other—generally both—had been able to obtain assistance from the infantry. Sheridan was confident he could beat their cavalry if he could get at them, and in opposition to the judgment of Gen. Meade, had at length obtained Gen. Grant's authority to bring the matter to a definite test. The corps was in superb condition and only too willing to try its strength with Stuart. The great desire of every officer and soldier was to get at such a distance from the armies that a decisive engagement might be had between the two bodies of cavalry, unassisted by infantry on either side. With this object in view, Sheridan marched all day past the right flank of the enemy and toward the North Anna river, which was reached and crossed by Merritt's division, in the advance, soon after dark.[12] Custer's brigade of this division was at once sent forward to Beaver Dam station, on the Virginia Central railway, which Custer destroyed, with an immense amount of military and subsistence stores. He also re-captured several hundred Union officers and soldiers who were on their way to Richmond as prisoners of war, and were greatly delighted at the sudden and unexpected change

[11] Sheridan does not mention the wagons, etc., but he does say that at the concentration of his corps at Aldrich's, late in the day on the eighth, "three days' rations for the men were distributed, and half rations of grain for one day were doled out for the horses." *Personal Memoirs*, I, 370.

Sanford's term "fully equipped" needs explaining. All unserviceable animals, unnecessary wagons and tents, etc., were left behind. "The necessary ammunition train, two ambulances to a division, a few pack-mules for baggage, three days' rations and a half-day's forage carried on the saddle, comprised the outfit." Theophilus F. Rodenbough, "Sheridan's Richmond Raid," *Battles and Leaders of the Civil War*, IV, 189.

[12] "The corps moved at a walk, the three divisions on the same road, making a column nearly thirteen miles in length.... Although the column was very long, I preferred to move it all on one road rather than to attempt combinations for carrying the divisions to any given point by different routes." *Personal Memoirs*, I, 372–73.

231

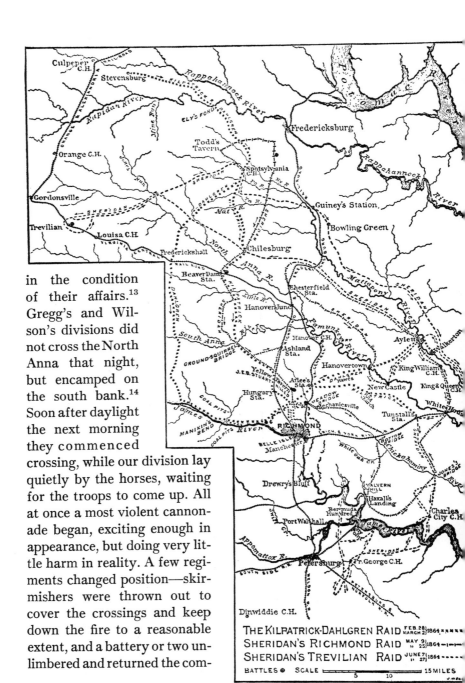

in the condition of their affairs.[13] Gregg's and Wilson's divisions did not cross the North Anna that night, but encamped on the south bank.[14] Soon after daylight the next morning they commenced crossing, while our division lay quietly by the horses, waiting for the troops to come up. All at once a most violent cannonade began, exciting enough in appearance, but doing very little harm in reality. A few regiments changed position—skirmishers were thrown out to cover the crossings and keep down the fire to a reasonable extent, and a battery or two unlimbered and returned the com-

THE KILPATRICK-DAHLGREN RAID FEB. 28 1864
MARCH 2
SHERIDAN'S RICHMOND RAID MAY 9 1864
" 25
SHERIDAN'S TREVILIAN RAID JUNE 7 1864
" 27
BATTLES ⊕   SCALE   5   10   15 MILES

FROM ROBERT UNDERWOOD JOHNSON AND
CLARENCE CLOUGH BUELL (EDS.), Battles and
Leaders of the Civil War (NEW YORK,
CENTURY, 1887), IV, 190

pliments of the rebels. They soon appeared to make up their minds
that they would never stop our career in that way, and their artillery
limbered up and the whole force withdrew. As we moved out in the
direction of Richmond, we could see occasionally through openings
in the woods the long columns of their cavalry evidently straining
every nerve to get ahead of us in the race and take up some position
of defense in our front. This they finally accomplished at Yellow
Tavern on the Brook Turnpike, six miles north of Richmond.[15]

This place we reached on the afternoon of the 11th of May and
found Stuart waiting for us with his whole force. The action commenced at once, by Gen. Merritt deploying his division and moving forward to the attack. As Gregg and Wilson came up with their
divisions, they were also deployed and moved into Merritt's support. Merritt soon drove the enemy beyond Yellow Tavern and got
possession of the direct road to Richmond—the Brook Turnpike—
but the enemy enfiladed the pike with artillery fire and for some
time Yellow Tavern was a decidedly hot place. Gibbs' and Devin's
brigades held fast on the pike, and Custer, with Chapman's brigade
of Wilson's division, charged the enemy's line, riding over their
guns which he captured and breaking the line.[16] Gen. J. E. B. Stuart,

[13] The freed Union prisoners numbered about 400 and had been recently taken
in the Battle of the Wilderness; included among them was one colonel, two lieutenant
colonels, "and a considerable number of captains and lieutenants." Custer destroyed
the station, three trains, and two "first-class locomotives." Also destroyed were
ninety wagons, "from eight to ten miles of railroad and telegraph lines," about
200,000 pounds of supplies, "amounting in all to about a million and a half of
rations, and nearly all the medical stores of General Lee's army." *OR*, XXXVI, Pt.
1, 817, and Sheridan, *Personal Memoirs*, I, 375.

[14] Sanford errs; read *north bank*. This is Sanford's first mention of another of
the "boy generals" in the war, Brigadier General James H. Wilson (1837–1925),
USMA, Class of 1860, classmate of Merritt and last surviving member of the class.
Wilson's career was most distinguished in the war, both in the East and West. Hon-
orably discharged at his own request in 1870, he returned to the Army in the
Spanish-American War, served in Puerto Rico and in the Boxer Rebellion.

[15] On the march from Allen's Station to Yellow Tavern Merritt's Division was
in the lead, followed by Wilson and then Gregg.

[16] "Custer's charge, with Chapman on his flank and the rest of Wilson's division
sustaining him, was brilliantly executed. Beginning at a walk, he increased his gait
to a trot, and then at full speed rushed at the enemy." Sheridan, *Personal Memoirs*,
I, 378.

For Gibbs, see n. 7 *supra*. Thomas C. Devin (1822–1878), who is to figure in
the later narrative, was finally commissioned brigadier general of volunteers in
1865. See p. 275 *et seq*. George H. Chapman (1832–1882) was to be promoted to
brigadier general in 1864.

the great cavalry commander on the Confederate side, was mortally wounded in this charge and died next day.[17] The enemy's force, which was cut in two, drew off with unusual rapidity, a part towards Ashland, the rest towards Richmond, and we went into camp on the battle ground. The camp, however, turned out to be scarcely more than a rest, for we had a cup of coffee, when orders came to mount, and by eleven o'clock at night we were on our way toward Richmond again.[18]

The general impression was that we were going *in*, and indeed there would probably have been little difficulty in doing so. How we would have got out is another story, and I suspect a doubtful one. However, it seems never to have been Gen. Sheridan's intention to try the experiment; possibly he had orders not to risk his command in such a way; at all events he passed through the first line of works, and then while Wilson's division made a feint against the second line, he moved with Merritt and Gregg around the city to the south side, where the Negroes reported Gen. Butler to be, with his army, within four miles of the city. We reached Meadow Bridge on the Chickahominy river about daylight, found the bridge torn up, the stream unfordable and the enemy posted on the other side in force. Take it for all in all, this ride from eleven at night until daylight next morning was one of the liveliest episodes within my recollection. The road was lined with torpedoes, which exploded at intervals, blowing some poor fellow into the air; the enemy was in front, in rear and on the flanks making things as uncomfortable as they knew how; it was thundering and lightning in the great style overhead, and the torpedoes blowing up under foot. Altogether, I certainly don't expect to see the like again, and don't especially want to. A little party of a corporal and some three or

---

[17] When he interposed himself at Yellow Tavern, Stuart's combat luck finally ran out. After the mortal wound, he was taken to Richmond, where he died. He was thirty-one years, three months old. "From facts obtained on the battle-field and from information derived since, I have every reason to believe that the rebel General J. E. B. Stuart received his death wound from the hands of Private John A. Huff, Company E, 5th Michigan Cavalry, who has since died from a wound received at Haw's Shop." From Custer's report, dated 4 July 1864, *OR*, XXXVI, Pt. 1, 810. See pp. 331–33.

[18] Down the Brook Pike.

four men dashed by us at one point and attempted to crowd into the columns just in front of my regiment. I was riding with the regimental commander, Capt. Sweitzer, and his Adjutant, Fred Ogden,[19] at the time, and Sweitzer began to remonstrate with the party in his usual forcible manner; but before he had spoken three words one of the luckless troopers rode on to a concealed torpedo and the whole set of fours went up into the air. It was a very lively night.[20]

As soon as day broke, every one was on the lookout of course for torpedoes and I saw one amusing incident in this connection. Someone discovered an iron bar lying in the middle of the road, which of course was supposed to connect in some manner with an invisible torpedo. The column was accordingly turned into the fields to go around it and a sentinel posted to warn all passers-by not to approach it too closely. Just as my regiment was passing, a blundering Irish orderly rode up at a gallop, and in spite of the challenge of the sentinel on one side of the road and the shouts of the passing troopers on the other, or perhaps bewildered by them, dashed directly down onto the dreaded missile and sent it flying twenty feet off, with one stroke of his horse's hoofs. The shout that went up from the men when the fact became apparent that there was no torpedo there might have been heard in Richmond. A small joke goes a good way under those circumstances, and it often seems strange to me now, when I think of how much fun we used to get out of pretty serious matters.

At Meadow Bridge about that time it looked as if the "Johnnies" were going to have all the fun to themselves and we were going to furnish the cause. The bridge was quite high about the water, and the roadway across it was entirely destroyed. The river was deep and sluggish at this point and the banks high and treacherous, so that it was out of the question to attempt swimming the horses. Scouts were sent out to hunt for fords, but there was no time for delay. The enemy had come out from Richmond and were pressing

---

[19] Frederick C. Ogden was commissioned a second lieutenant in the First Cavalry on 21 November 1861; first lieutenant, 17 July 1862. See pp. 243–45.

[20] No trooper was killed, but several horses were by these "torpedoes."

hard on our rear, while in front the approach to the bridge was swept by a heavy artillery fire. Custer's brigade was repulsed in an attempt to drive them off, and then Merritt with his whole division was directed to carry the bridge and the crest beyond at all hazards. The troops dismounted and, leaving their horses under charge of the "numbers four," dashed down on foot; the enemy were driven from the crossing and we swarmed across the bridge on the bare trestles, creeping, crawling—any way to get across. If a man was hit, of course he went into the water, there was nothing to hold on to, and certainly no way to help him.

As the head of the column reached the other side, skirmish lines were formed and the enemy driven rapidly back; planks were at once hurried on to the bridge and soon the roadway was repaired and the whole division crossed and attacked the enemy on the hill. They made strong efforts, but were undoubtedly badly weakened by the loss of their great leader the day before and by the severe handling they had received in the previous fights. Soon their whole line gave way and they were pursued rapidly by the 1st Division towards Gaines' Mills, near which point we camped.[21]

While we of Merritt's division were thus occupied in front, Gregg and Wilson were having an equally hot time in the rear and Wilson was at one time quite severely pressed. A charge by Gregg's division, however, relieved him, and the enemy were finally driven inside their works after which both divisions crossed the Chickahominy and encamped. A curious feature of this battle was the presence of a couple of enterprising young newsboys from Richmond who sold the morning papers on the skirmish line with the greatest coolness of our eager troopers, and who of course reaped a rich harvest by their undertaking.

[21] Merritt's report of this affair at Meadow Bridge asserts: "Our loss in this affair was serious, though not very heavy. It is thought that the resolute and impetuous manner in which the attack was made, when the time came for action, did everything to save many valuable men and officers, who must certainly have been lost if any other than the most vigorous attack had been made." *OR*, XXXVI, Pt. 1, 814. Merritt's losses amounted to one KIA, seventeen WIA, and eight MIA.

Sanford fails to mention the fact that Brigadier General James B. Gordon, CSA (b. 1842), was mortally wounded this day, 12 May. He died in Richmond on 18 May 1864. He had commanded a brigade (the North Carolina Brigade) in Rooney Lee's Division. His death was yet another serious loss to the Confederate armies.

236

The next day we marched to Bottom's Bridge on the Chicka-hominy, and on the 14th crossed White Oak Swamp and camped on the James river in sight of our gun boats and of our forces under Gen. Butler.[22] As we crossed Malvern Hill we came near getting into a hornet's nest, as our gun boats took us for Rebel cavalry and commenced pitching their enormous shells, which the men called "Lamp posts," at us. The signal officers soon estab-lished communication and succeeded in stopping the fire, as far as I know, without damage.[23] Our camp was on ground familiar to us all in the Peninsula Campaign of 1862, and we were much interested in noting the well-known spots. Our wounded were taken care of by the medical officers of Butler's army, and the supply departments furnished us with everything needed for our comfort. The Navy people also were wonderfully kind and allowed our of-ficers to purchase clothing for their own use from their ample stores. This was a great convenience as of course we had carried very little with us, and the severe work we had been engaged in had been very hard on clothes. It was rather an odd sight to see a cavalry officer rigged out with a blue sailor's shirt and broad collar and wide flapping trousers. The dark blue shirts worn as jackets, with-out a coat, were wonderfully comfortable and handy and many retained them during the remainder of the war for campaign use.

Our loss in this expedition was between six and seven hundred men and officers. The enemy's, I should judge to have been about the same, but we certainly secured the advantage in morale, as we were successful in every encounter, and proved conclusively, to our own satisfaction if not to theirs, that the Rebel cavalry could not hope for success without the help of its infantry. Subsequent operations in the Shenandoah Valley where the country was open

22 The Army of the James, Major General Benjamin F. Butler (1818–1893), of New Orleans occupation fame.

23 *ORN,* X, makes no mention of this but does print this dispatch from Acting Rear Admiral Samuel P. Lee, USN, North Atlantic Blockading Squadron, com-manding, to Secretary of the Navy Gideon Welles, dated 14 May 1864, 3:00 P.M.: "The cavalry corps of Major General Sheridan ... has just arrived at Turkey Island, left bank. ... Their timely appearance will relieve us from sharpshooters and facili-tate our operations now in progress for clearing out torpedoes." P. 56. Sheridan's camp was between Haxall Landing and Shirley on the James.

and better adapted in every way for cavalry operations than the tangled thickets of the Wilderness or the marshy low-lands of the Chickahominy and the James, settled this question for good and all.

On the 17th of May our return march to join the Army of the Potomac began.[24] It was by no means an easy problem, as we had received no news from that quarter, and the only thing certain was that Lee's army was between us, and that his cavalry were certainly on the lookout for a chance to get even. Gen. Sheridan sent expeditions in different directions to deceive the enemy as to his intention, and Gregg's command even went as close to Richmond as Mechanicsville, only five miles distance from the city. On the 22nd the whole command united at the White House, and after repairing the railroad bridge, we crossed the Pamunkey river and on the 24th rejoined the army at Chesterfield Station on the North Anna river.[25] Here we expected a little rest, and we got it, just one day.[26] On the 26th we were fighting at Hanovertown [Hanover], where we drove off Gordon's brigade and secured the crossing of the Pamunkey.[27]

On the 29th Gregg's division had a very severe fight at Hawes

[24] Sheridan's Corps crossed the James River on the sixteenth, crossed the Chickahominy at Jones' Bridge, and went into camp on 18 May at Baltimore Cross Roads and vicinity between the Pamunkey and Chickahominy rivers.

[25] Sheridan had decided to cross the Pamunkey River at White House. When it was discovered that the railroad bridge was only partially destroyed, Sheridan put Wesley Merritt to work on it, using the Second and Reserve Brigades. Sanford is too modest here and at the same time misses a good story: "An abutment and several spans of the bridge had to be replaced entirely, many stringers to be supplied, and the flooring for the entire bridge collected and transported from a distance. This was all done in about fifteen hours' work with poor facilities and no tools, save those ordinarily carried by pioneer parties." Merritt's report, dated 6 July 1864, *OR,* XXXVI, Pt. 1, 814. Merritt then singled out Captains Sweitzer, McKee, and Sanford for "especial notice," among other officers, "in this most important work." *Ibid.,* 815.

[26] When the corps arrived at Chesterfield Station, Sheridan's First Raid was over. "We lost but few horses, considering their condition when we started. The average distance traveled per day did not exceed 18 miles; the longest march being 30 miles. The horses which failed were shot by the rear guard, as they could have been easily recuperated and made serviceable to the enemy. I think the actual number lost would not exceed 300, perhaps not more than 250." Sheridan's report, *ibid.,* 792.

[27] Gordon's Brigade here is that of Brigadier General John B. Gordon (1832–1904), infantry, under Major General Jubal A. Early, CSA. The various skirmishes and battles following are part of the Operations on the Line of the North Anna, the Pamunkey, and Totopotomoy Rivers, which had commenced on 22 May and were to continue until about 1 June 1864.

Shop.[28] Custer's brigade of our division (Torbert's) was also seriously engaged and Merritt's and Devin's brigades were in support. The next day it was our turn, and the enemy attacked our pickets on the Matadequin Creek. Torbert put in the whole division and in a few hours we drove the enemy through Old Church and within a couple of miles of Cold Harbor. The battle was continued on the next day, and we eventually obtained possession of Cold Harbor about nightfall after very severe fighting, some of which was with the enemy's infantry.[29] Our regiment suffered a very severe loss this day in the mortal wounding of Capt. Samuel McKee, and I especially grieved for the death of a valued friend. I was by his side when the bullet struck him, just above the elbow, breaking the arm. He did not fall, and I supposed for a moment that the injury though serious and painful in the extreme would be confined to the loss of his arm. When however he told me that the ball had gone through the arm and into his side, I knew it was all over with him. Fred Ogden (the Adjutant) and I went to the hospital to see him that night; the first moment that we could be spared from the regiment, but he was under the influence of an opiate and did not recognize us. The surgeons had taken off his arm but they said there was no possible hope of his recovery, and I believe he died that same night. We never had another opportunity to go back, however, and indeed it was only a few days before my companion of that evening was himself "dead on the field of honor."[30]

After we got into Cold Harbor it became evident to Gen. Torbert that with our comparatively small force it would be out of the

[28] Haw's Shop took place on 28 May. Private Huff, slayer of Stuart, died here. See n. 17 *supra*.

[29] The set-to at Matadequin Creek was fought out on 30 May. During the morning of 31 May, Sheridan visited and conferred with Torbert and Custer and found that they had a plan to attack and capture Cold Harbor. Sheridan endorsed it, and in the afternoon of 31 May, the attack was launched. During these two days, Torbert's men were up against Major General Wade Hampton, Brigadier General Rooney Lee, and Brigadier General Matthew C. Butler.

[30] McKee died on 3 June of his wounds; see n. 4, Chap. II. In his report of the action around Cold Harbor, dated 4 July, Torbert called McKee's death "untimely" and said further: "A more gallant and accomplished soldier has not given his life for his bleeding country." *OR*, XXXVI, Pt. 1, 806. Merritt said McKee's loss "to the country and service was incalculable. A pure, unaffected, modest man, a chivalrous, educated, accomplished soldier." *Ibid.*, 849.

239

question to stay there and he accordingly withdrew his division and started back to a position nearer to the army. This was in accordance with Gen. Sheridan's instructions, but as soon as Gen. Meade heard that the cavalry had taken Cold Harbor he ordered Sheridan to hold on to it at all hazards, and no matter what it cost. Accordingly we turned around again and started back. The enemy fortunately had not noticed our withdrawal and made no attempt to interfere with us. We put our horses under shelter of the woods, and went to work at once building breastworks to resist the attack which we knew must come at dawn. So after two days' hard fighting and scarcely anything to eat, we spent the night marching and working on the defences. Why the infantry should not have been put at this we could not see, more especially as they had not done anything for several days, but there was no mercy for the cavalry as long as Gen. Meade controlled matters.

By daylight on the 1st of June we had scraped up a fairly good defensive line and were prepared to hold our position against a reasonable attack. Our Negro cook, Sam, had made a slight attempt toward providing something to eat for the Headquarters Mess. He had spread an india-rubber blanket on the ground and set out half a dozen tin cups of coffee, some fried bacon and hard tack, and announced "Breakfast, gentlemen," when the unmistakable Rebel yell and a perfect hail storm of bullets and shell announced something decidedly more important. Our commander, Sweitzer, who had already taken his seat on the ground, screamed to his orderly trumpeter to sound "To Arms," and at the same time made a dash at a cup of scalding hot coffee which he tried to swallow as he ran towards the skirmish line. I attempted to do the same, but Sam, who had mounted his old white horse at the first alarm and dashed up at the moment, reached down as he passed and caught the end of the rubber tablecloth which he carried off at a gallop, while the coffee, bacon and hard tack disappeared in the wildest confusion. For the next few hours we had no time to consider this episode, but I have laughed over it a good many times since, and can see the expression of that scared Darkey's face even now. The enemy, infantry as well as cavalry, made a most determined attack, but were as desperately resisted and repeatedly driven back after having actually reached the breastworks. About ten o'clock and when the men were becoming quite worn out besides being generally out of ammunition, word was passed along the line that the 6th Corps was coming up in our rear to relieve us. It was time.[31] About one P.M. we fell back through their lines and marched towards the White House, encamping that evening at Prospect Church, where we got our first regular meal in three days. We had to borrow tinware for our mess, though, and Sam did not hear the last of his "charge" that morning for many a long day.

For the next few days there was no very serious work, though we had some skirmishing and were under artillery fire more or less every day until the 7th of June.[32]

On that day we started on an expedition to break up the Virginia Central Railroad, and incidentally to meet and join Gen. David Hunter's command, which was supposed to be coming up the Shenandoah Valley and making for Gordonsville.[33] As it turned out, Hunter moved directly for Lynchburg and never turned in the direction of Gordonsville at all, so that of course that part of the expedition fell through. Our command consisted of the First and Second Divisions of cavalry, Torbert and Gregg commanding, with Sheridan in command of the whole. Wilson with the Third Division remained with the Army of the Potomac. Until the evening of the 10th we encountered none of the enemy at all, and actually began to forget that we were at war. On the evening of the 10th, however, the enemy's scouts appeared in our front, and when we went into

[31] The Reserve Brigade fought off a brigade of Confederate infantry in the first charge, made about 6:00 A.M.; the second charge, equally unsuccessful, was made a short time later.

[32] On 2 June, Torbert's Division marched to Bottom's Brigade, had a "slight skirmish"; 3 June, at Bottom's Bridge; 4 June, marched to Old Church; 5 June, marched to right of army; 6 June, marched to New Castle Ferry on the Pamunkey River.

[33] This is the well-known Trevilian Raid, 7–24 June 1864, Sheridan's second expedition. On 3 June, General Grant attacked Confederate positions at Cold Harbor, was repulsed with what he himself admitted were heavy losses—stultifying is most accurate; Lee's losses were light in comparison. In something like eight minutes, the Army of the Potomac lost anywhere from 7,000 to 12,000 men! Grant changed his strategy; he now pointed toward a siege of Richmond. Therefore, Sheridan was ordered to cut the Virginia Central Railroad to the west.

camp near Trevilian Station on the Virginia Central a strong line of videttes faced our own horsemen.

On the 11th we moved out towards Trevilian about daylight and at once became engaged in what proved to be one of the very hottest actions of the campaign.[34] The 2nd United States Cavalry of our brigade had the lead with the 1st Cavalry in support, and in a few moments Capt. Rodenbough, commanding the 2nd, was brought back badly wounded.[35] The whole brigade was immediately deployed in one of the thickest tangles of brush that I have ever seen. We were so close to the enemy that we could hear every word of command as distinctly as those of our own people, but the woods were so dense that we could see no one. Many men and officers on either side were captured by accidentally getting into each others' lines. Capt. Leoser, who succeeded Rodenbough in command of the 2nd Cavalry, was taken in this way while trying to establish connection between the left of his regiment and the right of the 1st.[36]

About noon the enemy began to give way and were soon driven rapidly and in considerable disorder through Trevilian. About this time Custer's Brigade came up on our left by another road and captured a large number of horses and caissons. These were however mostly re-taken by the enemy in our front who were driven back on to Custer, unexpectedly to him. About two in the afternoon our

[34] Merritt's Reserve Brigade was moving down Clayton's Store Road toward Trevilian Station, "a loading point with water tank and a few other buildings." On their left, along a woods road, Custer's Brigade moved. The two brigades were about a mile apart.

[35] Theophilus F. Rodenbough had been commissioned a second lieutenant, Second Regiment of Dragoons, 27 March 1861. He received five brevets for gallant conduct during the war. Here at Trevilian Station, he was awarded the Medal of Honor. In his report, General Merritt stated: "Captain Rodenbough handled his gallant regiment with great skill and unexampled valor." OR, XXXVI, Pt. 1, 849. In addition to the article cited earlier, Rodenbough also published "Sheridan's Trevilian Raid," Battles and Leaders of the Civil War, IV, 233–36, an interesting piece.

Second Lieutenant Patrick W. Horrigan was wounded here, and First Lieutenant Michael Lawless was killed. Both were natives of Ireland, both former enlisted men, both officers in the Second Cavalry.

[36] Charles McK. Leoser's captaincy dated from 9 June 1863. He had served eight months once (1861–62) as colonel, Eleventh New York Volunteers. He resigned the Army on 19 October 1865. Also taken prisoner in the battle was Major James H. Kidd, Sixth Michigan Cavalry, commanding, of Custer's brigade; he was later a colonel.

regiment, which was entirely out of ammunition, was withdrawn from the line for a new supply, and was then sent in again on the right to resist an attack which was seen to be impending in that direction. We moved down a steep hill and across a little valley through which ran a small stream bordered by willows. On the other side of the stream the ground rose again in high hills, on the crest of one of which was a large brick house and several farm buildings and a good sized orchard. Along the edge of the hill ran a stout stone wall, and as we reached the little stream in the valley, the enemy rose up from behind this wall and poured in heavy volleys. It was a very ugly position. They were well protected, and we had nothing bigger than a blade of grass. The hill was very steep and the grass slippery, and it looked exceedingly doubtful whether we could carry the crest. I was with my battalion on the right of the regiment, and my friend Ogden, the Adjutant of the regiment, was with me. As the enemy developed their force, he remarked, "Well, I must join Sweitzer," and jumping across the creek ran along the line towards the center of the regiment.

My battalion pushed straight up the hill and succeeded in carrying the stone wall and getting into the orchard. From thence we worked our way up to the brick house, and getting across the enemy's left flank, soon caused them to let go the whole line of the wall. About this time I noticed that we did not connect with anyone on our left, and one of my sergeants in that direction soon reported to me that the rest of the regiment was halted along the wall. Although we were in a capital position ourselves I knew it was useless to stay there as the enemy would soon find out our isolated position and probably take us all in; so I gave the order to fall back to the wall, which we succeeded in reaching, though with considerable loss, as the enemy made it very hot for us in crossing the open ground between us and it.[37] When I got over it and lay down to rest

[37] The engagement at Trevilian Station was mostly fought "dismounted by both sides, as had also been the earlier fights of the cavalry during the summer in the Wilderness, at Todd's Tavern, Haw's Shop, and Matadequin Creek. Indeed, they could hardly have been fought otherwise than on foot, as there was little chance for mounted fighting in eastern Virginia, the dense woods, the armament of both parties, and the practice of barricading making it impracticable to use the sabre with anything like a large force; and so with the exception of Yellow Tavern the dis-

a moment, Lieut. Hoyer of the regiment said to me, "Ogden is killed." Altogether it could not have been ten minutes since we had separated at the stream and it seemed impossible that my closest friend was gone. A bullet had struck him directly between the eyes and he fell dead without a word, within three minutes of the time I last saw him.

Frederick Callender Ogden was one of the most brilliant young men of his time and in all respects one of the most promising. He was graduated at Yale with the Class of 1860 and soon after had gone abroad to complete his education by foreign travel. The outbreak of the Rebellion drew him back to his native country and he was at once commissioned 2nd Lieutenant in the First Regiment of Cavalry, dating from November, 1861. Although without previous military training his great natural ability soon made up any deficiency in that respect, and his many accomplishments, affable manners and unusual personal beauty attracted the attention and won the admiration of all who came in contact with him. Added to this his conscientious discharge of duty and great gallantry in action soon marked him out for promotion, and soon after receiving his 1st Lieutenancy, he was appointed Adjutant of the regiment. It is with no intention of saying anything to the disparagement of the many gallant officers who have held that position during my term of service of nearly thirty years in that regiment that I say that I never saw his equal. All who knew him would willingly say the same. Our brigade commander, Gen. Wesley Merritt says, in his report of this action, "The modest, unaffected, generous Lieutenant Ogden, of the First, whom to see was to respect, and to know was to admire, poured out his life's blood at Trevilian."[38] We laid his body in a house at Trevilian that night, and next morning I went in to take a last look at him with Gen. Custer of the First Brigade.[39] We buried him in the yard of the house and put a board

---

mounted method prevailed in almost every engagement." Sheridan, *Personal Memoirs,* I, 424–25.

[38] *OR,* XXXVI, Pt. 1, 851.

[39] This was Sunday, 12 June 1864. Custer was fortunate to be able to pay his respects. The day before, he had barely escaped disastrous defeat at the hands of

at the head of the grave. The Chaplain of the 10th N. Y. Cavalry read the Episcopal service and all the men who could be spared from the regiment were present. The next year when the war was over, Ogden's cousin, Gen. Ranald MacKenzie, removed the remains and he now lies in the burying ground at Newport, R. I., where I have visited the grave.[40] The regiment never seemed quite the same afterward to me.

We buried our friend about eleven o'clock in the morning, and before we had quite finished, orders came to move out to the front. The battle began again at once and continued until long after nightfall by the light of the moon. This day we lost Lieut. John H. Nichols, killed. On the evening previous Nichols had brought me Ogden's watch and some trinkets he had taken from his body, saying that I as Ogden's closest friend was the proper person to take charge of them. This evening I performed the same duty for poor Nichols himself. He gave his life away—willingly taking a duty to which he was not sent.[41] Singularly enough he was shot in exactly the same spot as Ogden had been the day before, and like him fell dead without a sound. We lost many gallant fellows on each day, and Trevilian will always be a sad memory in my life.[42]

During the time we had been fighting, another portion of the command had been engaged in destroying the railroad track and

Generals Rosser, Butler, and Fitzhugh Lee. Surrounded, it looked hopeless for him when elements of Merritt's and Devin's Brigade broke through. See Jay Monaghan, "Custer's 'Last Stand'—Trevilian Station, 1864," *Civil War History,* VIII (September, 1962), 245–58.

[40] Ranald Slidell Mackenzie (1840–1889), USMA, Class of 1862, brigadier general of volunteers, 19 October 1864, another of the bright and talented "boy generals" under Grant.

[41] Merritt referred to him, affectionately, as "the frank and impulsive" Nichols. *OR,* XXXVI Pt. 1, 851.

[42] Trevilian Station was a nasty and costly battle. "Our satisfaction," wrote Merritt, "at our successes is allayed by the sad reflection that we lost so many brave soldiers and gallant comrades, who, while they fell battling in the cause of right, have left vacancies which, in too many cases, can never be filled; young officers who were just commencing a career of usefulness, of which the present offered such brilliant promise; others whose present services added fresh luster to the glories already won—all met the death of brave soldiers unflinchingly, leaving memories which cannot die." *Ibid.* Union losses were heavy. All told, Sheridan's Cavalry Corps sustained 1,007 casualties from 11 to 12 June 1864. *Ibid.,* 186–87.

bridges, in the vicinity of Trevilian.[43] This work had been pretty thoroughly accomplished, but the Junction with Hunter's forces was of course out of the question, as that General had not come in our direction.[44] Gen. Sheridan had learned from his scouts that large reinforcements of infantry were joining the enemy, and as he only had ammunition left sufficient for one more battle, he did not consider it advisable to remain longer in his present isolated position. Accordingly soon after midnight we moved back to the North Anna, which we crossed the next morning at Carpenter's Ford.

We had of course a very large number of wounded to take care of, and were further embarrassed by a body of prisoners, some five hundred altogether, which had to be guarded. About one hundred of our wounded, with a large number of the enemy's, had to be left behind in charge of the surgeons, and we hauled along in wagons collected from the country, perhaps five hundred more, who could bear transportation. Some two thousand Negroes, escaping from slavery, also followed the command.[45] During our return to the army the enemy made very little attempt to interfere with us—only watching us from a distance. We passed over the battlefield of Spotsylvania, and noticed the terrible destruction that had occurred there. In many places trees of ten or twelve inches in diameter had been cut in two by the hailstorm of bullets, and the smaller growth looked as if it had been swept by a cyclone. Fire had also broken out in the timber and we saw many instances where the seriously wounded had been burned to death in the flames. As there was no certainty as to the precise spot where we should find the Army of the Potomac, Gen. Sheridan marched in the direction of

[43] "The morning of 12 June Gregg's division commenced destroying the railroad to Louisa Court House, and continued the work during the day, breaking it pretty effectually." Sheridan, *Personal Memoirs*, I, 423.

[44] Instead of coming toward Charlottesville, as Sheridan had expected, General Hunter was in the neighborhood of Lexington, "apparently moving on Lynchburg." *Ibid.*, 422.

[45] Sheridan now had with him about 500 Confederate prisoners, 500 wounded Union soldiers, a number of Confederate wounded, and approximately 2,000 freed Negro slaves. At Trevilian, Sheridan left three hospitals "containing many Rebel wounded, and 90 of ours that were non-transportable, with medicines, liquors, some hard bread, coffee, and sugar." *OR*, XXXVI, Pt. 1, 797.

the White House, where he knew the gunboats were lying in the Pamunkey River, and where there was likely to be a depot of supplies. As we approached this place on the morning of the 20th we heard heavy artillery firing in our front,[46] and soon couriers came from Gen. Abercrombie, who was in command, bringing the news that he was attacked by a large force of the enemy.[47] Our approach, however, relieved the pressure on Abercrombie and we went into camp on the banks of the river. The next morning both our divisions crossed the river and drove off the enemy, after a sharp engagement.[48] We followed them up to Tunstall's Station where we had another engagement that evening, and the next day, the 23rd, we had a fight at Jones' bridge on the Chickahominy, which we secured.[49] On the 24th we pushed on towards the James river by way of Charles City Court House, Harrison's Landing and Malvern Hill. Torbert's division and Gregg's moved on parallel roads, and Gregg was sharply attacked at St. Mary's Church by the whole cavalry corps of the enemy. Owing to the dense woods and to some peculiar state of the atmosphere, not a sound of this engagement reached us, and as Gregg was entirely surrounded by the enemy not one of his couriers got through to Sheridan, who had accompanied our division. However, the gallant Gen. Gregg held his ground until after dark, when he was able to withdraw his command. By his splendid battle he had saved the train which we were escorting from the White House, and which never should have been left for us to guard.[50]

On the 25th we reached the James river at Douthat's landing and

[46] On 20 June, the route was across the Mattaponi by pontoon bridge, thence toward White House via King William Court House.

[47] John Joseph Abercrombie (1798–1877), USMA, Class of 1822, one of the eldest of Union commanders in the war, had until quite recently commanded at White House Depot—and apparently still did but had been relieved (at least on paper) on 12 June by Brigadier General George W. Getty. See n. 16, Chap. VIII.

[48] The Confederates occupied the bluffs, but the situation was not serious. During the morning of 21 June, Gregg's Division was crossed over dismounted and Torbert's Division mounted.

[49] Tunstall Station was also known as Black Creek, Jones' Bridge as Gowan's Bridge.

[50] Sanford echoes Sheridan's own words in his report of the operation; see *OR*, XXXVI, Pt. 1, 799. The train numbered some 900 wagons.

were ferried across in boats sent there for that purpose. There we found the Army of the Potomac on the south side of the James river settled down in front of the City of Petersburg and evidently "in for a siege." It was in fact a blockade of both Richmond and Petersburg, as Butler's Army of the James was now closely joined on our right, and the two armies were acting as one body under Gen. Grant's command.

We were of course greatly in need of rest and recuperation after such an expedition. The horses were actually reduced to skin and bone, and were greatly in need of shoeing. The men's clothing was in rags, and they were worn out and nervous from the constant strain of marching by night and fighting by day, with little sleep and less food, and incessant guard and picket duty. The infantry soldier, as a rule, knows little of the hardships experienced by his comrade in the cavalry. He sees him on reviews or inspections gotten up in a showy uniform, riding a sleek and well-groomed horse, and he is apt to think that he has the easy part of the campaigning, while his own duty of trudging along in the dust is the hard one. He knows also that when the armies are close-locked in battle, it is on the infantry that the brunt of the fighting falls, and that the fate of the campaign will be settled by the foot soldier. On the other hand, he does not see that where he marches one mile the trooper marches ten; that while he is lying quietly in camp with a neat tent over his head, a good supper being prepared for him by the company cook, and a reasonable probability of a good night's sleep ahead of him, the trooper is plodding wearily through mud and mire with the certainty of having his horse to take care of when he gets into bivouac—with no tent to lie in, for the scanty transportation will not admit of any being carried along, and with the certainty if he is wounded of being left behind to the tender mercies of the country people and the enemy, and the prospect of a prison should he be fortunate enough to recover. The infantry man decides the great engagements indeed; but where he is once under fire, the trooper is in twenty actions. When the battle is over, the infantry man can go quietly to sleep—his work is done—but the trooper must ride to the front, to the flanks, to the rear—everywhere—he is on the watch, and his rest only comes when the campaign is over.[51]

When we crossed the James we were ordered to draw forage and feed our exhausted animals on the south side of the river, but as we disembarked from the ferryboats, we were met with orders to hurry out to the extreme left of the army where we were needed at once. During our raid to Trevilian, Wilson with our Third Division had been on an expedition against the railroads south of the James. He had been entirely successful in his advance but on the return trip had run up against Lee's infantry in the vicinity of Reams' Station on the Weldon railroad, and been badly cut up. He lost all his artillery and large numbers of horses, besides many men killed, wounded and prisoners.[52] Gen. Meade had been notified before the expedition started, by Wilson, that he should return in that direction, and had promised to cover the ground. No relief however was sent until the return of Sheridan from his expedition. When we reached Reams' Station after a dreadful march through the heat and dust with our worn out horses and exhausted men, we found the gallant 6th Corps just getting up; but they were too late, as were we also. Wilson had been driven off, and a large number of his men captured. He made a long detour and eventually reached the army after suffering terrible loss.

As soon as Wilson was known to be safe, the whole cavalry corps was ordered to Light House Point on the James river, to rest

[51] Sanford's plea for the cavalryman is odd in this sense: during this entire period, Sheridan's men had fought dismounted (see n. 37 *supra*); they were mounted infantry. In his report on the raid, General Torbert commented on this also: "The cavalry fighting this year has been dismounted; the enemy had not dared to give us an opportunity to operate mounted, and when dismounted, they have had a great advantage of us from the fact that they have a very large brigade of mounted infantry armed with the rifled musket; but I am proud to say that the division has been signally successful in everything they have been called upon to perform. *OR*, XXXVI., Pt. 1, 810.

[52] Brigadier General James H. Wilson had been dispatched by General Meade on 22 June. Reams' Station is on the Petersburg & Weldon Railroad about eight miles south of Petersburg. Wilson suffered defeat at the hands of Brigadier General William Mahone, CSA, who captured twelve guns and all the wagons on 29 June. Sheridan marched down there on 30 June.

and refit.[53] They needed to do both. For fifty-six consecutive days we had been marching and fighting, and during that whole time had hardly ever had a decent meal or quiet night's rest. The limit of endurance had certainly been reached—for many poor fellows it had been passed—and probably there are few among the survivors whose lives have not been appreciably shortened by the hardships and privations of that terrible campaign.[54]

Light House Point was not an unpleasant place perhaps in the early Spring, but one would hardly choose it for a July residence. Still to us it was *luxury*. For the first few days no one cared to do anything but lie under the shade of the trees, and rest and smoke. Of course it was not all relaxation by any means. The whole command required equipment, the horses needed shoeing, and of course the regular service of picket and reconnaissance duty on the exposed left flank of the army went on as usual; but it was so different from the previous two months' work that it acted as a rest to body and mind.[55] In company with other officers of the regiment I took the opportunity thus afforded to visit the lines in front of Petersburg, which were curious and interesting, and also to call on old friends in the infantry and artillery, and at the different Headquarters. There were many gaps in the ranks, since the previous winter. In many regiments more than half, and in some, more

53 Sheridan's cavalry arrived here on 2 July and remained until 26 July. The original idea seems to have been for Sheridan to follow after Wilson. On 1 July, Sheridan wrote to Chief of Staff Major General Humphreys: "I will move in the morning, but it will be at the risk of dismounting my command. I marched from the river without forage and without preparation. My horses are worn out. Some of them have been without forage for forty-eight hours." *OR*, XL, Pt. 2, 573. This seems to have ended the matter.

54 To give the reader some idea of the extent of the raid, Merritt estimated that from 7 May (when he assumed command from Torbert) to 26 May (when Torbert returned), the Reserve Brigade (and the division) had marched 294 miles. In turn, Torbert estimated in his report that from 26 May to 26 June, the division marched about 400 miles—and both do not include the sally to Reams' Station.

55 "While at this camp I received about 1,500 horses. These, together with about 400 obtained at Old Church by dismounting recruits, were all that were issued to me while personally in command of the Cavalry Corps, from April 6 to August 1, 1864." *OR*, XXXVI, Pt. 1, 799–800. In his *Personal Memoirs*, I, 446, Sheridan complained that this number of horses was not "near enough to mount the whole command, so I disposed the men who could not be supplied in a dismounted camp."

than three-fourths of the officers had been killed or wounded since the beginning of the campaign. The position occupied by the enemy was very strong and as it covered both Petersburg and Richmond it was very long and of course impossible to surround. Gen. Grant's efforts were directed toward extending his lines farther and farther, toward his own left, and around the enemy's right—gradually getting possession of the railroads which supplied the two cities, and causing the enemy to extend his own lines to such an extent that they would become so weak as to be easily broken. These movements to the left were varied by an occasional feint towards the right, north of the James river. These last were generally entrusted to the forces of the Army of the James under Major General Butler; but occasionally troops from the Army of the Potomac were used.

The weather during July was intensely hot, and a good deal of sickness prevailed in the army.[56] The morale of the infantry was said at this time to have been a good deal impaired by the loss of so many excellent soldiers and officers in the terrible Wilderness battles and more especially at Cold Harbor, and by the influx of large bodies of drafted men to fill their places. These latter were additions in number, but generally speaking they were not acquisitions in any other respect. There was also a considerable element of substitutes purchased by drafted men to take their places, and of the class known as bounty-jumpers. These latter especially were a source of positive weakness. They deserted at the first opportunity, often to the enemy, and of course furnished information which was occasionally of value. As a rule the cavalry corps had none of these scoundrels in its ranks. The service was popular at this time, and when regiments were given an opportunity to recruit they had little or no difficulty in filling up the troops with a reliable class of men.

On the afternoon of July 26th the 1st and 2nd Divisions under Torbert and Gregg, with Gen. Sheridan commanding, moved out from Light House Point for the purpose of making a demonstration

---

[56] So warm was the weather, Sheridan says, that "almost an entire suspension of hostilities on the part of the Army of the Potomac" prevailed. *Personal Memoirs*, I, 446.

north of the James river.[57] The 2nd Army Corps under Gen. Hancock (who had command of the whole) and Gen. Kautz' small cavalry division from the Army of the James, moved also.[58] We crossed the Appomattox at Broadway Landing, and the James at Deep Bottom. Gen. Barlow's division of Hancock's corps moved in advance after crossing the James, and carried the enemy's works on that side of the river, capturing four pieces of artillery.[59]

The cavalry then moved to the right of the 2nd Corps and deployed in line of battle, finding the enemy also in line and protected by heavy breastworks.[60] The 2nd U. S. Cavalry deployed as skirmishers attacked the enemy's pickets and drove them in on their main body, which at once advanced and forced back our line a short distance.

Capt. Sweitzer, commanding the 1st U. S. Cavalry, having been taken ill during the march of the previous night, was obliged to relinquish the command; so for the first time I found myself commanding a regiment in action, on this day, July 28th, 1864. I sent word to Division Headquarters as soon as possible, and notified my senior officer, Captain Marcus A. Reno, who was at the time on the Division staff; but he very magnanimously declined to deprive me of the command, so I made up my mind to do the best I could with it. When the Rebel line advanced we fell back to the crest of a hill, behind which we lay down to get a little rest. The hill overlooked a valley perhaps three-fourths of a mile in width and bordered by a thick woods. In this woods the enemy halted— apparently to dress their lines, and we got a chance to reform also and to get our lines rectified. Soon they advanced again and as they came out into the open ground, we saw at once that it was an

[57] And, as Sheridan puts it, "if opportunity offered, to make a second expedition against the Virginia Central railroad, and again destroy the bridges on the North Anna, the Little and the South Anna rivers." *Personal Memoirs*, I, 446.

[58] August V. Kautz (1828–1895), USMA, Class of 1852, just recently (7 May) having been promoted to brigadier general of volunteers. His division was small: four regiments in two brigades and a section of artillery.

[59] Francis C. Barlow (1834–1896), commanding the First Division, Hancock's Second Corps, had enlisted as a private in 1861. He was ill during this maneuver, and on the evening of 29 July, he departed the Army on sick leave.

[60] The Confederate line extended across the New Market and Central roads, both leading to Richmond.

infantry force that we were fighting. The men sprang forward to the crest and poured in volley after volley from their breech-loading carbines. The Rebels faltered, then halted, and then turned and ran like good fellows for the woods. As our trumpets sounded the *charge*, the men sprang forward in pursuit and drove them clear across the valley and through the woods. My regiment captured the battle flag of the regiment in front of it and another was captured in the brigade. Our victory was complete, and the regiment was highly commended in orders and in the newspaper accounts of that date.[61] The enemy made no attempt to renew the attack, although we held the woods for one or two hours. On our side there was no desire to push forward, as the object of the movement had been accomplished. This purpose was to draw as large a force of Lee's troops as possible, from the South to the North side of the James river, in order to make it possible to break his lines after the explosion of the mine in front of the 9th Corps. This explosion was set for the 30th of the month, and great results were expected.

As I have said, our part of the affair was thoroughly successful. The enemy reenforced largely in our front, and all day of the 29th we lay in line of battle expecting an attack. This did not come, however, and towards evening the 2nd Corps with Gen. Hancock withdrew to the South side in order to take part in the battle next day. This left nothing but the comparatively small body of cavalry to hold the lines, and we were in a decidedly dangerous situation, as their force was amply strong enough to have completely crushed us if they had pushed forward. However they were undoubtedly unaware of Hancock's withdrawal and in addition were very possibly deceived by a ruse of Sheridan's. In order to deceive the

---

[61] Sanford has described the Battle of Deep Bottom, Virginia, also known as Darbytown, Strawberry Plains, or New Market Road. Sheridan reported taking 250 prisoners. The Union troopers were armed with repeating carbines. Major General Joseph B. Kershaw (1822–1894), CSA, was in command in this sector. The First Cavalry captured "the standard" of a North Carolina infantry regiment.

In point of fact, Sanford had commanded the regiment the day before in a "slight cavalry action on the North side of [the] James River." For his action on 28 July, Sanford had "the pleasure of receiving congratulations" from Merritt "for the conduct of the Regiment." Sanford to Brevet Colonel Charles H. Morgan, captain, Fourth Regiment of Artillery, in a letter dated 26 June 1866, written with a view to brevet promotion. See n. 41 Chap. X.

enemy, he sent the whole of our division over the bridge to the South side, before daylight in the morning, having first caused the bridge to be covered with straw so that the tramp of the horses might not be heard. Then leaving the horses on that side under guard, he moved the division back on foot by daylight, the straw of course having been removed and the troops allowed to make as much noise as they pleased. This naturally gave the idea that we were receiving large re-enforcements and tended to keep the enemy quiet.

On the night of the 29th we all withdrew and the whole corps reached the South side by daylight and moved rapidly towards the left of the Army in order to take part in the battle of the mine.[62] The explosion came off according to programme; but the 9th corps failed to make a lodgement beyond the enemy's lines. The whole matter has been the subject of a Court of Inquiry and can be found described at length in the Records of the Rebellion, so I will not go into it.[63] We saw as we passed along the lines, the broken and disordered remnants of the colored division, and also passed Gen. Meade and his staff—looking a good deal disgusted. One of the aides de camp (Sanders, 6th Infantry) in reply to a demand for news, would only vouchsafe the information that the General was "very mad indeed" and indeed that spoke for itself.[64] He certainly looked it, and he was none too amiable looking at the best of times.

Our services were not required at all events, and we went into camp, and I suspect everybody who was not on duty was asleep in about ten minutes. Sheridan says in his report of this affair, "The movement to the north side of the James for the accomplishment

[62] For some peculiar reason, Sanford, who is usually accurate in chronology, is badly confused. Surely the reader must be, too. After the affair at Darbytown on the twenty-eighth, the Second Corps withdrew to a line near the head of the bridge; Sheridan's cavalry was drawn back, too. That night, 28–29 July, Sheridan pulled off his ruse (he says he used moss and grass). Nothing happened on the twenty-ninth; after dark, the Second Corps was "hastily and quietly withdrawn" to the south side, and it was then that the Cavalry Corps felt anxious as Sheridan withdrew "by brigades" over the bridge. He said that "an offensive movement" by the Confederates would have annihilated his "whole command." Shortly after daylight, 30 July, the crossing was effected. *OR*, XXXVI, Pt. 1, 800–801.
[63] For the court of inquiry, see *OR*, XL, Pt. 1, 42–129.
[64] Captain William W. Sanders, commissary of musters.

of our part of the plan connected with the mine explosion, was well executed, and every point made; but it was attended with such anxiety and sleeplessness as to prostrate almost every officer and man in the command."[65]

That evening we were ordered to the Shenandoah Valley, so that our part in the Petersburg campaign was over for *that* year. Gen. Sheridan says that his casualties for this part of the campaign, May 5th, to August 1, 1864, were between five and six thousand men and officers, and his captures of prisoners from the enemy numbered two thousand.[66]

---

[65] *OR,* XXXVI, Pt. 1, 801.

[66] Sheridan did not boast; however, he did assert loudly that "we led the advance of the army to the Wilderness; that on the Richmond raid we marked out its line of march to the North Anna, where we found it on our return; that we again led its advance to Hanovertown, and thence to Cold Harbor; that we removed the enemy's cavalry from the south side of the Chickahominy by the Trevilian raid, and thereby materially assisted the army in its successful march to the James River and Petersburg .... In all the operations the percentage of cavalry casualties was as great as that of the infantry, and the question which had existed 'Who ever saw a dead cavalryman?' was set at rest." *OR,* XXXVI, Pt. 1, 802.

·CHAPTER VII·

ON THE 31ST OF JULY, the 1st Cavalry Division, Gen. A. T. A. Torbert commanding, embarked on transport steamers for Washington. We steamed down the James river and around Fortress Monroe, and up Chesapeake Bay, and the Potomac to Washington, where we disembarked, at Giesborough Point. On the evening of the 6th of August we marched through Washington and Georgetown to Tennallytown, Maryland, where we encamped. It was the turn of my regiment to take the lead that night, and as we passed out of Georgetown, an order came from brigade headquarters to throw out advance guard and flankers. "All right," said Captain Sweitzer to the A.D.C. "Four years of war, and marching out of Washington with an advanced guard." But there was need of it. Early had only just been driven away from the very ground we were marching over, and his cavalry were in our immediate front.[1] The march through Maryland was delightful. The weather was cool, as compared with the hot, stifling temperature of Southern Virginia, the farms were neat and well kept, and there was an air of thrift and comfort delightful to contemplate, after four years' experience of poor Virginia,—war-torn and battered as it was.

We reached Harpers Ferry on the 8th and there Gen. Torbert

[1] Early in July, Lieutenant General Jubal A. Early, CSA, entered Maryland from the Shenandoah Valley, met and defeated Major General Lew Wallace, USA, commanding Middle Department, at Monocacy on 9 July, threatened Washington on 11–12 July, retired back across the Potomac. Then he came across again; on his orders, the town of Chambersburg, Pennsylvania, was burned down on 30 July 1864. See n. 12 *infra*. Prior to this, Early had defeated Major General David Hunter, then commanding the Department of West Virginia, in the Lynchburg Campaign, 26 May–29 June 1864. Lee had sent Early into the valley after Cold Harbor.

reported for duty with his division to Gen. Sheridan, now commanding the Middle Military Division and the Army of the Shenandoah.[2] Torbert was at once assigned as Chief of Cavalry of the Military Division, and given command of a cavalry corps which was made up of his own 1st Division, thence forward under the command of Merritt; the 3rd Division of the Army of the Potomac, at first under Wilson, later under Custer; and a Division already belonging to the Shenandoah Army, at first under Averell, and afterwards under Powell.[3] We moved South from Harpers Ferry on the 10th and soon struck the enemy's pickets, and commenced skirmishing, driving them steadily during the day. On the 11th they resisted more strongly, and we had a very severe fight, for the possession of the Winchester turnpike, which we finally gained.[4]

At this time I was appointed Inspector General of the Regular Cavalry Brigade, and reported for duty in that capacity, but only served a day or two when I was offered by Gen. Torbert a position on his staff as Asst. Adjt. General of the Cavalry Corps. This I at once accepted, and performed the duty until the arrival of the regular Adjutant-General (Maj. Russell)[5] and thereafter the

[2] Sheridan arrived at Harpers Ferry on 6 August. That same night, he was busy and sent a telegram to Grant: "I find affairs somewhat confused, but will straighten them out....I am anxiously awaiting the arrival of General Torbert's command. General Averell has all the cavalry that belongs here." At the moment, Averell was pursuing Brigadier General John McCausland, CSA, who burned Chambersburg, Pennsylvania. *OR,* XLIII, Pt. 1, 710. On 7 August, Sheridan was assigned temporary command of the newly constituted Middle Military Division, consisting of the Middle Department and the Departments of Washington, the Susquehanna, and West Virginia. Thus begins the famed and successful Shenandoah Valley Campaign, 7 August–28 November 1864, against Early.

[3] Torbert assumed command as chief of cavalry, Middle Military Division, on 9 August 1864. To clarify the eventual organization of his cavalry: Brigadier General Wesley Merritt, First Division; Brevet Major General William M. Averell, Second Division; Brigadier General James H. Wilson, Third Division. Averell's Division was to come from the Department of West Virginia and as yet was not a part of the Cavalry Corps. Wilson's Third Division had not yet arrived from Petersburg. See p. 258. Colonel William H. Powell commanded the Second Division at Cedar Creek after relieving Averell. See n. 36 *infra.*

[4] Action on 11 August occurred at Toll-Gate, near White Post, Virginia, Newton, and near Winchester.

[5] Major William Russell, Jr., assistant adjutant general of volunteers, to rank from 15 April 1863. General Orders No. 11, dated 8 September 1864, relieved Sanford from duty as acting assistant adjutant general and announced him as commissary of musters for the cavalry, Middle Military Division. See *OR,* XLIII, Pt. 2, 52.

duties of aide de camp and Commissary of Musters of the Corps until the end of the war.

The next few days we marched up the valley, crossing Cedar Creek and driving the enemy beyond Strasburg, but on the 17th the whole command was ordered to fall back down the Valley. The infantry (6th Army Corps) under Gen. Wright had already gone and the cavalry covered the rear, closely followed by the enemy.[6] The cavalry with the exception of one brigade under Col. Lowell, was ordered to Berryville.[7] Gen. Torbert with that brigade went to Winchester, where he was joined about noon by the 3rd Division of Cavalry under Wilson, just arrived from the Army of the Potomac.[8] A small brigade of infantry under Col. Penrose, also reported for duty,[9] and with this command Torbert was directed to hold the position as long as possible, to enable the main body to take posts near Harpers Ferry.

In the afternoon the enemy advanced and attacked our lines in strong force, and Gen. Torbert soon found that he was engaged with the whole Army Corps of Maj. Gen. Breckinridge. He held them off splendidly until nightfall, though with considerable loss; when satisfied that he had accomplished his object, he gave orders to fall back to the other side of Winchester, and thence to proceed to Summit Point where Gen. Sheridan had by this time concentrated

6 Horatio G. Wright (1820–1899), USMA, Class of 1841, commanded the Sixth Army Corps under Sheridan. Wright had been brought to Washington with his corps to oppose Early in July, thence to the valley. This was the second time Wright had been a major general of volunteers; his date of rank now was 20 May 1864. Until 1861, his service had been with the Corps of Engineers; he returned to the corps after the war and in 1879 became brigadier general chief of engineers, USA.

7 Colonel Charles R. Lowell, Jr., commanded the Third Brigade, First Division, about 700 muskets. Lowell was commissioned captain, Sixth Regiment of Cavalry, 14 May 1861; colonel, Second Massachusetts Volunteers, 10 May 1863. He died 20 October 1864 of wounds received at Cedar Creek. See n. 34 *infra.*

8 Indeed, Wilson just then arrived at Winchester—on the seventeenth at 11:00 A.M. On 5 August, he broke camp before Petersburg, marched to City Point, and embarked for Giesborough Point, much the same procedure as Torbert. On 12 August, Wilson received orders to proceed to the Shenandoah Valley, via Leesburg, through Snicker's Gap.

9 Colonel William H. Penrose, First Brigade, First Division, Wright's Sixth Corps, composed of three New Jersey regiments, the so-called Jersey Brigade. He was a top-notch officer and garnered five brevets during the war. When he retired in 1896, he was colonel, Sixteen Regiment of Infantry.

his army.[10] The aides de camp were sent in different directions with orders, and my own required me to go in to the town of Winchester, directly in our rear, and to start the wagon trains down the road toward Summit Point. This duty I performed of course, and having done so, it occurred to me that it would be an exceedingly proper thing for me to drop in at our friend Mrs. M.'s and warn the family of what was about to occur.

The M.'s were very lovely people and great lovers of the Union, and had shown great kindness to our troops on numerous occasions. There were two young ladies in the family—most attractive girls in all respects. As I knew the battle was over, it being at this time quite dark, and I took it for granted that the main body of our troops must fall back on the main street, in which the house stood, I never doubted the perfect safety of the visit. For that matter I do not suppose the thought occurred to me. I accordingly rode up to the house and dismounted, leaving my horse in charge of my little trumpeter, John Powers, a boy of perhaps fourteen. Immediately after another aide, Lieut. Goldsmith of our staff, rode up with the same idea in his mind that I had.[11]

We were warmly welcomed by our kind hostesses, and possibly remained longer than we expected. At all events, we were suddenly startled by Powers crying out, "Run, Captain! Run, Lieutenant! here come the Johnnies!" We did run, and fortunately our horses stood quietly for us to mount, and we swept down the street with a clatter of hoofs and a hailstorm of curses and pistol balls close about and behind us. My most vivid recollection, however, of the whole thing is the sight of those two brave girls, standing in the bright light shining out from the door—clapping their hands and calling "good bye" while the bullets flew all around them. They showed me the marks of several bullets in the swinging blind doors, when I returned there for winter quarters some months later.

[10] Major General John C. Breckinridge (1821–1875), CSA, a native of Lexington, Kentucky, commanded a division under Early. Sanford neatly glosses over what was a defeat at the hands of Breckinridge on 17 August. Torbert lost 200 infantry and 50 cavalry as prisoners, but states that he withdrew in good order. Sheridan bluntly said that Breckinridge drove Torbert out.

[11] First Lieutenant Howard H. Goldsmith, Fifteenth New Jersey Volunteer Infantry, aide-de-camp to General Torbert.

Goldsmith and I were well mounted and knew the country well —or rather he did—and we had little difficulty in throwing off our pursuers; but we were not out of the woods yet, for as we rode through the outskirts of the town we were fired at several times from the windows. Then as we came up to our own rear guard, the troopers, supposing us to be scouts of the enemy, took a crack at us all around, and on the whole, as Goldsmith remarked at the time, "I doubt whether this thing pays." The worst was to come and *we knew it*. Gen. Torbert, like the fine soldier he was, was in the place of danger at the moment, well to the rear of his force. He heard the firing, and was quite ready to greet us on our arrival, when he found what the occasion of it was. He had been exceedingly worried at our non-appearance, and had given us up as dead or prisoners. He gave us a pretty severe scolding, and we deserved it, for we had no right to cause him the anxiety we had done. He often laughed about it afterwards, and always ended up by saying that we deserved to have been shot. We found out afterwards that the brigade which was ordered to withdraw through the town, had taken a back street, and not being pressed by the enemy at the moment, had gone by without our knowledge.

It was a remarkable coincidence that about six months later an incident of precisely the same nature in every respect occurred on an expedition of the Cavalry Corps to Charlottesville on the Virginia Central Railroad. On that occasion the gentleman who was saying good bye and was only narrowly saved from capture by the courage and address of his orderly (Sergt. Bates, 1st Cavalry), was Bvt. Maj. Gen. Torbert, commanding the Cavalry Corps. The fact was that one never knew what to expect at that time. The enterprising partisan chief, Mosby, assisted by a crowd of lesser lights such as McNeill, Payne and Gilmor, kept the whole country so thoroughly covered by scouts and spies that you would not move a hundred yards from camp without an escort.[12] They knew the

---

[12] Lieutenant Colonel (later Colonel) John S. Mosby, CSA, Forty-third Virginia Cavalry Battalion, commanding, had recently and successfully brought to a close a period of operations from 1 May to 3 August, but he was out again from 9 August to 14 October. Without a doubt, he was the most successful of partisan chiefs.

Sanford's list includes Major (later Lieutenant Colonel) Harry W. Gilmor, CSA,

country thoroughly, and every man, woman and child in it was a friend, ready to give them every possible information and comfort, and equally prepared to deceive and injure us. Of course it was quite natural that it should be so, and in some respects it would seem that no blame could be attributed to them. But on the other hand it has to be remembered that they were accepting our protection, and many of them were engaged in traffic with us. Then the laws of war are perfectly definite as to the position of a citizen in a country occupied by hostile armies, and afford no mercy to one who takes an actively hostile attitude. Should he join the enemy as a soldier, he is entitled to all the treatment afforded soldiers, should he be taken prisoner; but should he prefer to remain a citizen and yet be proved guilty of hostile acts, martial law says he shall suffer death. Many of Mosby's people were said to be, and doubtless were, citizens of the neighborhood, who joined him for a scout or a raid and left him at the conclusion of it, ready to respond to his call when again needed. By this means the Rebel government was saved the expense of supporting a large command, and at the same time had an efficient body of spies at all times within our lines. They were a most dangerous element, and caused perhaps more loss than any single body of men in the enemy's service. Their favorite mode of attack, was to lie in ambush on some road along which they knew one of our supply trains was moving. Through spies clothed in our uniform, and from information furnished by the citizens, there was never any difficulty in ascertaining when a train would be at a certain point, nor in finding out the strength of the train guard and the kind of troops of which it was composed.

With this information in his possession it was not a difficult thing for Col. Mosby to make many successful attacks, and he certainly was very successful. About the time of which I am writing,

Second Maryland Battalion of Cavalry, who set Chambersburg, Pennsylvania, afire (see n. 1 *supra*); Captain John H. McNeill, CSA, Virginia Partisan Rangers; and Captain William H. Payne, CSA, Thirty-seventh Virginia Cavalry Battalion. In September, 1863, six companies were mustered into service as a battalion of partisan rangers under Gilmor; he operated independently until late summer, 1864, when he joined General Bradley T. Johnson. Harold R. Manakee, *Maryland in the Civil War,* 137.

For another section on Mosby and his guerrillas, see pp. 300 ff.

he attacked a large train near Berryville, Va., capturing some fifty or sixty wagons and killing and wounding a large number of men. This train was guarded by a brigade of troops under command of a brigadier general, and Mosby probably had not to exceed one hundred men. The train was composed of at least six hundred wagons, and moving over a bad road and through wooded country it was necessarily more or less strung out. Then the brigadier general in command had directed the march to be made at night, and the men composing the guard were consequently tired out and exhausted by daylight, at which hour the attack was made. The number of men actually at the point where the attack was made seem to have been less than Mosby had with him, and from all accounts they made little or no resistance. The enterprising partisan "cut out" the train nearest him, which happened to be the supply train of the Reserve Cavalry Brigade, took such of the mules as he wanted, and set the wagons on fire. Then as the guards of the remainder of the train began to approach, he drew off his men and disappeared. Only one wagon of the Reserve Brigade was saved, and that wagon, as the report states, "contained officers' baggage of the 1st U. S. Cavalry." It contained about everything which I possessed in the world at that time, and I was glad enough to find it was safe, after the report came of the capture of the train.[13]

[13] It is interesting to examine this Mosby feat in some detail, compare it with Sanford's account and feelings on the matter. On 13 August 1864, Mosby attacked the Union supply train, guarded by Union forces (mostly "100-day men") under the command of Brigadier General John R. Kenly, with the rear guard under the command of Lieutenant Colonel Frederick R. Miller, 144th Ohio. The train numbered about 525 wagons.

Mosby tells the story: "Completely routed the guard, with a loss of over 200 prisoners, including three lieutenants, besides several killed and wounded. Captured and destroyed 75 loaded wagons, and secured over 200 head of beef-cattle, between 500 and 600 horses and mules, and many valuable stores. My loss two killed and three wounded. My force numbered something over 300 men, with two mountain howitzers." *OR*, XLIII, Pt. 1, 634. Union sources would dispute the losses, but not seriously.

A board of inquiry was convened on 8 September to consider the disaster. It met off and on until 13 November, when it announced "that the guard was insufficient for the number of wagons constituting the train; that the loss of the wagons was occasioned by the officer in charge, Captain E. P. McKinney, commissary of subsistence of the Reserve Brigade, who, at the instance of First Lieutenant William Dean, acting quartermaster, assumed to take charge of the train, failing to look after his train personally, and without orders permitting the train to go into the

This was a fair sample of Mosby's attacks about which so much has been said and written. They have been regarded as wonderful, on account of the small number of men he controlled, as compared with the results he accomplished; but the fact was that his safety lay in the very fact that he only employed a small force. A brigade or even a regiment would have been hunted down and destroyed in a week had they attempted the role successfully taken by Mosby for several years.

After concentrating the forces on the 18th, Gen. Sheridan remained in his lines in front of Charlestown, Va., for several days. During this period the cavalry were constantly engaged at different points in front of the lines, and in every encounter were successful. This "mimic war" was an excellent thing for the cavalry corps as it resulted in a feeling of confidence on the part of the soldiers, to such an extent that they went into battle with a full expectation of defeating the enemy whenever they met him. Of course a corresponding depression obtained in the ranks of the enemy, and as Gen. Early himself said in his official reports later in the campaign, "It is impossible for our cavalry to compete with him" (Sheridan's). "It would be better if they could all be put into the infantry; but if that were tried I am afraid they would all run off."[14] These remarks refer to a state of affairs which existed some weeks later; but at the time now under consideration, there was still some feeling of hope and enthusiasm among the Rebel leaders and their subordinates.

On the 25th of the month Torbert was ordered to move with the 1st and 3rd Divisions of the cavalry to Kearneysville[15] to develop

park, the drivers to unhitch and unharness their animals and lie down and go to sleep, so that when attacked the wagons could not be moved.

"The Board cannot ... fix negligence upon any individual officer of the train guard, but is of the opinion that there was no sufficient picket established whilst the train was halted to prevent surprise." *Ibid.*, 632.

[14] *OR*, XLIII, Pt. 1, 559, in a report dated 9 October 1864 and addressed to Lee. For another quote from this same report, see p. 285. Jubal A. Early (1816–1894), USMA, Class of 1837 (a class which included Braxton Bragg, Townsend, Sedgwick, Pemberton, and Hooker), served about a year in the U.S. Army and then resigned in 1838; he returned to service during the Mexican War as a major of Virginia volunteers. He was promoted brigadier general, CSA, to rank from 21 July 1861; major general, 17 January 1863; and lieutenant general, 31 May 1864.

[15] West Virginia.

the enemy and ascertain what they were doing. On the march we ran against his force advancing in our direction, but supposing that it was only a brigade or so of cavalry making a reconnaissance, Gen. Torbert deployed a portion of his force and attacked with great vigor. In a few moments it was discovered that we were engaged with a large body of infantry and artillery, and later we found that it was Maj. Genl. Breckinridge's division, and that we had the whole Rebel army directly in our front. The attack was made, however, with so much vigor and determination, that the enemy, taken by surprise, were at once brought to a halt, and then driven back in confusion for nearly a mile.[16] Their loss was reported at two hundred and fifty killed and wounded, including one brigade commander. Of course Gen. Torbert was not out there for the purpose of fighting the whole of Early's army, and accordingly after this exceedingly creditable success, he directed a retreat. This took place in good order, the 3rd Division falling back on one road toward the right of our army, and the 1st Division on a parallel road.[17] The enemy pursued with infantry and artillery on this latter road, and made it exceedingly warm. I rode with the skirmish line of my own regiment, which was covering the rear of the Reserve Brigade, and was greatly pleased with the coolness of the men.

They seemed to be rather pleased than otherwise at the idea of contending with infantry, and constantly made joking remarks as to the closeness of their shots and those of the enemy. As the country was quite rough and covered with scattered trees and stone walls the skirmishers were dismounted, and their horses sent forward to the main body, while the fighting line delayed the enemy as much as possible. As we drew near the Potomac however the Confederates pressed the retreating Federals more rapidly northward and finally it became necessary to send Custer's brigade

16 Sheridan writes that "this engagement was somewhat of a mutual surprise, our cavalry expecting to meet the enemy's cavalry and his infantry expecting no opposition whatever." *OR*, XLIII, Pt. 1, 45, in Sheridan's report of operations, 4 August 1864–29 February 1865.

17 Wilson's Third Division took the road from Kearneysville, via Duffield's Station (on the Baltimore and Ohio Railroad); Merritt's First Division took the direct road to Shepherdstown, West Virginia, two and one-half miles distant on the south bank of the Potomac River.

264

mounted, to the rescue; Custer accomplished his object with his usual magnificent dash, but going too far to the rear was himself cut off with his whole command from the rest of the corps, and forced to retreat across the Potomac at Shepherdstown. As the river was fortunately quite low, he accomplished this without much loss. The rest of the cavalry took position on the right and left of the army which was at this time in the vicinity of Halltown, Va.[18] For the next few days we had constant skirmishes with Early's cavalry and occasional ones with his infantry. On the 28th the 1st Division under Gen. Merritt had a very gallant fight near Leetown, and drove the enemy across the Opequon Creek by a splendid sabre charge.[19]

On the next day this division was attacked by a strong force of infantry and cavalry and driven back on to our infantry, when the gallant 6th Corps came to the rescue, and soon brought the Rebels to a stand.[20] Gen. Torbert had an uncomfortable habit of riding along the skirmish line, attended by his full staff, orderlies, headquarters flag and cavalry escort. Of course this made a small army in itself and was calculated to attract attention anywhere. It most certainly did from the enemy and they never omitted to send all the compliments of the season in the shape of lead and iron which they had at command. Torbert was a very handsome man himself and always beautifully mounted and conspicuously dressed. He liked his staff to follow his example in the latter respects, and they were perfectly well aware of it, and naturally anxious to please him. On the day of which I am speaking, the General was riding on the line of skirmishers of Merritt's division as they were falling back and talking rather strongly to the troopers about their unnecessary expenditure of ammunition; Surgeon Rulison the Med-

[18] A mile and a half or so from Harpers Ferry in present-day West Virginia.

[19] Merritt met Major General Lunsford L. Lomax's cavalry near Leetown, drove them to Smithfield, then out of Smithfield and across Opequon Creek.

[20] Merritt's units were on reconnaissance toward Bunker Hill (across the Opequon) when attacked by Confederate infantry. "The brigade was withdrawn to the right bank of the Opequon, and the entire division, after a stubborn resistance, fell back toward Charlestown, about two miles." Merritt's report, dated 5 October 1864, *OR*, XLIII, Pt. 1, 441. Torbert says the Third Division, Sixth Corps, Ricketts' Division, relieved the First Division and drove the Confederates back across the creek. *Ibid.*, 426.

ical Director of the Corps, and I were riding by his side, and he had just pointed out to a trooper who had fired his carbine that "you couldn't his a barn-door at that distance" when a bullet from an enemy's rifle struck poor Rulison in the side just above his belt. He died in a few moments, and was greatly regretted by all who knew him including the General himself, but it made no difference in his habit of riding among the skirmishers.[21]

From this time until the 19th of September we were moving forward and backward from Halltown to Berryville, skirmishing more or less each day, and endeavoring always to draw the Rebel cavalry away from its infantry. This they would not allow, and plainly showed their indisposition to fight without the assistance of their foot troops. In one of these skirmishes my regiment, the 1st U. S. Cavalry, especially distinguished itself. Gen. Merritt says "by a splendid charge against double its numbers of the enemy, repelling his charge and driving his column back in confusion. In this charge Lieut. Hoyer of the 1st, a gallant and promising young officer, fell mortally wounded while leading his squadron."[22] The regiment to which the 1st Cavalry was opposed in this encounter was known as the Jeff Davis Legion, and was regarded by the enemy as one of their best cavalry regiments. Hoyer's was a singular case. He was shot at very close quarters with a pistol ball, but said nothing to anyone and retained command of his squadron until the enemy were driven off; then he rode up to Capt. Sweitzer and saluting him, asked permission to leave the column. "What for, Mr. Hoyer?" said Sweitzer, naturally a good deal surprised at the request under the circumstances. "Because I am mortally wounded, sir," answered poor Hoyer, without changing countenance. He was taken charge of in a moment and everything possible done

21 Surgeon William H. Rulison, Ninth New York Cavalry, medical director of Sheridan's Cavalry Corps. Torbert says Rulison was hit by a minié ball. He was thirty-nine years old when he was commissioned assistant surgeon, 15 February 1862, Fifteenth New York Engineers (Veteran). Mustered out on 15 July 1862, he was promoted surgeon, Ninth New York Cavalry, 31 July 1862, with rank from 16 July.

22 OR, XLIII, Pt. 1, 441; but inexplicably, Sanford is referring to the engagement of 28 August (see p. 265 and n. 19 supra). He seems to have forgotten the previous discussion. Joseph S. Hoyer had been commissioned a second lieutenant, First Cavalry, 6 March 1862. His brigade commander that day, Colonel Alfred Gibbs, Nineteenth New York Cavalry, called him "a most excellent officer." Ibid., 488.

COLONEL GEORGE B. SANFORD

for him, but his case was perfectly hopeless as he knew from the first, and he died in a few hours.

On the 18th of September the army was encamped on the "Summit Point" line, some eight or ten miles north of Winchester, the cavalry divisions of Merritt and Averell guarding the right, and that of Wilson the left, of the army.[23] Early in the morning of the 19th the whole army advanced toward the Opequon Creek, the 1st Division, with which Gen. Torbert rode, striking the creek at Seivers' and Locke's fords. These were guarded by infantry posted behind breastworks of logs and dirt. The cavalry charged these with great spirit and drove the defenders off, pursuing them for about a mile and a half when they rallied in a second position previously prepared, along the crest of a hill overlooking the valley of the Opequon. The ground between the stream and the crest was generally open and cultivated, much of it being planted with buckwheat. The charge of the 1st Division across the open ground was a very gallant effort, and a beautiful sight. The position however was too strong to be carried by a front attack, and after the first attempt Merritt was ordered to confine himself to demonstrations, while Averell with his 2nd Division still farther to the right was ordered to drive off the Rebel cavalry and get around the left flank of the infantry force holding the crest. This duty was rapidly accomplished and as soon as the enemy heard Averell's guns thundering in their rear they commenced their retreat and soon the two divisions were in line again, Gen. Averell on the right and Merritt on the left of the Valley Pike and within four miles of Winchester.

The whole command then advanced driving the Rebel cavalry before them and when within sight of Winchester, came square against the left flank of the Confederate infantry then hotly engaged with our own. The 1st Division instantly charged the infantry by brigades, breaking their lines and driving them in confusion. The Reserve Brigade especially distinguished itself riding

---

[23] Actually, east of Winchester is more accurate, for the Union forces had to cross Opequon Creek in their advance. Merritt commanded the First Division and Averell the Second (from the Department of West Virginia). Wilson had the Third Division.

over a large redoubt and capturing the earth-work and battery which it contained. Averell at the same time drove the Rebel cavalry at a gallop around Winchester, and on to the turn-pike beyond it. The 1st Division captured this day over eight hundred prisoners including seventy officers, seven battle flags, and two pieces of artillery, besides a large number of small arms.

The whole Rebel army was driven in confusion through and beyond the town of Winchester, into which we entered just before sundown. The land north of the town, bordering the Valley turnpike on either side, is level or gently rolling, and the sight that evening as the sun was setting was a most magnificent one from a soldier's point of view. East and West stretched the long line of the Union forces in beautiful order, the infantry pressing the Rebel foot steadily before them, while the great mass of Torbert's cavalry, in one grand charge, bore down all opposition, sweeping everything before them in wild disorder.[24] Gen. Sheridan, as was usual with him, was up with his advanced lines, and entered the town with the first of his troops. As I rode up to him with some message from Gen. Torbert and saluted him in the customary formal manner, he responded by saying, "Well, isn't this bully!" at the same time giving me a hearty slap on the shoulder. This was not the ordinary style of receiving an aide de camp among the Major Generals and was not at all in Sheridan's line, but he was feeling unusually happy, and well he might, for he had gained a great victory.

Once before during the battle of that day, I had seen and spoken to him, and had happened to witness a characteristic incident. I was riding along a narrow lane leading through a piece of woods which the enemy was shelling heavily. Just in front of me a light battery was moving in column at a gallop endeavoring to get into an open space to take position, when a shell from a Rebel battery landed squarely on one of the caissons, and sent the whole concern flying into the air. I got by this as soon as possible and out to the front

[24] Sanford was not alone in his exulted feelings. General Merritt was carried away, too, with the action, calling it "a noble work well done—a theme for the poet; a scene for the painter ... trailing the rebel banners in the dust in the Valley of the Shenandoah, the former valley of humiliation to Union armies." *OR*, XLIII, Pt. 1, 445, 446.

of the woods. Here I came upon another battery commanded by Lieut. Cuyler of the 3rd Artillery.[25] His horses were exhausted, one of his pieces was down in a deep rut; it seemed impossible to move it, and it was blocking the way of all the rest. Cuyler was in despair for he wanted to be up in front where the tide was turning in our favor, and where he knew he was badly needed. He stormed and swore, and almost cried for he was only a boy, though a very gallant one, but the horses were "done" and they would not pull. Just then Gen. Sheridan rode up, entirely unattended as was often the case with him, his aides and orderlies being off with messages. He saw at once what was wanted, and dismounting, while half a dozen gunners sprang to help him, he raised with their assistance the wheel and then the horses easily pulled the piece out on the level ground. Then springing on his horse, with a smile and a nod to Cuyler, he said, "That's the way to do it, my boy," and was off at a gallop.

He was a wonderful man on the battle field, and never in as good humor as when under fire. This pre-supposes, however, that everyone about was doing his duty as he deemed it should be done. If he judged the contrary one might as well be in the path of a Kansas cyclone. Explanations were not in order, and the scathing torrent of invective that poured out, his shrill voice rising ever higher as his anger grew, while his piercing eye seemed absolutely to blaze, was a sight once seen not likely to be forgotten. I was the witness of more than one of these explosions, but fortunately never their object. On the contrary, I am glad and proud to say, that I never received any but the kindest treatment from the General, as indeed was the case from most of my superiors. People who knew Sheridan in the later years of his life would not recognize him from this description. Soon after the war he became deeply interested in religious matters, and this exercised a softening influence; but more especially after his marriage a marked change was visible.

---

[25] William C. Cuyler was commissioned second lieutenant, Third Regiment of Artillery, 19 February 1862; first lieutenant, 17 April 1863. He was brevetted captain for his services in this battle and at Cedar Creek. By late 1869, he was dead.

The Third Artillery, Batteries C and F, was horse artillery and a part of the Cavalry Corps.

His voice, once noticeable for its piercing shrillness, was soon equally marked for its softness, and his whole manner showed the refining influence of the beautiful and cultivated woman he was so fortunate as to marry.[26]

This battle of the 19th of September, 1864, is often called the Battle of Winchester, but the official name is "The Opequon." So many battles have been fought in the vicinity of Winchester that the name has ceased to be a distinguishing title—no less than nine are given in the official list of battles, to say nothing of numberless skirmishes long since forgotten. This was the first great victory ever won by the Union troops in the Valley, and was eagerly hailed by the whole country as a fore-taste of better days to come. Sheridan was appointed next day a Brigadier General in the Regular Army, his previous rank being that of Captain in the 13th Infantry.[27]

It was a very happy night in Winchester, at least at Torbert's Headquarters. The cavalry had done marvelously well and had been successful in everything they had undertaken. The 3rd Division under Gen. Wilson, which acted on the left flank during the battle, had gained equal credit with the 1st and 2nd Divisions on the right. Gen. McIntosh of the 1st Brigade of this division who was also a Captain in the 5th U. S. Cavalry, lost a leg, and Gen. Chapman, of the 2nd Brigade, was wounded.[28]

On the 20th the army again moved forward, the 1st Division on the Valley Pike, the 2nd on the Back road to the right of the army, the 3rd on the Front Royal pike, to the left. We marched to

26 Irene Rucker, youngest daughter of Colonel Daniel H. Rucker, assistant quartermaster general, USA. She and Sheridan were married on 3 June 1875; she was twenty-two and he was forty-four.

27 Sheridan's Army of the Shenandoah lost rather heavily; 697 KIA and 3,983 WIA; the Cavalry Corps, 68 KIA and 304 WIA. *OR,* XLIII, Pt. 1, 118. The chief result of the action was the restoration of Union control of the lower valley from the Potomac to Strasburg. Another result was Sheridan's being assigned permanent command of the Middle Military Division on 21 September 1864, one day after he was made permanent brigadier general, a leap in promotion reminiscent of John J. Pershing's similar move upward in the early 1900's.

28 John B. McIntosh (1828–1888) was a very junior captain in the Fifth Regiment of Cavalry; he had entered the Army as a second lieutenant on 8 June 1861. His brother, James McQ., was a brigadier general in the CSA. See n. 31, Chap. I; for Chapman, see n. 16, Chap. 6.

270

Cedar Creek and beyond to the town of Strasburg, and found the enemy in a very strong position along the crest of Fisher's Hill,[29] and the adjoining high ground stretching from the Massanutten mountain to the North mountain chain.

Our army went into position in about the same shape that it had marched, except that Merritt's division was placed on the right of the infantry instead of in front. On the 21st Torbert with Merritt's and Wilson's divisions, started on an expedition up the Luray Valley, hoping to get around the right flank of the Rebel army and come back into the Valley Pike at New Market, and thus cut off the Rebel army in case Sheridan should have been victorious in the attack he was preparing to make at Fisher's Hill. Torbert left behind him with the main army Averell's whole division of cavalry and also Devin's brigade (2nd) of Merritt's division. The Luray Valley is a part of the Shenandoah valley, but is separated from it by the bold chain called Massanutten.[30] This is about thirty or forty miles in length and is very abrupt and heavily wooded, with only a few practicable passes from which troops can move from one valley to the other. Of course the enemy was certain to guard the valley strongly, and the whole success of the plan rested on Torbert's making a desperate push through whatever opposed him and getting possession of the pike at New Market, before the main body of Early's army could reach there. Unfortunately as it turned out, Torbert, when he struck the enemy's forces at Milford on the 22nd, considered the position very much too strong to be carried by a front attack, and quite impossible to turn as it was protected by the high mountains of the Blue Ridge on one side and the Massanutten on the other. The bridge across the stream had been destroyed and the banks were held by the enemy in force. He skirmished some time at this point and then determined to withdraw and seek some other way of getting up the Valley.[31]

[29] Both Strasburg and Fisher's Hill are along the North Fork of the Shenandoah River.

[30] The Luray Valley is bound on the west by the South Fork of the Shenandoah River and the Massanutten Range, on the east by the Blue Ridge Mountains.

[31] Torbert's own report is valuable here: "About 11 a. m. . . . the advance came upon the enemy posted in a still stronger position on the south bank of Milford Creek, their left resting on the Shenandoah, which runs so close under the mountain

In the mean time he determined to report the state of affairs to Sheridan, and I was sent back to Strasburg with the despatches. When I reached this point however I found that a great battle had been fought that day at Fisher's Hill; that the enemy had been completely routed and driven in utter confusion up the Valley, and then I realized the tremendous opportunity that Torbert had lost.[32] I pushed on with my despatches as rapidly as possible and overtook Gen. Sheridan on the afternoon of the 23rd beyond Woodstock. The infantry were in camp, or rather bivouac, at this point, drawing rations, which they were greatly in need of, and the cavalry which does not need rations, or at least are not supposed to, were some miles in advance confronting the enemy near the village of Edenburg.

Sheridan was very angry, I was told by his Chief of Staff, Col. Forsyth.[33] In fact there was a suggestion of suppressed trouble in the air, in the whole appearance of his Headquarters. Forsyth's first question to me when I rode up was, "For God's sake, where is Torbert?" When I told him of our fight at Milford and subsequent withdrawal, he gave a prolonged whistle and threw up his hands. "Look out for squalls," he said, "the General's in there; go in and

it was impossible to turn it, and their right rested against a high mountain. The length of their line was very short, and the banks of the creek so precipitous it was impossible for the men to get across in order to make a direct attack.... Not knowing that the army had made an attack at Fisher's Hill, and thinking that the sacrifice would be too great to attack without that knowledge, I concluded to withdraw to a point opposite McCoy's Ferry." *OR,* XLIII, Pt. 1, 428. Brigadier General Williams C. Wickham, CSA (1820–1888) commanded the Confederate forces.

[32] On 22 September 1864, Sheridan had smashed the Confederates at Fisher's Hill under Ramseur, Pegram, Gordon, and Wharton in a battle that featured a "secret march" by General George Crook. But again, Early, as he had at Winchester, escaped Sheridan.

At Strasburg, Sanford sent a dispatch to Torbert: "I have just reached here. General Sheridan has gone to Woodstock with the army; great victory here last night .... Their army is in full retreat. Colonel Devin is in advance, following them up rapidly. His guns have been heard this morning. Our trains have all gone up the Valley." To his name, Sanford added "aide-de-camp." *OR,* XLIII, Pt. 2, 157–58.

[33] Lieutenant Colonel James W. Forsyth, USMA, Class of 1856, assistant inspector general and chief of staff to Sheridan, held a permanent rank of captain in the Eighteenth Regiment of Infantry. Quite talented and professional, Forsyth won five brevets in the war, served as aide-de-camp to Sheridan from 1869 to 1873, commanded at the Battle of Wounded Knee, and was promoted brigadier general in 1894.

report." "In there" was a little wall tent, just off the side of the road. I did not feel very cheerful. I was tired and faint for want of food and sleep, and from desperately hard riding. But I felt sure that Torbert had acted for what he thought to be the best, and I meant to say so. I had crawled up, the morning before, with the gallant Lowell, to the edge of the bank overlooking the crossing at Milford, and I knew that it never could have been carried without a most awful sacrifice of life, if at all. Lowell, who was in command of the Reserve Brigade and who gave up his life less than a month later at Cedar Creek, was known as one of the very bravest men in the whole army. He was a fatalist and believed that one must die when his time came and that no possible precaution could alter the fact, but he shook his head when he looked at that place. He desired me to report to Torbert what I saw, but declined to express an opinion himself, other than that the Reserve Brigade was ready for action.[34]

I went in to Sheridan's tent, and found the General lying on a little cot with a wet handkerchief over his face, which he removed as I came in, and dipped in water from time to time. He was very much flushed, as from anxiety and fatigue and looked worn and harassed. His manner however was quiet and pleasant to me, and when I gave him my despatches, he read them at once, and slapping them again and again against his hand, he only said, "I thought so; I thought so." Then he began to ask me questions about the situation of affairs in the Luray, what others thought, etc. His manner got more animated and excited as he began to say what should have been done, and I was afraid that the trouble was coming, when Forsyth appeared at the tent door, looking more ominous than ever, and said "General! Major Kip is here from Averell's command."[35] "Tell him to come in," said Sheridan, and sat up on the cot. "Has Averell crossed that creek at Edenburg?" he broke out before Kip

[34] See n. 7 *supra*. Lowell (b. 1835) was a nephew of James Russell Lowell. For his death, see pp. 297–98.

[35] Lawrence Kip, a non-graduate of the Class of 1857, USMA, had been commissioned second lieutenant, Fourth Regiment of Artillery, in 1857. The rank of major is not altogether clear, but it may have been a courtesy one, since Kip served as major aide-de-camp of volunteers, 20 August 1862–15 August 1863. His permanent rank was first lieutenant, Third Regiment of Artillery.

could fairly speak. "No, General," answered Kip, "but he thinks the enemy will go back tonight." "He does, does he?" fairly shouted Sheridan. "Well he'll go back in the morning," and threw himself back on the cot, as if exhausted. When Lawrence Kip first came in, I had started out, supposing the General might want to see him alone, but Sheridan said "Sit still, Sanford; I want you to hear the news from Averell"; so I had remained, but now Forsyth, who had also been standing at the door, beckoned to Kip and myself to come out, and we accordingly followed him, the General saying nothing. I went to Forsyth's tent and got a good supper and a good rest after having seen that my orderly and our horses were being equally well taken care of.

On the next morning I woke feeling perfectly rested, and was told by Forsyth that we were to march at once; that the General had sent orders to Torbert to push on up the Luray Valley at all hazards, and to join the main army at New Market, and finally that I was to accompany Headquarters that day. Breakfast followed in a few moments and shortly after, the Staff mounted and followed Gen. Sheridan up the valley. I rode in the early part of the day with my friend Major Lawrence Kip, and talked with him about matters relative to Averell's Division. He told me the details of the Fisher's Hill battle, and of Averell's failure to pursue the enemy vigorously which coming on top of Torbert's failure had so greatly angered Gen. Sheridan. I also heard that orders had been sent to Averell relieving him from command of his division, and ordering him to report at Wheeling, Va., to await further orders. Col. Powell of the 22nd West Virginia Cavalry was placed temporarily in charge of his division.[36]

36 In his *Personal Memoirs*, II, 43–45, Sheridan considers Averell's failure to follow up Early in some detail. Sheridan is furious to think that Averell had left "to the infantry the work of pursuit." He further says that Averell utterly failed "to accomplish anything." Then there was Averell's own dissatisfaction with the setup within the Army of the Shenandoah: the fact that he ranked Torbert by about two months on promotion to brigadier general of volunteers. Says Sheridan: "I therefore thought that the interest of the service would be subserved by removing one whose growing indifference might render the best-laid plans inoperative." *Ibid.*, 45.

But Sheridan was almost as unhappy with Torbert: "To this day I have been unable to account satisfactorily for Torbert's failure. No doubt, Wickham's position

274

After a short ride we reached Mt. Jackson, and here I saw Gen. Averell sitting in front of a tent just on the left of the pike, as we rode up. Gen. Sheridan and his staff halted just north of Averell's tent under some trees on the opposite side of the road. The General did not approach or speak to Averell, and as far as I know, no communication took place between them. I went over myself, though I cannot remember that any other officer did. I felt very sorry for Averell. He was dreadfully depressed and broken. I believe he started for the rear within a few moments after we left him, and never was employed again during the war.

Gen. Averell graduated from the Military Academy at West Point in 1855. He was promoted through the various grades to a Captaincy in the 3rd Cavalry, which latter grade he reached in July, 1862. In the Volunteers he rose rapidly from a Colonelcy to the position of Major General by Brevet. He resigned all his appointments at the close of the war, and went into business in Washington, but was not particularly successful. He eventually succeeded in having his name restored to the ranks of the Army in 1888 as a Captain of Cavalry, on the retired list. I have never felt that he was quite fairly treated.

We stopped at Mount Jackson only a few moments and then proceeded up the Valley. Gen. Devin with his small brigade of the 1st Division had the advance on the pike, and I obtained permission to join him. I found "Old Tommy" in great force.[37] His whole brigade was deployed as skirmishers, and there were not very many skirmishers either. As far as I could judge the only reserve con-

near Milford was a strong one, but Torbert ought to have made a fight...his impotent attempt not only chagrined me very much, but occasioned much unfavorable comment throughout the army." *Ibid.,* 42. Sheridan refers to Brigadier W. C. Wickham of Fitzhugh Lee's cavalry division, who held the position at Milford with elements of the First, Second, and Fourth Virginia Cavalry. Map 1, Pl. LXXXIV, *Atlas to Accompany the Official Records,* III, shows plainly enough Torbert's difficulties.

Colonel William H. Powell, Second West Virginia Cavalry, succeeded to command of the Second Division on 24 September 1864 in obedience to Special Orders No. 41. See *OR,* XLIII, Pt. 1, 505. He would soon be promoted brigadier general of volunteers for service at Cedar Creek. See n. 3 *supra.*

[37] See n. 16, Chap. VI. The cognomen "old" does not quite match Devin, who was all of forty-two years of age.

sisted of the General and his staff and Frank Taylor's battery of the 1st Artillery. The old man, however, was not bothered about reserves at that particular time. He was "loaded for bear," as they say out West, and didn't propose to stop until he had to. Gen Sheridan had ordered him to "pursue the enemy." He was going to "pursue" and it was the enemy's business to keep out of his way. Half a dozen times that day, I saw their rear guard of at least five times his strength drawn up, in commanding positions to stop him, but each time they fell back before his determined advance. It was a remarkable instance of successful "cheek." Of course the Rebels could have stopped him and thrown him back on to our infantry, but equally of course that would have entangled them in a conflict that it was their policy to avoid, for it was a life or death matter for them to reach New Market, where the Luray Valley road came in to the pike, before Torbert got there. Torbert in the meantime having received his peremptory orders, had gone up to the Luray again determined to force his way through. He found however when he reached Milford that the enemy had evacuated that strong position and he crossed the stream without other difficulty than that caused by having to ford or bridge a rough and deep mountain stream. Of course this caused delay to a certain extent, but he eventually got over and pushed on to Luray Village where he had a very sharp encounter with Lomax's cavalry, defeating and driving them through that village. Lomax however had fully accomplished his object, having detained Torbert to such a late hour that he was obliged to go into camp at the end of the fight, and Early with his army, joined also by Lomax, had safely passed the junction of the roads at New Market.[38] Sheridan with Devin still in advance had also pushed up the Valley, Devin having a sharp fight on the streets of New Market, and the whole command

[38] Again to read Torbert's report of these important days: "The next morning at daylight, the 24th, both divisions moved up the valley, the First Division (Brigadier General Merritt) in advance. The advance came upon the enemy in position about three miles from Luray. They were immediately engaged, and in a gallant charge of the First Brigade, First Division, led by Brigadier General Custer, capturing some seventy prisoners. The command passed through Luray on the pike leading to New Market, crossed the Shenandoah River, and bivouacked at the foot of the pass." *OR,* XLIII, Pt. 1, 429.

finally went into camp shortly before sundown about six miles south of that village.

At this hour however we still had no news whatever from Gen. Torbert, and Gen. Sheridan was very anxious to make sure that he was carrying out the orders he had sent him the previous day,[39] so he sent for me and gave me instructions to push directly across the Massanutten mountain and into the Luray Valley, find Torbert and give him orders to press forward in the morning at all speed and overtake the army. This was a cheerful state of things. We knew nothing whatever positively in regard to the position of Torbert or his command, and we did know that wherever Torbert was, there, close by, was Lomax and his troopers. More than that it was well known that the mountains were full of stragglers from the disastrous Fisher's Hill fight, making their way as best they could to join Early's army, and last, but by no means least, Mosby, Mc-Neill, Gilmor and all the rest of that ilk were so to speak everywhere on the watch for just such stray innocents as I should be, when I had ridden two miles away from our camp.

Of course I did not volunteer any of these suggestions to Gen. Sheridan but received his directions and made my preparations, so that I was ready to start in a few moments. Forsyth informed me with a certain grim humor that I half enjoyed, that I ought to have at least a troop of cavalry to escort me through, but as there was none to spare, perhaps it was just as well. If I met no enemy at all, I could get through, and if I met Lomax I would "go to Libby" anyway, troop of cavalry or not. So my escort consisted of my orderly, Powers. When we had ridden about two miles and were just entering the woods at the base of the mountains, I noticed that that enterprising young soldier had disappeared. As this was not at all his style of doing things, I waited for a few moments for him to catch up, and then found that his horse had cast a shoe, and was dead lame. That settled all questions of escort. I ordered him to return at once and report to Gen. Forsyth, and struck out myself up the mountain. In a few moments I had reached and passed our line of videttes, receiving the consoling information

[39] Torbert had received orders to push on at about 4:00 P.M., 23 September.

277

from the officer on duty that the "woods were just full of Johnnies, some of them horse-back and more of them foot."

After I got into the woods, the night shut down as black as a pocket, but I rather liked that at first, as I knew it would render my chance of escaping observation much better. My plan was to get across the mountain and strike the Luray Valley pike as soon as possible, then to endeavor to ascertain from the signs whether any troops had passed up, and if possible which army they belonged to; then if I should find myself behind (north of) our forces, my duty would be clear and tolerably easy; all I would have to do would be to follow the pike in a southerly direction until I caught up. On the other hand if I were in front (or south) of them, or still worse, between the two, my position would be decidedly ticklish, and my chances "for Libby," as Forsyth remarked, would be more than favorable.

As it turned out this was exactly the state of things that existed. I was between the two forces when I reached the pike, but more owing to good luck perhaps than good management, I avoided capture. Going through the woods I got along comparatively comfortably, although the darkness of the night rendered my progress very slow. As far as possible I kept in the trees and off to the sides of the mountain trails. About an hour before dawn I crossed the summit, and almost at once came in sight of a few low fires which I knew of course were picket fires, but at the distance I was from them it was impossible to tell whether of our men or of the Rebels. I got my horse into a clump of pretty dense timber and tied him securely, and then made my way as cautiously as possible in the direction of the fires, on foot. I know that I could not get up to the fires without running across a line of videttes, for no fires would be on the vidette line, but back with the reserve. What I hoped to do was to locate the line without being seen myself, which I thought I might probably do in the darkness and then wait until the relief came along, when I could judge from the direction they took, as to what army they belonged. It turned out nearly as I had hoped. Before I got sight of the videttes I heard the tramp of horses and the jingling of the sabres. I kept perfectly still for some time until

I found that instead of posting reliefs they were apparently with-drawing their videttes. As the light began to increase, so that I could see a little, I ventured to crawl to a spur of a ridge from which I could get an outlook; then the matter was settled in a few moments. Quite a distance to the North of me in the Valley was a large camp, which I had little doubt was of our cavalry and on the road to the south I could hear the retreating tramp of the small body of horse which had evidently been left behind by Gen. Lomax to watch Torbert and give timely notice of his movements.

Although they were thus early drawing in their videttes I knew quite well that the main body would not move until Gen. Torbert's command was en route, and that if I attempted to get through I should most certainly be picked up; so I crawled back into the thickest brush I could find, and lay quiet for an hour or two. It was a pretty critical situation, but once or twice I dozed off to sleep from exhaustion after the anxieties and perils of the night. From time to time also I heard the tramp of horses at greater or less distances and at these times I was desperately anxious lest my horse, Prince, should neigh, and thereby disclose my hiding place. By patting him and talking to him in a low tone however I pre-vented this, and that danger was passed. Finally when it was quite light I mounted and determined to make a rush for it, if necessary.

Almost as soon as I had crossed the ridge that screened the Luray Valley from me, I caught sight of our troops in motion, and in a few moments the advanced guard came up and my ride, or rather the dangerous part of it, was over. I reported to Gen. Torbert and rode with the staff to New Market, and thence to Harrisonburg, where we camped that night.[40] The next day, 26th of September, we moved with the 3rd Division under Wilson and the Reserve Brigade under Lowell to Staunton, which we entered just before sundown, capturing a large amount of ordnance, subsistence and medical supplies. On the afternoon of the 28th, after destroying such of the captured stores as we could not carry, we moved East

[40] Early had long since passed through New Market. This laconic comment from Sheridan: "Late in the afternoon of 25 September Torbert's cavalry came in from New Market arriving at that place many hours later than it had been expected." *Personal Memoirs*, II, 49.

to Waynesborough at the mouth of Rockfish Gap in the Blue Ridge Mountains. This place was on the Virginia Central Railroad, which here crossed the South Fork of the Shenandoah, on a substantial iron bridge.

On the 28th we destroyed this bridge and burned the depot and Government buildings; while attempting to destroy the railroad tunnel east of the bridge, we were attacked by a large force of infantry, cavalry and artillery. This occurred about five o'clock in the afternoon and very soon after, a regiment of cavalry which had been sent to Piedmont, came in, bringing despatches from the Headquarters, 2nd Cavalry Division, that a large force of the enemy was moving from that vicinity to cut us off. Gen. Torbert accordingly determined to fall back nearer to the main body which was still at Harrisonburg, and we commenced the march in excellent order. The Reserve Brigade under Col. Lowell was in rear, and the whole body deployed on the skirmish line, was fighting with its customary coolness and vigor. With Gen. Torbert and the rest of the staff I was watching this conflict, when a battery which had been brought up under cover of some houses, opened with canister at short range, knocking over several men and horses in the Staff. My horse was struck and I was hit in the side of the head and stunned.[41]

Gen. Torbert who was close by my side caught hold of me and supported me until we got out to the side of the road and out of the press of men and horses, many of which were down. It was a bad time to be hit as the enemy were pressing us hard and we had every reason to expect another attack in flank from the force of which we had already received notice. I soon found however that my wound was a slight one, and as soon as the blood was staunched and I had got another horse I mounted and rejoined the staff. Not long after in riding along a sunken road between two lines of timber we were greeted by a tremendous volley from the force on our flank which had succeeded in getting ahead of us and selected this place for an ambush. Fortunately for us, only a small party had reached this point and owing to the fact that the road was considerably below the level of the woods most of the bullets passed over

41 This is the skirmish at Waynesboro.

280

our heads. The brigade was under perfect discipline and while a portion charged up the road and held possession of the outlet, another body skirmished through the timber and drove back the force there to a sufficient distance to render the passage practicable. This ended the adventure of that night though we marched until nearly daylight, camping at Spring Hill on the back road from Staunton to Harrisonburg. During the latter part of the march I was obliged to give up my horse and lie down in an ambulance wagon.

·CHAPTER VIII·

Fᴿᴏᴍ ᴛʜɪs ᴛɪᴍᴇ until the 6th of October, by which date I had entirely recovered, the army lay in the vicinity of Harrisonburg, the cavalry being engaged in frequent reconnaissances to the front and flanks, during which the detachments concerned had many sharp encounters. On the 6th, 7th and 8th the army moved back down the Valley, the 1st and 3rd Cavalry Divisions covering the rear. The object of the movement was to take position at some point nearer the Baltimore and Ohio Railroad from which we drew our supplies.[1] The enemy pressed on our rear with considerable pertinacity and especially so on the 8th of October which so exasperated Gen. Sheridan that he was especially bitter in his comments as to the efficiency of the rear guard.[2] Of course he did not really mean all he said for no one had a higher opinion than he of the cavalry or was better aware of their efficiency in this brilliant campaign.

I happened to be the only Aide de camp who accompanied Gen.

---

[1] There were several reasons why the Army of the Shenandoah was moving back. Sheridan discusses the problem in part: "I was also confident that my transportation could not supply me farther than Harrisonburg, and therefore advised that the Valley campaign terminate at Harrisonburg, and that I return, carrying out my original instructions for the destruction of forage, grain, &c. . . . I therefore, on the morning of the 6th of October, commenced moving back, stretching the cavalry across the Valley from the Blue Ridge to the eastern slope of the Alleghanies, with directions to burn all forage and drive off all stock, &c. . . . fully coinciding in the views and instructions of the lieutenant-general [Grant], that the Valley should be made a barren waste. The most positive orders were given, however, not to burn dwellings." *OR,* XLIII, Pt. 1, 50.

[2] Brigadier General Thomas L. Rosser, CSA, commanded the pressing cavalry; he had just joined Early in the valley with his Laurel Brigade.

Torbert when he rode up to Gen. Sheridan's Headquarters that evening and I heard a portion of the conversation—as much of it as I deemed it advisable to hear. Then I rode off a short distance and waited for my Chief. I can testify quite freely that Sheridan was "mad clear through" and was quite willing that everybody should know it. Among other things that he said to Torbert was: "I want you to go out there in the morning and whip that Rebel cavalry or get whipped yourself."[3] Gen. Torbert was "mad too," but he had a different way of showing temper. He said nothing at all as he went back to his own headquarters, but seemed to be in a brown study. On arriving he sent orders to Gen. Custer on the Back road and Gen. Merritt on the Valley Pike to move at an early hour in the morning, and attack the enemy as soon as they were encountered. The two roads were parallel to each other and about three miles apart.

Gen. Custer had a few days before been placed in command of the 3rd Division vice Gen. Wilson who had been ordered out West as commander of the Cavalry of Gen. Sherman's army.[4] His division moving quite early on the 9th soon struck the enemy and became sharply engaged. Immediately after the sound of their guns were heard, Merritt's division opened on the forces of Lomax and Bradley Johnson on the Valley Pike.[5] The Reserve Brigade which was moving on the Pike were very sharply engaged and for about two hours were quite unable to drive the enemy from their position. Repeated charges were made but in each case counter charges by the enemy would regain any ground captured. Gradually however, the 2nd and 1st brigades succeeded in working to the right and at length established connection with Custer's division, so that we had a continuous line from one road to the other.

[3] "That night [*i.e.*, 8 October] I told Torbert I expected him either to give Rosser a drubbing next morning or get whipped himself, and that the infantry would be halted until the affair was over; I also informed him that I proposed to ride out to Round Top Mountain to see the fight." Sheridan, *Personal Memoirs,* II, 56.

[4] Custer had relieved Wilson on 30 September 1864; Wilson, on orders from Grant, proceeded to Atlanta, Georgia, and reported to Sherman as chief of cavalry, Military Division of the Mississippi.

[5] Bradley T. Johnson (1829–1903), brigadier general, CSA, 28 June 1864, had served under McCausland at Chambersburg, Pennsylvania.

The country was tolerably open and rolling—on the whole well adapted to cavalry operations—and magnificently did the cavalry take advantage of it. A vigorous charge in front and on the flanks, at length started the enemy and in a moment Merritt saw his opportunity. Lowell's Reserve Brigade, with the 1st Cavalry leading, captured five pieces of artillery and then dashed on in pursuit. It was a great sight and the men were wild. I was greatly disappointed at this moment to receive instructions from Gen. Torbert to ride as fast as I could go across to Gen. Custer, tell him what had happened on the Pike and direct him to crowd the enemy back at all speed. As it happened I was able to see more of this fight, on this account, than anyone else who took part in it, probably, for I found Custer when I reached him just forming for a charge. I told him that the 1st Division had captured five pieces of artillery and was about to ask him whether he had taken any, when he said, "All right, hold on a minute and I'll show you six"; and immediately ordered the charge sounded. The division charged with a will and got their six pieces of artillery in less time than it has taken me to write about it.

Custer then pursued at a gallop and I returned across country to the 1st Division which was all this time driving the enemy at top speed.[6] When I caught up with my own gallant regiment at the head of the column, it had just stopped to breathe the horses at the brook at Edenburg. Devin's 2nd Brigade then took up the pursuit and followed some miles further. Gen. Devin made a gallant attempt to capture the only piece of artillery remaining in the possession of the enemy, but their retreat was too rapid and he was unable to accomplish his object.[7] The command, after awaiting the return of Gen. Devin's brigade from Mt. Jackson, went into

[6] Custer's comments on the rout are worth considering: "Before this irresistible advance the enemy found it impossible to stand. Once more he was compelled to trust his safety to the fleetness of his steed rather than the metal of his saber. His retreat soon became a demoralized rout. Vainly did the most gallant of this affrighted herd endeavor to rally a few supports around their standards and stay the advance of their eager and exulting pursuers." *OR,* XLIII, Pt. 1, 521.

[7] But Devin had captured one piece at Hawkinstown. Lomax continued his retreat with the remaining piece, and Devin chased him through Mount Jackson trying to get it. He failed.

camp near Woodstock and on the 10th and 11th returned to the main body of the army which was found not far north of Cedar Creek. The result of the fighting of the 9th, generally called the battle of "Tom's Brook" or the "Woodstock Races," was the utter demoralization of the enemy's cavalry in the Valley. They were driven twenty-six miles nearly all the time at a gallop. Eleven pieces of artillery were captured with their caissons and battery wagons and all their wagon trains, with ordnance, subsistence and quartermaster supplies; also two standards and many provisions.[8] In Gen. Early's report of this affair to Gen. Lee, he says: "This is very distressing to me, and God knows I have done all in my power to avert the disasters which have befallen this command. They cannot fight on horseback, and in this open country they cannot successfully fight on foot against large bodies of cavalry; besides, the command is and has been demoralized all the time."[9]

From this time until the 15th of October the whole army occupied the line of Cedar Creek and the cavalry were engaged in frequent reconnaissances up the Valley and on the flanks of the army. On the 13th the enemy made his appearance with a large force of infantry, artillery and cavalry and forced back Gen. Custer's pickets on the right of the army. On Custer moving out with his division, however, the Rebels retired and our line was reestablished.[10] On the 15th Gen. Torbert moved after dark with Merritt's 1st Division to near Front Royal, with orders to proceed the next day with Merritt's and Powell's divisions and on a raid against the Virginia Central Railroad at Charlottesville and Gordonsville. Gen. Sheridan accompanied this command as far as Front

[8] There must have been twelve guns captured, if we count Devin's piece. No matter, really, for as Torbert reported (and he had certainly obeyed Sheridan's orders): "There could hardly have been a more complete victory and rout. The cavalry totally covered themselves with glory, and added to their long list of victories the most brilliant one of them all and the most decisive the country has ever witnessed." *OR,* XLIII, Pt. 1, 431. True to his word, Sheridan had observed the battle from the summit of Round Top. Despite this defeat, Rosser was promoted major general.

[9] More or less accurately quoted from Early's report, dated 9 October and sent from New Market. See *OR,* XLIII, Pt. 1, 559. But *cf.* p. 263, where Sanford quotes from the same report.

[10] This action took place at Cedar Creek.

285

Royal from which point he went direct to Washington to consult with the authorities there in reference to the future movements of his army.[11] On arriving at Front Royal however on the 16th, Sheridan had received information from Gen. Wright, whom he had left at Cedar Creek in command of the army, that an attack was threatened by the enemy. Gen. Sheridan had little faith in the attack himself, but he decided to abandon the contemplated cavalry raid, and send Gen. Torbert back with his command to report to Gen. Wright. The 1st Division accordingly, returned at once taking position on the right of the infantry and on the left of Custer's division. Powell's division guarded the left of the army from near Front Royal to the left of Crook's corps.

The position from left to right was now Powell, 2nd Cavalry Division; Crook, 8th Corps (Army of West Virginia); Emory, 19th Corps; Wright, 6th Corps; Merritt, 1st Cavalry; Custer, 3rd Cavalry Division.[12] Powell's division, however, although it watched the country between the left of the infantry and the village of Front Royal, was not closed in to the right as it should have been. The main force was on the Front Royal pike and when the attack came the division concentrated there, leaving the left flank of Crook's corps entirely exposed. Early on the morning of the 19th the camp of the army on the north bank of Cedar Creek[13] was aroused by heavy musketry firing from the direction of the left flank. The men turned out of their shelter tents with great rapidity and seized

[11] The paragraph is badly constructed and the second half of this sentence is out of sequence. After Torbert was ordered to return to General Wright, Sheridan went to Washington, where he arrived at 8:00 A.M. on 17 October. He, Secretary of War Stanton, and General Halleck held about a four-hour conference in regard to Sheridan's operating "east of the Blue Ridge." Sheridan opposed such a plan; the others more or less agreed with him. Sheridan would now hold a defense line while "the bulk" of his troops were detached for duty at Petersburg. At noon, Sheridan returned to Martinsburg, Virginia, arriving about dark. He spent the night of 17–18 October there. Next day, 18 October, he very slowly made the twenty-eight miles to Winchester, spent the evening there, and went to bed about 10:00 P.M. Sheridan, *Personal Memoirs,* II, 66–67. See n. 19. *infra.*

[12] All familiar names by now except that of George Crook (1828–1890), USMA, Class of 1852, a brigadier general commanding the Department of West Virginia since 30 August 1864. He was to gain subsequent fame in the West after the war.

[13] Flows into the North Fork of the Shenandoah River.

[14] The Valley Turnpike. Belle Grove House was maybe a mile outside Middletown.

their rifles and equipments, falling in to ranks in readiness for battle. The Headquarters of the army had been established in a large stone house on the west side of the turn-pike known as the "Belle Grove" house.[14] Gen. Torbert's Headquarters were in the orchard near the house and a little nearer the road. Gen. Emory's were close by and the lines of the 19th corps were just south of us. The 6th corps were in rear of the 19th in echelon, and the cavalry stretched along the creek to the right as far as the back road. When I got outside of my tent, in a good deal of a hurry, I could see a great swarm of disorganized men coming across the pike from the south east, while tremendous volleys of musketry were going on in that direction. Directly south of us the musketry and artillery fire was also very heavy, but there was also more appearance of discipline in the ranks. Far off to the right could be heard artillery firing also, and in the cavalry camps of Merritt the trumpets were sounding "To horse" and I could see the squadrons forming.

It was very plain to almost a tyro in war that the camp was badly surprised. Our left flank was completely turned and the centre driven in. In a very few moments it was probable that the Rebels would have possession of the turnpike and of the shortest road to Winchester. With that would go all our supplies, and without doubt the ruin of the army would follow. It was certainly as bad a lookout as could well be imagined.

Gen. Torbert was mounted and hurrying about trying to get his camp struck and his wagons started off. I did what I could to help, but after a few moments, noticed with some surprise that my own tent was still standing though everything else in the Headquarters was down. I had just called Sergt. Tully to "get that tent down" when Gen. Torbert dashed up and asked what that tent was standing there for. The sergeant who had been in to the tent to see, came out and saluting the General said, "Capt. Coppinger is taking his bawth, sir!" I thought Torbert would ride him down as he screamed, "Cut those tent ropes. Cut the ropes, I say." The tent came down in short order and in five minutes was in the wagon. It seemed that my gallant tent mate had concluded that things were not particularly desperate, and that at all events the rebels would not be so ungentlemanly as to interfere with his toilet.[15]

Altogether it had only been a very few minutes from the first alarm till we were in the saddle and following Gen. Torbert at a rapid gallop towards his command on the right of the army. We soon reached the cavalry lines and found our own troops in beautiful order. Gen. Merritt had his whole command mounted and much of it deployed, endeavoring to rally the retreating soldiers of the 8th and 19th corps, who were streaming by thousands from left to right, evidently heading for the back road and Winchester. We could see that the 6th corps had preserved its formation and that one of its divisions (Getty's) was fiercely engaged with the triumphant enemy.[16] The attempt to rally the demoralized troops was utterly futile, and it was evident that the first thing to do was to support the 6th corps in its attempt to hold the pike and prevent the enemy from getting entirely around our left flank. Torbert accordingly directed Merritt to move his division at once to the left of the pike, joining his right flank on to the left of the 6th Corps, and directed Custer to support him. This movement was soon executed and soon after eight o'clock a line consisting of the cavalry and the 6th Corps had been established well in advance of Middletown, which stopped the forward movement of the enemy—for the time at least.

In the meantime Emory was endeavoring to rally and reform the 19th Corps and had been so far successful that he had a pretty fair line established in rear and to the right of the 6th.[17] The state of the 8th corps was considerably worse, and it was some hours later before they appeared in any condition to render assistance.

[15] John J. Coppinger, a native of Ireland, who had been directly commissioned a captain in the Fourteenth Regiment of Infantry, 30 September 1861. This ludicrous incident should not mask the fact that this man was a first-rate officer and would be promoted brigadier general in 1895 and serve as major general in the Spanish-American War in 1898.

[16] George W. Getty (1819–1901), USMA, Class of 1840, a truly professional soldier, was a brigadier general commanding the Second Division, Sixth Corps.

[17] Brigadier General William H. Emory, commanding the Nineteenth Corps and a veteran of the Red River Campaign earlier in 1864, was last mentioned in the narrative on p. 156.

About nine o'clock Gen. Torbert, who was at this time a short distance to the left of the pike and about two miles in front (south) of Middletown, received a despatch from Col. Powell commanding the 2nd Cavalry division near Front Royal. There had been great anxiety as to the safety of this command up to this time, as should it have been captured or cut off there was nothing to prevent the enemy coming down the Front Royal pike behind us and taking possession of the Valley pike at Newtown, half way between us and Winchester.

It now appeared that one brigade under Col. Moore had been cut off from our army by the advance of the enemy, but its commander with excellent judgment had hurried his wagon train back to Winchester and had taken his brigade safely round the enemy's right flank and come in on the pike in front of the enemy.[18] He was then attached temporarily to Merritt's division and placed on the extreme left of the line. Soon after his arrival news came from Col. Powell commanding the division that with the rest of his force he was falling back on the Front Royal pike and would come in at Newtown, that the enemy's cavalry under Gen. Lomax were pressing him hard with the evident intention of getting possession of the pike and attacking our wagon trains. During the remainder of the day this threatening attitude of the enemy in that direction was a constant menace and considerably delayed the action for the recovery of our lost ground.

As soon as Gen. Torbert received the information as to the position of Powell's forces he sent me to Gen. Wright, the temporary commander of the army, to acquaint him with the facts. I found the General half or three quarters of a mile west of the pike and on the line of his own 6th corps which was in magnificent condition, and doing its duty as the 6th Corps always did. One division under Getty was well to the front holding the enemy, the other two in line of battle in rear supporting the first and holding off the enemy on the right flank. Gen. Wright himself had just received a wound

[18] Colonel Alpheus S. Moore, Eighth Ohio Cavalry, commanded the First Brigade in Powell's Second Division. At Winchester, he had commanded a detachment of the Eighth Ohio Volunteer Cavalry in this same First Brigade. His commission as colonel was dated 9 May 1864. He resigned 4 January 1865.

from a rifle ball in his face, just between the lower lip and the chin, and was staunching the blood with a pocket handkerchief when I reported to him. He looked faint and tired but was his usual courteous self in manner. I remained with him but a moment or two and started back to join my own chief.

As I approached the turnpike my attention was attracted by two or three horsemen approaching from the direction of Winchester, and riding quite rapidly. There was nothing particularly remarkable about this, as officers and orderlies were riding rapidly in all directions at this time, but something about them did fix my attention and in a moment or two I saw that the officer in the lead was Gen. Sheridan and the other was his aide de camp Sandy (George A.) Forsyth; one or two orderlies followed at a short distance in the rear.[19] I turned down the road, of course, and met the General who asked eagerly after the condition of affairs at the front, and then as to where he could find Gen. Torbert. I told him about where I had left him, but added that I had just come from General Wright and could take him there at once if he preferred. He said that was precisely what he wanted and spurred up his horse at once and dashed forward. He was riding his great black war horse "Rienzi," so well known to every participant in the campaign of the Shenandoah.

We turned into the fields in a few moments to the west of the pike and rode along a ridge from which he could look down on the line of the Reserve brigade and Getty's division of the 6th corps, both of which commands were quite hotly engaged with the enemy. He said: "Is this all?" at the same time moving his hand towards the line. I explained as well as I could, as we galloped on, that the rest

[19] See fn. 11 *supra*. To continue the story, Sheridan had been awakened about 6:00 A.M. on 19 October by an aide, who reported hearing artillery fire in the distance. In his *Personal Memoirs*, II. 68ff., Sheridan tells quite well the story of coming upon his shattered army, reforming it, and going on to victory. Unfortunately, he does not mention meeting Sanford.

Sheridan was riding with two of his aides-de-camp, Major George A. Forsyth (not to be confused with Lieutenant Colonel James W. Forsyth; see n. 33, Chap. VII) and Captain Joseph O'Keefe. The latter is an interesting person. Born and bred an Irishman, O'Keefe was listed in the *Official Army Register* as an additional aide-de-camp with rank of captain, to date from 24 April 1862, and appointed from Ireland.

of Merritt's and all of Custer's divisions were still further to the left and that all of the 6th and a good portion of the 19th corps were in pretty fair condition. He asked a question or two as to how Custer came to be on the extreme left when he had left him on the right. I explained that he had been ordered there at the time of the break of the 8th corps and that by Gen. Wright himself; that I knew that Torbert did not approve of the change in the position, as I had heard him say so; but of course he obeyed the order. The General said "Yes-yes."

We had been all this time riding in a south-westerly direction and had now got close down on the line of the 6th corps. Sandy Forsyth, who was an enthusiastic fellow and full of fire and spirit, rode considerably closer to the line and I could see that he was endeavoring to rouse the spirit of the men by telling them Sheridan had come. In a moment or two the news began to spread along the line and the men commenced cheering. Forsyth waved his cap and encouraged them, and by this time we reached Gen. Wright there was a good deal of excitement. Wright was just where I had left him, but had dismounted, and was sitting on the grass on the hill-side. He looked tired and a little disspirited. As Sheridan rode up he said: "Well, we've done the best we could." Gen. Sheridan answered quite brightly: "That's all right; that's all right." At that moment Gen. Emory rode up on a big chestnut sorrel horse and said to Gen. Sheridan: "General the - - - division (I don't know which one) of the 19th corps is formed and in good order to cover the retreat to Winchester." Sheridan replied like a flash: "Retreat —Hell—we'll be back in our camps tonight."

When I listened to this conversation I did not exactly appreciate the fact that it was going to be an historical occasion, but I did understand that it was an interesting one, and the more so from the fact that until that moment it had never occurred to me that it was possible to even hope for anything more than an orderly retreat to Winchester, and an opportunity there to recuperate and recruit, preliminary to a new effort for the control of the Valley. This put a new aspect on affairs and considerably surprised me, and I suspect it did most of the people within hearing. I do not think that Gen.

291

Sheridan was ordinarily what would be called a profane man. I knew him long and well, and for several months at a time had been in the habit of meeting him and hearing him talk daily, but that is the only time I can positively say I can remember hearing him use profane language. Probably I should not remember so distinctly as I do had it been his ordinary custom. At all events, I remember perfectly well what he said then, how he looked and the faces of Wright and Emory and two or three others. I recall perfectly the line of the 6th corps and the appearance of the troops of the enemy in our front. My stay here, however, was short; after a very few moments' conversation with Gen. Wright, Gen. Sheridan directed me to go at once to Gen. Custer and direct him to move his whole division across the pike and take position on the extreme right of the army, then to rejoin Gen. Torbert and report the fact to him. Ordinarily this message would have been sent by Gen. Sheridan to Torbert, the Corps Commander and by him transmitted to Gen. Custer, but Sheridan evidently wanted the change made at once and did not intend to lose any time about it. I took for granted that was it anyway, and went off at a gallop and came near having an absurd accident, owing to my rather reckless riding.

Just before you reach the turnpike on the west of the road there is a mill, and a mill race in which was a good deal of water running very swiftly. As I came down towards the edge of this as fast as I could run my horse, a shell struck square in the mill race dashing the water up almost into my face. My horse almost sat down in his fright and came within an ace of sending me into the middle of the stream. It was quite all I could do to keep my seat and I did not keep my hat which went into the stream and disappeared. I went on however, across the pike and almost immediately met Gen. Custer and communicated the orders as I had been directed, and Custer with his division at once started for the right of the army. For some time after this, perhaps as much as two hours, there was quite a lull in the fighting and this time was taken advantage of by Gen. Sheridan to bring up his troops and rectify his line. Gen. Torbert took his station just to the east of the pike and behind the line of the Reserve Brigade of Merritt's division. A light battery of the 1st Artillery under Lt. Frank Taylor was in position at this point, but not firing at the time.[20] The staff and orderlies were ordered to dismount and I suppose in two minutes most of us were sound asleep. I know I was, and from later developments I suspect I must have slept for over an hour. At all events, the first thing I knew was that my orderly was leaning over me and calling in an excited way: "Captain, Captain, the General is mounted." I jumped up in a hurry and found that Taylor's battery was firing furiously and that the whole line was hotly engaged. I was soon on my horse and followed the General to a position a little in advance of where we had been and about half way between the road and a belt of timber which bordered the open field in which we were standing. The enemy had a plain view from his position of this field, and was shelling it furiously so that it seemed impossible for any troops to cross it. Torbert was very anxious about our left flank, as repeated messages had come from Col. Powell that the enemy were forcing him back on the Front Royal pike, and it was not known at what moment our flank might be attacked.

At length Torbert rode to the left himself, to take a look at the country beyond the woods, and called to me to accompany him, leaving the rest of the staff where they were. He examined the ground carefully and then rode back into the timber and just as we reached it the enemy opened a number of guns directly on the woods. I scarcely ever saw such destruction as occurred in the next few moments. Fortunately for us, their shots were generally high, but the crashing and tearing among the high branches of the trees was fearful. Limbs were falling in every direction and our horses were wild with terror, while the bursting of the shells and the shrieking of the shrapnel and canister shot exceeded almost anything I have ever heard. In one spot a rail fence, which I was obliged to jump, crossed my path and as my horse cleared it, the patter of bullets against the boards sounded like hail on a tin roof. Why we and our horses were not struck is beyond my comprehension.

[20] First Lieutenant Frank E. Taylor, who had the same date of rank for both second and first lieutenant, 5 August 1861. He commanded the Horse Artillery, Companies K and L, First Regiment of Artillery, during the battle and was cited by Torbert for "invaluable service."

Torbert was about as cool a hand under fire as I ever met, but as we rode out of the woods into the open, he looked at me with a little shrug of his shoulders as much as to say that it was pretty lively. The open plain was by no means a desirable spot for a family picnic, but it was a long way preferable to the wood with the splinters flying in every direction. This tremendous artillery duel continued for about an hour or perhaps an hour and a half, and was followed by an advance of the enemy against the line of the 19th corps, which was repulsed by Gen. Emory. At about four o'clock in the afternoon, Gen. Sheridan ordered an advance of our whole line, which was executed in grand style; the men cheering and shouting as they ran forward. The cavalry advance, which of course I was able to see most plainly, was simply magnificent, each brigade being formed in line of regiments, each regiment in close column of squadrons. The double rank formation which we used in those days gave a much more solid appearance to the cavalry than the formation now in use.

The enemy could not stand this counterblow, and it was at once evident that their movement to the front had been simply a feint to cover the attempt to remove the great mass of property they had captured from us in the morning. The left of their line overlapped our right, and again they essayed an attack on the 19th corps. Gen. Custer, who was guarding this flank, was ordered to charge with his division, and at once dashed in heavy masses on the enemy, cutting off the flanking force. Gen. Merritt on the left at the same time charged the enemy's right which gave way in wild confusion, and the infantry advancing, their whole line fled in disorder. Merritt found a ford to the left of the pike on Cedar Creek and Custer one to the right, and both divisions crossed the Creek and rushed on the confused masses of the enemy. By this time it was dark and almost impossible to distinguish friend from foe. The pike on which the enemy was traveling in his effort to get to the protection of the works on Fisher's Hill was packed with guns, wagons, mounted men and stragglers from the ranks. Gen. Devin's brigade of Merritt's division supported by Lowell's Reserve Brigade charged this mass from one side of the road while Custer dashed into them from the other, and the whole thing fell into our hands. Had it not been for the darkness of the night, I do not see how the enemy could have escaped. Gen. Early says in his report to Gen. Robt. Lee: "I found it impossible to rally the troops, they would not listen to entreaties, threats, or appeals of any kind. A terror of the enemy's cavalry had seized them, and there was no holding them. . . . The rout was as thorough and disgraceful as ever happened to our army. . . . I went to Fisher's Hill with the hope of rallying the troops there and forming them in the trenches, but when they reached that position the only organized body of men left was the prisoners, 1,300 in number, and the provost-guard in charge of them."[21]

Certainly the Rebel army was in a dreadful condition, but our own forces were by no means particularly well off. The 6th corps and the cavalry it is true were in excellent order, but they had been fighting all day without even a mouthful of food, and were tired and weary. Gen. Sheridan at first only directed the cavalry to pursue the enemy—later after he had heard of the capture of all of Early's artillery and wagons, he ordered a division from the 19th corps to cross Cedar Creek and support the cavalry. By that time, however, the cavalry had followed the enemy to Fisher's Hill, and had there given up the pursuit. The horses were scarcely able to carry their riders and the troopers themselves were faint from hunger and worn out with the labor and excitement of the day. When Gen. Sheridan decided to suspend the general pursuit, he proceeded with his staff to his former Headquarters at the Belle Grove house, and as usual Gen. Torbert and his staff accompanied him. Of course we were without tents or baggage or anything else, except what we had on our backs, but I knew where our hay stack had stood in the morning, and judging that some of it at least would still be there, I made up my mind to crawl in under the hay, and had no doubt as to my ability to sleep well. Before attempting this, however, I walked over, with one or two of our own staff, to a big fire which some of Sheridan's aides had started near the house.

[21] *OR*, XLIII, Pt. 1, 562–63, in a report from New Market dated 21 October 1864 and addressed to Lee.

Everyone was excited and delighted with the day's work of course, and when somebody came up from the wagon train with a supply of bacon and hard bread, we soon had a welcome feast.

Not a man at Headquarters was aware at this time of what had been accomplished on the other side of Cedar Creek by the Cavalry, but as we were sitting laughing and talking an aide de camp of Gen. Merritt's, Lt. Trimble of the 1st Cavalry, rode up with despatches for Gen. Torbert.[22] I think Forsyth carried the despatches into the house, where Torbert and Sheridan were together while Trimble stood telling the news. In a moment Gen. Sheridan himself came out evidently very much excited by the despatches, and commenced questioning Trimble with great rapidity. He broke off in a moment to send orders to Gen. Emory to hurry a division of the 19th corps across, and then gave other directions. The news spread rapidly and the excitement was intense.

For some purpose which I have now forgotten the General directed me to go into the Belle Grove house, where his quarters were. The surgeons had taken a part of the house for a hospital and in one room I saw a very distinguished looking officer, Major General Stephen D. Ramseur of the Confederate Army, dying of wounds received that day. Ramseur had graduated at West Point only four years before, but had resigned his commission to join the Southern army.[23] Custer, who had been three years at the Academy with him, came into the room while I was there and greeted Ramseur in his bluff, hearty manner, but he scarcely responded. His aide de camp soon came in under a flag of truce, and next morning returned with Gen. Ramseur's remains to the Rebel lines.

Our loss in this day's battle was about six thousand and the

22 Joel G. Trimble, first lieutenant, First Regiment of Cavalry; he had served as an enlisted man in the First and Second Regiments of Dragoons and the Second Regiment of Cavalry from 1855 until 19 February 1863, when he was commissioned a second lieutenant.

23 Ramseur was twenty-seven when he died on 20 October; his class at USMA was 1860, but he had resigned the Army on 6 April 1861 after serving as a second lieutenant in the Third and Fourth Regiments of Artillery. On the battlefield at Cedar Creek, he was shot through both lungs. He commanded a division under Early.

enemy's probably about the same.[24] In all other respects there was an immense difference; we re-captured whatever property the enemy had taken from us in the morning and an immense amount beside, guns, caissons, flags, wagons, ambulances and prisoners. The enemy retreated all night in disorder; it is said not a company organization was intact and only got together again at New Market, nearly thirty miles away. It was probably the most thoroughly decisive battle of the whole war, and entirely settled the question as to the ownership of the Shenandoah Valley which was never seriously disputed afterward.[25] One great loss occurred in the cavalry this day, which was indeed a loss to the whole army. Col. Charles Russell Lowell commanding the Reserve Cavalry Brigade was an officer of singular merit and great gallantry. He was a captain in the 6th Regular Cavalry and Colonel of the 2nd Mass Vol. Cavly.[26] He was wounded early in the day but utterly refused to leave the field, even concealing from the staff the nature of his injury which was afterwards found to be quite severe.

Toward the close of the day and when victory was quite assured, he met his death blow while leading his splendid brigade in a most gallant charge against the enemy's right. He was quite young, probably not more than twenty-five years of age, of unusually fine appearance, and most courteous manners. He commanded the re-

[24] Total Union casualties at Cedar Creek were 5,665, of whom 644 were KIA and 3,430 WIA. The cavalry got off lightly, suffering only 196 casualties in all. *OR*, XLIII, Pt. 1, 137.

[25] And one of the most celebrated victories, too, in song and poetry, the thanks of Congress, etc., etc. Sheridan was satisfied. "The direct result of the battle was the recapture of all the artillery, transportation, and camp equipage we had lost, and in addition twenty-four pieces of the enemy's artillery, twelve hundred prisoners, and a number of battle-flags. But more still flowed from this victory . . . for the re-occupation of our old camps at once re-established a *morale* which for some hours had been greatly endangered by ill-fortune." *Personal Memoirs*, II, 92–93.

Elsewhere, Sheridan reported that Cedar Creek "practically ended the campaign in the Shenandoah Valley." *OR*, XLIII, Pt. 1, 54.

Another result that cannot be overlooked was Sheridan's promotion to major general in the Regular Army, to rank from 8 November 1864.

[26] See nn. 7 and 34, Chap. VII. Sheridan spoke of him as "gallant Lowell." Torbert waxed most expansively in his report of the battles: "Thus the service lost one of its most gallant and accomplished soldiers. He was the beau ideal of a cavalry officer, and his memory will never die in the command." *OR*, XLIII, Pt. 1, 434.

Lieutenant Colonel Caspar Crowninshield, Second Massachusetts Cavalry, succeeded to the command of the Reserve Brigade; he later attained the rank of colonel.

spect of all who knew him, and in his own brigade was regarded with the warmest admiration and affection. A few days after the battle, I had the pleasure of carrying to Gen. Merritt his Brevet as Major General of Volunteers, and of being the first to congratulate him on its receipt. Lowell's commission as Brigadier General had come in the same mail, too late, and I well remember Merritt's emphatic remark, when I told him of it: "I would gladly give up *this,* if he could only take *that.*"[27]

I had a curious adventure on the night of the battle; or rather the next morning, which shows that war, like poverty, brings strange bedfellows—sometimes. After talking the battle over with my friends on our own and Sheridan's staff until quite late, I concluded to hunt my "haystack" bed, and accordingly started off with Lieut. Wallace of the Michigan Cavalry, one of our aides.[28] It was very dark and we had to walk carefully to keep from stumbling over sleeping soldiers; but we managed to find some vacant spots in the hay, and as each of us had an overcoat for a pillow we were soon all right. I slept like a top until daylight and was suddenly awakened by my hand coming into contact with an icy cold face of a man. I started up in a moment, and looking closely at my neighbor, I saw that certainly he would never awaken again until the last reveille. He was a Confederate private, and stone dead. Near him lay an officer of the same army, of the grade of Captain, and scattered about were numerous others. The sight was decidedly eerie, and I had no inclination to turn over and try another nap. I remember that the Captain, poor fellow, had evidently tried to take a last smoke before he died. His tobacco bag lay beside him, half open, and in his hand was his brier root pipe,—filled but apparently never lighted. Either his strength failed him or possibly another shot struck him and ended his career and his smoke together.

It seemed that the Confederate surgeons had attempted to estab-

---

[27] For his own services at Cedar Creek, Sanford was given a brevet promotion. See n. 41, Chap. X.

[28] First Lieutenant Robert C. Wallace, Fifth Michigan Cavalry, although records indicate a captaincy dated 24 August 1864. He had been promoted first lieutenant on 2 November 1863. Torbert cited him for his services during the Shenandoah Valley Campaign. He was subsequently promoted major.

lish a field hospital at this point, and that numbers of the wounded had been brought here only to be killed in the final charge.

We of the cavalry had little time, however, to look about us that morning. Boots and saddles sounded before we had finished our coffee and bacon and we were soon on our way up the valley after the flying remnants of Early's army. Merritt and Custer had already started when Gen. Torbert and the staff rode across Cedar Creek and we had a fast gallop to overtake the head of the column. The pursuit lasted for two days, and only terminated beyond Edenburg, when it was found that there was no prospect of bringing the enemy to a stand. A large number of wagons, caissons, ambulances, and small arms abandoned by the enemy in his flight were captured or destroyed.[29] After this the command returned to the camp on Cedar Creek, and took up the routine duties of a cavalry corps in the field. During November and December there were several skirmishes with light parties of the enemy, but no more heavy fighting on the part of the main body of the army.

In one of these conflicts early in November, all three of the cavalry divisions were sharply engaged and Gen. Powell's captured some two hundred and fifty prisoners, two pieces of artillery and two battle flags from the Confederate cavalry under Lomax. Custer's division lost a very gallant officer—Col. Walter Hull—who was killed while leading a charge.[30]

[29] The pursuit lasted two days more or less. On 20 October, Merritt's First Division moved to Fisher's Hill, where Rebel cavalry was encountered and driven on. Merritt pushed on for Woodstock. Crowninshield's Reserve Brigade went ahead now, alone, into and beyond Edenburg, but, finding no enemy, returned to the main body. On 21 October, the cavalry encamped near Fisher's Hill.

[30] Action against Confederate cavalry near Cedar Creek, Ninevah, and Newton on 12 November 1864. Lieutenant Colonel Walter C. Hull, commanding the Second New York Cavalry, was instantly killed. Memory slips Sanford and he treats this action again, somewhat differently; cf. pp. 306–307.

·CHAPTER IX·

ABOUT THE 20TH OF THE MONTH Gen. Torbert made a reconnaissance some forty miles up the valley to Rude's Hill. Here he developed a force of some ten thousand infantry and artillery, and a division of cavalry, with which he had a very sharp action.[1] Gen. Merritt with the 1st Division also made an expedition into the country east of the Blue Ridge, with the hope of being able to catch and crush Mosby's band, or failing that, to destroy the supplies in that section which afforded subsistence to his men and indeed contributed in a measure to the support of the Confederate Army. In his primary object he was unsuccessful, but he destroyed or gathered up a large amount of forage of various kinds and large quantities of cattle and horses.[2] As for catching Mosby or any of his men, it was about as easy as the traditional hunt for a needle in a haystack. This enterprising partisan during the whole period of our campaign in the valley had kept the country between the army and

[1] On 21 November, Torbert, with the Second and Third Divisions, began a reconnaissance up the Shenandoah Valley. He engaged the enemy next day at Rude's Hill, near Mount Jackson (about forty miles from camp), and sustained thirty WIA but captured fifteen to twenty prisoners.

[2] Expedition from Winchester into Fauquier and Loudoun Counties, 28 November–3 December 1864. Crowninshield's Reserve Brigade alone destroyed 23 barns, eight mills, one distillery, 10,000 tons of hay, and 25,000 bushels of grain and captured 87 horses, 474 beef cattle, and 100 sheep. *OR,* XLIII, Pt. 1, 673.

Merritt responded to orders from Sheridan, dated 27 November, directing him to operate against the guerrillas in this "hot-bed of lawless bands."

[3] For an earlier treatment of Mosby's operations, see pp. 260 ff. After his raid into the Blue Ridge Mountains, Merritt had this to say: "The country on every side of the general line of march was in every instance swept over by flankers from the columns, and in this way the entire valley was gone over. The guerrillas were exceedingly careful to avoid any encounter with any of the parties. *Ibid.,* 672.

the base of supplies in a state of terror.[3] Even within the lines of the army itself it was by no means safe to ride without a strong escort.

A tragical incident illustrative of this statement was the death of Lieut. John R. Meigs of the Engineer Corps early in October.[4] I was within an ace of being involved in this affair and only the merest accident apparently prevented my accompanying him, when I should have undoubtedly shared his fate. I had received orders from Gen. Torbert on the evening of October 7th[5] to carry certain despatches to Gen. Custer who was lying beyond the village of Dayton, some miles from Headquarters, which were near Harrisonburg. The General explained that as the ride was a long one and there was no probability of our moving next day, I might as well put off the trip till early in the morning. However I could suit my own convenience in that respect. I strolled over to Gen. Sheridan's Headquarters which were close by, undecided whether to go at once or wait till daylight. On the one hand was the prospect of a good night's sleep in my own tent; on the other the prospect of a jolly evening with the fellows at Custer's Headquarters. It was, after all, a question of companionship en route and I concluded if anyone happened to be going that way from Gen. Sheridan's staff I would go too; otherwise I would wait till next day.

Just then I met Meigs, who was Engineer officer on Sheridan's staff, and after a few moments' conversation it came out that he was on the point of starting for Gen. Custer's, with reference to some work he had to do in that neighborhood, connected with a survey he was making. We agreed to go together, and to start as soon as possible, as it was almost dark. While we were talking it clouded up suddenly, and threatened a heavy shower. I had no overcoat with me and thought it foolish to get soaked for nothing, so I decided not to go until morning, and urged Meigs to do the

[4] First Lieutenant John R. Meigs, Corps of Engineers, chief engineer, Department of West Virginia, and aide-de-camp to Sheridan's headquarters. He had entered service on 11 June 1863.

[5] Sanford is in error here, for all records indicate that Meigs was killed about dusk on the evening of 3 October beyond Harrisonburg, beyond Dayton, Virginia. He was twenty-two.

same. He had a big rubber coat and with that and his cavalry boots he said he should be all right, so off he went and I went back to my tent.

The next morning I rode over early to Custer's Camp and delivered my despatches. They said Meigs had been there and returned. I paid no especial attention to the matter, as I supposed of course he had reached Headquarters before I left, but that I had not happened to see him. When I returned to camp that afternoon I found the Headquarters in a great state of excitement. One of Meigs' orderlies had made his way in on foot and wounded, and reported that the Lieutenant and the other orderly were killed. Parties sent out at once found poor Meigs' body and brought it in. The soldier was not found and it was not certain whether he had been killed or taken prisoner. As well as could be ascertained, Meigs with his two orderlies, were riding along a trail or country road through a piece of woods, when they caught up with a small party of cavalry soldiers riding in the same direction. They were miles inside of our picket line, and it probably never occurred for an instant to Meigs that they were not some detail from Custer's division. At all events he rode up to and partly by them. All of both parties were enveloped in cloaks or rubber ponchos on account of the rain, and there was nothing to indicate by their dress to which side they belonged. They seem to have kept along parallel to each other for a few moments and then suddenly the strangers, at a signal from their leader, turned and fired shot after shot from their revolvers into the unsuspecting soldiers by their side. Meigs seems to have been killed at once, and the trooper of the 6th Cavalry who escaped believed the other soldier was also. He himself was wounded, and his horse also wounded fell with him and in the darkness and confusion he managed to crawl into the bushes and hide.

Of course the whole thing was murder—no more, no less.[6] Meigs was well inside our lines, on a peaceful errand, looking for no enemy and expecting none. He was not halted or challenged and was given no more chance for his life than any murderer gives his

[6] Sheridan called it murder, too, and an "atrocious act."

victim. This sort of work is not war, and is not so regarded in any civilized community. In years long after I saw plenty of horrors of this description among the Indians of the Southwest; but I can scarcely believe now that soldiers of our own blood could be guilty of such crimes. Gen. Sheridan was wild with indignation, and ordered every house within a radius of five miles to be burned to the ground. His theory was that the murderers were citizens of the vicinity, and that all of the inhabitants were in sympathy with and affording assistance to the criminals. The order, however, was never carried out to its full extent, nor, I suppose, did he intend it should be, though he did intend to give the people a severe lesson.[7] A few days later, as I remember, McNeill, one of the principal guerrillas of the vicinity, and the leader who perhaps next to Mosby was most feared, was mortally wounded and fell into our hands. He was placed in a house near Middletown where I saw him and had considerable conversation with him.[8]

I have never quite understood how I failed to find poor Meigs' body on my ride to Custer's camp, as I must certainly have passed close by it. He was one of the most brilliant young men of his day, and a great loss to the service. In age he must have been about twenty-one or two, as he was graduated from the Military Academy only the year before his death. He was at the head of his class, and I have heard it stated that his average mark was higher than that of any man who had ever been graduated at that institution.[9] He

[7] Never fully carried out, it is true; on the other hand, Sheridan did order the houses burned, and in a dispatch to Grant dated 7 October 1864, he said that "all the houses within an area of five miles were burned." *OR*, XLIII, Pt. 1, 30. In his *Personal Memoirs*, II, 52, Sheridan modifies the action somewhat. Custer was detailed for the work and began on 4 October. "The prescribed area included . . . Dayton, but when a few houses in the immediate neighborhood of the scene of the murder had been burned, Custer was directed to cease his desolation work." The itinerary of the Third Division states this: *"October 3 to 5.* In camp. Pursuant to orders the Fifth New York Cavalry was detailed to burn houses in vicinity of camp in retaliation for the murder of Lieutenant Meigs." *OR,* XLIII, Pt. 1, 99.

[8] On 7 October 1864, Colonel Oliver Edwards, Thirty-seventh Massachusetts Volunteers, who had commanded the First Division, Sixth Corps, at Cedar Creek, reported that "Captain McNeill, guerrilla, is mortally wounded, lying at Middletown." *OR*, XLIII, Pt. 2, 315. See n. 12, Chap. VII.

[9] John R. Meigs, a good student, stood No. 1 of twenty-five, Class of 1863, USMA. He was first on the list of distinguished cadets reported at the examination in June, 1863, and excelled in an extraordinarily long list of subjects. See *Official*

was a son of Major General Montgomery Meigs, Quartermaster General of the Army, who like himself had been an officer of the Engineer Corps.[10]

From this time on Mosby and his bandits made the lower valley a perfect place of terror. No party of less than fifty men was safe a mile from camp, and the loss in men, animals and supplies was enormous. No less than three officers of Gen. Sheridan's own staff were killed by these guerrillas, and numerous others. I can remember the names of Col. Tolles, the Chief Commissary of Subsistence of the Army; and Dr. Ohlenschlager, the Medical Director; Dr. Coover, Medical Director of the Reserve Brigade; Lieuts. Walker, 1st Cavalry, and McMaster, 2nd Cavalry. The latter was robbed and killed after he had been taken prisoner.[11] These were all personal friends or acquaintances of my own, and their names remain in my memory; but the list could be swelled to many pages, by reference to the reports of that year.

About this time I had business which took me to Martinsburg on the Baltimore and Ohio Railroad, and took advantage of an escort of the 17th Penna Cavalry which was going to that post from Winchester. The party consisted of, I think, a troop of the regiment with one or two officers, and Captain Ira W. Claflin of the 6th Cavalry, and myself.[12] As the troop was quite small we

---

Register for 1864, p. 117. Wrote Sheridan at a later date: "This young officer was endeared to me on account of his invaluable knowledge of the country, his rapid sketching, his great intelligence, and his manly and soldierly qualities." *OR,* XLIII, Pt. 1, 56–57.

[10] Brigadier General Montgomery C. Meigs (1816–1892), Class of 1836, USMA, served as Quartermaster General of the Army, 1861–82.

[11] Lieutenant Colonel Cornelius W. Tolles, chief quartermaster to Sheridan, who had entered service on 14 May 1861, and Acting Assistant Surgeon Emil Ohlenschlager, acting medical inspector on Sheridan's staff, were ambushed on 11 October 1864. Tolles is reported to have died on 8 November; he had been shot in the head. Ohlenschlager was shot in the bowels.

The other officers in Sanford's list are Surgeon John B. Coover, Sixth Pennsylvania Cavalry; First Lieutenant John S. Walker, regimental commissary, First Cavalry, killed on 15 August 1864; and Second Lieutenant Charles McMaster, killed 20 September 1864. The last two officers had been in service a little more than a year at their respective deaths.

[12] Captain Ira W. Claflin commanded General Sheridan's escort, comprised of men and officers of the Sixth Regiment of Cavalry. He had been around in the

probably did not number much over thirty men all told. It was a beautiful moonlight evening when we rode out of town, and we expected to reach our destination soon after midnight if all went well. The road at this time was considered so excessively dangerous, that all traveling was done at night, the danger being regarded as less in the dark, as the guerrillas were then unable to perceive a command at great enough distance to complete their plans for an ambush in time. They, on their part, did not dare to lie in ambush near the road for any length of time as they would then be liable to surprise themselves. We rode along without incident for an hour or two, enjoying the beautiful freshness of the night, and the little spice of adventure in the trip. Claflin and I were old friends, and as we of course had nothing to do with the troops, being simply guests as it were, we felt relieved of all responsibility, and were delighted with the experience.

Shortly before reaching the village of Bunker Hill, one of the officers of the troop rode up and joined us and pointed out the site of the village. "That," he said, "is Bunker Hill, and it is about half way to Martinsburg. When we get through there the worst of the trip is over, and I think we are all right." With this he dropped back to his troop, which was a few yards in rear, and gave some directions to his men, relative to keeping silence, and not lighting matches. About a hundred yards in front of us we had a small advanced guard and on either side of the road a few flankers at a short distance from the column.

Claflin was a jovial sort of a youth; he had a leave of absence in his pocket and he was going home to be married, so that he felt pretty good. Just at this time we saw one or two dead horses lying by the side of the road in our front. It was nothing particularly startling, as dead horses were by no means uncommon in that country in those times; but it afforded Claflin the opportunity to take a flask of whisky out of his saddle bags, with the remark, as he handed it to me, "I always make a point of taking a drink when I pass a dead horse, out of compliment to what the poor fellow has

Army since 1857 and was brevetted captain for services at the Battle of Valverde, New Mexico, in 1862.

done." He didn't get that drink just then, nor did I. A piece of pine woods ran down nearly to the road on the west side, but on the east it was open and a short distance in front the ground rose in to quite a little hill. The advanced guard had reached and were passing over this elevation, and we were just abreast of, and but a few yards from the little woods, when there came a volley of pistol bullets, and then with the well-known Rebel yell, Mosby and his men were upon us, their sabres flashing in the moonlight, and the sound of their horses' hoofs like thunder on the hard ground.

The Pennsylvanians were old hands at this work, and in their own brief but incisive language, "they didn't stampede worth a cent." There was no time nor opportunity to form and meet the charge, but the whole column swept on to the hill in front where the advanced guard and flankers had already gathered, dismounted and opened fire from their carbines. The troop almost instantly drew up in their rear and poured in a heavy fire, which stopped the guerrillas. Then they drew sabres and charged in their turn, sending the "Johnnies" flying to the shelter of their woods. The whole thing didn't last ten minutes, and is only mentioned as an instance of what was occurring on that road and every road in the Valley pretty nearly every day during that campaign. We had one or two men wounded and some horses shot; but they were pistol wounds and not serious, I believe. The enemy's loss I don't remember, or even whether any occurred. Probably there was some, as the Pennsylvanians used carbines and a number of them were dismounted and had that advantage in their favor. Then we repaired damages as well as we could, and Claflin got his drink in quiet. During the rest of our ride we were not troubled by any similar attentions from the enemy, and reached Martinsburg in due season.

About the middle of November the usual routine of camp life was varied by a threatened attack of Gen. Early on our forces. He moved his own command down the Valley as far as Cedar Creek which he crossed to the north bank, probably under the impression that the 6th Corps had been sent back to the Army of the Potomac. The whole cavalry corps under Torbert was at once moved to the front and Early immediately fell back. The pursuit was continued on all the valley roads to a point beyond Harrisonburg, more or less fighting occurring in all the commands. Powell's Division in particular had a very gallant fight on the Front Royal pike, in which they completely routed Lomax's Cavalry, capturing guns, caissons, wagons, battle-flags and prisoners.[13] After it was evident that Early did not intend to make a stand with his main body, our forces were withdrawn to the lower valley and both armies soon went into winter quarters.

Army headquarters and cavalry headquarters were established in the town of Winchester, and the troops took up a defensive line covering the city, and extending from the Shenandoah to the North Mountains. The railroad was repaired and completed to Stephenson's Depot on the Opequon, which became the principal depot of supplies. As soon as the troops were comfortably quartered, drills were resumed and with the usual schools and picket and reconnaissance duty occupied the time of the command. The weather was magnificent for out door work, and many horse races were gotten up, which afforded much amusement, especially in the Cavalry Corps.

Captain Parsons, of the Adjt. General's Department on Sheridan's staff, became very famous for his success as a light weight rider, and quite carried off the honors in that line.[14] The sporting interest at Torbert's Headquarters made many efforts to find something to beat him, but though they imported horses from the North at considerable expense, nothing was ever able to distance little Parsons on his famous black racer.

Of quieter amusements there were plenty. Many of the inhabitants were Union people, and even among the Confederate sympathizers the younger generation were quite willing to join in the festivities incident to so large a population as had been gathered together in Winchester that winter. Whist clubs and reading clubs were formed and balls, parties and private theatricals often oc-

[13] It will be recalled that Sanford has already dealt with Brigadier General Powell's fight on 12 November 1864; see p. 299.

[14] Captain Enos B. Parsons, assistant adjutant general of volunteers on Sheridan's staff, dated 29 February 1864; major, assistant adjutant general of volunteers, 24 December 1864.

curred. Occasionally a great review would take place, and one of the whole cavalry corps I remember in particular as a magnificent affair. My own regiment, the 1st Cavalry, was detailed early in the winter for escort duty at our Headquarters, and that fact added greatly to my pleasure, as it enabled me to meet my brother officers very much more frequently than when they were off with one of the divisions.

Of course in such a great assemblage of young men in a winter camp, with a good deal of time on their hands, many things took place which were not as agreeable or harmless as those I have mentioned. There was, as there always will be in such times, and under such circumstances, a good deal of card playing and hard drinking, and as a consequence some bad feeling, terminating in challenges and duels. These were very quietly conducted, however, and few persons besides the actual participants knew anything about them. Probably the majority of officers would say that no such things as a duel ever occurred in the Army of the Potomac, but I have personal knowledge of several.

One of them was an exceedingly sad affair, as it terminated in the instant death of one of the principals and resulted in completely wrecking the career of the other, one of the most brilliant young men I have ever met. As the facts in the case are perhaps not known to more than three men now living, I shall not indicate the time or place when and where they occurred, but the circumstances were as follows: The Cavalry Corps went into camp one evening after a hard day's marching and fighting, and a number of young officers met in one of the camps and engaged in conversation over the results of the day's battle. Pipes were lit, and whisky was passed around. Everything was jolly and comfortable and there was no thought of any hostile movements except such as they were sure to encounter on the morrow in the way of business; when a game of poker was proposed. This was warmly welcomed by a certain number, and cards were produced and the game began.

Things went on as usual in such cases. The wary old birds played their hands cautiously, abstained from liquor, and made their coups with deliberation and judgment. The younger or more reckless grew noisier as they won or lost, venturing more heavily, and drank more deeply as the game went on. Finally the more careful or sedate players, withdrew one by one and the interest of the game was centered in the contest between two young men neither more than twenty-five years old, and both men of high reputation in their respective regiments. Fortune clung steadily to the side of one of them, and the reckless betting and smothered anger of the other only tended to make his play more hopeless and his losses greater as the game went on. Finally in a paroxysm of excitement, he dashed his cards in the face of his opponent, and springing to his feet charged him with cheating. The few men present were sobered in an instant, and rushing between the unhappy young fellows, carried them off to separate tents. Day was breaking and everyone knew that a battle was certain with the rising of the sun.

Nothing could be done to prevent the hostile meeting between the poor misguided young men. No apologies were offered or perhaps would have been accepted, and by the time it was light enough to see, they stood facing each other at a few yards from the camp. Two shots rang out together on the air, and the poor boy who had offered the insult fell dead with a bullet through his heart. The picket lines were already engaged. "To Horse" was sounding in the camps, and the whole corps was in action long before sunrise. Captain A. was reported as "killed in action" at the battle of blank, and his more unfortunate opponent, his heart eaten out by remorse, and his brilliant faculties stupefied by the liquor vainly swallowed to deaden his regrets, has long filled a drunkard's grave in the cemetery of one of our far Western posts. That is the history of an army duel, known to but few at any time and now to almost none.[15]

Many, however, still remember that gallant soldier whom I consider

[15] There is no reason to doubt this tale, and Article 26, Articles of War, lends ironic underpinning to this minor tragedy: "If any commissioned or non-commissioned officer commanding a guard shall knowingly or willingly suffer any person whatsoever to go forth to fight a duel, he shall be punished as a challenger; and all seconds, promoters, and carriers of challenges, in order to duels, shall be deemed principals, and be punished accordingly. And it shall be the duty of every officer commanding an army, regiment, company, post, or detachment, who is knowing to a challenge being given or accepted by any officer, non-commissioned officer, or soldier, under his command, or has reacon to believe the same to be the case, immediately to arrest and bring to trial such offenders."

much the more unhappy of the two, and he is seldom spoken of without expressions of wonder as to the astonishing breakdown of such a strong character, and the utter collapse of so promising a career. In the above story we have the key to the secret.

My whole experience in the army has satisfied me of one thing, and that is that of all possible forms of vice that a man can fall a victim to, the most degrading, the most utterly hopeless, is the vice of gambling. From anything else a man may recover, but from gambling never; for the habit so hardens a man to all the finer sentiments that he soon loses any possible desire for reformation. I have heard of reformed gamblers and reformed drunkards. Of the latter I have seen a few; but of the former, none. In my younger days gambling was the curse of the army, but thank Heaven, it is scarcely known in the service now, and the reason for the change is evident. Twenty or thirty years since, the time of the young officers was divided between periods of intense activity and hardships in the field, and what was called rest, but would be more correctly styled stagnation in camp. As there were no comforts of any description to be had, few officers among the younger were married, and still fewer of those who were cared to expose their families to the hardships of camp or frontier life. There were no schools or libraries worthy of the name; the mails reached the posts only at long and indefinite intervals; there was no society or refining influence; and in fact no social intercourse of any kind, and some such intercourse a man must have or go mad; the officers were driven to the back room of the sutler's store, with its regular accompaniment of whisky, tobacco and cards. The wonder is, not that many young fellows "fell by the wayside,"—many careers which opened with the most brilliant promise went out in blackness and gloom—but that any at all escaped. When I run over the list of the young men of my date, and follow up their history, I am struck with horror and amazement, and can only marvel at my own escape. But I have been led into a long digression, from thinking of the gay winter of 1864–5, and must return to my story.[16]

[16] This is as good a place as any to mention the fact that General Torbert, in his report on cavalry operations in the Shenandoah Valley, listed a number of staff

The summer and fall of 1864 in the valley was, as has been seen, one long succession of victories for the Union cause. In the Army of the Potomac proper no such brilliant results had been obtained, but there had been bloody and desperate fighting during the whole time, and Grant held Lee fast locked in an embrace which it was apparent to all must end in surrender, unless some almost miraculous interposition occurred. In the West the brilliant Atlanta campaign; the magnificent march to the sea, with the capture of Savannah and the crowning victory at Nashville by that grand soldier George H. Thomas had practically closed the Rebellion in that quarter. Day after day we heard the cannon booming out salutes in honor of some new victory gained, and everyone knew that with the first advent of the spring, the final struggle must occur, and few, if any, doubted as to what the result would be. Late in December the magnificent 6th Corps was sent back to the Army of the Potomac, and though the cavalry were left behind in the valley, we all understood perfectly that our separation was but temporary, and that when the time came for the final wrestle, the Cavalry Corps of the Army of the Potomac were sure to be in at the death.[17]

So during the last months of the winter every nerve was strained to bring the command up to the highest pitch of discipline and efficiency. The ranks were filled to the maximum, and almost to a man, with veteran soldiers. The horses were in splendid condition, the clothing and supplies of all kinds were of the best and in the greatest abundance, and when finally on the 27th of February, 1865, the trumpets rang out "To Horse" and the Cavalry Corps rode out to the South on the valley turnpike, no finer body of ten thousand sabres could be found on this planet.[18] The command

officers for special praise—and among them was Captain George B. Sanford. Torbert described them as "fit recipients of higher honors than lay in my power to bestow, for gallantry and courage . . . braver and more efficient staff officers never drew rein or saber." *OR,* XLIII, Pt. 1, 435.

[17] "By the middle of the month [*i.e.,* December] the whole of the Sixth Corps was at Petersburg; simultaneously with its transfer to that line Early sending his Second Corps to Lee." Sheridan, *Personal Memoirs,* II, 99.

[18] Here begins Sheridan's well-known Expedition (raid) from Winchester to the Front of Petersburg, 27 February–28 March 1865, but Sanford must disgress and does not deal with it until Chapter X.

consisted simply of the Army of the Potomac cavalry with its proper complement of Horse Artillery. The 1st Division was now under command of Gen. Thos. C. Devin, and the 3rd under Gen. George A. Custer. Gen. Merritt commanded the corps in the room of Gen. Torbert, absent on leave. Torbert had applied for and received a twenty days' leave of absence shortly before we started, under the supposition that no movement would take place for some weeks. He took for granted, of course, that he would be notified should anything necessitate his return, and indeed his staff officers would have telegraphed him at once had they been allowed to do so, but Gen. Sheridan forbade it.

The fact was that Gen. Sheridan had never forgiven Torbert for his failure to press the enemy more vigorously at Milford in the Luray Valley, at the time of the battle of Fisher's Hill. His gallant conduct at Waynesboro, at Tom's Brook and at Cedar Creek should seem to have blotted out the error of judgment then committed, if error it was; but nothing satisfied Sheridan for a fault once committed. Again late in December on one of the numerous expeditions which I have passed over as unnecessary to mention, Sheridan had been dissatisfied with our failure to capture Gordonsville, although even he could find no fault with the conduct of the affair. The intensity of the cold and the icy condition of the roads delayed the marches to such an extent that the enemy were enabled to bring up large reenforcements to infantry by rail from Richmond; and though Gen. Torbert made, as always, a very gallant fight, capturing even a battery of artillery, besides prisoners and large quantities of supplies, still he did not succeed in the main object of the expedition. So Gen. Sheridan had determined to leave him behind at Winchester, and adopted this rather curious way of getting rid of him.[19]

His successor in the command of the corps was Gen. Wesley

[19] In his *Personal Memoirs,* II, 112, Sheridan is brutally explicit: "General Torbert being absent on leave at this time, I did not recall him, but appointed General Merritt Chief of Cavalry, for Torbert had disappointed me on two important occasions— in the Luray Valley during the battle of Fisher's Hill, and on the recent Gordonsville expedition—and I mistrusted his ability to conduct any operations requiring much self-reliance." Torbert had commanded the expedition to Gordonsville, Virginia, 19–28 December 1864.

Merritt, of whom I have already frequently spoken. Merritt was and is a splendid soldier, and a gentleman for whom I had the greatest personal respect and admiration. He was so kind as to propose to retain me in the same position on his staff that I had occupied on Gen. Torbert's, and I highly appreciated and was most grateful for the confidence displayed. At the same time I recognized thoroughly the exceedingly uncomfortable position in which I was about to be placed. The corps was moving to battle, and I felt that I must go with it; there was no doubt about that; and yet I was leaving my own chief, when under a cloud for what I regarded as no fault of his own, and at a time when I knew he would be most bitterly hurt, and most in need of the sympathy and assistance of his trusted staff officers.

I did what I thought I ought to do, and went with Gen. Merritt, but owing to a most unfortunate complication of affairs which occurred later, I eventually became entangled in a web of difficulties, from which there was no possible escape without wounding the feelings of both of these men, and laying myself open to the charge of ingratitude in either case. Yet now after the lapse of all these years, I can see no possible way in which by any act of mine I could have avoided the result. It was simply one of those cases in which there is "Some divinity which shapes our ends, rough hew them as we may."[20]

Well, both of these gallant soldiers and accomplished gentlemen have been my good friends since,—Torbert up to his sad but noble ending and Merritt till now; but the wretched misunderstanding in which we were involved, has always been a matter of great regret to me. To the best of my belief, it was the one solitary disagreeable incident in my relations to my superiors in all my army life. I will mention the circumstances when I come to them in due course.

[20] More or less correctly recited from *Hamlet,* Act V, scene 2, lines 10–11.

·CHAPTER X·

THE SPRING OPENED LATE THAT YEAR, and the hilltops of the Blue Ridge and the North Mountains were white with snow as our long column trotted up the valley turnpike.[1] The roads, however, for the first day or two were excellent, and they were the very last good roads we saw during the war, for the frost already was beginning to come out of the ground, and almost simultaneously with our starting the rains descended and the floods came, and from the 1st of March until the end of the campaign the army absolutely floundered in a sea of mud. However, on the 27th and 28th of February, the traveling was good, and we made about thirty miles each day, which is good marching for a column of ten thousand horsemen with their trains. The enemy kept out of the way until March 1st, when Gen. Rosser attempted to dispute the passage of the middle fork of the Shenandoah at Mt. Crawford. Two regiments of Capehart's brigade swam the river and drove him off after a very gallant little fight, in which Capehart captured a number of prisoners, and some twenty or thirty wagons and ambulances. I was so fortunate as to be with this part of the column

---

[1] Torbert was left with the First Brigade, Second Division (Department of West Virginia), Brevet Brigadier General William B. Tibbits commanding, and the Reserve Horse Artillery Brigade, Captain James M. Robertson commanding. On 26 February, Sheridan estimated that in all, there were about 2,000 cavalrymen in the valley when he left. "This seems to me to be ample for the defense of this frontier." *OR*, XLVI, Pt. 2, 711–12.

Sheridan's orders were "to destroy the Virginia Central Railroad, the James River Canal, capture Lynchburg if practicable, and then join Major General Sherman wherever he might be found in North Carolina, or return to Winchester." *Ibid.*, Pt. 1, 475.

314

at the time of this affair, and very much admired the spirited action of Col. Capehart's troopers.[2]

On the morning of the 2nd we rode into the pretty town of Staunton, but found no enemy to oppose us. The citizens, however, said that Gen. Early with what was left of his army, had gone to Waynesborough, where he meant to fight us. This sort of challenge was always welcome to Sheridan, and our stay at Staunton was consequently very short indeed. Gen. Merritt moved out of the Waynesborough road with Custer's division in the advance, closely followed by Devin. When Custer's head of column reached Waynesborough, Early was discovered with a few brigades of infantry and one brigade of cavalry, occupying a line of intrenchments just west of the town. I looked at this piece of country with a good deal of interest, as it was just the spot at which I had had my misadventure some four months earlier. Custer made short work with Early and his army. A hasty reconnaissance disclosed the fact that the enemy's left did not quite reach the Shenandoah river, and sending Pennington with his brigade dismounted to threaten that flank,[3] he, with his remaining two brigades, mounted, drew sabres and dashed in a wild charge at and over the intrenchments, capturing all the infantry and artillery, and trains. Gen. Early himself, with some few of his generals and about twenty men, escaped across the Blue Ridge, and Rosser with the cavalry managed to get around the command and make his way back to the upper valley; but everything else fell a prey to the victorious Custer, who was in high feather when I saw him a few moments later.[4]

[2] Colonel Henry Capehart, First West Virginia Cavalry, commanded the Third Brigade, Third Division (Custer), formerly the Second Brigade, Second Division. Capehart lost five WIA; the Confederates lost thirty POW, a few KIA, twenty ambulances and wagons with contents destroyed. Capehart had entered service in 1861 as a surgeon.

[3] Colonel Alexander C. M. Pennington, Jr., USMA, Class of 1859, Third New Jersey Cavalry, commanded the First Brigade in Custer's division.

[4] Sheridan called this a "brilliant fight" which netted the Union forces 11 artillery pieces, 200 wagons and teams (all loaded), 17 battle flags, and 1,600 officers and men as POW. How Early and his fellow generals ever escaped baffled Sheridan, "unless they hid in obscure places in the houses of the town." *OR,* XLVI, Pt. 1, 476.

In Staunton, Sheridan had to make a most important decision: should he pursue

I rode through the village and up to the bank of the stream as the sun was setting, and just then caught sight of Custer coming down to the east bank of the river at a gallop. As he recognized me he called out, "Is Gen. Sheridan over there, Sanford?" I said, "Yes, he is just riding in to the village." "Well, tell him I have got two thousand prisoners, seventeen battle flags and eleven pieces of artillery." I carried the message back, which was the first authoritative news we had, and of course there was great rejoicing. Before long up came Custer himself with his following, and in the hands of his orderlies, one to each, were the seventeen battle flags streaming in the wind. It was a great spectacle and the sort of thing which Custer thoroughly enjoyed.

He was certainly the model of a light cavalry officer, quick in observation, clear in judgment, and resolute and determined in execution. Brave as a lion himself, he seemed never for a moment to imagine that any subordinate, down to the meanest private soldier in his command, would hesitate to follow him even to the death, and indeed he had reason to be firm in this belief. It was said that he was ambitious and grasping; but as far as I could see, or can now judge, his ambition seemed to be more to surprise and startle both friend and foe with the brilliancy of his deeds, than anything else, and his claims for special honor were always for his Division rather than for his personal account. As I never belonged to Custer's Staff or served under his command, and on the contrary was well known to be a firm friend and strong partisan of his great rival, Gen. Wesley Merritt, I have the less hesitation in making this statement. To my mind there never was any good reason for invidious comparison between the two men, whose ability, each great in its way, would have naturally developed along

---

his course toward Lynchburg and leave Early in his rear, or should be seek out Early, fight him, defeat him, "and open a way through Rockfish Gap, and have everything" in his own hands in order to accomplish that part of his orders which directed the destruction of the railroad and the James River Canal? Sheridan decided on the latter course.

Very pleasing to Sheridan after the victory at Waynesboro was the fact that the crossing of the Blue Ridge, "covered with snow as it was, at any other point would have been difficult." *Ibid.*

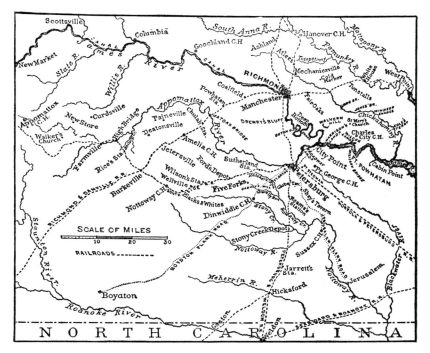

THE PETERSBURG AND APPOMATTOX CAMPAIGNS
FROM JOHNSON AND BUELL (EDS.), *Battles and Leaders of the Civil War,* IV, 569

quite different lines. Custer was the typical *beau sabreur* "sudden and quick in quarrel, seeking the bubble reputation even at the cannon's mouth."[5] Merritt was cool, calm, judicious, slow to conceive but prompt to act when the time for action had arrived, and so acting that there was never opportunity for doubt in the mind of friend or foe as to what his intention might be. Both were at this time young men of wonderful brilliancy and great promise and well worthy of the devoted allegiance in which they were held by their troopers of the 1st and 3rd Divisions.

On the morning of the 3rd Merritt marched for Charlottesville, Custer's Division having the advance. As we approached this beautiful old town Gen. Custer was met near the entrance to the grounds

[5] *As You Like It,* Act II, scene 7, lines 151–53.

of the University, by a deputation of citizens and officials who handed to him the keys of the public buildings and one of the University of Virginia.[6] The College officials (at least I suppose they were) I remember had long white wands, and the whole ceremony reminded me greatly of a passage in one of the romances of Sir Walter Scott. One circumstance which perhaps detracted from the scenic effect was the appearance of our own command. Our four years experience of Virginia mud might be thought to have accustomed us to its effects, but all previous records were broken on this campaign. It was literally knee-deep, and how the wagons ever got through it after ten thousand horsemen had kneaded it up, is more than I can tell. As it was they did not reach the town for more than two days after we got there, and even then the mule teams were dreadfully used up. After receiving the surrender of the City, which didn't occupy him long, Custer pushed on with great ardor, and just beyond the town ran against a small party of cavalry with three pieces of artillery all of which he promptly captured. The whole command then went into camp in the outskirts of the city, and as it was understood that we should probably have to remain two or three days, while waiting for the trains, everyone settled down to getting the mud off and a good rest preparatory to a new start.[7]

At this time nobody knew exactly what we were going to do—not even Gen. Sheridan himself. His orders from Gen. Grant had given him considerable discretion as to his course after destroying the Virginia Central Railroad and the James River Canal, which was the main object of the expedition. Both lay now at the mercy of Sheridan, to deal with as he pleased, but his subsequent course was still in doubt. One suggestion of Gen. Grant's was that he

[6] In his report, dated 20 March 1865, Custer mentions "a deputation of the citizens . . . headed by the mayor and common council." He arrived about 4:00 P.M.

[7] And to a good deal more than rest and washing away mud, namely, destruction of the Virginia Central Railroad. Parties were sent out toward both Gordonsville and Lynchburg for a distance of about fifteen miles and accomplished what Sheridan called "a thorough and systematic destruction."

General Alfred Gibbs, Reserve Brigade, First Division (Devin), was in charge of the trains. The delay because of the mud forced Sheridan to abandon the idea of capturing Lynchburg.

should cross the James river and join Gen. Sherman who was at this time advancing through North Carolina,[8] and it is more than likely that this plan would have been carried out, had it been possible to have crossed the James river. Several attempts however to seize bridges had resulted in failure, the Rebels in each case setting them on fire as soon as our troops appeared. The tremendous rain also had resulted in a greatly swollen condition of the James, so that it was simply impossible to ford it, and our pontoon train was nowhere long enough to reach across. The other alternatives were to return to Winchester, or push through to the Army of the Potomac. Everybody knew that Sheridan would never go back, so that question was settled in our minds in very short order. Before striking out for the Army about Richmond, however, he determined to make a demonstration towards Lynchburg, destroying the railroad and canal, as completely as possible on the way. The 1st Division under Devin was accordingly ordered to strike the James river at Scottsville and break up the canal to the westward, while Custer with the 3rd Division moved along the railroad in the same direction, destroying it as he went.[9]

Attached to the cavalry headquarters was a small party of "scouts" who usually preceded the command a few miles on the march, and in various ways obtained information as to the movements of the enemy. They were under command of a young West Virginian named Fanquier,[10] and were a dare-devil lot of youngsters, mostly natives of that section of the country, and all of them ready at all times to risk life or limb in the pursuit of intelligence of the Rebels, not to speak of the chance of "gobbling" a good horse occasionally on their private[11] accompany these fellows on

[8] In Sheridan's orders; see n. 1 *supra*.

[9] "I decided to separate into two columns, sending General Devin's division, under immediate command of General Merritt, to Scottsville, thence to march along the James River Canal, destroying every lock as far as New Market, while with Custer's division I pushed on up the Lynchburg railroad ... destroying it as far as Amherst Court House, sixteen miles from Lynchburg, and then moved across the country and united with General Merritt's column at New Market." *OR*, XLVI, Pt. 1, 477.

[10] This person cannot be identified.

[11] The manuscript is defective at this point; at least one line, perhaps two, is missing.

some of their trips, and learn something of their methods, but they evidently fought shy of close inspection, and preferred to have their operations judged by results rather than by an examination into the details.

I prevailed on Fanquier however to accept my valuable aid on the morning we left Charlottesville for the James, and he finally agreed on certain conditions and considerations, insisting however that I must go in disguise. He and his men all wore Confederate uniforms and this of course was out of the question. I didn't propose to assume the part of a spy. As it happened, I had among my traps a long linen duster, which completely covered and concealed my uniform when on horse back, and it was at length agreed that I should wear that. Finally I was obliged to promise that under all circumstances and whatever might happen, I was to stick close to him and his principal assistant, whose name I have forgotten, and to follow the lead of one or the other of them in case the party should become separated. We had quite a jolly ride across the country; there were about twenty I should think in the party, when we started, but they scattered out at once like a flock of quail, and during the greater part of the day there were never more than three or four visible at a time. They had some secret understanding or signal however, for on one or two occasions the whole party came suddenly together and exchanged intelligence.

On the last occasion of this kind, as we rode over the crest of a little hill, Fanquier pointed out in the valley below a little stream with a bridge, over which the road ran, and said, "There are the Johnnies." Sure enough I could see a few videttes at the bridge, and a small party back on the road. At the same moment our own men began to scatter in to the road from the clumps of woods to the right and left. There was no deliberation or consultation of any kind, but all hands took the gallop, each man for himself, and were down at the bridge before the Rebels appreciated the fact that we were enemies. Then they fired and ran as hard as their horses would carry them, and we after them. One after another of the Rebels jumped off his horse and took to the woods, but in each case some one of our own party followed suit.

320

I stuck by Fanquier as agreed upon, until he dashed off into the woods in this manner, but as I was engaged in an animated exchange of pistol shots with a gentleman a few yards in front of me, I could not well accompany him. My friend and I were soon left entirely alone upon the road, and as my horse was gaining on him at every stride, I soon had him entirely at my mercy. As he had to turn in his saddle and fire while at full speed, he expended all his ammunition without hitting me, but he was a plucky fellow and hated to give up. There was no way out of it, however, and he finally called out that he surrendered, and pulled up his horse and dismounted. Then I saw that he was hit, and I got off my horse and gave him some water, while he rested on the grass by the road side.

In a few moments the men began to gather in with their prisoners, and plunder, which was evidently much more important in their eyes. One man had a fine gold watch. I asked him where he got it, and he said he had taken it from an officer. An enquiry as to the officer's whereabouts elicited the fact that he was at a house just below, wounded. Accordingly I rode down there, leaving Fanquier to gather up the prisoners, none of whom were much hurt as far as I recollect.

I soon reached the vicinity of the house, which was a fine old Virginia mansion of red brick, standing some distance from the road with a fine avenue bordered by great trees leading to it. At the lodge gate was standing a young Confederate officer in the full uniform of a Colonel. He was a handsome young man, but pale and delicate looking as if he were recovering from a fit of illness. He said in fact that he was there on "invalid furlough" and that his name was Slaughter, a name well known to me as belonging to a celebrated Virginia family.[12] I took his verbal promise on honor to report to Gen. Sheridan as soon as he came up, and was turning away when he spoke of having been forced to give up his watch. Of course I got it for him, and then I began to understand why the scouts did not care to have officers accompany them in their expeditions. The fellow who had the watch was very surly about

[12] Very possibly Colonel Philips Peyton Slaughter, Fifty-sixth Virginia Infantry.

giving it up, and I have no doubt would have refused had he dared. Horses captured in this manner were a legitimate prize, and the scouts were tacitly allowed to keep them although strictly speaking, they were Government property. My capture on this occasion I turned over to the scouts, so I suppose they were satisfied.

We captured also on this occasion some wagons and military stores, and I obtained an article of clothing which as far as I can remember was about the only piece of "loot" I acquired during the war. It was a new cavalry great coat of French manufacture, and had evidently just run the blockade. It was not unlike our own coat in color (light blue) and cut, but was much longer and heavier, and in every way a finer garment. It was lined throughout with fine red cloth and trimmed with the same, and altogether was a very handsome and most comfortable garment. Years afterwards it was stolen in the mountains of Idaho. I have often wondered what its subsequent adventures were, and whether anyone ever did pay anything for that coat, first or last, or whether it was always "captured."

Devin's and Custer's divisions under Merritt's supervision did their work very thoroughly, joining forces at New Market and carrying their operations to within less than sixteen miles of Lynchburg. It was known from the reports of the scouts that the fortifications of that City had been greatly strengthened and that Pickett's famous division had arrived there from the Army of Northern Virginia to aid the garrison in its defense. Consequently Gen. Sheridan did not consider it advisable to attack it, and after making one final attempt to seize the bridge across the James river at Duguidsville, which was burned by the Rebels just as we reached it, he turned the heads of his columns eastward toward Richmond and the Army of the Potomac.[13] It was known that Gen. Longstreet was in the City of Richmond preparing a heavy column to

[13] The Confederates also burned the bridge across the James at Hardwicksville. Sheridan was left the "master of all the country north of the James River." He had eight pontoons, which would traverse about one-half of the river. Says Sheridan: "It was here that I fully determined to join the armies of the lieutenant general in front of Petersburg, instead of going back to Winchester, and also make a more complete destruction" of the canal and the railroads which connected Richmond with Lynchburg and Fredericksburg. *OR*, XLVI, Pt. 1, 478.

interpose between us and our destination, and that Fitzhugh Lee with all the cavalry would be in our front, and Pickett in our rear, while the Richmond forces were ready to take us in flank. Sheridan, however, guarded against the latter contingency by determining to march down the north side of the Pamunkey river to the White House, relying on Gen. Grant to send supplies and a pontoon train to meet him at that point. To deceive the enemy as to his intentions, he concluded to push rapidly down the James river to Goochland Court House, and having drawn the enemy in that direction, to turn north and cross the North and South Anna rivers which together make up the Pamunkey, above their junction. He ordered Fitzhugh's brigade of the 1st Division to march night and day with all speed to Columbia and thence to Goochland, which he was to take and hold until the main column could arrive.[14]

I was directed to accompany this column and send back frequent reports as to its success and progress, which I did. I think it rained every minute of that march and that the mud was generally at least three feet deep. Take it altogether I look back upon it as one of the hardest marches I ever made, but we were completely successful, and carried out Sheridan's instruction as thoroughly as he desired.[15] My impression is that the main body did not get up to Goochland for two or three days after we did, but as my duties ceased on my arrival, I believe I slept pretty much all the time until they did come, and I have not as accurate a recollection of events as in some other cases. From this point we turned north and marched through Hanover Junction, Ashland, and Mt. Carmel Church where we crossed the North Anna to King William Court

[14] Colonel Charles L. Fitzhugh, Sixth New York Cavalry, Second Brigade, First Division (Devin), commanding. He had been a cadet at USMA, 1859–61, then a first lieutenant, Fourth Regiment of Artillery; commissioned colonel, 24 December 1864; served as colonel commanding from 18 February to 17 June 1865.

[15] Among his instructions was the order to destroy "every lock upon the canal" and cut the banks "wherever practicable." Fitzhugh did that, and Sheridan said: "Colonel Fitzhugh had destroyed the canal about eight miles east of Goochland, thereby reducing it to a very small length." *OR*, XLVI, Pt. 1, 478.

The command reached Columbia on 9 March. "The march from Warminster to Columbia, a distance of fifty-six miles, was made in seventeen hours, and was a most severe one, owing to the rain and mud encountered." Fitzhugh's report, dated 19 March 1865, *ibid.*, 498.

House, and thence to the White House, which we reached on the 18th of March. The night we camped near King William, Gen. Merritt's Headquarters were in a very nice house, and the staff officers were scattered about in the various rooms, one of which I occupied in conjunction with one or two other aides.

In the morning we left our valises, etc., to be packed away in the wagons as usual by our servants, but on our arrival at the White House that night my baggage was missing and I blamed my man for carelessness in the matter. He could not say positively that he had seen it put in the wagon, but as the different servants had always been in the habit of helping each other with their work, it was not unusual at all for one to pick up another's things, and the only certain information I could get was that "all the baggage was packed."

Less than a month later I was in Richmond and the war was over. I sent out to this place, offered rewards and did everything possible to get those valises, but I couldn't get them or any track of them. My reason for being so especially anxious in the matter was that during the whole war I had kept a journal from day to day of the events occurring in my vicinity, or of which I had any accurate knowledge. The little journals containing these records were all packed away in that luggage. I knew the war was practically at an end (although I must say it came sooner than I expected) and all my records were gone.

Twenty-seven years later I was in command of the military post of Fort Robinson in the north-western corner of Nebraska, and received there one morning a letter from a lady in Roanoke, Virginia, telling me the whole story of the missing property.[16] She had often tried to get some trace of me, she said, but had never happened to find anyone who had ever heard of my name until shortly before she wrote, when by mere accident she procured my address. She proposed to return what was left of my property, and for a time I hoped I was to recover my missing journals, but eventually I received only a few books, Tennyson, Longfellow,

---

16 Sanford was ordered to command Fort Robinson, Nebraska, in December, 1891, seven months before he retired from the Army. See Introduction, p. 94.

The Odes of Horace, *Lucille,* etc. It was a disappointment and I would much rather she had kept them, but after all I might have known that the journals would not have been preserved, or even have been allowed to remain in her possession.

Her story was a curious one and I will endeavor to condense it into as short as possible, as she gave it to me in different letters during our correspondence: At the time mentioned Miss C. was a young girl, scarcely in her teens, visiting her grandmother who lived in King William County. She belonged to one of the best of the old Virginia families, and like all of her class, was a bitter Rebel. A near relative of hers was a young officer in Gen. Lee's army and was on duty in the section of the country through which we were marching. He happened to visit her house while on a scouting expedition on the evening we encamped near by. While Parkinson (as his name was) and his cousin were talking, Mr. Rider, who owned the place which we occupied as headquarters that night, came to the C.'s house on some business. He was of the poorer class of Virginians and worked at his trade of harness-making, I think, and it was for something of that kind he was wanted at the time. At all events he seems to have been a garrulous fellow and the young Confederate officer who was in disguise of course pumped him pretty effectually as to his knowledge of our party. He bragged a good deal about his distinguished guests, their fine horses and fine clothes, etc. I have no definite recollection of the man myself, but I suppose I must have had some conversation with him for at all events he knew my name, rank, and position on the Staff, which he gave them.

After Rider had gone, Miss C. and her cousin in the course of conversation concluded it would be a magnificent joke to get possession of my property—perhaps obtain information relative to our army which would be useful to Gen. Lee, etc. Half in fun and half in earnest she wrote a note to Mr. Rider (which Parkinson was to deliver) purporting to come from me, and to which she "signed" my name. The letter stated that I was wounded and a prisoner and on my way to Richmond, but that my servant had been paroled to come back and get my baggage which I needed and take it to me. Parkinson disguised himself as an Irish soldier of our army and hung back about the place until the Staff had started and then presented himself boldly while the orderlies were still busy with their breakfast; demanded and obtained the two valises, and in less time than it takes to tell the story, had them in a place of safety whence they were eventually taken to Miss C.'s house; there they were opened and the contents distributed.

The journals of course became official property, and I suppose went to the Confederate Headquarters. Miss C. retained the poetry and two photograph albums and the private letters of which there seem to have been a good many, judging from her statement. She assures me that all were burned unread, and I have no doubt at all as to the truth of her statement. The photographs she retained for some time, hoping that eventually she might be able to restore them, but during the reconstruction period affairs in Virginia were so precarious that she became frightened and destroyed them all. In fact everything that could lead to suspicion of any kind was effectually disposed of. Of course the whole thing was improper and unwarranted by the laws of war, but she was only a girl, and evidently a romantic one at that, and probably thought she was doing a great service to her country. It had however worried her ever since, and I suspect she was glad enough to get the last "evidences" off her hands.

At the White House we found the supplies for which Sheridan had sent to Gen. Grant, while we were well up the James river. The message was carried by two scouts named Campbell and Rowan who rode that long distance, every foot of the way through a bitterly hostile country, literally taking their lives in their hands for every single instant of their journey. Twenty years later Campbell served under my command at Fort Custer, Montana, as Chief of Scouts.[17] He was still strong and active and ready for a hundred mile ride at any time. He was as brave a fellow as ever lived, and a very worthy man.

Horses and men were all pretty badly used up when we reached

[17] Sanford was stationed at Fort Custer, Montana, 1884–85. See n. 69, Chap. I, and Introduction, pp. 67 ff.

the White House, and needed rest and recuperation. We knew quite well the sort of rest we would get from Gen. Meade when we reached the Army of the Potomac, so no one expressed any especial grief when it was given out that we should "lie up" for a few days. We had hoped for some new horses as a great many of them were dismounted owing to the severity of the march and the frightful condition of the roads. Gen Sheridan says: "The hardships of the march far exceeded those of any of the previous campaigns by the cavalry," and "almost incessant rains had drenched us for sixteen days and nights."[18] Personally I cannot call to mind any hour of that expedition when it didn't rain hard; but I suppose it did let up a little sometimes.

While at White House we were kept pretty busy re-shoeing the horses and replenishing the supplies of rations and forage.[19] The enemy under Pickett and Fitzhugh Lee had made several attempts to attack us, but the frightful weather and swollen condition of the streams had interfered with their plans quite as much as with ours, —perhaps more. At all events they never succeeded in getting possession of any position in our front that they could hold against us, and as for attacking us in the open, they probably thought it wouldn't be safe. When we at length reached the White House they had moved up as far as Hanover Junction, and we saw no more of them, as from the point they withdrew to Richmond.

On the 25th of March Gen. Sheridan started with the cavalry for Harrison's Landing where he camped that night and whence he took a boat to City Point on the other side of the James, to consult with Gen. Grant at his Headquarters there as to his future movements. Gen. Merritt was directed to cross the cavalry over in boats to the south side of the James, and thence to move to Hancock Station on the military railroad in front of Petersburg. Before leaving the command Gen. Sheridan gave directions as to certain matters he wished attended to, and among others he wished to send an officer to Washington and thence to Winchester to transact cer-

18 *Personal Memoirs,* II, 123.
19 "Our loss in horses was considerable—almost entirely from hoof-rot." Sheridan's report, *OR,* XLVI, Pt. 1, 480.

tain business. I was selected by him for this purpose, and reported to him in person for his private instructions, which he gave me, referring me afterwards to Col. Forsyth, the Chief of the Staff, for my official orders. I did not much like leaving the command just at this particular moment, for we all thought this was to be the last campaign of the war, and everyone naturally desired to be on hand. I said something of the kind to Forsyth, but he assured me that as my duties would not require me to be absent more than ten days, I would be certain to be back in time for the Spring campaign, and very justly remarked that judging from past experience, whatever occurred in the fighting line, there would be "quite enough to go round and possibly some left over,"—which sentiment I cordially concurred in. The fact was none of us would have dared to think, much less express the opinion, that in less than two weeks the great Army of Northern Virginia would have surrendered as prisoners of war, and that the Rebellion would be practically at an end.[20]

Such was the fact, however, little as I thought it when I went sailing down the James River on a steamboat bound for Fortress Monroe and Washington. The journey was an easy and pleasant one after our long "mud campaign" and I reached Washington, and after transacting such of my business as was practicable there, went on to Winchester. Here I found my old chief, Gen. Torbert, and those of my comrades of the Staff who had not accompanied the column to the Army of the Potomac.[21] The General, who was fretting and chaffing at his inactivity, as well he might, greeted me cordially and seemed to be very glad to see me, though he was disposed to chaff me a little about deserting him. He appreciated the situation, however, perfectly, and I knew attached no blame to me; but when he approached the subject of my applying to transfer back to him and saw my hesitation, I think he was hurt. It was a desperately hard place to put a man in, and I think he

[20] A most unceremonious anticlimax—the Winchester or Great Raid, certainly one of the most destructive ever accomplished was over—for on 27 March, by direction of General Grant, Sheridan's cavalry went into camp at Hancock's Station in front of Petersburg.

[21] In official correspondence, General Torbert was still called chief of cavalry, Headquarters, Middle Military Division, at Winchester.

328

should have seen it. I could not ask to leave troops who were on the point of beginning a bloody campaign, to take service with a man who was virtually out of the war for good. At all events I wouldn't do it, and said that my duty was plain enough, and however much I might prefer to stay with him, that I must at all events complete my business and return to make my report to Gen. Sheridan.

It happened that Capt. George A. Gordon, of the 2nd Cavalry, who occupied the same position on Merritt's Staff which I did on Torbert's prior to the commencement of the campaign, had been also left behind when we started, owing to his being on leave.[22] He had of course rejoined at Winchester where his leave was up, and Torbert had taken him in my place. He was very anxious to get back to the army and suggested to Torbert that he could send him down in my place and keep me at Winchester. Without any knowledge on my part, this matter was arranged, and Torbert telegraphed to the War Department, stating that he had two officers there on the same duty, and asking authority to keep one (myself) and send the other (Gordon) to report to Cavalry Corps Headquarters at the Army of the Potomac. The War Department people who probably neither knew nor cared anything about Gordon or me, but saw on the face of the thing that there were two officers up in the mountains at Winchester, doing nothing, and here was a chance to get one of them down to the front, approved the request at once, and the first thing I knew, the order was issued. I was really overwhelmed and did not know what to do, but orders have to be obeyed, whether agreeable or the reverse.

Still I determined to go to the War Department in person and state my case in the hope that at all events I might make a clean record in the affair. The business on which I had been sent to Winchester was by this time finished, and I obtained permission from Gen. Torbert to go to Washington and complete what I still had to do there. We had known for a day or two that the Army of the

[22] George A. Gordon, USMA, Class of 1854; his captaincy dated from 30 May 1861. Considering the rapid promotion, etc., in the Army, one can but wonder at this case.

Potomac was moving, and that there had been some heavy fighting on the extreme left, notably at a place called Five Forks and Dinwiddie Court House.[23] But details were wanting, and as there was always "heavy fighting on the extreme left" and had been for the last six months, no-one quite realized how critical the position was. When I reached Washington I found that there was a great deal of subdued excitement and a general undefined impression that "something" was going to happen. I hurried up and finished my business, determined to go to the War Department that day and have an understanding about my future—when all of a sudden came the news that Lee was in retreat; Richmond evacuated, and our forces in full possession of the City. This was on April 3rd or 4th, less than ten days since I had started, and I certainly had not lost a minute.[24]

In a short time I met Col. Robert N. Scott, of Gen. Halleck's Staff,[25] who informed me that he was "looking for me"—that I was to proceed to Richmond at once, and report for duty on the Staff of Major General Silas Casey,[26] who was entrusted with important duties needing prompt action. I explained to Scott that in spite of myself I was at present actually on the rolls as a member of the Staff of two Brevet Major Generals (Torbert and Merritt); that I was on private and confidential staff duty for a third, and that the third was no less a personage than Major General Philip H. Sheridan, and that I could not stand a fourth; and that fact was I wanted to go back to my regiment and quit staff duty altogether. Scott laughed and said he was "sorry for me, but there was no help for it. Go I must and the very next day too. I could not go

[23] Dinwiddie Court House, 31 March, and Five Forks, 1 April 1865, in which Sheridan's cavalry was engaged. Sanford's luck in battles was not good throughout the war.

[24] Union forces occupied Richmond and Petersburg on 3 April.

[25] Robert N. Scott had entered service as second lieutenant, Fourth Regiment of Infantry, 21 February 1857. At the time Sanford encountered him, he was serving as major assistant adjutant general of volunteers, to date from 28 September 1864.

[26] Silas Casey (1807–1882), USMA, Class of 1826, was major general of volunteers (31 May 1862) and permanent colonel of the Fourth Regiment of Infantry (9 October 1861). On 28 February 1865, he was listed as commanding provisional brigades (all Negro troops) in the Middle Military Division, scarcely an important post. It appears Casey was sent to Richmond in connection with Negro recruiting.

back to Winchester or anywhere else but straight to Richmond." It was hard lines, and I saw that do what I would, it must be difficult for me to straighten out my record with Merritt and Torbert, to say nothing of Gen. Sheridan.

That night Washington was illuminated and there was great rejoicing over the fall of Richmond. I went about the city with a party in which I remember were Captain N. B. Sweitzer of my own regiment, and also Colonel of the 16th N. Y. Cavalry; Major Robert Williams, of the Adjutant General's Department and since Adjutant General of the Army; Doctor Notson, of the Medical Department; and some others.[27] It was a great sight and I had never imagined how mad with joy the people would be at the idea of peace.

The next day I went down to Richmond, taking up my quarters at first at the Spotswood, then the famous hotel of the city. I reported for duty to General Casey, but there seemed little to do at first. Everything was in such a state of confusion and turmoil that anything like steady work seemed out of the question. More than half of the city had been destroyed in the conflagration which was started by the Confederates under Gen. Ewell when they commenced their weary march southward.[28] The first were still burning here and there, but the principal source of danger was from the insecure walls of the ruined buildings, many of which I saw fall in the next few days after my arrival. Capt. Frank Shunk of the Ordnance Department and I had taken a room together and spent considerable time in wandering about what was left of the city and its environs.[29] Among other places which we visited was the beautiful Hollywood Cemetery, on a noble site overlooking the James river; and here we had a little adventure which has always

[27] Major Robert Williams, USMA, Class of 1851, in the Adjutant General's Department, had entered service on 1 July 1851. He served as Adjutant General of the Army, 1892–93.

Assistant Surgeon William M. Notson entered service on 16 April 1862.

[28] Lieutenant General Richard S. Ewell (1817–1872), CSA, USMA, Class of 1840, commanded the defenses of Richmond.

[29] Captain Francis J. Shunk, Ordnance Department, had entered service on 1 July 1853 after graduation from USMA. By a coincidence, he died in Richmond at the age of thirty-five on 15 December 1867.

caused me annoyance owing to the probable misconstruction placed on our action.

As Shunk and I were rambling about the burying ground, admiring the charming bits of landscape, and occasionally reading an inscription on a monument, we came suddenly on a small, wooden slab, painted white, with an inscription in black paint, about to this effect: Maj. Gen. J. E. B. Stuart, C. S. A. Died May 12, 1864.[30] Of course we were greatly interested. Shunk had been at the Military Academy with Stuart for years, and was an intimate friend, and in common with all of our cavalry I had a great admiration and respect for the brilliant Confederate leader. So we went up to the grave and on approaching it closely found to our disgust that some wretch had defaced the monument by opprobrious remarks in pencil.

Mortified and ashamed that anyone wearing the Federal uniform should be guilty of such outrageous indecency, we sat down by the grave and went vigorously to work to erase the writing. Shunk was working away with his knife, and I rubbing with my handkerchief, when chancing to look up, I saw two ladies clad in the deepest mourning approaching the grave. Of course there was nothing to be said or done, except to get away as quickly as possible. We could not offer explanations to people in their circumstances, their affliction and distress. We wore the uniform of the cause they hated, and it was doubtful whether they would believe our statements if they even condescended to listen. So we silently withdrew as they advanced, and the last I saw of them they were kneeling at the grave in attitudes of heart-felt grief.

I have always supposed they were the wife and mother of Gen. Stuart, as one was evidently very young, and the other a middle aged woman apparently, but both were too closely veiled to afford any special indication. I have often wondered what they thought, and whether they appreciated what we were trying to do, or be-

---

30 See n. 17, Chap. VI, for Stuart's mortal wound at Yellow Tavern, 11 May 1864. After the battle, Stuart was taken to the home of his brother-in-law, Charles Brewer, a physician, in Richmond. Here Stuart died at 7:38 P.M., 12 May 1864. He was buried in Hollywood Cemetery on 13 May.

lieved us to be the contemptible scoundrels that the circumstantial evidence would have seemed to indicate.

For the next few days after my arrival the city was rapidly filling up with officers and soldiers, Union and Confederate. Among the latter were many of the famous men of the Confederacy, who had been captured and paroled in the final battles, and at the surrender of Appomattox Court House on the 9th of April. Many of them I had the pleasure of seeing and talking with at various times, and others were pointed out to me. Pre-eminent among them all I remember Gen. Robert E. Lee, the great chieftain of the Confederacy and one of the great soldiers of all time. He never appeared on the streets in Richmond during my stay there and it was only by accident that I saw him, standing at the window of his own house a few days after the surrender. His sons Gen. W. H. Fitzhugh Lee and Gen. G. W. C. Lee I saw frequently and also his distinguished nephew, Gen. Fitzhugh Lee, who had commanded the cavalry opposed to us after Stuart's death.[31] Also I remember Longstreet, Pickett, Hood, Gordon, Butler and many lesser lights in that galaxy of gallant soldiers. The surrender of Lee at Appomattox on the 9th of April of course ended the war, as far as the Army of the Potomac was concerned, and the various corps commenced moving back to Petersburg and Richmond at once.

On the night of the 14th occurred the terrible tragedy at Ford's theatre in Washington, which plunged the nation so suddenly in grief and mourning. I had been sent on some duty across the river, and as far down as City Point and Petersburg at this time so that, as well as I can now remember, it must have been about the 16th when I first heard the news. Everyone seemed to be stunned by it for a time, but no one seemed to know what would be the result. The attitude of the defeated Rebels in Richmond was quiet and reserved, but at the same time showed marked disapprobation of the dreadful crime. In fact they had for a long time past been learning to know the great qualities of Mr. Lincoln, and to appreciate that in his heart as he said himself, there was "Charity for all

[31] Rooney Lee and George Washington Custis Lee (1832–1913), Robert E. Lee's oldest son, a graduate of USMA, Class of 1854, and major general, CSA.

and malice toward none." The path towards peace which all believed to be clearly marked out in his mind, was now obstructed if not entirely obliterated, and no one could foresee the terrible events which might be impending. There can be no stronger proof of the law abiding sentiments so deeply instilled in the hearts of our citizens, as they were thirty years ago, than the conduct of our army at this time. Occupying as they did a recently conquered city, which had been the very head and front of the rebellion, and was even then filled with the principal leaders of the revolt, it would hardly have seemed unnatural if some outbreaks of anger or revenge had occurred; but to the best of my knowledge and belief, and I had every opportunity of knowing, not one unpleasant incident occurred, not one officer or soldier of the late Confederacy was insulted. They moved about the streets as quietly and safely as if their own troops were in charge of the city, and many of them expressed their astonishment and admiration at the conduct of our troops. That such moderation would have been displayed in any city in Europe under similar provocation, I do not believe. The condition of the city of Paris six years later is an instance.

A few days later came the news of Johnston's surrender to Gen. Sherman. Just prior to this General Henry W. Halleck was sent to Richmond to take command of the Department, and commenced a series of "marching reviews" for the troops passing through.[32] Among the first to pass was the 5th Corps, then under the command of Gen. Charles Griffin.[33] During the passing of this command I saw an instance of what might be called the ruling passion strong in death, which struck me at the time as interesting and rather pathetic, and also as indicating a favorable outcome perhaps for the future relations between the lately bitter enemies, North and

[32] General Orders No. 65, dated 16 April 1865, assigned Major General Henry W. Halleck to the command of the Department of Virginia; then, on 19 April 1865, in General Orders No. 71 (revoking No. 65), the Military Division of the James was constituted (*i.e.*, in the Department of Virginia, such parts of North Carolina not occupied by Sherman, and the Army of the Potomac). Halleck was assigned to command this military division. *OR,* XLVI, Pt. 3, 788, 833.

[33] Charles Griffin (1825–1867), USMA, Class of 1847, recently (2 April) commissioned major general of volunteers. He had replaced Major General Gouverneur K. Warren on 1 April.

334

South. Gen. Casey's Headquarters at this time was in a big double brick house on the main street. One half of it was occupied by our Staff and the other half by a number of gentlemen belonging to the late Staff of Gen. Robert E. Lee. Across the front of this double house extended an iron porch or balcony on to which the windows of the second floor opened, and on which the occupants of both houses often sat and smoked their cigars. When the 5th Corps passed by of course all hands were out on the balcony and many favorable comments were made by our late enemies on its splendid appearance. But some of them at least had been officers of our army before the war, and when the splendid Regular Brigade of the 5th Corps made its appearance, the old feeling asserted itself in spite of four years of hostility. As the 3rd Infantry came by, one of them jumped to his feet and exclaimed "There they are! The old Third, God Bless 'em!"[34] Poor fellow, I heard years after that he went to Mexico on one of the foolish colonization schemes that were gotten up in Maximilian's interest, and died there.

Many other commands passed through Richmond at this time on their march to Washington, and at length came the great army of the West under Gen. Sherman himself. After receiving the surrender of Gen. Johnston's army, Sheridan had gone south by steamer to Savannah and Charleston to settle up various matters connected with his command, and now joined his army, which meanwhile had been marching northward, at Manchester, opposite Richmond. I rode over there with some other officers to see this great army and pay our respects to its wonderful chief. I was much pleased to find that he had not forgotten me, and our association at Benton Barracks.[35] He was very talkative and genial in his manner, and was evidently much pleased at his reception in the streets of Manchester. It seems that some young woman had come out as he was riding by and thrown a beautiful wreath of flowers over his horse's neck. Among other things which I remember of this conversation, was a story the General told me about a large

[34] Sanford's wet-eyed memory betrays him: the Third Regiment of Infantry may have been in the review, but not as a part of the Fifth Corps; rather, as Provost Guard, Army of the Potomac.

[35] See pp. 137–38.

diamond which had been found in Manchester some time before. It was picked up by chance in some gravel, as a peculiar looking stone, and on examination is proved to be a gem of the first water. When cut it was valued at several thousand dollars—my recollection is fourteen thousand, but I do not feel certain of the amount, though I know it was very large. As far as he knew no other stones of the kind had ever been discovered there. I have often wondered since at the cheerful, pleasant manner, and utter lack of care which General Sherman evinced that day. He was really in the heart of a great crisis in his life, and yet from his whole appearance no one would have supposed he had an ache or a care physical or mental.

After his arduous campaign from Savannah through the Carolinas he had finally compelled Gen. Johnston to surrender, on the 18th of April, 1865, near Durham Station, North Carolina.[36] Unfortunately Gen. Sherman, instead of confining himself to the purely military aspect of the situation, allowed certain specifications to be placed in the treaty binding the Government of the United States to a general amnesty, etc. This was quite outside of his authority as a soldier, and the treaty was at once disapproved, on its reception at Washington, and Gen. Sherman instructed to force a surrender on the same terms as that of the Army of Northern Virginia. To this Gen. Johnston acceded at once, he having in fact no other resource; but in the mean time the awful tragedy of President Lincoln's death had resulted in a feeling of most intense bitterness against the Confederate Leaders, and possible sympathizers with them. Secretary Stanton issued bulletins violently characterizing Gen. Sherman's course, and even implying serious doubts as to his loyalty. Gen. Halleck went still farther, and issued orders to all commanders within his reach to obey no orders of Sherman, and in fact for some days it looked as if Sherman might at any moment be utterly disgraced.

Fortunately wiser counsels soon prevailed, and the quiet good sense of the mass of the people refused to believe that their great general who had for years been doing everything to bring peace

[36] General Joseph E. Johnston, CSA, surrendered to Sherman at Bennett's House, near Durham Station, North Carolina, on 26 April 1865.

and prosperity back to the country, was now at the very culmination of affairs, false to his trust. Still the blow had been struck, and though it left no scar on Gen. Sherman's fair fame, the sting remained, and the army watched him closely to see how he would resent it. Resent it he did, and in the most public manner, both to General Halleck at Richmond, and afterwards in the case of Mr. Stanton, on the President's reviewing stand in Washington the day of the great review. To Gen. Halleck's proffer of hospitality at Richmond, he replied by telegraph that he considered his conduct insulting, and declined to meet him. He also forbade the review of Gen. Jeff C. Davis' 14th Corps which Gen. Halleck had ordered.[37] At Washington after passing in review before the President at the head of his army, he mounted the reviewing stand and shook hands with the President and each member of his Cabinet until he reached the Secretary of War. Then as Mr. Stanton offered his hand, he publicly declined to take it, and I think every soldier who saw the act, approved his course.[38]

The utter collapse of the Rebellion east of the Mississippi did away with the necessity for the work which Gen. Casey had been sent to do in Richmond, and afforded me the opportunity I had long desired of rejoining my regiment. I think it must have been early in May when I received my orders and rode over to the Cavalry Camp then near Petersburg. My regiment was now attached to Gen. Sheridan's Headquarters for escort duty, but before joining it, I went to Corps Headquarters to report my return to Gen. Merritt. He, I knew, had taken umbrage at the unfortunate state of affairs in which I had been placed by Gen. Torbert's application and the ensuing orders, and had been inclined to believe me at least partially responsible for it. In this he did me great injustice, but I am glad to think he afterwards changed his opinion, and our service together in after years was never darkened by any cloud whatever as far as we were personally concerned, though singularly enough it was once again my fortune to be placed

[37] Fourteenth Army Corps, Sherman's army, Brevet Major General Jefferson C. Davis commanding.
[38] Sherman's troops were reviewed in Washington on 24 May 1865.

in a position of great difficulty between him and another officer of high rank.

Shortly after reporting to my regiment we received our marching orders for Washington and started North.[39] The march of course took us over many of the old battle fields of the preceding four years, and was of great interest to us all; but it was inexpressibly saddening to think of the many fine fellows who had given up their lives in that dreadful struggle, or perhaps sadder still, were condemned to a lingering life of pain and illness from desperate wounds. We reached Washington soon after the middle of May and at once commenced to get things in order for the grand review before the President, which it was understood would occur about the 23rd. I hoped then to obtain a good leave of absence and visit my home in New Haven, preparatory to our departure for the frontier. There was a great cleaning up of saddles and arms and furbishing up of uniforms the night of our arrival, and many plans made for the morrow, when most of us hoped to get a good dinner for the first time in many months. These hopes however were completely dashed by the arrival of an order to proceed to the Baltimore & Ohio Railroad depot in the morning and there take the cars for Parkersburg, West Virginia, whence we would be transferred to steamers and go down the Ohio and Mississippi rivers to New Orleans. It was a great disappointment of course, but I do not think we quite realized how great at the time. Four years of constant marching and moving about had so accustomed us to sudden changes, that anything seemed natural except lying still. The Administration had determined to force Maximilian and the French out of Mexico at once, and had selected Gen. Sheridan to command the forces to be employed.[40] As my regiment was his

[39] Sheridan's cavalry left Black and Whites Station, Virginia, on the evening of 1 May; the unit was in Petersburg on 3 May.

[40] General Orders No. 95, Washington, D.C., dated 17 May 1865, relieved Sheridan from command of the Middle Military Division and assigned him "to general command west of the Mississippi River, south of the Arkansas River." *OR*, XLVI, Pt. 3, 1165.

Grant wrote to Sheridan: "Your duty is to restore Texas, and that part of Louisiana held by the enemy, to the Union in the shortest practicable time, in a way most effectual for securing permanent peace." Sheridan, *Personal Memoirs*, II, 208.

338

Headquarters' Guard and personal escort it was necessary for us to go. The General made application to remain over for the review, but it was considered advisable that he should start at once, and I think we left about the 20th on our long journey, and the War of the Rebellion was over.

I received some time after a Brevet as Major U. S. A. to date from October 19th, 1864, "for gallant and meritorious conduct at Cedar Creek," and one of Lieut. Colonel, U. S. A., to date from March 13th, 1865, "for gallant and meritorious services during the war."[41]

On 27 June 1865, General Orders No. 118 directed that the United States be divided into military divisions and subdivided into military departments. Major General Sheridan was assigned to command the Military Division of the Gulf, comprising the Departments of Mississippi, Louisiana and Texas, and Florida, with headquarters in New Orleans.

[41] Sanford was stationed at Fort McDowell, Arizona Territory, when, on 28 December 1866, he accepted the brevet promotions.

General Order No. 73, dated 24 March 1863, authorized Lincoln to confer brevet rank upon commissioned officers for gallant conduct or meritorious conduct. Such brevet rank did not entitle the officers to any increase in pay or in command (usually); it was an honorary rank. Like so many things during the war, this honor was misused, mistreated, and misunderstood until affairs reached a point bordering on the absurd.

Note that Sanford's brevet of lieutenant colonel is dated 13 March 1865; so were perhaps thousands of others. "It at once became a standing joke in the Army to refer to 'that bloody day, the 13th of March.'" Francis A. Lord, *They Fought for the Union*, 230–31.

·BIBLIOGRAPHY·

Introduction

Army and Navy Journal, XVI–XIX, XXI, and XXIII–XXVII, *passim.*

Arnold, R. Ross. *Indian Wars of Idaho.* Caldwell, Idaho, Caxton Printers, 1932.

Baird, George W. "General Miles's Indian Campaigns," *The Century Magazine,* XLII(July, 1891), 351–70.

[Bishop, J. B.]. "Cost of Our Latest Indian War," *The Nation,* LII (January 22, 1891), 63–64.

Brown, Mark H. "Yellowstone Tourists and the Nez Percé," *Montana,* XVI (July, 1966), 30–43.

Congressional Record Containing the Proceedings and Debates of the 44th Congress, 2nd Session. Washington, Government Printing Office, 1877. Vol. V.

Congressional Record Containing the Proceedings and Debates of the 45th Congress, 1st Session. Washington, Government Printing Office, 1877. Vol. VI.

Crook, George. *General George Crook; His Autobiography.* Ed. Martin F. Schmitt. Norman, University of Oklahoma Press, 1946.

Downey, Fairfax. *Indian-Fighting Army.* New York, Bantam Books, 1957.

Dupuy, R. Ernest. *The Compact History of the United States Army.* New York, Hawthorn Books, 1956.

Fee, Chester A. *Chief Joseph: The Biography of a Great Indian.* New York, Wilson-Erickson, 1936.

Fuller, George W. *A History of the Pacific Northwest.* New York, Alfred A. Knopf, 1931.

Hagemann, E. R. "Scout Out from Camp McDowell." *Arizoniana,* V (Fall, 1964), 29–47.

———. " 'Thou Art the Man,' " *Journal of Arizona History,* IX (Spring, 1968), 30–38.

Heyman, Max L., Jr. *Prudent Soldier: A Biography of Major General E. R. S. Canby, 1817–1873.* Glendale, Calif. Arthur H. Clark Co., 1959.

Howard, Oliver O. "Causes of the Piute and Bannock War," *The Overland Monthly,* Second Series, IX, (May, 1887), 492–98; "Outbreak of the Piute and Bannock War," *ibid.* (June, 1887), 586–92; "The Bannock Campaign," *ibid.,* Second Series, X (July, 1887), 95–101; "Battle of 'Old Camp Curry,' " *ibid.* (August, 1887), 120–23; "A Mountain Chase," *ibid.,* (September, 1887), 310–15; "Birch Creek," *ibid.* (October, 1887), 347–52; "Captain Miles's Engagement," *ibid.* (November, 1887), 533–39; "The Back Tracks," *ibid.* (December, 1887), 653–59; "Close of the Piute and Bannock War," *ibid.,* Second Series, XI (January, 1888), 101–106; "Results of the Piute and Bannock War," *ibid.* (February, 1888), 192–97. Grouped under the general title "Indian War Papers," Howard's articles are more detailed and expansive than the chapters on the Bannock War in *My Life and Experiences.*

———. *My Life and Experiences Among Our Hostile Indians.* Hartford, Conn., A. D. Worthington & Company, 1907.

———. *Nez Percé Joseph.* Boston, Lee and Shepard, 1881.

Jackson, James. "The Modoc War—Its Origin, Incidents, and Peculiarities," *The United Service,* VIII (July, 1892), 1–12.

Josephy, Alvin M., Jr. *The Patriot Chiefs: A Chronicle of American Indian Leadership.* New York, Viking Press, 1961.

King, Charles. "The Leavenworth School," *Harper's New Monthly Magazine,* LXXVI (April, 1888), 777–92.

[Mallery, Garrick]. "The Lessons of the Bannock War," *The Nation,* XXVII (25 July 1878), 51–52.

New York Times, July 14, 1908.

Office of the Adjutant General, Records of the War Department, Record Group No. 94. National Archives, Washington, D.C. Microfilm.

Official Army Register. Washington, Adjutant General's Office, various years.

"Operations of Troops in Modoc Country." Senate Executive Documents,

No. 1, 44th Congress, Special Session. Vol. II. Report of Colonel Alvan C. Gillem, First Cavalry.

"Report of the Commissioner of Indian Affairs, 1873," *Report of the Secretary of the Interior, 1873–1874*. House Executive Documents, 43rd Congress, 1st Session.

"Report of the Commissioner of Indian Affairs, 1881," *Report of the Secretary of the Interior, 1881–1882*. House Executive Documents, 47th Congress, 1st Session.

Report of the Secretary of War, 1872–1873. House Executive Documents, 42nd Congress, 3rd Session.

Report of the Secretary of War, 1874–1875. House Executive Documents, 43rd Congress, 2nd Session.

Report of the Secretary of War, 1877–1878. House Executive Documents, 45th Congress, 2nd Session.

Report of the Secretary of War, 1881–1882. House Executive Documents, 47th Congress, 1st Session.

Report of the Secretary of War, 1882–1883. House Executive Documents, 47th Congress, 2nd Session.

Report of the Secretary of War, 1884–1885. House Executive Documents, 48th Congress, 2nd Session.

Report of the Secretary of War, 1885–1886. House Executive Documents, 49th Congress, 1st Session.

Report of the Secretary of War, 1886–1887. House Executive Documents, 49th Congress, 2nd Session.

Report of the Secretary of War, 1888–1889. House Executive Documents, 50th Congress, 2nd Session.

Report of the Secretary of War, 1889–1890. House Executive Documents, 51st Congress, 1st Session.

Report of the Secretary of War, 1891–1892. House Executive Documents, 52nd Congress, 1st Session.

Sanford, George B. "Arizona Record Book, Reports of Scouts by 'E' Troop, 1st Cavalry, in Arizona Territory, from May 1866 to May 1871." Manuscript, n.d. Reports for 1867 and 1868 are missing.

———. "Idaho Record Book." Manuscript. Partial record; pp. 64–112 only.

———. "Scrapbook." In possession of William K. Wallbridge, Short Hills, N.J.

———. "Papers." In possession of William K. Wallbridge, Short Hills, N.J.

Tyler, Barbara Ann. "Cochise: Apache War Leader," *Journal of Arizona History*, VI (Spring, 1965), 1–10.

"War with Modoc Indians in 1872–1873." House Executive Documents, 43rd Congress, 1st Session. Adjutant Generals' Office, dated 7 January 1874.

Weigley, Russell F. *Towards an American Army: Military Thought from Washington to Marshall*. New York, Columbia University Press, 1962.

Wood, Charles E. S. "Chief Joseph, the Nez Percé," *The Century Magazine*, XXVIII (May, 1884), 135–42.

———. "Famous Indians: Portraits of Some Indian Chiefs," *The Century Magazine*, XLVI (July, 1893), 436–45.

TEXT

Sources

Atlas to Accompany the Official Records of the Union and Confederate Armies. Washington, Government Printing Office, 1891–95. 3 vols.

Bosqui, Edward. *Memoirs*. Oakland, Calif., Holmes Book Co., 1952. Reprinted from the 1904 private edition.

Castel, Albert. "The Jayhawkers and Copperheads of Kansas," *Civil War History*, V (September, 1959), 283–93.

———. "Kansas Jayhawking Raids into Western Missouri in 1861," *Missouri Historical Review*, LIV (October, 1959), 1–11.

Grant, Bruce. *American Forts, Yesterday and Today*. New York, E. P. Dutton & Co., 1965.

Heitman, Francis B. *Historical Register and Dictionary of the United States Army, from Its Organization, September 29, 1789, to March 2, 1903*. Washington, Government Printing Office, 1903. 2 vols.

A History of the Class of 1863 of Yale College. New York, Little, 1889.

Hoffsommer, Robert D. "Jackson's Capture of Harpers Ferry," *Civil War Times Illustrated*, I (August, 1962), 12–13.

Johnson, Robert U., and Clarence C. Buel (eds.). *Battles and Leaders of the Civil War*. New York, Century Co., 1888. 4 vols.

Lobdell, Jared C. "Nathaniel Lyon and the Battle of Wilson's Creek," *Bulletin of the Missouri Historical Society*, XVII (October, 1960), 3–15.

Lord, Francis A. *They Fought for the Union*. Harrisburg, Penn., Stackpole Co., 1960.

McClellan, George B. "The Princes of the House of Orléans," *The Century Magazine*, XXVII (February, 1884), 614–23.

Manakee, Harold R. *Maryland in the Civil War*. Baltimore, Maryland Historical Society, 1961.

Mies, John W. "Breakout at Harpers Ferry," *Civil War History*, II (June, 1956), 13–28.

Monaghan, Jay. "Custer's 'Last Stand'—Trevilian Station, 1864," *Civil War History*, VIII (September, 1962), 245–58.

Myers, William S. *Study in Personality: General George Brinton McClellan*. New York, D. Appleton-Century Co., 1934.

Naval History Division, Office of the Chief of Naval Operations. "Civil War Naval Chronology, 1861–1865, Part II, 1862; Part III, 1863; and Part IV, 1864." Washington, Government Printing Office, 1962–64.

Nevins, Allan. *Frémont: Pathmarker of the West*. New York, D. Appleton-Century Co., 1939.

Official Army Register. Washington, Adjutant General's Office, various years.

Official Records of the Union and Confederate Navies in the War of the Rebellion. Washington, Government Printing Office, 1894–1917. Series I; 27 vols.

Osterweis, Rollin G. *Three Centuries of New Haven, 1638–1938*. New Haven, Yale University Press, 1953.

Paris, Louis Philipe Albert d'Orléans, Comte de. *History of the Civil War in America*. Tr., Louis F. Tasistro. Philadelphia, Joseph H. Coates & Co., 1875–88. 4 vols.

Patten's New Haven Directory, for the Year 1840, 1844–1845, and 1845–1846. New Haven, Price & Lee, 1840–46.

Phisterer, Frederick. *New York in the War of the Rebellion, 1861 to 1865*. Albany, J. B. Lyon Co., 1912. 6 vols.

Powell, William H. *List of Officers of the Army of the United States . . . 1779 to 1900*. New York, L. R. Hamersly & Co., 1900.

Revised United States Army Regulations of 1861; With an Appendix Containing the Changes and Laws Affecting Army Regulations and Articles of War to June 25, 1863. Washington, Government Printing Office, 1863.

Rodenbough, Theophilus F. "Sheridan's Richmond Raid," *Battles and Leaders of the Civil War*, IV, 188–93.

———. "Sheridan's Trevilian Raid," *Battles and Leaders of the Civil War*, IV, 233–36.

Scott, Henry L. *Military Dictionary*. New York, D. Van Nostrand, 1862.

Sheridan, Philip H. *Personal Memoirs*. New York, Charles L. Webster & Co., 1886. 2nd ed. rev.; 2 vols.

Sherman, William T. *Memoirs*. New York, D. Appleton Co., 1887. 2 vols.; 2nd rev. ed.

United States Adjutant General's Office. *Official Army Register of the Volunteer Force of the United States Army for 1861–1865*. Washington, Government Printing Office, 1865–67. 8 vols.

United States War Department. *List of Field Officers, Regiments, and Battalions in the Confederate States Army, 1861–1865*. Washington, Government Printing Office, 1891.

United States War Department. *List of Staff Officers of the Confederate States Army, 1861–1865*. Washington, Government Printing Office, 1891.

Warner, Ezra J. *Generals in Gray*. Baton Rouge, Louisiana State University Press, 1959.

————. *Generals in Blue*. Baton Rouge, Louisiana State University Press, 1964.

The War of the Rebellion: A Compilation of the Official Records of the Union and Confederate Armies. Washington, Government Printing Office, 1880–1901. Series I; 128 vols.

West Point Alumni Foundation. *Register of Graduates and Former Cadets. 1802–1953, of the United States Military Academy*. Ed. Robert M. Danford. New York, West Point Alumni Foundation, 1953.

Background

Barnett, James. "The Bounty Jumpers of Indiana," *Civil War History*, IV (December, 1958), 429–36.

Catton, Bruce. *Mr. Lincoln's Army*. Garden City, N.Y., Doubleday & Co., 1962.

The Civil War Through the Camera. New York, Trow Directory Printing & Bookbinding Co., 1912.

Johnson, James R., and Alfred H. Bill. *Horsemen, Blue and Gray*. New York, Oxford University Press, 1960.

Kautz, August V. *The Company Clerk: Showing How and When to Make Out All the Returns, Reports, Rolls, and Other Papers*. Philadelphia, J. B. Lippincott & Co., 1864.

McClellan, George B. *Regulations and Instructions for the Field Service of the U. S. Cavalry in Time of War.* Philadelphia, J. B. Lippincott & Co., 1861.

Miller, Samuel H. "Yellow Tavern," *Civil War History,* II (March, 1956), 57–81.

Monaghan, Jay. *Custer.* Boston, Little, Brown and Co., 1959.

O'Connor, Richard. *Sheridan the Inevitable.* Indianapolis, Bobbs-Merrill Co., 1953.

Rhodes, James F. *History of the Civil War, 1861–1865.* New York, Macmillan, 1917.

Stackpole, Edward J. "Showdown at Sharpsburg," *Civil War Times Illustrated,* I (August, 1962), 6–11, 42–43, 45–50.

———. "The Battle of Fredericksburg!" *Civil War Times Illustrated,* IV (December, 1965). Published separately as a special issue.

Steele, Matthew F. *American Campaigns.* Washington, United States Infantry Association, 1939. 2 vols.

Stine, J. H. *History of the Army of the Potomac.* Philadelphia, J. B. Rodgers Printing Co., 1892.

Stinson, Dwight E., Jr. "The Battles of South Mountain," *Civil War Times Illustrated,* I (August, 1962), 14–17.

United States Adjutant General's Office. *General Orders Affecting the Volunteer Force,* 1863. Washington, Government Printing Office, 1864.

Williams, T. Harry. *Lincoln and His Generals.* New York, Alfred A. Knopf, 1952.

·INDEX·

351